THE NAVIGATOR'S DREAM
VOLUME 3

THE NAVIGATOR'S DREAM

VOLUME 3

Seatime

Julia A. Turk

iUniverse, Inc.
Bloomington

The Navigator's Dream
Volume 3
Seatime

This is a work of fiction. All of the characters, names, incidents, organizations, and dialogue in this novel are either the products of the author's imagination or are used fictitiously.

iUniverse books may be ordered through booksellers or by contacting:

iUniverse
1663 Liberty Drive
Bloomington, IN 47403
www.iuniverse.com
1-800-Authors (1-800-288-4677)

ISBN: 978-1-4697-4789-7 (sc)
ISBN: 978-1-4697-4791-0 (hc)
ISBN: 978-1-4697-4792-7 (e)

Library of Congress Control Number: 2012900897

Printed in the United States of America

iUniverse rev. date: 1/16/2012

Contents

Prologue –
Leaving the Bar and Passage to the Islands in the Mystic SEA

Joana chirped loudly in her cricket cage, which I had hung over the chart table on our 36' sloop. I had the charts spread out on the table, but we were running into uncharted waters. The coastline behind us, where we had left the safety of the Bar, was wavering on the radar and dissolving, and nothing was visible ahead. To the West, only depths, marked in fathoms, showed on the chart. The water - black as I gazed down into it - was rapidly getting deeper, and the soundings on our depth meter were already below the level of the Mariana Trench.

I took Joana out of her cage, stroking her wings, and held her up to my ear. She knew the weather signs intimately, and I could hear her telepathic weather report clearly.

"A low pressure cyclone is approaching from the northwest and intensifying rapidly. All vessels in the area west of the Bar should shorten sail and prepare for sudden squalls and high winds. Barometric pressure will drop below 26" and wave height may reach 33 feet. Small vessels should batten down the hatches."

I looked at Joana, wondering whether this worrying report could be true, for the sea was still relatively calm, but I did notice a heavy swell beginning to come in from the northwest which sent a shiver through me. Putting the cricket back in her cage, and giving her a tidbit, I rolled up the useless chart and gave instructions to Pompeybou and Endevvy to drop the genoa jib in favor of a smaller storm jib, and put three reefs in the mainsail. They looked at me in surprise.

"Why are we doing this?" Pouted Pompeybou, who always thought he knew best when it came to boat handling. "It's going to slow us down. The weather isn't that bad, surely?"

I looked stern. "Joana has given us a serious weather report. I can already see swells coming in from the northwest. We need to shorten sail." I paused. "If this blows over, we can continue under full sail again."

"That's a lot of work for nothing." Grumbled Endevvy, who knew very little of sailing techniques. "I don't believe it's necessary. How can you be so certain?"

"Joana is an expert forecaster. She never lies and I believe her."

My moods were no longer attracting my entities, since they had matured and broken away when we reached the Bar, which lay between the Lagoon and the Mystic SEA. It was hard to handle them now that they had taken on a life of their own. I wished, in a way, that they had remained mere projections of my moods, but in order to clarify my behavior, I found it necessary to separate them from me. In that way, I could examine my own reactions clearly. With a glare, I insisted they obey, so they reluctantly reefed the main, but stubbornly kept up the big jib, to make speed, as they pointed out.

We kept on our course, close hauled with the wind fine on the starboard bow, and the boat well heeled over to port with the seas sloshing over her lower decks. Numbyling had difficulty steering, dropping off course as the wind was becoming gusty and laying the boat over on her ear. This caused us to lose speed as the boat floundered in the large swells. I stationed Pompeybou beside her to take the wheel in the increasing squalls, so that Numbyling could learn how to head up and spill the wind. The genoa jib was flogging fiercely each time we did this. I ordered Endevvy to go forward, drop it, and raise the storm jib, as I had asked him to do earlier. He looked somewhat guilty as he gingerly edged his way to the foredeck, holding onto the grab rails, and struggled with the flapping sail. With annoyance, I noticed that he had not put on his safety harness.

We continued on the starboard tack, with sail finally reduced, as the seas grew larger and the sky darker, heading down into the troughs and up the immense crests, when I would look around for land. Endevvy returned from the bow cautiously and slipped below to check the filters in the engine room, and I asked Numbyling to slacken sail and bear away on a course of 225 degrees to reduce the heel of the boat. I was glad that I had stowed everything tightly below, as I learned my lessons in rough seas a long time ago.

The motion of the boat eased as we bore away and, leaving Numbyling to handle her, Pompeybou and I went down for a quick snifter of rum. I could hear Endevvy cursing from the engine room as he bled the fuel system, which had taken on an air bubble from the unsteady slamming of the boat. The engine had to be ready to start if we needed it. The engine room was the worst place to be in a storm.

Suddenly, without warning, the boat lay over on her side, knocked down by a huge wave. Hearing a shriek, I saw Numbyling lose her grip on the helm and slide down the deck and over the lifelines into the churning sea. I rushed on deck, shouting "Man Overboard," accompanied by Endevvy, who had just emerged from the engine room. Numbylings' bobbing head popped over a wave and then disappeared, her arms waving frantically. Before I could stop him, he leapt into the water in an attempt to save her, and disappeared under a large wave. I wrenched the man overboard pole from its position and tossed it after them, then a lifebuoy with a flashing Epirb emergency beacon attached to it, which fell short of them.

Fortunately, it was still light and I put Pompeybou on the bow, clasping the rail tightly as he pointed to the two in the water, who had joined up and were hanging grimly onto the lifebuoy, the beacon flashing their position. I swung the boat into a Williamson turn, the standard method of finding our reciprocal course, and came down on them, keeping them on the lee side of the boat. Putting the vessel up into the wind, Pompeybou and I were able to lower a jib sheet to Endevvy, who made a quick bowline around Numbyling, passing the rope under her arms. We hoisted her in, straining at the winch as she came heavily out of the water dripping, gasping, and throwing up the seawater she had swallowed. Endevvy, who was a good swimmer, came up next, soaking wet and coughing violently, and we thrust them down into the cabin, where Pompeybou stripped off their wet clothes and wrapped them in blankets, giving them a hot toddy.

I was furious, even though I had had little time to think, but had acted automatically throughout the emergency. Endevvy had to learn that if someone went overboard, it was a very bad idea to jump after the victim. We could have lost two members of the crew at once! I resolved to discuss the matter with him later. Meanwhile, Numbyling had shown me that she was not yet capable of handling the boat in bad weather. I should not have allowed myself to carouse with Pompeybou over a glass of rum. That was bad stewardship, and I weakly reminded myself that we must only drink in the future during clement weather.

Leaving Pompeybou on the helm, we ran the boat off in front of the ferocious storm, setting a course, still under reduced canvas, of 180 degrees due south, as the wind shifted to the north. Joana chirped smugly in her swinging cage above me, as I descended the companionway to find Numbyling on her knees, shivering in her blanket and praying earnestly to get off the boat. Endevvy crouched up in the forepeak amongst the sails, his head hidden silently in his arms. I noted the time of course change and our speed in the log, so that when we could head upwind once more, I would know what calculations to make to allow for our previous heading. I then sat with Numbyling, who seemed more apathetic than ever, and reassured her that the boat was strong and had good gear. The storm would be over soon, and calm would return. There was nothing to worry about. After a while, she lay down in the bunk and I tucked her in and told her to relax and get some sleep.

With time to think, I knew I had made some serious mistakes. I had forgotten to make sure that the crew had their lifejackets on, and I had not arranged to rig a lifeline along the deck so that everyone could clip on their safety harness as they went forward to douse sails. As helmsman, Numbyling should have been wearing a harness clipped to a secure point, to keep her from being swept overboard. I mentally made sure that my previous nonchalant method of sailing was no longer acceptable, since it put my less experienced crew in danger, and, kicking myself, I resolved to take more precautions in future.

Little did I know what the future held for us as I settled down to catch some much needed rest? All I knew was that I must complete the journey I had begun in a tiny coracle, I knew not how. Fate also had her say, as an event lay ahead for which we could take no precautionary safety measures, and that would be far more serious than any mere storm at sea.

Forty-eight hours passed as we ran before the storm, setting us far to the south of our original course, before the gale blew itself out and we were able to emerge and dry out our wet clothes and blankets. Pompeybou and I had taken spells on the helm as we continued downwind under sail. I had made the decision not to heave to because of the hanging wave crests that bore down on us. The boat could have rolled over, possibly breaking her mast and destroying the entire rig. Now I heaved a sigh of relief as the sun came out, and Numbyling was well enough to cook us a simple meal, which we ate gratefully, as we had been living on cans of sardines for several days.

Tacking the boat back towards her original course, I calculated that we had run off 336 miles to the south during the gale, and therefore I set a course to intercept of 315 degrees, which put us on a fast point of sailing, a port beam reach, for the wind had backed to the southwest. We barreled along at a great clip, Numbyling and Endevvy together sitting by the helm, where I noticed they were holding hands surreptitiously.

What next! My entities were becoming totally out of my control! Fortunately, Pompeybou seemed the same as ever. He was probably one of the closest to my real self, anyway. However, who was I? Torn in twenty different directions by all the entities, I needed to wrestle with my separate selves in a final bout, before the worst happened and I splintered off from myself in psychic disintegration. My experiences on the river and in the lagoon had taught me much, and I hoped that I was strong enough to survive my next trials on the path of Knowledge.

With the boat back on course and sailing fast, I sat up at the bow, thinking about my potential psychic collapse and watching the waves as the vessel cut through the water silently. We had not used the engine, as I wanted to keep it for emergencies and maneuvering in port. The only sound was the thrumming of the rigging, the steady bubble of the wake behind us, and the low sound of voices as Endevvy and Numbyling sat talking in the cockpit.

The sun was sinking and we had just had our evening meal when a low rumbling bellow echoed over the sea. It sounded like an earthquake, but there was no land close to us. This curious sound was followed by a snorting that repeated itself, the breathing - in and out - of something gigantic coming from the north on our starboard bow. I narrowed my eyes to see in the failing light, hearing the wash of water as ripples started breaking on the boats' hull. To the north, I could make out tossing waves, which appeared to come from a central hump that gyrated in a spiral through the sea towards us.

I cursed the twilight as the sun disappeared under the horizon, for the shape was definitely moving in our direction. Its snorting breaths were louder, while the sound of its body thrashing the water came closer. I snatched the searchlight from above the chart table, afraid to switch it on for fear of what I would see. When the creature, for it must be alive, was about a quarter of a mile away, I aimed the light and, swallowing bravely, pressed the switch.

A sharp beam illuminated the heaving water, which had turned blood red, and as I raised the light, led in a trail of red flashes to the approaching creature. I cowered back in terror at the horrifying shape that raised itself from the sea, pushing a small bow wave in front of it. There was no head! A mere torso cut through the water, a headless torso from the shoulders down, covered with small flashing points of light that, as it approached, became small, insidious eyes. Yes! The creature was dotted with hundreds of eyes that glared at me malevolently. I shut off the searchlight and shrank back into the cabin in dismay.

The three members of my crew abandoned the cockpit and the helm in fear, leaving the boat to head up into the wind with her sails flapping forlornly. They scrambled down the steps and jammed themselves into the forepeak, where they pulled the spare sails over their heads for cover. Useless to hide, of course, since the intruders' torso alone cleared the surrounding water by several feet, and I knew not how much more of it there was under the sea.

Looking out from the cabin, the creatures' dark bulk raised itself above the stern of the boat. I switched on the light again and ran it over the shape. Close up, it was at least ten feet tall and half as wide, and made of metal, since the light glinted off its round belly. I had seen similar shapes on the prow of submarines in the shipbuilding yard in New Haven. The eyes blinked at me from niches in their metallic abode, while a seam that ran across the surface cracked open to reveal a pale mouth, and a tinny voice came over a microphone.

"You, I want you." It sputtered. "You come with me. I know about you. You have been deficient in your duties and have placed your crew in peril. We like that! You are one of us when you make bad mistakes." The mouth curled into a malicious grin, then continued. "Besides, we always welcome those who are mentally confused and have lost control of their entities, for they are either weak or deluded."

The narrow mouth closed and the spiteful eyes winked at me.

"I may not be a perfect skipper, but I can't abandon this boat and its crew." I protested shakily. "I'm not coming with you, so go away. Leave now, and let us continue our journey to the Island of Malkuth in peace."

The mouth opened and let forth a sizzling snort. "I am from Malkuth, idiot! You're no longer necessary on this boat. Your entity Pompeybou, who is now free of your damned insolence, can skipper it himself safely to Malkuth. You must come with me now."

"I'm not going to, and that's flat!" I had my back to the forward bulkhead below, but the creature could still see me as it cocked itself to one side. "Get away from me!"

"Too bad!" The thing rumbled, "You're not very cooperative, which is a pity. We'll have to come and get you. My friends are waiting to greet you in the Dark Ground. You remember that, don't you? That's where we live."

A small door quickly opened in front of the metal shape and four figures came out. I saw their identity immediately as they climbed over the stern rail of our sloop. They were some of the Shells that Trid, the Page of Pentacles, and I had seen on our journey into the mine. They were the Qliphoth! Before I could cry out, they were in the cabin and had grabbed my arms and legs roughly and manhandled me up the steps, over the steering wheel, off the boat and in through their door. It began to close, and I called out despairingly as I heard the faint cries of my crew.

"Don't leave us, Navigator! We need your help to complete the passage to Malkuth. You are the best at navigation. Come back, please."

There was no escape for me; however, for the Qliphoth held me tight as the door slammed shut behind us.

I was so scared that I could not find my legs, which turned to jelly, and I sank down onto the floor. A long tunnel stretched in front of me, with bunks on either side and tools and equipment everywhere. The monster was, in fact, the inside of a World War I submarine, and by the barnacles that clung everywhere, it must have been lying underwater for a long time.

As the four Shells pushed me rudely along the narrow walkway, I saw skeletons of long-dead mariners – the crew of the submarine – ready in their attack positions on each side of the passage. Some, in fact, still lay in their bunks, caught unawares by a depth charge that must have rolled off an ancient destroyer.

I felt a change in the atmosphere as the metallic creature sank down into the deep, taking me with it. It became hard to breathe and each breath I took was a painful struggle. My lungs felt as if they were closing up, and the increasing pressure caused me to pass out, as I was dragged along the endless metallic passageway. I never saw the end of it, for, sinking into blackness, I knew no more......

Encounter with the Qliphoth

The sweat poured off me as I awoke and dashed drops of moisture from my eyes. A red glow suffused everything, and the clanking of metal tools and harsh voices filled my ears. It sounded as if I was back in the deepest area of the mine where we had first encountered the Qliphoth, and the foul stench of them filled the air.

Looking down, as I attempted to sit up on the hard metal floor, I found my legs held firmly by something heavy and soft, like a big sack of corn, that rested on my feet. It was hard to make out exactly what was there in the dim light. Its silhouette was illumined by sparks from the metal works clattering away beyond, and I could distinguish some sort of head that swung to and fro, as if it were watching something I couldn't see.

My labored breathing barely allowed me to draw in enough stagnant air to remain conscious. I could hear the sound of great bellows and the intermittent roar of flames, the clatter of hammer against anvil, the sizzle of red hot metal hitting water, which all indicated that we were in the clandestine blacksmiths' forge near the mine upon which Trid, the Page of Pentacles, and I had stumbled. The pressure on my eardrums signified that I was deep underground. This posed a problem, as they had captured me at sea over one of the deepest trenches known to exist. I felt sure we were underground, but where could we be? Deep beneath the ocean trench, or below some unknown island, I could not imagine. Maybe it was another forge – there could be dozens of them everywhere.

Meanwhile, it was necessary to focus on the heavy object that pinned down my legs. I leaned forward, stretching out my arms to give it a push, but found I could not reach it. My legs seemed to have grown much longer, and the creature that sat there seemed to slide further and further away, but I still felt the weight of it. I fell back to the floor, banging my head, and lay there enduring the pain. Thoughts of food flashed through my mind, and I realized that I had not eaten for some time.

A movement by my side and a brief puff of clear night air made me turn to the left. I saw the prow of a boat, made of copper, and in it sat my banished entity, Aquirot, she who represented my greed for money, now vanquished. Above her rose the graceful form of the goddess Isis, who bent down and, handing me a plate of bread and a skin of wine, spoke to me softly.

"Do not despair. To you, it seems as if you are deep under the earth, but you are not. The land of the Qliphoth is neither above nor below, neither beside nor behind, nor is it in front of you, but it is within you. The molecules of the evil ones exist within your body, side by side with those of blameless virtue. You have made mistakes, of course, and you have been brought here by the Shells to atone for your errors." Isis continued with a smile. "Aquirot asked me to come to you, for she also lives in this eternal passageway because of her desire for material wealth. She is not a bad entity, and I feel that one day she will be able to leave her prison if she becomes more moderate and frugal. I am here to tend the dead, and to feed the living to give them strength to pass through this endless tunnel. The passage is spiral shaped, yet the end of the spiral is also the beginning, like a Moebius strip, so that one needs special powers to escape from it by traversing its outer limbic membrane." She sighed, and then went on. "You must first remove the sack of garbage across your limbs. This baggage is stopping you from moving on. You have been collecting it for years and it has now taken on a life of its own. The gold anklet that you stole from Endevvy, during your adventures in the Six of Cups, attaches it to you. See how it moves its head? The Shells and their mining operations fascinate it. Above all, you must not allow it to become attracted to the Seven Shades, for they are intent on capturing it. Remember, the more you try to reach for the creature, for it is alive in your mind, the more difficult it is. You must remain detached, only knowing that this obstacle has been placed on you by the Hoodwinker, your Shadow self, who is nearby and watching."

Swallowing hard, I whispered to Isis. "How can I remove it, then?" I didn't want anyone to hear my plans, for I knew that others were listening closely.

"The Bride gave you a steel triangle, open at one corner, with a small bronze rod beside it. That triangle will summon her, for she rules over all virtues and vices that exist in the Island of Malkuth. She may be willing to assist you. Do you have the triangle with you?"

I had placed several objects, gifts received during my earlier journey down the river, in my pockets and in the hem of my cape before I sailed away from the Bar. I searched around anxiously, relieved to find the triangle. I struck it with the rod, and it gave out a humming noise, as of many bees in a hive. I peered anxiously into the fiery gloom, not noticing that Isis had faded away, I was intent on the search for she whom I loved – the beautiful Bride of Malkuth, the World Dancer. Would she appear before me?

But, no! The moments passed, and still I heard and saw nothing but the dismal clanking of hammers and the raucous voices of the Shells as they worked. Their reason for existing was to extract lead from gold, and manufacture the counterfeit coins that my parents had received long ago and sent out into the world. My sack of garbage seemed to become heavier and heavier, until the pain in my immoveable legs eased as they gradually became numb. I wriggled and tried to throw the weight off my feet until I gave up in despair, I saw no way out of my predicament.

In desperation, I held up the little triangle once more and struck it again, once, twice, three times the humming noise reverberated in the fetid air. This time it roused the workers, who straightened up from their toil and turned towards me in a sinister way. Several of them began to advance upon me. I looked fearfully at these horrific metal objects, searching for their faces - their eyes - but all I saw was a twisted mass of bloody metal shards, for the Shells had no eyes, no faces. Four of them grabbed me by my arms and legs and dragged me across the floor towards a round opening in the far wall that was a continuation of the tunnel.

They rudely shoved and pushed me into a small annex at the side of the tunnel. A figure, dressed in medical clothes, lifted me onto a table and took the heavy sack off my legs, removing the gold anklet by snipping through it with chain cutters and, instead, attaching the sack to my ankles with a large elastic bungee cord. Then the faceless Shell massaged my legs until the blood flowed into them once more.

"Thank you, thank you," I murmured gratefully. "Now I can walk again."

"Don't thank me, you ignorant fool." It responded rudely. "My aim was to recover the gold anklet, which is ours, for you told the mango vendor a lie, saying that the anklet was poisoned, so that you could keep it. Your dishonesty means the anklet belongs to us now, for we claim all objects obtained by theft, Ponzi schemes, and outright deception, and we can melt it down to hide the lead that we manufacture. All gold is valuable at this time, but beware of those who would buy it cheap, for they will profit from you."

The Shell sniggered and went on. "We have only shifted the weight of the baggage you are carrying so that you can proceed on your own legs along the tunnel to your next encounter. You will still have to drag the sack along with you, so don't imagine that you are free of the hindrance. In fact, most people find it particularly exhausting to haul their sacks of garbage behind them. Your task is to free yourself of it, for as long as it is attached, you won't be able to pass through the tunnel membrane. Think of the triangle, for Isis has given you a hint. Think of three sides, three only is the number to hold in your thoughts. Go on, now. The Council of Eight is waiting for you in the conference room ahead."

I gingerly placed my feet on the ground and took my first step, wondering who the Council of Eight could be. The sack, strapped to both my ankles, made each step forward a burdensome jerk as the cord rebounded and slapped the back of my legs. I tried shuffling without lifting my feet off the ground, to lessen the effect on the cord. The sack twisted this way and that, catching on snags protruding from the floor of the tunnel, as I made my way slowly into the conference room.

This was an ugly metal box, about twenty feet long, with a stainless steel table and matching chairs, the arms of which stuck out like cactus spikes and looked very uncomfortable. To my dismay, the figures that sat around the table were all too familiar. The horrible Seven Shades lounged rudely around the table, assembled to pass judgment on me, I assumed. At the head of the conference table sat the Hoodwinker herself, and I felt sure she was grinning in a most discomfiting manner, although I couldn't see her face.

I sank to the ground, fear striking me as I curled into a fetal position with my head buried in my arms. I yearned for the comforting arms of Paragutt fastened around my back, but he had apparently remained at the amethyst tower of Belvedere. One by one, the foul Shades came up, some of them kicked me, and some beat me over the head, while others pinched me and used their little whips on me. I did not move or cry out, which must have disappointed them, for they took their seats again, grumbling amongst themselves.

The Hoodwinker spoke to me sternly. "Stand up and look me in the face."

Struggling to my feet with difficulty, I searched for her face, but it remained hidden deep within the cowl of her cloak. The faces of the Seven turned towards me were also in shadow, so this command was impossible to obey. I shrugged my shoulders helplessly.

The dark voice continued. "You are here because you have made many mistakes during your long journey. Now you have entered the domain of the Mystic SEA, which holds many terrors. My friends and associates, who assemble here, each dominate one of the seven lower Paths in the Mystic SEA and hold their position relative to the secret significance of that particular Path. When you reach that place, you will encounter the appropriate Shade, who will teach you many things – although you may not enjoy their lessons!"

A low and musty giggle of approval ran through the group and they wagged their heads up and down, coughing and spitting grossly onto the metal floor while they searched their garments for fleas and other irritating pests, scratching and muttering amongst themselves.

I found the courage to speak up. "I really don't see that I've done anything so terrible. All I want is to be left alone, and return to my sailboat. The crew may need me. Please let's forget this and let me go."

My pleading was fruitless.The Hoodwinker responded smartly. "Alas! Alas is my favorite word, by the way. Your journey has reached the stage from which you can never return. You made that choice on the day that you set out. This is a process, which you can only resolve by true understanding of the paradox between good and evil. As you must realize, pain and suffering are better teachers than a life of ease and plenty." She paused, taking a small bandanna decorated with crocodiles from her sleeve and passing it under her cowl, where she dabbed her eyes for a few seconds. "We - who are the embodiment of bad choices, are here to initiate you and enable you to move into the life of – I would like to say Riley, but I desist – a fuller life, let me suggest."

Again I was roused to reply. "I already have a very full and busy life! I don't need any more challenges. I'm tired of meeting people who need help and advice. Can't anybody stand on their own feet these days? I just want to relax and have fun. Please allow me to leave and return to the Bar, and I won't trouble you again." I began to sniffle, and wiped my nose on the hemp sleeve of my tunic. The straps around my ankles hurt sorely. Strangled with sobs, I managed to stutter out. "Pl…please, le..t me out of here and…" snivel "…take off this dreadful sack that I'm dragging behind me…."

A howl of delighted laughter filled my ears. The Shades bent over the table, holding their sides, and almost choking with mirth. They rolled in their seats, slapping each other on the back and crying out "Bravo!" as they mimicked my hunched attitude.

How cruel they were! I hated them to the core of my being. I was entrapped, stuck in a situation that I felt was none of my fault, neither was it my choice. Why, the whole affair was out of my control! My entities, whose manifestation I had relied on to take my part in every situation, had abandoned me. They had branched out in their own lives and, instead of being grateful to me because I had birthed them and nurtured their attitudes throughout my own existence; they felt they owed me nothing. Now I had lost control of my self, too. I was at the mercy of my Shadow self and its minions.

The Hoodwinkers' sharp voice broke through my misery. "Pull yourself together! You are weak. You wallow in pity for yourself. Now, you cannot avoid what lies in front of you. However, we will divide your journey into sections, which is very considerate of us, so when you approach each Island by the allotted Path, you will only have to deal with the elements relating to its correspondences. We must complete this voyage cautiously, taking each of the ten spheres – or Islands, as you call them – one at a time, in a set order that has been ordained since time began. Each of my compatriots here -" She made an indicative sweep of her cloak, "is assigned to one of the seven lower Islands. You will deal with them one at a time, for your stupid Paragutt cut the copperhead snake into seven pieces while Knight Ignitia watched. He should have killed the snake as one, which would have eliminated all the Shades at once. Your journey through the Paths and the Spheres is the reverse order of Divine Emanation, and it is called the Way of Return. We who are lost down here wish to participate in that release, and we must reach towards the mysterious root of it in gradual stages. If we did not, the overload would drive us mad. Mad! I say, believe me."

She threw back her head archly and the cowl suddenly slid from her face.

I gazed in bewilderment and shock, drawing back in amazement. This could not be! The face revealed to me was none other than the Bride herself. Greedily I ran my eyes over her beautiful features, cast in a silky skin of pale green, while her eyes, the color of bark on a young tree, regarded me somberly. She had a long, aristocratic nose ending in a charmingly curved mouth, while a tendril of her mossy hair escaped from the dark cowl that now lay on her shoulders. I had always believed that the Bride of Malkuth was sacred, and carried in her veins nothing but good for the earth. However, the Hoodwinker was adept at shape shifting, for she had demonstrated that ability when we attacked the hermit Hugh, who was incubating the negative egg full of demons, and destroyed it by hurling it off a cliff.

So, was this the Hoodwinker? Alternatively, was it really the Bride? I did not have the answer yet, but I was determined to find out the truth behind her astonishing metamorphosis.

The meeting between me and the Council of Eight ended abruptly, as metal began to drip and cascade down the walls of the room and all that it contained dissolved into a mist. I found myself standing in the middle of the tunnel, still attached to the sack of garbage that trailed behind me. My next question was how to get rid of it? I knew I could not pass through the tunnel membrane into Malkuth as long as I possessed it.

Some thought, originating long in the past, swept through my mind. Isis had given me a hint. The triangle! That had not worked, or had it? The Bride had appeared to me, if, indeed it was she. The triangle had three sides. When in difficulties, find three witnesses to talk to, and they would listen and resolve the problem one was facing. Nevertheless, where could I find these witnesses? I floundered clumsily along the tunnel, dragging my baggage and looking to either side for the entrance to a second room, which might contain a witness or two.

I had traveled some half a mile with great exertion, when I came to a sort of cross section. The tunnel stretched on in front of me, always turning slightly to the left, and two closed doorways faced each other across the corridor. I hesitated, trying to decide which of them I should attempt to open, the door on the right, or the one on the left.

With a shiver of fear, I tried the handle on the right hand door first, but it was locked. I rattled it fiercely in frustration, and a wheezy moan came from within the room. Someone was imprisoned in there! Maybe it was a witness. I struck the triangle forcibly with the bronze rod and it set up a strong vibration. A click immediately came from the locked door, and it swung open to reveal a dank and musty darkness. Faint groans came from a bundle that lay at the back of the room, just visible in the dim light from the corridor. Cautiously I moved in, yanking my sack after me, and bent over the shivering form, drawing back the thin blanket that covered it. The face that peered up at me, blinking its bleary eyes in the shadows, was that of – could it be? – my long-lost friend and mentor Swollup! I tore off the covers and took her thin body gently in my arms, carrying her out into the tunnel in order to see her more clearly. I laid her down and crouched over her, ignoring my unwanted baggage for a moment.

Swollup, my lustful entity, had passed away shortly before the end of my river journey in great sorrow, but she had made me a promise on her deathbed that she would return in a different form, and that her name, in the future, would be Pullows. I now addressed her, calling her new name softly.

"Pullows, Pullows, is it you? Can it really be you?" I hugged her to my breast in fervor of tenderness. "I thought you were gone for ever. How did you get here? What has happened to you? You are so thin and weak. Have you been tortured by someone?" A rush of questions poured from my lips as I sought the answer.

Pullows responded in a faint voice. "I have been left here for many aeons, the time that has passed while you were surmounting the trials set for you by the Court Cards around the Lagoon. I have neither slept nor wakened, I have not eaten or drunk, since you bade me goodbye on my bed of death that day. Now, the time has come that I may arise in my new form. You will remember that I represented your lustful self. Since you have now overcome that side of you, I am free to rise with you into the land of another kind of bliss, and I will help you, for I am your first witness."

Feeling elated by her renewed presence, I helped her to her feet and we turned towards the left hand door. "Should we open it, do you think?" I wondered. "I'm a bit nervous. We don't know what's inside, do we?"

"Go ahead and open it." Pullows advised. "Whatever's in there, we must meet it and deal with it one way or another. It might be the second witness, too. That would be very fortunate for us."

Knocking on the door brought no response, so I turned the knob slowly, but someone had locked it. Again, I struck the triangle. A brilliant flash of light streaked through the crack and temporarily blinded me as the door shifted slightly. Pullows stepped forward and pushed the door a little further, so that we could see inside. The object that I saw spinning in the middle of the room sent forth bright flashes and sparks that bounced and ricocheted off the walls in a continuous fireworks display. The round, spiky creature was fizzing like a bottle rocket about to take off, and the result was quite alarming.

I called loudly to the object that was causing all the fuss. "Bazoom! Bazoom, is that you? If it's you, calm down and come to the door so we can see you."

The spiky ball stopped spinning and the flashes subsided. I was able to make out the form of my angry entity, Bazoom, who, of course, was now leading his own life.

Bazoom flew over to us. "Yes, it is me! Who's that with you? Do I recognize her?" He was very excited.

"This is Pullows. She was Swollup, you know. She has inverted herself and she's my first witness. Will you be my second witness, please? I need three."

"What do you need three witnesses for?" Asked Bazoom. "I know where there is another one. Would that do?"

"Who is it?" I questioned him. "It has to be someone with power. I must rid myself of a terrible load."

"Let me show you the way," was his answer as he joined us, and he led us along the tunnel until we came to an opening in the ceiling above us, set up as a bat house. A large number of fruit bats, long-eared bats, vampire bats. and other kinds of bats were hanging there, and greeted us merrily. However it was the green figure, who hung amongst them upside down, his arms folded neatly across his chest, that surprised me the most.

"Paragutt! What are you doing up there? Come down and see us – we need a third witness quickly."

I held up my hand to help him down, but he seemed unable to move. "What's wrong? Can't you come down?"

"I'm stuck. My feet are glued to the ceiling. Strike the triangle, it might free me."

I obliged, and little Paragutt swung down and slid to the floor beside me, giving my leg a hug. I was relieved. "Hello! How did you find your way here?"

The little fellow replied. "Ever since I was awarded the Order of the Nonexistant Empire, or ONE, by Ignatia, the Knight of Wands, I've been absorbed by you. Now, although I've become part of you, and therefore inseparable, I can still operate on my own in your sight and presence. We three, Pullows, Bazoom, and I, represent the three strongest urges in your personality, namely, Lust, Rage and Fear. In fact, these three primal impulses can, and do, overpower our rational mind and invade our dream world, in the Island of Yesod, on a constant basis. However, the main thing now is to rid you of that stinking sack of garbage that you've been dragging around. By listening while you address the evil remains of these urges, trapped in your sack, we can objectively monitor you. Then you'll be free of your baggage."

Paragutt paused and looked up the tunnel. "There's a safe place further along where we can turn off into an alcove and sit down. There you must return to your past lives and review the mistakes you've made, not to mention some of the nasty things that you did, like throwing away that deck of tarot cards. Oh! Yes, - we know about that, too. Come now, let's sit together and listen so we can get this over with." He moved speedily along the tunnel and indicated a small alcove on the left, furnished with a large empty shell. It looked as if an enormous hermit crab had once lived inside.

"Bend down and crawl into the shell." Paragutt ordered. "Squeeze right to the end and crouch down in the little point up there. Then we can start."

It was hard enough to get into that space. I had to crawl around and around the spiral, dragging the wretched sack behind me, until I got to the tiny chamber at the very depths of the shell. I sat down and then saw that my three witnesses were also crawling along, and they soon joined me. We were packed into a very small space, and it was fortunate that I knew them so intimately, for otherwise I would have felt quite claustrophobic.

Our meeting lasted for some hours. Pullows was able to regress me to earlier times by gently pressing her fingers onto my eyelids and murmuring a charmed sentence, while the other two listened intently to what I said, nodding their heads from time to time, and occasionally suppressing a grin as they heard me talking about them and their antics. When I had told my tale, the cords around my ankles holding my sack of garbage sprang open, and my three witnesses pulled the despised sack out of the hermit shell. I followed them, feeling a great sense of freedom now that the shackles were off and I could move on with my journey.

We pulled the garbage sack back along the tunnel and rolled it towards one of the great ovens that the Shells used to melt their gold coins. With a terrifying hiss, it hit the open mouth of the oven and succumbed to the fire, gyrating wildly and spewing forth the gobs of vile accusations, hot conflicts and exploding resentments hidden inside it. At the same time, a tremendous relief flooded over me and I laughed out loud. At last! My baggage was gone!

My three witnesses clapped their hands in glee – at least, Paragutt and Pullows did – for Bazoom had no hands, of course. He zoomed around happily and bounced off a few walls instead, much to the horror of the watching Qliphoth. The four of us returned to the tunnel and made rapid progress along it, passing the two rooms, the bat house and the alcove with the hermit shell, and made for an area of the tunnel where the membrane was particularly thin.

Paragutt went ahead, being a careful fellow, tapping on the walls to find the fragile spot. He stopped presently, a finger above his head. "Here it is. We should be able to pass through here. Give me a leg up, and I'll test it."

I stood him on my shoulders and he pushed against the shiny metallic membrane. The wall curved around his finger and then the center section gave way, allowing some of the outside grey light to filter in.

"O.K. Let's go!" Paragutt said. He pushed aside the shuddering metal as it bent and broke under his thin fingers and disappeared through the gap. His arm came back through the opening, and drew Pullows up, and then she helped me wedge aside the opening, followed by Bazoom, who simply leaped through the gap as it closed after him.

We were all safely outside, and I was relieved that we had not been followed. No one had tried to stop us! Little did I know that there was no need for them to pursue us, for many a trap lay ahead, and the Qliphoth had more than one way of catching us.

Island of MALKUTH

We were standing in an enormous bowl, whose sides rose gently up towards a jagged rocky crest ringing the deep, dark valley that completely encircled us. A faint stench of rotting material hung in the airless surroundings. There were many paths leading off in different directions, and I couldn't decide which one to follow. I wondered if we had arrived in an extinct meteor crater, for dark grey ash dusted the ground and puffed up around our feet as we began to move. Bazoom darted ahead and led us towards a small hut beside a pile of natural boulders, made of a grey shimmering material that was barely visible in its surroundings.

As the four of us approached, a grey shape seemed to separate itself from the shack behind and formed into the figure of an old fellow with a parrot on his shoulder. In such a lonely spot, who could this be?

I racked my brains as I strode forward, the dim remembrance of a person who, in the past, had been my advisor and aide. But, who was it? I could not recall either his face or his name, and yet I instinctively knew him.

Arriving at the hut, the old man looked at me quizzically and then doubled up with laughter. The parrot cocked its' head and mimicked his cackles. I wondered what he found so funny, and looked at my companions, but there was nothing particularly strange about them, I thought.

The old man patted me on the back. "Never you mind." He said. "You wouldn't remember me very well. You've been focused on material problems while the Court Cards were testing you in the Lagoon. Now, don't forget! I can often find the answer to your problems if you have trust in me."

I stared at him, wrinkling my brow. I did know him, and I tried to place him, but could not. I felt embarrassed. How could I have forgotten who he was? Was he one of the Kings, a missing entity, or someone I had adventured with during my river journey? I gave up and shrugged my shoulders in perplexity.

Without a further word, he invited us into the hut, placing the parrot on a perch in the corner, and I glanced around. On the back wall was a shelf with various flasks, pipettes, and bottles containing strange objects. Below them hung clothing made from animal skins, and there was a small iron stove in the corner with a pot of stew bubbling away.

It was then I remembered who the ancient man was! The delicious smell of stew gave away the secret. I turned to the old fellow and was about to embrace him, when he stepped back with a warning sign.

"You know who I am now, don't you? I am your Guide. Welcome to the land of Malkuth. We're in the Dark Ground, which I warned you about many Aeons ago. It is dangerous to tread here, for there are many snares set in ambush on your path. I stopped you all - to warn you and advise you how to proceed." He smiled at me kindly. "You may not touch me here – it is too dangerous. My energy in this dread place is too powerful for you in your present state. I can help and counsel you, though. Let us sup and relax together, and then I will tell you how to proceed from here."

We sat down and gratefully took the bowls of stew, devouring them voraciously. With a full stomach, I felt a lot better, for I had not eaten since Isis had given me the bread and wine in the Qliphoths' forge.

"Tell us what to do." I asked my Guide eagerly. "I must move on from here. As for my three companions, they may stay with me, or leave, as they like. They were my entities, but now they are free to lead lives of their own."

"That is an important step for you." The old man nodded sagely. "You must understand that your entities, which come when you experience certain conditions of behavior, are not actually a part of you. They are under the guidance of your ego, Belvedere – the wretch! So realizing this is a big step towards your independence. Detaching yourself from their attitudes will help you to take the Middle Path amongst the Islands of the Mystic SEA, although you will find yourself frequently pulled to one side or another by your emotional and rational selves." He continued. "Now I cannot make your decisions for you, but I will allow my parrot, Arty Weight, to show you the design of the Mystic SEA."

The old fellow walked over and placed the parrot on a covered table in the hut that consisted of a few planks set on two sawhorses, carefully removing a sheet that covered a beautiful painting. The brightly colored motif shone out from a swirl of abstract forms in the background.

The Parrot, who I now recognized as the bird I had met on the island in the Seven of Pentacles, spoke in a raucous voice. "Here we have what is known as the Pattern on the Trestleboard, namely, the Tree of Life of the Hermetic Cabala. This is like a map that you can follow as you progress. First of all...." He paused and pointed to the lowest sphere on the design. "This is the island, or sphere, as we call it, of Malkuth. It is divided into four quarters, which are represented by four impure mixes of colors that have specific meanings. The quarter that you have appeared in is the Black section of the island, attached to the location of the Qliphoth beside it. The Shells, as we call them, are the evil remains of all human mistakes, ignorance, and wicked thoughts. To the east of the Island, the color of the sphere of Hod, orange, is mixed with black to form a Russet hue."

Looking at the orange sphere, I saw in the design that it lay on the left hand side, which I felt must be the west, if we assumed that the map would have north at the top like most others. The parrot must be mistaken. This map was inverted, obviously, so I interrupted him rudely.

"Why is the design upside down?" I remonstrated. "It doesn't seem right?"

"I will explain that in due course." Arty Weight said firmly, frowning at me. "Now let us continue. As I was saying, Hod...."

"Oh! Yes." I burst in again. "I have met some of the Hodians. They have a place down in the dunes, where they took Koorong, exploded his body and hung his head on the wall. I don't like them much."

The parrot continued, ignoring my outburst. "The quarter to the west is the green color of the sphere of Netzach, also mixed with some black to form the color Olive, and the main quarter to the south is colored Citrine, which is a mixture of the gold of Tiphareth rendered impure, again, by the infiltration of black from the Qliphoth. These colors are important to remember."

"Why are the pure colors of these three spheres merged with black?" I asked in perplexity. "What has spoilt them?"

The parrot glared through a yellow eye. "Malkuth is the lowest sphere, or island, on the Tree of Life, which is the background design of the Mystic SEA. Therefore Malkuth is close to the origin of evil, the Qliphoth." He paused, deep in thought. "You may remember the story of Lucifer, the angel who fell from Divine grace, carrying with him a great emerald. Lucifers,' influence is paramount in Malkuth, and although these three higher spheres send their emanations into Malkuth to some degree, the Qliphoth blurs their essential message. You must reach these three spheres separately to fully understand what they mean."

Noticing that two of the colors he referred to, Orange and Green, were secondary colors, and one color - that of Tiphareth - was a pure primary color, Yellow, I asked the parrot. "Where is the third secondary color, then? That would be Purple, the mixture of blue and red, wouldn't it? Which are the two spheres that are blue and red? You haven't mentioned them. What about the purple sphere?"

"This is difficult for me to relate, for we are moving up the Tree of Life into greater clarity and power. The Red sphere, Geburah, and the Blue sphere, Chesed, mix their colors to form the Purple of Yesod, the sphere of the dream world. Yesod is also the seat of your ego, Belvedere, as you might have noticed when we met him in his amethyst tower."

"I don't understand you." I was frustrated. "Why is Belvedere in the same sphere as the dream world? I thought that dreams were not part of the ego."

"Who says that?" Interrupting, the sage gave a chuckle. "The material world separates them because people think that when they are asleep their ego is also asleep beside them. That may not be true. Ego is not, necessarily, defined as the conscious mind. It reaches into the sub-conscious, and thus it can influence the dream world."

This was a new idea for me to consider. I studied the design of the Tree of Life and noticed that the three spheres on the middle pillar had dropped down, and they were in a lower position than their counterparts on the two outside pillars of the design. Above them, there was a gap in the Tree.

I pointed to the gap, turning to enquire of my Guide. "Why is there a gap here? It looks as if these three middle spheres should be higher on the Tree, otherwise the design is not symmetrical."

He raised his bushy eyebrows. "I am not surprised at your comments. Sometimes my parrot does not give clear explanations. Although you tend to make assumptions, you have great ability to discern such things. For now, I cannot tell you the meaning of this pattern. You will learn it soon enough, when you reach the sphere of Tiphareth, which is my second home. There I will reveal the secret, but not before. Now, it is time for the four of you to depart. I can tell you no more at present. Go on your way safely, and I will be watching to see the paths you choose. Be careful and beware of traps set by the Shells, who lie in wait for you. Farewell, and remember to call on me this time!"

My Guide picked up the parrot, who squawked disconsolately, and opened the door of the hut, ushering us outside. "You will find a friend waiting for you," he chuckled.

To my surprise, a familiar figure stepped forward and bowed low before the old man. It was Trid, the Page of Pentacles. "I'm glad to see you, Trid. How is your training as a squire going? Well, I hope." I commented.

"I've passed all my tests, and the Knight Terramud from the Castle of Earth has sent me on this quest. He feels that you may need me here in Malkuth, and I have experience of the Qliphoth, too. I hope I can be of service to you."

"I'm sure you will be very helpful. We have to investigate all four quarters of the Island of Malkuth, and the Black quarter is going to be the most difficult. Your knowledge of the lower worlds will be invaluable."

I shook his hand, turning around to find the old man, the parrot and his hut had vanished, and we stood at the crossroads marked in the center of the crater, deciding which path to take. Since there were now five of us, it made sense for us to split up, and each take one of the paths. I knew I must be the one to go further into the Black quarter of the Island, for I did not want to put my three friends in peril. I therefore announced that I would take the Black section.

Bazoom spoke up. "I'll take the Citrine Path, to the South. I'm best equipped to face any heated topics!" Here he laughed shortly.

"The Path to the Olive section is best for me." Pullows announced. "I'm closer to Netzach emotionally, and I've always favored that group mentality."

The Russet path to Hod was left to Paragutt, and he objected, on the assumption that he should be the one to explore the Black section, since he represented fear, and that I should go towards Hod, since I had a rational mind.

"I'm not so sure about that. It's very brave of you to offer. I will agree on one condition, that you take Trid with you as a companion."

Paragutt was relieved. so, giving each of my entities a high five, I placed my foot on the path to the Russet quarter, gazing anxiously at the little figure of Paragutt disappearing into the North, with Trid striding at his side.

The Navigators Story of the Russet Quarter

The Eastern path I was following - a stony and uneven trail - led towards some high mountains that wavered like smoke on the horizon. As I trudged along, the wind picked up, puffing at my face anxiously as if seeking solace, and the grayish black earth underfoot gradually took on a rusty color, similar to the red loam of my long lost native country. Feeling an increasing loneliness, I paused to look back for my three companions, searching the skyline for any sign of movement. They had vanished, each on their own trail of discovery, and the circular valley was empty of life.

I turned again into the increasing wind, bending my head down as my plodding steps followed the path, which was well marked. I settled down for the night behind some boulders, chewing frugally at some strips of dried meat and fruit that my Guide had provided. It was hard to sleep, and strange thoughts floated through my brain. The most horrifying moment I relived, time and time again, was the metamorphosis of the Hoodwinker into the Bride that I instinctively loved and admired. Could it be true? Was this the real Bride, the beautiful one on the white camel that I had observed on my river journey? Or was it a cruel trick, a shape-shifting, an illusion, caused by the proximity of the Qliphoth?

Sleeping fitfully, I woke in the morning to the sound of snuffling close by my ear, and as I turned over, a loud bray shocked me into life. There, in front of me, stood a donkey. It was no ordinary ass. It was Mandrake, my old friend and support, on whom I had ridden many miles during my previous adventures. The donkey came up and nuzzled me as I gave him a piece of dried fruit. Now, with a surge of joy, I knew I had transport that would ease the blisters already appearing on my feet. I gratefully climbed onto little Mandrakes' bony back, and with a waggle of his long ears, we were heading for the far-off peaks.

We reached the foothills of the mountains after five days of hard riding through a land that became increasingly boulder-strewn and barren. The wind had strengthened considerably, yet Mandrake trotted on stoically, his muzzle bent against the gale, and I was very thankful for his undemanding help. It would have been impossible to make headway on my own feet. The russet path narrowed, and began to climb in zigzags towards the highest snows. Resting from time to time, the donkey munched on dried bracken and leaves stripped from the few bent trees dotted around us.

When we reached the pass, I strained to see against the howling wind that battered my face, blowing loose tears from my eyes. Barring our path was a large gate slung in between two rough stone towers, and in front some very military looking guards marched in serried ranks, their weapons at the ready. They had evidently closed the trail into the Russet quarter, and as we got nearer, I was worried they would not allow us through.

Arriving at the gate, several soldiers with Asian features, dressed in costumes that looked Japanese in design, halted us. Glancing through the gate, I saw a precipitous slope on the other side of the mountains that led down into a valley divided into neat squares of farmed land, surrounded by reddish sand dunes that shimmered in a rising heat.

A harsh shout, which made Mandrake start and begin to tremble, interrupted my reverie. One of the soldiers, who carried a viciously gleaming sword, ordered me to dismount. I hung on to Mandrakes' stubby mane tightly as he gestured with the sword for me to kneel down. I wasn't going to let go of the donkey, so I ran my hand down his foreleg as I knelt, bowing my head in false supplication. The soldier seemed satisfied.

"What is your mission here?" He asked. "I am surprised to see an ass expecting to enter the Land of Rational Thought. Or are there two asses here?" He threw back his head and laughed. "Are you stupid fools imagining that the fallen Hodians who live here will accept you?

I don't think so. However, on second thoughts, you seem worth investigating. We have very good communication skills here, so I will ask the Head Hodian for permission to allow you to pass. Then you may be permitted to cross the barrier."

The soldier did not move away from us, nor did he appear to have any type of telephone or radio. Instead, he brought out a small mirror and, catching the sunlight, flashed a message in Morse code towards a building that sparkled in the sunlight far down in the valley. A series of quick flashes replied, and his face brightened.

"The Head Hodian, whose name is Dominus, will let you enter, as he is curious to find out what your IQ is. Personally, I think it must be in the low 60's, or you would not have been so stupid as to come here, and, as for your dumb friend …." Here he laughed again "We all know how intelligent a donkey is!"

At this joke, all the other soldiers, who had gathered around us, went into peals of glee. I felt utterly humiliated, but Mandrake just stood there and winked at me, so I knew it was all right and that he forgave them for their error.

"Good luck getting down to the plain." Our soldier grinned sarcastically as he opened the gate. "I'm aware that you have dropped in – now, don't drop off the precipice!"

Leaving behind the carousing soldiers, we carefully wound our way down a very steep and narrow path, one side of which plunged into a jagged canyon thousands of feet below. I would have been nervous, yet I trusted Mandrakes' sure footedness completely, and I let him have his head as he cautiously picked his way down the rock-strewn terrain. Every loose pebble served to remind me of the terrifying drop on one side of us and the powerful wind that was still blowing up out of the valley, carrying a hint of red dust with it. I wondered why the soldier had communicated with his boss, the Head Hodian, in such an outmoded fashion. The world had abandoned Morse code many decades before, and new communication equipment had replaced it. Were the Hodians that lived here backward, by any chance? I was looking forward to finding out how rational they really were, since they had been exiled from the Island of Hod.

Three days later, we were safely down off the mountain, thanks to Mandrakes' bright and steadfast intelligence. The red path widened and soon we came to a second gate barring our way. To one side was a collection of buildings where horses and other beasts of burden hung their heads over the half doors and whinnied at Mandrake.

A groom came up to us. "This is where your donkey stays. Dominus will not allow asses into his kingdom, so we have made provision for all animals that have inferior intelligence to remain here." I slipped off Mandrakes' back doubtfully, as he continued. "However, we have a friend of yours waiting for you, and she will accompany you in the Russet quarter." Here he motioned to a figure behind me, and the Page of Swords, Breata, hurried forward and gave me a quick hug.

"I'm so glad to be here with you." She smiled. "I recently graduated Summa Cum Laude from the University of the White Pyramid. Braimind, the Ace of Swords, was my insructor. You remember him, don't you? I'm a fully fledged logician now, and I can sort out many philosophical questions. I'd like to help you here in the Russet quarter."

"You're more than welcome." I was overjoyed to see her. "We'll go on together."

An impatient voice interrupted our reunion. "You will continue to the city on our own sled. It's over there. Move along, now."

We went towards a large sand sled with eight jackals wearing orange collars harnessed to the traces, each animal clad with a set of small snowshoes to prevent it sinking into the fine sand beneath its' feet. The driver, a wildcat in goggles, looked ferociously at us as the groom led my donkey away. The cat let out a loud screech, beckoning us with a long claw. Reluctantly, we climbed into the sled, the gate swung back, and the cat whipped up the jackals, which set off at a furious pace towards the buildings I had seen earlier, whirling across the giant dunes. A rusty radio mast, obviously unused, stood at the summit of each dune, and from there I strained my eyes to see the patches of farmed land, but they were no longer visible. The dunes stretched on each side for mile after mile, and after an exhausting ride, we drew up outside a large group of metal buildings with glass windows that seemed to shiver in the hot and squally wind. I gazed in awe at the main building, for the place was constructed entirely of quicksilver, so that its sections seemed to run into each other like a river, while windows floated in the spaces between.

The wildcat rudely motioned us to get out of the sled, and we entered an undulating doorway, edging carefully past the moving walls to avoid any poisonous mercury brushing off onto our clothes. Once inside, we found ourselves in a cool atmosphere created by the constant fanning of thousands of birds' wings, which flew about the building freely. The room was octagonal, and evidently used for an anteroom, as there were uncomfortable metal seats around the walls. From it led a square corridor leading to a closed door with a jackal head imprinted on it in blue metallic tones.

I shuddered at my surroundings, for on the walls of the room hung seven heads, each mounted on a varnished oaken shield, with the description of the person, the date of capture, and a short obituary carved in gold lettering under it. I felt I must look at these unfortunates more closely and try to identify them. One of the shields was empty, and six of them I did not recognize, but the seventh I knew, only too well. It was my aborigine friend Koorong, who had come with me to the Hodians many aeons ago, and whom they had beheaded in a most cruel manner. I had seen his body flung at me, and I had escaped in terror by summoning the wildcat with the sled to return to my boat. It all came back to me now.

Poor Koorong! I gazed up at his head in sadness, yet it really didn't look at all shriveled or dead, but rather healthy. In fact, were the lips moving? I couldn't quite make out. Then the head smiled. Yes, it recognized me! I smiled back, and it nodded slowly. I returned to my seat beside Breata in astonishment. Now, were the other heads still alive, as well? I must inspect them more closely. I got to my feet again.

But, wait! Before I could observe the heads in detail, the metal door opened, and a cold voice ordered us to enter the room at the end of the corridor. Dismayed at seeing the severed heads, I moved nervously towards the door with Breata, while the Hodian standing in the entrance impatiently tapped his foot.

"Hurry along, now! We have no time to waste Nobody here is allowed to be late." He spat at me. "Step up to the panel and bow to Dominus, our Head Hodian, immediately."

Slowly edging forward, I raised my eyes upwards to where a figure, clad in a brilliant metal suit, glared at me from – two sets of eyes! There was no doubt, Dominus possessed two heads and both of them looked at me with a supercilious stare, while behind him a large group of people, all in orange suits, stood to attention in neat rows.

His left head spoke to me in a cold voice. "You have stumbled into our territory, idiots. Now, we want to find out where you came from. First of all, who are you? What is your IQ? Have you seen us before? Why did you bring that ass with you, moron? Are you here intending to subvert our culture?"

This barrage of questions continued, and it was impossible for me to answer any of them, so I waited as calmly as I could until Dominus paused to draw breath.

I then interjected. "I'm the Navigator, and I'm on a quest. I've traveled far, for many aeons, and finally I arrived here on the Island of Malkuth. Breata, the Page of Swords, Summa Cum Laude, is also with me, and ready to answer your questions. I have chosen to explore the Russet quarter, where you are living....."

He cut in impatiently. "You haven't answered all my questions. What do you mean – the Island of Malkuth? I've never heard of it. How dare you say that our land is only a quarter! It is complete, a whole, and there are no other lands nearby to usurp our power, for we have vanquished the darkness with our rational ideas and the Qliphoth are no more."

"On the contrary," I burst out. "The Hodians actually only occupy a quarter of the Island of Malkuth. There are three other entities at this very moment searching the other three quarters, and I can prove it!"

I suddenly realized I had made a foolish error and I tried to sound defiant, but I felt fear when I thought about the empty oaken shield outside. Would they try to mount my head in that space? I had to apply cunning to avoid such a fate. I thought quickly. My insubordinate attitude would only irritate them. Instead, I should appear humble and willing, if I was to outwit the domineering attitude of their Head Hodian.

I assumed a sycophantic manner, my voice wheedling. "By your leave, now that I'm here in your land, I can see that I was mistaken. Of course you own the entire space here! In fact, I was very interested in your farming methods, for I saw, as I crossed over the pass, that you had many cultivated fields, and I wondered if I might analyze the soil, as it seems so fertile?"

"Are you a soil analyst, then? Where did you train? Which college did you graduate from? What degrees do you hold? Who employs you? How do you work in your laboratory?"

He shot the questions at me like bullets. I responded as best I could. "I work for the government of a far land. They have abolished the idea of universities, for they found that the system was inefficient and too many stupid people obtained degrees."

At this, Dominus permitted himself a thin smile. "So, what do they do instead? After all, learning by rote and logic is the only way to move forward. We know that here. It seems that your companion Breata has learned that system."

"Yes, that may be true. My country is run by a hierarchy, now. Our government nurtures each individual from birth to reach his or her highest potential, and then we pick the very best people for our top jobs." Lying through my teeth, I continued. "I'm their chief Soil Expert, as I've studied mud, earth and all types of dirt since I was born, and I am proud to say that I have dissected every molecule of shit I could find." Here I raised myself to my full height and tried to look disdainful.

Dominus leaned forward. "Oh! That is very interesting. But - the most interesting thing is that you are lying, my friend. There is no cultivation here. What you say you saw must have been an illusion – a mirage, caused by the heat rising from the dunes. No, we don't need to farm vegetables and fruits, for we have plenty of other things to eat." Here he gave an evil smirk. "Especially the very stupid people who wander across our border, for they taste quite exotic and spice up our regular menu."

Oh! Damn! He had foiled me, but I replied quickly, fearing their cannibalistic greed. "Alas! My lord, my flesh has been spoilt by passing through the dread land of the Qliphoth, and I am contaminated. Don't try to eat me, for I am poisoned by their evil ways."

"The Qliphoth! My God! I thought that we had vanquished them! They have touched you?" Dominus' right head looked aghast. "Do you mean they are still around here?" All at once, he seemed to have shrunk to half his size.

"It's true!" I glanced swiftly behind me. "They are near your borders in greater numbers than ever! You need to ready your army, for they intend to invade this land of Hod."

At this juncture, I felt sure that I had him under my thumb. He was clearly a man who was easily roused to anger, and one who would not tolerate an enemy for long. If I could get him to start a war with the Qliphoth, I would be able to kill two birds with one stone. "May I offer my services as advisor to you, our Head Hodian? I am skilled in foreseeing the future and what it portends. I have ways that can assure you victory over the Qliphoth, who even, now, are gathering at your gates."

Dominus hesitated, frowning. I could see the inner struggle he was having. One moment he had thought I was a stupid liar, and now, he dared not totally dismiss the prospect of attack by the Qliphoth, for it might be true. "I will send a message in Morse code to the guardians of our gates. That will take a little while, as we have eight gates. They will signal back if there is any sign of impending attack. In the meantime, I will arrange for a private audience with you, and you will tell me how to win any battle that we might have to fight. I am not interested in psychic rubbish regarding the future, only in battle strategy. If you are skilled enough in warfare, I will use your tactics. That is all."

I bowed low, for I had formed a plan. "I am at your service, my lord." Secretly, I hoped that the soldiers at one of the eight gates would be able to run down some stalking Qliphoth, for there were always a few around. If not, my luck might run out.......

Our private consultation took place in a large room, where tables with maps of the area around each of the eight gates stood. Before focusing on the maps, we had to await news from the gatekeepers. This took some time, and I was again surprised by their outmoded methods of communication. They didn't appear to even have the telepathy I used to talk with my cricket, Joana. That made me recall the fate of my three crew, abandoned on our boat. My sudden kidnapping by the Qliphoth had left them alone with the cricket in her cage. Were they alive? If so, how were they faring?

Dominus distracted my thoughts. "Here in the land of the fallen Hodians, we don't use the methods of intuition, feelings, or sensations. These techniques are false, and we don't consider those methods when we make important decisions. Only a logical approach works for us." He paused, furrowing his brow. "The irritating question is, our rational thought should always work, but sometimes we seem to slip up, and I can't understand why."

"Problems can't always be solved rationally." I ventured. "A balanced person needs to consider each of the possible ways to a solution." I looked up at him cautiously, judging my words, for I did not want to upset him. "I have passed through the White Pyramid, where the four Aces of the elements hold sway, before sailing for the Island of Malkuth. The Ace of Swords, Braimind, who is the Root of the Powers of Air, would be your compatriot. Have you ever met him?"

He looked astonished. "No, I have not. Indeed, I have never heard of him. Where is the White Pyramid?"

"It lies in the center of the Lagoon, where the four castles of the Court Cards are. I've traveled far and wide over their territories, and I have learned much about the four different elements." I paused, casting him a sly glance. "Do you understand that you have been exiled here? Exiled from the Sphere of Reason, Hod? You are referred to as the fallen Hodians because your philosophy is polluted by the influence of the Qliphoth, who led you to believe that you had vanquished them. That is not the case."

"You speak strangely, but I believe you. None have ever come here with such a tale." Dominus was having difficulty maintaining his strict expression, for a tear hung and glittered at the corner of an eye. His left head was obviously struggling to hold back emotion, while his right head stared woodenly into space. "We have never asked why we are named the fallen Hodians. Do you mean we are not part of the Sphere of Hod now?"

"You have a tenuous connection with them. Indeed, you may be able to return to that place, but only if you clear the surrounding territory of the Qliphoths' influence, for it is still rankling here and causes you to allow prideful thoughts."

I heard a knock on the map room door, and a messenger entered, bowing low.

"Your Dominance, I bring bad news. The Qliphoth are already storming the fourth gate, located due east of here, and there are signs they are also gathering to attack at the sixth gate, to the south. Between these two gates, our only escape is through the fifth gate that leads directly onto the Path of the Sun. We do not have the forces to hold them back on two simultaneous fronts." The messenger raised his head and pleaded softly. "Please do not strike off my head and eat me. I am speaking the logical truth."

"He's right." I emphasized. "As long as you and your people remain here, attacks from the Qliphoth will never cease, even though you think you are the winners. Their ranks are constantly replenished by the cast-off evil thoughts and unfinished plans of the world. I can accompany you to the fifth gate, if you will gather your people and prepare them for their journey back to the Sphere of Hod. I will not accompany you to Hod, for I must remain here awaiting news from my three entities, who are exploring the other three quarters of the Island of Malkuth." Here I took a sideways look at Dominus to see if he was going to absorb this information.

"Something in my gut tells me you are right." Dominus patted his stomach. "I have never felt this way before. You have come to our land for a Reason, Ha! Ha!" He became serious and turned to the messenger. "Send Morse code instructions to everyone – they must hurry to pack up their possessions and prepare for flight. Maybe it will be better there. I am heartily sick of the blowing sand here, anyway."

Saluting, the messenger sped away, and, gathering the fallen Hodians together, Breata and I marched at a furious pace towards the fifth gate, which led to the southeast, and arrived there before nightfall. As the vast crowd of terrified Hodians stood on the dock awaiting the boats that would carry them across the Mystic SEA, the Path of the Sun was clear before us, lighting up the waves cast by the boats as they moved in to pick up everyone.

After they were all aboard, Breata accompanying them, I made sure they had cast off, and then I turned to make my way back towards the gate where, I hoped, Mandrake awaited me, for we had to return to the circular valley to find my three friends, Bazoom, Paragutt and Pullows, and hear their tales of adventure on the Island of Malkuth. Finding Mandrake in the abandoned stables with a large group of other animals, I quickly opened all the doors of their stalls to let them escape. They would do fine roaming in the deserted quarter of the Hodians, and would multiply without number. Leaping onto the donkeys' back, we began the ascent over the pass, finding the gate between the two stone towers swinging open. Fortunately for us, the Qliphoth were busy attacking the other gates, and we reached the center of the circular valley without trouble.

Bazooms Story of the Citrine Quarter

Dismounting, I gave Mandrake a pat on his rump and he trotted off. I sat down to wait for one of my entities to appear, and it was only a few hours before I spotted a bouncing ball of fire in the air, rapidly coming towards me. Bazoom landed on my shoulder.

"Ouch! Dammit!" I yelled. "You always forget how spiky you are. Please land on the ground, and then I can pick you up carefully and put you in my lap." Crestfallen, he did so, and I bent down to hear what he had to say about the Citrine quarter. Bazoom recounted his tale.....

"I headed south, as you requested, and soon came to a land of green meadows and mysterious bogs, surrounded by low vegetation. Brushing the mists from my eyes on a handy bullrush, I threaded my way cautiously among the tussocky humps of grass that spread across a stretch of swampy ground. Ahead, the mist grew thicker, and soon I could barely see in front of my face. It was important to pick the path warily, for the slightest bound into the citrine swamp cabbage that grew on either side could land me in a quicksand up to my topmost spike.

Tall rushes blocked the path, but I shouldered them aside. They cut and tore at me, but I warded them off with my tough prickles. Creeping through the mist, I emerged by a lake with a floating platform in the center that spiraled from side to side without pause. It was astonishing! On this platform was the statue of a torso, built in silk gossamer and radiating from the center of its stomach, transparent, pulsating lavender light in regular bursts, rather like a lighthouse with its orderly flashes.

I do not like to swim, as cold water tends to reduce my fiery nature, so I opted to cross the water in a short flight instead, landing squarely on my frontal spikes before the statue. On closer inspection, I became aware that there was a doorway in the center, held open invitingly by a young man dressed in the costume of a Page, and I decided to investigate. The light bathed me in its radiance as I entered behind him and we began to descend a tight spiral staircase that led down below the lake. A humming noise, as of thousands of bees, filled the air, and lulled me into a pleasant trance, so that it became harder and harder to focus on my mission.

Bejaysus! A series of painful thumps told me that I had missed my footing, falling down several flights of stairs to land on an enormous purple mattress at the bottom. Slipping on its satiny surface, I attempted to roll over the side, my eyes blurring as if from a deep sleep. The Page helped me up and whispered his name. "I am Ripskin, the Page of Wands. I have shed eight of my skins, and now I am extremely vulnerable to the material world. I have been expecting you and I will accompany you on your adventure here, but I will remain in the background, as an observer. Now that I have reached Malkuth, I hope to ascend to the Island of Yesod as quickly as possible."

I accepted his story, as a thin, reedy voice whispered in my ear. "You are disturbing our solitude. Please make less noise." The faint breaths fanned my face. "Do you wish to join our prayer meeting, or are you here for the dream work?"

I had difficulty adjusting myself to the wavering scent of joss sticks that hung in the air, while a soft chant sounded from a chapel nearby. I made a quick decision.

"I am here to have my dreams interpreted." I announced hastily, not knowing what I was in for, especially since I never remembered any dreams. "Where is the Interpretive Unit?"

"Ssshuh! Keep your voice down. Nobody here is allowed to be loud." I could make out in the dim light a small figure close by that seemed to hover a few inches off the ground. "Please both take off your shoes and follow me. Oh! Dear - I see that you have no feet. I am so sorry to embarrass you. Whatever happened?"

I felt annoyed. "I've never had feet. That's not the way I'm made. I bounce, and I fly, and I am very good at being thrown at people. I am called Anger in my world."

A gasp, followed by shocked silence, made me glance around and see the little creature scurrying away, as if I had slapped its face. What a strange thing, I thought. Doesn't anyone down here get aggressive? Oh, shucks, I might as well have a look around while I'm here, since that was what the Navigator asked me to do.

Motioning to Ripskin to follow me, I bounded along an endless corridor with rooms leading off it, trying to be as quiet as I could, but arousing incredulous glances from several people that evidently felt our presence intruded upon their reflections. I stopped at one of the rooms, carefully making myself as small as possible as I observed the activity inside, where a number of the diminutive people were hovering in a lotus position about nine inches off the floor. It seemed strange that they did not fall, and I wondered how they attached themselves to the ceiling. Possibly by invisible threads? In another room, monks in purple vestments recited a long prayer in Latin, raising and lowering their arms above their heads as if flying. A row of dark hermit cells followed. I looked through the grille in one of them and saw a starving figure lying on a simple cot, staring at the ceiling. A plate of untouched food lay nearby.

Continuing, I came to a room on the left where some feeble activity was taking place. On a gurney, wired up to several machines, lay another figure, snoring faintly. Three people dressed in doctors' outfits bent over the prone dreamer and made rapid notes on their pads. A whirring noise frequently broke the silence.

"Excuse me. Is this the Dream Interpretive Unit?" I said as quietly as I could, but the words seemed to come bursting forth, and the three doctors jumped in unison, their hair standing up on their heads as if they had received a powerful electric shock.

"Ssshuh! Can't you see that we are entering a critical phase of REM sleep with our patient? Who are you, anyway?"

Whispering, I crept into the room with Ripskin, who remained silent, sliding through the air as silently as I could, and abandoning my usual flamboyant style. "I am here for dream interpretation. Where should I wait?"

"You must, first, be received by the Priestess of Diurnal Hours. She is half of the one whose effulgent dew permeates the Land of the fallen Yesodians, in the divine hope of resurrection from their lowly state." One of the doctors detached himself from the group and led us along the corridor to a gap in the floor, covered by a transparent trapdoor.

"Down there – in the Longing Room, the Priestess Semra rests on her couch." The doctor pulled back the trapdoor to reveal a long slide down into blackness. "Jump on this slide and it will take you to her. Then she will answer your questions." Here the doctor gave me a little push, and I found myself traveling down the slippery surface towards a meeting with a strange lady, while Ripskin waited at the trapdoor above."

Bazoom paused, taking a sip from my water bottle, then continued.

"I landed in a large tub of salt water, which was very discomfiting, and made me sizzle. Shaking the droplets from my eyes, I looked up and saw a long couch upon which a lady, dressed in purple satin, lay idly playing with a cats' cradle, her fingers moving across the threads with dexterity. From her eyes dropped large tears, which fell into the tub from which I had emerged. She regarded me tenderly.

"My little prickly one! So, you have come to see me at last. Have you managed to control your Anger yet?" She smiled sympathetically.

Irritated, I flashed back at her. "How do you suppose I can control my Anger? I am the Navigators angry entity! If I am not allowed to represent Anger, I fear I will no longer exist! The Navigator would not like that, because I can be thrown at people when they appear menacing. By the way, have I seen you before? Weren't you at the entrance to the badgers' burrow during our battle against the Seven Shades?"

"Yes, I was. I do remember you because you fought so bravely! My name is Semra. I suppose that controlling your Anger would not be the best thing for you." She sighed. "Nevertheless, I am sure that if you used your Intuition more often, you would find that your immediate and uncontrolled reaction could be curtailed, although that might lead to hidden resentments."

"How can I do that? What is this Intuition, anyway? I just don't work that way."

"It is – the knowledge of the situation. One must see below the surface of a problem. My only dilemma is, being a dreamer, I find it difficult to make up my mind about anything, and I tend to procrastinate. Then, the opportunity slips by. I have to leave it to the Priestess of Nocturnal Hours, Qamra, to solve. Whereas you don't even stop to think before you act! There must be a middle way, somehow."

Semras' voice trailed away, as she became distracted by a small fish that jumped from the tub, landing on her lap. She spoke to it firmly. "You can't come out now. We have company. Go back and take another breather underwater. I will bubble when I am alone again, and we will do as I promised."

I wondered what that was, as Semra slid the fish back in the water and gazed reflectively into the surface, from which now came a gentle greenish glow. "Ah! I see the pathway to Yesod, our native land. How I long to return there….. it has been many a Moon since we were ostracized and forced to come down, first to the material realm, and then to the Island of Malkuth. The influence of the Qliphoth penetrated our dreams, and wrought havoc, for we could not tell the difference between their good and evil messages, and we followed the wrong path. We set fire to the Transmitters that kept clear communications going between Yesod and Malkuth, and we have been punished for that."

"Maybe I can help you to restore the Transmitters?" I offered. "Certainly my organizer, the Navigator, would know what to do. I myself am an outsider – a stranger in this land. I am not under the influence of dreams, for I never remember my nocturnal adventures. Is there a gate through which you may go to find the path to Yesod?"

"Indeed there is. The path is due south, and it is named the Universe. We must travel through that dangerous World to reach the seat of our dreams in Yesod. The Transmitters are there, mounted upon the pinnacle of a great mountain. We need a leader to take us there, for we are not given to making practical plans. We are too idealistic." Semras' face softened and her eyes gazed into the surrounding darkness. "One day, that person will come, and we will be released from our bondage in Malkuth."

"I believe I know that person, who has passed many trials and is gaining great knowledge. That is the Navigator, who would be able to solve the problems of the burned-out Transmitters. I 'll find the Navigator." I looked determined.

Semras' eyes brightened. "That would be wonderful. And now, you look like a practical sort of fellow, and we don't have many people here who are into mundane matters, as they prefer to day dream. While you are here, would you fix our Reception Vats, which are used to contain the ether that is poured into them from Yesod. They have been leaking at the bases, as gluttonous rodents repeatedly gnawed upon them. We had to cut off our supplies of ether, which has resulted in many people dying of depression. Can you do this for us?" She widened her azure eyes in a look of supplication.

I squared my rounded shoulders. "Where are the Vats? I will take a look at them if you show me the way."

Semra rose unsteadily from her couch, brushing a puddle of water from her lap. Gliding to the back of the dim space, she pulled on a cobwebby bell rope that hung from the ceiling. A distant carillon sounded a melody and within a few seconds, two black vultures appeared, flapping their wings and squawking vehemently.

"There you are, my brave devourers!" She cried with delight. "I have a task for you. Take this – er- gentleman down to the Reception Vats, and provide him with every tool he may need, rubber, concrete, plastic or West system, in order that he may mend the bottoms of the vats. As you both know, we are in urgent need of more ether here."

The vultures looked glum. Then one of them spoke up. "Your highness, I think it would be a bad idea to restore the supply of ether."

The other vulture chimed in. "Indeed, we have been feasting well lately. So many people have died of depression, their corpses are scattered everywhere. All our friends in the flock are trying desperately to clear up the mess, which they are thoroughly enjoying."

"That's not the point." Semra murmured. "These people aren't supposed to die here. They have gathered in great numbers with the hope of restoration to Yesod, where they will be able to dream their hearts away. What's more, you had a perfectly good diet of rodents, but you turned up your beaks at them. It's your fault we became overrun with rodents, and they ate the bottoms of the vats. Everything can be blamed on you."

The larger vulture fluttered his eyelashes. "We got really bored of eating rodents – same, same, all the time. If you can spice up our diet with some little tarsiers, now, we would be more willing to help the prickly fellow."

"Oh! I suppose so. Tarsiers are hard to find, though. They live down with the Qliphoth, for they are night dwellers. Qamra knows more about them. But, if you insist, we'll make a deal. Get this fellow to mend the Reception Vats, and then I will send him down to catch some tarsiers for you." She cocked her head on one side enquiringly. "How does that sound?"

The two vultures nodded their heads. "Fair enough. Tarsiers are a great delicacy. In fact, they are nearly extinct in the World, as far as I know, whereas there are many of us. We will take your prickly friend to the Vats."

I followed the two vultures as they hopped and squabbled along a faint path, until they came to a huge underground cavern. Dozens of rock crystal containers, scattered randomly over the dirt floor, filled the area from floor to ceiling high above Each vat had an open trumpet-shaped valve at the top, to receive the ether, which was purified and deoxygenated as it arrived from Yesod and, therefore, settled to the bottom of the vats.

On inspection, I could see that each vat had dozens of tiny holes at the base, the signs of rodent teeth being evident around the chewed edges.

"I turned to the vultures. "I can fix these. We will need the West system. You can mix it up in batches while I go around patching the holes quickly. There's one thing I don't understand. Rodents aren't into ether, especially since laboratory assistants often use ether to suffocate them. They have bad memories of that, and avoid the smell, so why would they attack the vats?"

A guilty glance passed between the two vultures. "Shall we tell him the truth?" One said. "We're in trouble anyway."

"I suppose so. The game is up, for sure." The second vulture lowered his eyes modestly. "I must tell you, we devised a trick. We smeared the base of the vats with gorgonzola cheese. The rodents went mad for it! They couldn't get enough. The fools thought that the vats were completely filled with cheese, and they wanted to get at it. When they gnawed through and the ether dissipated, we knew that people here, who are mostly melancholic, would sink further into depression, and would stop eating. Especially since they loved gorgonzola cheese, and it was all gone. We fed on the bodies one by one, as they died, since we have no Prozac here. It was wonderful! But it turned into a catch 22 situation, as we couldn't keep up with all the corpses, and Semra got to hear of it because of the terrible smell."

The vultures were mixing up the batches of epoxy as they talked, and I went around, patching up all the vats with my right hand spike. When they had finished, my heart sank, as I knew the next task would be to descend into the realm of the Qliphoth once more, to capture as many tarsiers as I could before leaving the Citrine Quarter and returning to the circular valley to make my report to the Navigator."

Bazoom sighed, took another sip of water and chewed thoughtfully on a piece of dried meat. Then he continued.

"I didn't want to go back to the dark land of the Qliphoth, but I was honest enough to fulfil my part of the bargain in order to leave the Citrine Quarter as soon as possible. This time, the vultures led me to an elevator, loaded me in, and pressed the button that said 'Nadir.' The elevator descended at rocket speed, and I clung to the bars around the walls to keep from flying up to the ceiling. It finally stopped and I stumbled outside, leaned over, and threw up my last meal.

A shriek of delight greeted this. "Vomit! Fetch your spoons and come quickly for this rare treat!" A shuffling of feet came along the passage and I turned away as they – the hideous creatures – bent over and began to eat. Ugh! I rushed away down the endless corridor, knowing I had to find the enclosure where the Qliphoth kept the tarsiers and get out of there as fast as I could.

I soon began to smell something rank, which got stronger and stronger as I moved along. It smelt like a zoo – raw meat, animal droppings and lion breath – so I reckoned there would be some tarsiers there. The passageway widened and gave way to an open area where dozens of cages were huddled. Peering into each cage, I saw, to my horror, not a live animal, but the skeleton of an animal instead. In the lions' cage, two skeletons were mounted, and the rear door opened as the keeper placed some fresh meat on the ground. Immediately the two skeletons leapt off their mountings and began to tear at the meat, blood dripping from their bony jaws. When they had finished, they returned to their pedestals, and all was still.

I moved on to another cage in trepidation. The skeleton of an elephant was happily munching on some hay, while a hippopotamus skeleton bathed in a dirty pool, swishing the water over its back. I heard a movement beside me, and a voice snarled.

"Who are you? This zoo is private. Do you have a ticket of admission?" I found my largest spike grabbed roughly by horny fingers, and I was almost yanked off my metaphorical feet, as the Qliphoth beside me pulled me along the path. This creature was not human, but shaped like a mortar shell, somewhat broken at the edges and with the most horrible expression on its face.

Face? There was no face. Merely a semblance of one, approximately in front of what should be the head. I was terrified! What could I do? Nothing. I must remain calm, until I knew where they were going. Would they imprison me? Hopefully, they did not realize that I had special powers, and was a skilled escape artist. Besides, Ripskin would wonder where I was and be sure to raise the alarm, if he could focus his attention for five minutes.

Yes! That was it. I could get away from any situation if I chose, by letting go of a barrage of Anger, and then retreating behind it as the stunned recipients tried to recover their equilibrium. All was not yet lost, I decided.

We stopped by the door of a large cage. The Qliphoth chuckled to himself. "You won't last long in here – the python is hungry and hasn't had food for a month. Enjoy being swallowed!"

The evil one swung open the door and pushed me roughly inside, where I quickly used my strength to bounce upwards onto a convenient branch. Moving gingerly along the branch, I brushed up against several tiny, trembling creatures. In the dim light, I made out ten pairs of large, luminous eyes. The animals were huddled in a high corner of the pythons' pen, their tiny, human hands clutching tightly onto the branches of a dead tree, while their long tails drooped miserably. I asked them who they were, and why they were here in the pythons' cage.

"We are the ten tarsier martyrs. The Qliphoth took a great liking to our kind many years ago, because we can see in the dark and turn our heads 180 degrees to each side. They made us work for them, searching for evil in the world outside, constantly sneaking through the night shadows, when the bad things raise their heads." The closest tarsier blinked swiftly, then continued. "The Qliphoth eventually became annoyed with us. They wanted us to be able to turn our heads around the full 360 degrees, and they began to force the issue. Many brave tarsiers lost their heads, for the Shells became frustrated and broke them off when they wouldn't turn far enough."

I gave a gesture of commiseration and questioned them again. "That is so weird. I am sorry about that. Did the ten of you disobey them?"

"We refused to have our heads turned, and we went on strike. They singled us out for python meal time, but at least that was better than being beheaded. Of course, we don't want to die, but what can we do? We're trapped here."

"Now you're going to become a meal, and so am I, unless we find a way out of this cage. Let me think about it." I peered down from the branch and looked at the python, which was asleep, a large bulge showing in its stomach. "Hhmmm…This snake has recently eaten, so we have some time. I see that the Qliphoth lied. He made out the python was hungry and hadn't eaten for a month. I suppose lying is a natural thing down here."

The tarsiers looked hopeful. Examining the cage, I saw a weak spot in the top of the cage where the bars were slightly dislodged. Forcing some prickles into the gap, I made myself get as angry as I could by thinking of all the unfair things that had happened to me during my life, storing up the resentments until they burst out of me in a great rush, and then, pushing against the bars, I was able to bend them aside. They parted with a snap, allowing the tarsiers, who were close behind, to follow me to safety.

We crept along the tops of the cages swiftly to escape from the zoo. I had to find the elevator again! The tarsiers would follow me now. The problem was that I would be leading these innocent little creatures to another, even more terrible death at the claws of the vultures, who would be waiting impatiently above. Somehow, I had to save them.

I did not dare warn the tiny animals of their potential fate as we arrived back at the elevator. The Qliphoth had not detected their silent flight. Piling into the elevator, I directed one of them to press the button marked 'Zenith', and we shot up, leaving our stomachs behind us in haste. As we staggered out of the elevator door, dazed, several of the waiting vultures raised a cheer. Their eyes gleamed as they saw the tender little tarsiers that huddled behind me in terror.

I faced down the group of vultures with an insolent grin, their sharp beaks whetted, and their appetites aroused. As the vultures lunged towards the tarsiers, I dodged from side to side, protecting them with my prickles, punching and butting the birds and drawing a considerable amount of blood. Their feathers flew and the vultures grew angry, but I was angrier. As our fight grew fiercer, the noise of the conflict reached Semra, and she came gliding up her slide from the Longing Room, accompanied by her badger.

"What is going on here?" She exclaimed. "Birds! This is not the way to behave, my little devourers! Be polite and sit down at table with your bibs on, and stop jumping and quarreling all over the place, or I will take away your meal and you can go without."

"We're hungry! We have been waiting a long time for your stupid messenger to bring back the meal he promised us. Now, let us eat, or there will be trouble."

Oh! Dear. I had to think of something. An idea came to me, as I continued to dodge back and forth in front of the tarsiers. A python would make a very large and satisfying meal for the birds. All I had to do was promise them a better deal, and lure them into the elevator. I would tell them where the pythons' cage was, and how to get in through the broken bars. They could pounce on the snake while it was asleep, and overpower it. I announced a brief cease fire, and told them of my plan.

"Devouring birds! I have something far more delicious than these meager morsels for you. At the bottom of this elevator sleeps a massive snake, the likes of which you have never seen. It will provide you with food for several months. I will tell you how to find it - if we do a deal. Let those scrawny little creatures go, and descend among the Qliphoth to eat your fill."

The leader of the vultures cocked his head and placed a glittering eye on me. "Snake – you say snake? That is one of our favorite foods." The other birds nodded vigorously. "If what you say is true, we will make the swap. These tarsiers are nothing but skin and bone, after all, and vanish in a gulp, allowing us no pleasure in tearing and mauling our dead prey." I slid open the elevator door and the vultures trooped in, then pressed the 'Nadir' button and quickly hopped out again. The elevator went down with a whoosh, carrying thirteen vultures with it. Nobody ever saw them again, and whether they found the snake, or not, is another story.

Meanwhile, the tiny creatures clustered around me to thank me. They could not hug me, for I am sharp, and not given to clinging at all. Semra, who had been watching, now made a suggestion. "We don't want these animals to stay here indefinitely, for the nuisance of having to feed them and look after them would disturb our reminiscences and distract us from using our intuitive powers. I have recently heard that the World Dancer, who lives in the Universe, is looking for some pets. Once you have found her path, you can take them with you as a gift to the World." Semra looked thoughtful. "It may take some time for you to find the Path of the Universe, for you may take other paths through the labyrinth of the Tree of Life that will be false, and will lead you nowhere. Until you return here, ready to face the World Dancer and unveil her, we will look after the tarsiers. Do not be gone for too long, for they will be waiting."

"Are my tasks complete?" I asked her. "Now can I return to the Dark Ground?"

"Yes, you may return with your report to the Navigator, who will be relieved to see you. Do not forget us, for I know we will meet again. Ripskin will remain here with us, and he will guide you on the path of the Universe. Here is a gift for you that you will need to keep you safe." She hung a bow and a quiver of arrows on my spikes as she spoke. "When we have enough ether in our vats, we may also transcend the World and live once again in the dream Island of Yesod. I wish you well."

I turned and bounced sadly back up the path that led to the circular valley, and here I am." Bazoom finished his story. I felt that it was most interesting. The Citrine Quarter would, hopefully, be restored to Yesod one day. As I mulled over this thought, clumping footsteps sounded close by, and I looked up to see the well loved figure of Pullows, who held out her ample arms and embraced us both, never fearing Bazooms' prickles. She had returned safely from the Olive Quarter of Malkuth, and tried to tell us something, but her words were lost in a sudden puff of wind.

Pullows Story of the Olive Quarter

Bazoom and I were delighted to welcome Pullows, and anxious to hear her story about the Olive Quarter to the West, whence she had journeyed. First, we soaked a portion of the dried fruit and meat in puddle water, and then we rubbed Bazoom against some rocks to produce a small fire to cook the meal. I was getting tired of this staple fare, but none of us knew when we would get a decent meal, and it was better than nothing. Sitting by the fire in the middle of the circular valley, the precipitous cliffs rising around us, we listened to Pullows' adventures.

"I had only been traveling for a single day when, all around me, small stubbly bushes began to grow, and soon the vegetation changed into scrub pine and grew denser and thicker. It was hard to push my way through, as the branches seemed to catch at me with spiteful intent. By nightfall, the trees were full grown, and getting larger and the path became easier to follow, as the dense tops of the huge trees shut out all sunlight and prevented any undergrowth from blocking my way. At regular intervals in the forest, I found grassy spaces that seemed to echo with the sound of dancing feet, yet there was nothing there but the smell of crushed leaves and stems and a few broken branches. A few stray dogs sniffed my feet and then disappeared into the bushes.

The wood surrounded me, its solemn silence broken occasionally by faint gusts of tinkling laughter and barely audible giggles, but although I looked around to see who was hiding, there was no one there. On the third day of walking, sustaining myself with the plentiful berries and fruits that hung from the bushes at the edge of each glade, the forest began to darken and grow menacing. A hush dropped over the murky trees, as if the moon had eclipsed the sun, and I abruptly felt the bite of a noose around my leg, dragging me down onto the mossy sward. I flailed my arms in panic and tried to regain my feet, but sweaty hands held me down and cast a heavy blindfold over my eyes, quickly secured behind my head by deft fingers. A chuckle arose from the people who were moving rapidly around me, and they were talking excitedly about a barbeque they were evidently planning.

I was soon bundled onto a litter, which was made of supple branches woven together, and carried off at a trot along the path. I had no idea where I was going, and I had, wisely, remained silent, fearing to give away the reason for invading their territory. After a bumpy two hours, I felt the warmth of sunlight on my face and knew we must be clear of the trees. My captors deposited the litter on the ground without ceremony and walked away, their voices fading into the distance. For a while, I lay there, expecting them to come back at any moment, but as the time passed and nothing happened, I attempted to sit up. The bindings around my hands were tightly tied and impossible to remove, so that I was unable to slide the rope off my leg and stand up. Fortunately, a voice beside me offered to help, and I felt quick hands untying my bonds and removing the blindfold at the same time.

My helper was a young lady, named Rivula, the Page of Cups. She said she would accompany me to the ousted people of Netzach. We were in a large clearing in the forest, about five or six acres of grassy meadow land. In the center of this field stood a large wooden structure, somewhat like a longhouse, and attached to it haphazardly were small huts, thrown together in a crazy shambles and leaning this way and that, their crumbling walls propped up by stakes driven into the ground. There was no sign of anyone around this village, so we began to explore the area cautiously while a large pack of the stray dogs followed us in mild curiosity.

Beyond the edge of the meadow, we came upon a path through the encroaching wood, which led, after a short distance, into a sloping grove of olive trees that stretched as far as we could see. Distant shouts and wild laughter drew our attention towards a winding river that moved sluggishly through a wide channel cut into the surrounding fields. Now we could see dozens of very excited people sporting in the shallows, splashing each other, screaming and yelling, and ducking each other under the water, in a frenzied game that seemed to have some elements of cruelty in it, for all their merriment. Concealing ourselves behind one of the larger trees, we observed the scene. The people were nude, and did not appear to have left any clothes on the bank, but at least the air was warm. After a while, the revelers began to climb out of the water and ran nakedly up the slope between the olive trees, heading back to their village. They did not spot us crouched behind the tree, where we could hear them good-naturedly teasing and joking amongst themselves.

When the last bare behind had disappeared into the forest, we made our way cautiously back to the village, where there was much excitement, as several people were running about between the empty litter and the longhouse, waving their arms and calling to each other. Soon a group had gathered at the litter, arguing amongst themselves and looking around them. After a while, they began to trickle back to their huts, shrugging their shoulders as if to say they did not really care that their victim had escaped.

It was clear that these people were both male and female, and there were many children among them. It seemed to be a nudist colony, but, to my surprise, it appeared I was wrong, for after a couple of hours, as the sun began to go down, an amazing assortment of people in costume came out in front of the longhouse. Three very strange musicians piped up, and the whole crowd began to whirl around in a fanatical dance to their pagan melody. One player was half-human, half goat, and played a set of Panpipes. The second figure, clad entirely in green from head to foot, had leafy hair and leaves growing out of his mouth, as he plucked a lyre, and the third wore a white Punchinello mask with a long nose and beat on a large drum.

The crowd was very festive and I loved the way they were dressed in vivid costumes of every imaginable design. Their faces were heavily made up, some with clown features, others in drag with huge wigs of blonde hair balanced on top of their nodding heads, and more in the skins of various animals, such as dogs, wolves and bears. Rivula became very excited, and begged to link up with them. She dressed herself in a wild costume and joined the dance that went round and round, the people weaving in and out, singing and evidently partaking generously of some sort of black drink from a very large barrel.

Twilight crept over the revelers, and yet night seemed to drive them to new frenzies, as they lit blazing torches at a huge bonfire and spread out further into the meadow, their little points of light disappearing in pairs towards the bushes at the edge of the forest. I knew what they had in mind, remembering my parlor with the striped awning nostalgically, as if in another life. Now I was free from those lusts and could focus my energy on this new quest.

The noise died down towards dawn, and I curled up in a hollow and slept a little. When I opened my eyes, the meadow was deserted and there was no sign of life around the longhouse, but there were clothes strewn everywhere. I could hear faint cries, shouting, and laughing from the river. It was a good chance to investigate their houses, so I decided to camouflage myself. I picked a number of leafy branches and draped them over my head, and set out on all fours to cross the meadow. Crawling is not my favorite method of progression, but it did make me look smaller and blend in with the surroundings. I reached the wall of the nearest hut, my knees torn and scraped, and cautiously peered around the corner. Assuring myself that the place was deserted, I quickly slid into the nearest doorway, and immediately stumbled over a stinking pile of garbage, containing hamburger wrappers, chicken bones, cans and all sorts of other things, including torn clothes, burnt pans and battered books. The place was a mess! Several cots stood around the walls, piled high with dirty linens and cast-off decorations from the night before. There was a small dresser with a spotted mirror, dusted with spilled make up in various jars, and brushes filled with hairballs. An empty bottle of perfume lay on the floor.

Leaving the first hut, I checked out some of the others, and found they were equally filthy. I moved on to the longhouse, arranged as a banqueting hall with long tables and benches. This room was dense with the smell of stale cooking, rotting food, and spilt wine that dripped from a spigot in the wall. The tables, littered with dirty plates, led to sinks full of unwashed dishes. I was disgusted and was about to leave, when the door darkened and someone slipped through. It was too late to hide, so I faced the newcomer bravely, shaking my leafy headdress down to cover my features.

A piercing scream burst forth from the person, who had not expected to find anyone there. He, for it was a naked man, leapt into the air, yelling at the top of his voice. He fled from the hall, shouting and running back towards the river. I had to move out quickly before they all came to find me. I did not know their intentions, and I had already formed a very bad opinion of them.

Darting out of the banqueting hall, I sprinted across the meadow towards the safety of the surrounding trees. Unfortunately, a trailing branch from my disguise tripped me up, and I fell flat on my face as the first people came running up from the river, dripping wet. They crowded around me, poking me in the back, and then turned me over. I saw a sea of inquiring faces above me as small hands reached down and pulled me to my feet. Everyone started to talk at once, putting innumerable jumbled questions that were hard to understand. I waved my hand in front of my face in a warning gesture, and they reluctantly pushed forward one of their number.

He spoke up nervously. "I'm the one who found you in our dining room. I'm not used to speaking as an individual, so you will have to forgive me." Here he paused uncertainly. "What were you doing there? We want to know why you are alone. Where is your group?"

"I don't have a particular group. I am an individual and I often travel by myself. I suppose you could say that I am part of the Navigators group, but we now have our own lives and personalities, and we are free and can think for ourselves." I gave a faint smile.

"Good heavens! We've never heard of such a thing. How can you survive without belonging to a group?" He shook his head in amazement. "We're always together and we do everything with each other. I would be very lonely if I didn't have someone by my side all the time."

"That would drive me mad." I said in a resolute voice. "Do you mean you don't treasure solitude? That is so important to us."

"Solitude? What good would that be? How could we exchange ideas if there was nobody to talk with? Relationship is very important to us, and even if we are alone for five minutes by mistake, we always have the radio on, just to make noise, so that we are not afraid."

"That's very surprising. As you now know, I've been inside your homes, and they are awfully untidy. Don't you ever clean up and get organized?"

"What for? It would only get dirty again. That would be a waste of a beautiful day. We just wash the dishes when we need them, in fact, some of us prefer to have the remains of our last meal still on the plate, as it adds flavor and saves water. We like water to bathe in, to amuse ourselves."

"Well, I was disgusted by your living quarters." I looked at them sternly, my natural motherly inclination taking over. "Would you like me to teach you how to keep your village in order? I could begin with the first hut, and you could all help me."

They looked at me with horror. Then their spokes person began to weep inconsolably, and with one accord, they all burst into tears, sobbing on each others' shoulders and mopping their eyes with strands of their companions' hair. I was astonished. Had I said something dreadful? They turned, and began trailing back towards the river, their backs bent, as if by a great tragedy, leaving me alone.

Oh, dear! They were obviously very upset and insulted by my suggestion. I followed them, trying to understand why they preferred to live in disorder. Walking down to the river, I saw, to my surprise, that as each person reached the water, they began to shout with joy, and soon everyone was splashing and playing as before, their cares immediately cast aside. I sat and watched them until the sun started to go down, when they began to leave the river and return to the longhouse. Several of them beckoned to me, so I joined them, somewhat annoyed by their loud and continuous chatter, and went with them to see how the evening would turn out.

"Please join us for dinner," one of the men volunteered. "We don't want you to eat alone," he added. "You must spend an awful lot of time cleaning up after yourself."

"Yes!" Another slim girl said shyly. "That's such a waste of a wonderful day – we can play all day and into the night as well. It's a great life here."

A third spoke more solemnly. "We only have a single regret, and that is, to understand why we have been cast out from the Sphere of Netzach, our real home. We have asked ourselves this many times, but we have not found the answer."

Pullows stopped and sighed deeply, then continued....

"I see that your way of life has many advantages." I volunteered. "You're all easy to get along with, and you don't hold grudges. Indirectly, however, you are being selfish, for you are amusing yourselves without considering ways of using your great talents as entertainers to raise the spirits of people who are less fortunate."

"Oh! I get it. You mean we should reach out to new people who live in Malkuth? We do know that the other three quarters of the world of Malkuth are not as happy as we are."

"You may be happy, but it is a superficial thing. Unless you do reach out to the Malkuthians, all of whom are going through their own difficulties, you won't feel that ultimate satisfaction of touching those who are strangers to you." I continued. "I have an idea. You have some very talented musicians, and you dance very skillfully. Can you also tell jokes?"

"Oh! Yes. We have several performing magicians who live here, and we are always joking around and playing tricks on people. It makes us laugh. Could we learn to do a performance?"

"It would take dedication and more discipline." I said. "I can be your director, because I have learned to pay attention to my inner voice. We will put on a Gypsy Opera, for I am sure you also have wonderful singers, isn't that so?"

"What a great idea!" They all shouted and jumped up and down like little children. "Let's have dinner and then sit down and put our ideas together. We'll come up with something."

Everyone rushed to the benches and wriggled into their places, and I sat down at the end of a table. A plate of food was set down before me, and the plate seemed clean, which was a relief. Someone must have been dishwashing and cooking, after all.

"Who came back to cook the dinner?" I asked them as I cut into a vegetarian steak of pea-goat. "It is delicious."

"Oh, we always order out. Nobody here wants to take the time to cook. There's a very good franchise about ten minutes from here, and they deliver our meals."

The dinner went well, although it was hard for me to concentrate on the meal amid all the chatter, laughter, and cat calling that went on amongst the diners, some of them playfully flicking spoonfuls of tapir-okra pudding at each other. Afterwards, when they rose from the clutter on the tables, throwing down their knives and forks with a rattle, they sat down outside the longhouse around the big bonfire, and discussed the lyrics for their opera.

It was agreed by all that some of the music should be from Gypsy heritage. They liked the idea of Lizards' Hungarian Rhapsody and themes from Rave-ons' Bolero, and the musicians thought optimistically that the scores would be easy to play on the pipes, lyre and drum. The dancers got into an argument about the choreography, but finally worked out some steps that included a break dancing minuet, and the singers decided that the main voice would be a parody of pantomime, Pucchin-ello and Pavarotti. The costumes were easy. They already had full closets of different styles, although quite a few of them needed mending, so somebody organized a sewing bee and they got started with needle and thread.

The next problem, with the opera written and rehearsed, was to get in touch with the other Malkuthians and arrange a central spot on the Island where they could all meet. They first sent a group of envoys to the Citrine Quarter. These received a somewhat lackadaisical welcome, which was only to be expected, considering the nature of the fallen Yesodians. However, once Semra received them in the Longing Room, she did promise to attend with her meditators, for they had all finally received plenty of ether from Yesod, and they were in a mood of outward gregariousness.

The envoys who went to the Russet Quarter found a scene of great confusion. The boats containing the escaping Hodians had reached the shores of the Sphere of Hod, but to their disappointment, they had been turned back without an explanation. They had returned to the Russet Quarter, only to find it usurped by thousands of animals, who had escaped and were breeding indiscriminately. The one good thing about this situation was that the Qliphoth had given up their conquest in disgust, as the odor of manure hung heavily over the dunes and the quicksilver building was occupied entirely by millions of munching fruit bats. The Hodians could not reoccupy their land, and they were camped on the shore in disarray, and, instead of cleaning up their campsite, they were quite eager to have some entertainment to break the monotony of constant drills, and agreed to come as long as the opera had a logical conclusion.

The third group of envoys that were sent to the Black Quarter had been captured by the Qliphoth the minute they crossed the border, and made to swear that the opera would include an evil, satanic actor that they supplied themselves. Furthermore, they wanted the plot to write in at least five dramatic murders. They produced their repulsive actor immediately, and with great distaste the Olive envoys promised to rewrite the script, as they were forced to bring him back to their Quarter and house him in one of the huts, which he immediately tore apart looking for a box of Alaskan cigars.

To end with, the troupe of actors were ready and assembled on the meadow, their costumes, draperies for the stage settings, and backdrops loaded on to the horde of dogs that scavenged around the village. They all set out for the circular valley with me, singing and clapping their hands, dancing and making merry. As several days passed on the trail and they had not bathed, they began to carouse less, and by the fifth day of walking, they had all fallen silent. Each one was lost in his very own thoughts and focused on putting one foot in front of the other, for they were exhausted and longed to return to the river.

I led the hushed crowd to the circular valley, reaching out my arms when I saw the Navigator and Bazoom awaiting me, as they tried to catch the words that fell from my lips.

"Look at all these people! They have come to perform a Gypsy Opera. We have invited many of the Malkuthians, so that they may come together and be united at last!"

As I turned around to introduce the crowd of actors, a puff of wind swept across my face, and my words vanished into thin air, along with the multitude that had accompanied me.

Paragutts Story of the Black Quarter

Pullows looked rather taken aback as she sat down with us around our small fire. We ate, and then she tried to explain how there really had been a multitude of people following her, and that they had rehearsed a Gypsy Opera that they wanted to perform. It was hard for Bazoom and I to believe her, but she seemed genuine. In any case, they had all vanished, so there was nothing further to be done, except to wonder about the strange people in three of the quarters of Malkuth, and to look anxiously along the path to the North, searching for the little figure of Paragutt, who was overdue.

Five days passed, during which I became increasingly worried. Our food had run out and we were chewing on twigs and finding the odd cockroach for dinner. I always took off the legs before I swallowed them. On the evening of the fifth day, I saw the small figure of Paragutt limping slowly towards us, and I ran to greet him. He was badly wounded, I could see, with a bandage around his head, one arm in a sling, and his feet completely raw and bloody.

"What has happened to you, Paragutt? Here, jump on my back, and I 'll carry you. Have a leg up." He was used to climbing up easily, but this time it was hard for him.

He sighed with relief. "I thought I wasn't going to make it. The Black Quarter is horrifying, even for someone who is Fear itself. I saw every kind of demon you could imagine – why, I honestly believe that artist – not Breugel – the other fellow, Bosch – must have visited the Qliphoth before he did those amazing paintings." He laid his head down on my shoulder and relaxed. "After that experience, we'll never be afraid any more, since you and I are unified now. I must remember that I have the Order of the Nonexistent Empire, or ONE, awarded me by Ignitia, the Knight of Wands."

"That's right. That's why I allowed you to go and investigate the Black Quarter. I was with you in spirit." I laid him down gently by the fire, and Pullows attended to his wounds.

"When you are rested, you must tell us your story. Here's some food – only a few cockroaches, but they are very nutritious – and then you should get some sleep."

Paragutt was much improved the following morning, with a fresh bandage made from Pullows petticoat and his feet dressed with Vaseline. We sat down and he began his tale of terror under the influence of the Qliphoth.

"Trid and I set out along the path that led North, and kept straight on as night fell. At a dim crossroads, I was able to make out four signposts, but I could not read the signs. A tall, dark figure of a woman, trailing long skirts behind her, accosted us.

"Which way are you going, little yellow one and companion? I am Hecate, Keeper of the Crossroads, and I will read the signs for you, because my eyes are sharp, even in dim light. Which road do you choose?"

"We have already chosen." I said. "The road to the North Quarter, if you will let us pass."

"Oh! Foolish one. That is a dangerous path. You can change your mind, if you like. I am offering you a more sensible choice."

We hesitated, then I pulled myself together and insisted that I had decided on the road to the Black Quarter. I wasn't going to pull back now, for I remembered I had made a promise to you. I bowed to Hecate and moved on down the path, towards the dread adventures awaiting me. Trid, however, hesitated.

"I don't feel comfortable on that path," he said. "I'm going to go this way instead."

He turned and strode firmly off to the south without another word.

It was a blow to lose my companion so soon, and I felt I secretly despised his lack of bravery. There was nothing for it however, so, traveling all night as the dawn must be near, I looked east expecting to see the sun rising, yet the twilight remained and at the hour of dawn the horizon barely brightened to a faint glow. I could see well enough, for all fearful creatures like me have good night vision. After a short distance, I came to a long wall of black stones crudely placed on top of each other to about ten feet high. In the wall were two lych gates, spaced about ten feet apart. I tried the knob of the left one, but it was locked. I went over to the other gate and was about to put my hand on the latch, when a sonorous voice addressed me from above.

"Which gate will you choose? The wych gate or the gate of the witches? I can open the one you choose, or you can choose the one I open, or the one that opens will be the one you choose, or the open one will choose you. Ha! Ha! Ha! Confusing, isn't it?"

I braced my narrow shoulders, gazing from one gate to another. They were exactly the same with their dark and ancient woodwork. I decided to try the left hand gate, and pointed to it.

"O.K. Be ready. I'm going to open it. Now, you don't have to choose that gate, remember, there is always the other one." A smothered chuckle came from what I now saw was a gatehouse at the top of the wall.

The gate swung open with a screech of rusty hinges, and I was about to step through when I saw that the path leading away from it was no thicker than a strand of wire that stretched across a deep chasm. The tightrope that crossed the dark, bottomless abyss in front of me made me draw back uncertainly.

"Aha! Didn't like that one too well, eh?" Mocked the voice from above. "The other one appears easier, I can tell you. Mind you, appearances are not always as they seem, and who would know that better than yourself?"

I ignored the provocation and walked over to the righthand gate, which opened noiselessly, as if it had been oiled frequently. Ahead I saw a reasonably broad road leading into the vague distance. The land on each side was flat and featureless. It seemed much safer than the left gate, so I walked through.

"Goodbyeee! Have fun! I wonder if you chose the right gate or the correct gate? I guess you'll have to find out, won't you? Ha! Ha!" The sonorous voice teased.

I set out on the grey road, heaving a sigh of relief that I did not have to walk a tightrope to get into the Black Quarter. I wished there was better light, but my eyes were accustomed to the dark by now. It was just....that there might be something hiding behind the low bushes that now began to sprout on either side of the road. It was impossible to see any movement clearly.

To my relief, the road ended briefly in a walled staging area, where a row of gun carriages, pulled by skeletal horses, stood in line. The driver of the first carriage, who resembled a mortar shell, beckoned to me with a trailing arm of shattered metal and indicated that I should climb up and sit behind it on the steel seat that swung on top of a large, spiral spring. My light weight made the seat wobble frenetically and it was hard to hold on, so I braced my feet firmly against the large cannon below me as the carriage rumbled off.

The ride was incredibly uncomfortable. The carriage was very heavy, and had solid iron wheels that jolted and crunched over every dip in the road. I leaned forward and asked the driver, who seemed oblivious to my discomfort, whether another form of transport was available. There was no reply. I put my hand on the smooth curve of its shoulder, and tried to peer into its face. I could just see two gleaming metallic eyes, a sharp nose like a fin, and a thin slit of a mouth. I thought maybe it could not speak.

The road began to slope upwards and, reaching the top, I saw in the dim light that we were overlooking a deep, flat valley divided into ten sections, the road winding down and passing through the middle of each section in turn, twisting and turning as if in a labyrinth. As we rumbled on, the sound of quarreling and restless crowds below came faintly on a cold wind that seared my face. The unpleasant sound grew louder as I leaned forward, nerving myself to face whatever was in store. The gun carriage tipped gently as it began to roll down the side of the hill, gaining speed rapidly. I hung on and yelled to the driver to put on the brakes, but my cries were ignored. We hurtled to a stop and panting, my heart thudding, drew up outside the first section, and the driver rang a sonorous bell. A door in the high walls that now enclosed the rough road opened, and revealed the space inside to be a large office, although I had never worked in one with the Navigator. It was huge, and divided into about 50 cubicles, in which sat apathetic workers who all looked the same, staring inertly at their computer screens. The driver took out a prod and gave me a brief and startling electric shock, at which I jumped from the carriage with a shriek, and ran inside.

In spite of my agitation, there was an air of indifference about the place, and I could see that many of the people were not focusing on their paperwork, but were spending the time playing computer games, drinking coffee and stealing out to smoke cigarettes. I wondered how much they were getting done? As I watched and passed among them, they didn't seem to notice me. I knew that if I was invisible to them, they would not be disturbed at my appearance.

Out of the blue, a fierce curse resounded through the office as a tall, thin man with an eagle eye came striding down the hall, glancing into each cubicle as he passed. A rustle of whispers hastily alerted the workers, and they began to type, but it was too late for one of them, an immensely fat woman who sat, perspiring, her stomach overflowing onto the keyboard. The boss had already spotted the Free Cell game she was playing, and although she quickly flipped to Excel, he stopped at her desk with a scowl.

"Don't try to hide from me! I'm sick of your indolent ways." The man snatched up a pile of papers from the desk and shook them angrily.

"Look, you were given these forms to file last week, and they still aren't done! Don't try to kid me – you were playing games on your computer again."

He slammed his fist into the side of the cubicle, smashing a large hole in the flimsy wood. "Goddamit! I've given you so many chances. Now I've had enough. You're fired!"

The woman began to cry. "Please don't fire me! I'm so tired. My mother is very sick at home, and I'm caring for her. She is tossing and moaning with pain all night, so I can't get any sleep. I just can't focus on my work at the moment." She mopped her eyes with her sleeve.

"You know, I really don't give a damn about your mother. Old ladies get sick all the time – just leave her with some sleeping pills and let her be. If you're lucky, she might take an overdose by mistake. That would save you the trouble of looking after her."

He spat on the floor and turned his shoe in it. "That's what I think, and that's not going to change my decision. Pack up your desk and I'll escort you to the door. You have five minutes."

"Please, please let me stay on. I desperately need the money. My mother has no health insurance, and we are broke." She turned tearful eyes up to him, but he was not impressed.

"Oh! I can't stand weeping women. Get moving, now, and don't waste my time. I'll be back in a few minutes."

With that, her boss strode out angrily and, sobbing quietly, she began to open her desk drawers and empty out the contents. I rushed to help her, catching hold of her arm in sympathy. She turned to see who was there, but her glance encountered empty space. In spite of that, she seemed to calm down at my touch, and dried her eyes. By the time the boss came back, she was composed and ready to leave.

I walked invisibly beside her as he pushed her roughly out of the door, her briefcase thrown after her. I followed her home and made sure she was safe. Then I turned with a heavy heart, and thought that it was a cruel way to treat someone who needed help, and if her boss had not been so cold hearted he could have arranged for her to keep her job. The Black Quarter did not seem very nice, but little did I know this was just the beginning of a series of unjust actions that I would have to witness under the spell of the Qliphoth.

The gun carriage with its horrible driver was waiting, and it ordered me back on board. As we traveled to the next section, the driver commented rudely. "Serves her right! Lazy time-waster. I love it when people don't do their work properly. It creates a back log, and their co-workers get upset. That's very satisfactory."

I chose not to reply to this sarcastic remark. After a short and bumpy drive, we came around a bend and arrived at a run-down singlewide trailer, from which came the sounds of conflict. The shouts, slaps, and gurgling screams I heard made me jump from the carriage before the driver could prod me, run up to the door and fling it open. Facing me across the room was a big brute of a woman, with a leather belt dangling from her fist, and a small man crouched in a corner, his hands over his face, trying to shield himself from her blows. I stood in the doorway, appalled.

"Damn door blew open again, Bob!" The woman bawled. "Another thing you never got around to fixin' – yer useless son of a bitch! Ter hell wiv yer – get outta here or I'll give you somethin' ter remember the rest of yer life."

With that, she leapt forward, bringing the heavy leather belt down across Bobs' shoulders and face, again and again. She then seized the unfortunate man by the scruff of his neck and dragged him to the open door.

I, of course, was invisible, and I had to jump aside quickly as Bob was bundled down the steps. "Please, Gertie! Let me come back in. It's cold out here. You know I don't have the money for a bed."

He paused, his teeth chattering, then, as the door slammed shut, a grimace twisted his thin face. "You cleaned out my bank account, you greedy fuckin' bitch. I'll report you to the authorities. Yes, I'll report you to the IRS, too. You've been cheating on your taxes for years. Yes, I'll do that, and you try to stop me, bitch!"

With that, Bob got to his feet and made off at great speed along the road before Gertie, who was watching from the window, could land him another blow.

I followed scurrying Bob along the road towards a large ugly building with the words "St. Astaroths Hospital" written above the door. He paused, then edged towards the door slowly. Immediately, a long, hairy arm grabbed him and drew him inside. I followed, keeping to the side of the lengthy, grey passageway. I could hear the hairy doctor, who looked very much like a chimpanzee, muttering and chattering at Bob. Two heavy doors opened and slammed shut behind them. I pushed at the doors but they were firmly closed, and I couldn't pass through. The last thing I heard was a long drawn out, gurgling scream. Then there was silence.

Considerably shaken by these two unpleasant incidents, I climbed back on the carriage and we drove to the next bend in the road. The driver sniffed disdainfully.

"I really enjoy these passive-aggressive types like Bob! They think they're a cut above open violence. The real truth is that hidden aggression is more subtle and damaging, by sending out a powerful message of secret rage. This sort of conduct is much more interesting than a mere blow to the head."

I began to think the driver had a decidedly nasty streak, and kept my counsel. Then the smell of slopped beer and liquor greeted me as we halted outside a greasy looking tavern, where the foul odor of cigarette smoke rolled from the door in a dense cloud, accompanied by the sounds of drunken carousing. I took my last breath of the already fetid air, and dived inside to inspect the scene.

"Well, fuck you too! You cheated again. I saw you palm a card, Dick!" An angry voice fell on my ear. "I declare this game null and void, dammit!"

"Oh, come on, Jake." A voice wheedled. "You can't say any of us are honest, now, can you? How are we supposed to win if we don't cheat?"

"How dare you! I don't cheat," insisted the first speaker. "My wins are pure luck. Or maybe, they are your stupidity?"

"You're insulting me!" The second man sounded furious. "I'll take it outside. Or are you too chicken to face me? Come on, double dealer, how about it?"

"Right! You're on. Son of a bitch, do I have to break your ass again? You know what happened last time."

The men both jumped up and made for the door, pushing past me as they rolled up their sleeves for a fight. Leaving them to their conflict, which, in any case, I could not control, I moved through the smoky atmosphere to another table, where the rattle of dice, accompanied by rasping coughs, heralded the announcement by the dealer that red-6 would be paid. Being invisible was a distinct advantage, I decided, as I walked to a third table, where a sad looking woman was placing a large pile of counters on a number. The roulette wheel spun, as her eyes followed it with anxious hunger, then her face fell as the dealer swiped away her counters. She had lost her last bet.

Rising from the table, she stumbled through the dense atmosphere towards the door. As she reached the threshold, it slammed open and a man appeared, blood dripping down his face. Mumbling through broken teeth, he went to the bar.

"For fucks' sake, get an ambulance! I think he's dead. Oh, God! I hope I haven't killed him. I'll be in real trouble then. Hurry! There's no time to lose." He lurched back outside, knocking the astonished woman aside.

"Where's my husband? Where's my man, you asshole?" She spat at him and followed him out of the door. A terrible scream cut through the air.

"Dick! Oh, Dick! Are you all right? Say something to me, Dick." She shook the prone man on the ground. "Dick – oh my God! He's not breathing, oh God, help me. Someone get an ambulance." She rose to her feet and began screaming hysterically. "Oh God! It's my fault. I shouldn't have come in here. I knew he would follow me and get in trouble again." She knelt down over the body, covering her face and choking with sobs. A clanging noise announced the arrival of the ambulance.

"Where's the problem? Lady, move out of the way, now. Is this your husband?"

"Yes, I think he's dead. That bastard Jake floored him again. Please, please hurry."

The medic bent over the man, taking his pulse. "We need CPR immediately. Get the defibrillator."

Paragutt began to weep copiously. Pullows and I bent over him, holding him gently and drying his tears. After a few minutes, he gulped, and went on with his story.

"I could take no more. It all seemed so unfair. I left the scene and jumped into the carriage, turning around the next curve of the road. The driver remarked sardonically. "Gambling dens are one of my favorite places. They always create violence and can lead to murder, which is at the top of my list of pleasures."

I ignored this ugly remark as we arrived at a large and hideous building, where a milling crowd had gathered, looking upwards. Following their gaze, I saw a figure in a business suit clinging to a ledge on the 32nd floor of the corporate headquarters.

A group of people, dressed in suits, were yelling up to him. "Don't! Don't jump, Henry! We'll work it out. The money isn't that important. Think of your wife and kids, Henry. Go back inside, carefully now."

A fire truck with a long ladder was up against the building. The ladder only reached to the 27th floor, but I could see firemen leaning out of the window above the man, talking to him calmly, while below, others were spreading a large canvas tarp to catch the man if he fell.

"What's happened here?" I asked, not really wanting to know. "What made him so upset? I hope he decides to give up any thoughts of suicide and go inside again."

Someone near me answered. "It's the corporation. They just heard today that it's failed and faces bankruptcy. He's the director, and he blames himself. Had a corporate jet, and all that, you know, millionaires' house in Florida and all the perks."

"Yes." Added another onlooker angrily. "He awarded himself those huge bonuses. I hope he jumps! His life isn't worth living now. There are plenty of people down here who are ready to tear him apart. They've lost all their money – it's a Ponzi scam. Disgusting, I call it."

As he spoke, the desperate man let go of the ledge and plunged downwards, screaming. The firemen holding the canvas positioned themselves under his falling body, but, in a flash, a woman bystander jumped into the middle of the tarp, and they had to move it, for fear she would be crushed by the falling body. The director landed onto the concrete sidewalk with a horrible thump as the crowd fell back in a hushed silence. Then, all mayhem broke loose as cops arrested the woman.

"I'm his wife! He deserved to die! He's been having an affair with his secretary. Now, at last, I'm rid of him and his philandering." She was laughing hysterically as they led her away.

"Ha! Ha!" Roared my driver. "Greed, adultery, suicide and manslaughter, all in one episode. I'm enjoying myself tremendously on this trip."

What a horrible place, I thought, as the gun carriage rounded the next bend in the road. I was dreading what I would find next. Was there nothing good here? Nothing worthwhile? No happiness or peace? Yet, I knew that I had to observe further experiences, for I had seen ten separate partitions on the winding road of the Black Quarter. Was I going to hell and back, I wondered?

The carriage jerked to a halt again. I was in an urban park with a skateboarding ramp, where several teenagers were scooting around, doing jumps and wheelies. Across the brown and deadened grass, two or three ragged people were waiting on a corner furtively, their hands in their pockets. A car drew up, and the driver leaned out, handing over some money and receiving a small packet.

Two of the teenagers were watching. I crept closer to hear what they were saying. They could not see me, of course.

"Have you never tried it, then? It gives you a real buzz." Said the taller one. "Want to buy some?"

"I don't know. Don't you get hooked on it?" His friend replied "I've hears some scary stories. I don't think I want to try it. Anyway, my parents would have a fit. I'd have to hide it from them."

"You're not really worried about them, are you? Good heavens, they probably did it themselves when they were younger. They just won't admit it to you. Come on, now, just once. It won't harm you – it will make you feel good."

"OK. I will try it, if you say so. You do it and you seem perfectly normal. Will you get some for me?"

The taller teen walked over to the dealers and bought a small packet, then came back to the skateboarding park. As he was about to hand over the packet to his friend, two cops stepped forward out of the bushes and arrested him, pinning his arms behind his back and taking the packet.

"You're under arrest! When are you going to learn? Too much of a party man. You should leave the younger teens alone – you'll get them all hooked, if you're not careful. Anyway, this time you're going to be away for quite a while."

They moved towards the younger boy, wrestling his arms into handcuffs. "Why me? What did I do?" He yelled in fright. "I didn't get any of that stuff."

"You're guilty by association." The cops told him, as they led the two culprits away and placed them in a police car that drove off towards the local jail.

Shaking my head sadly, I moved too slowly, and the driver managed to get in a sharp electric shock with its prod on my butt. As I jumped and clutched my scraggy rear end, a metallic clockwork chuckle came from somewhere inside its chest.

The driver was positively ecstatic. "Drugs! What a boon they are to the dark side. Of course, there's nothing wrong with the substance itself. What

I enjoy is the mess people get into when they abuse the drug in ignorance. Wrongful arrest, too. Those cops are good at profiling."

I jumped back onto the carriage in some haste as we moved on to the next section, where a five-barred gate separated us from several fields of a small farm. A grumpy-looking old man stared at me from the entrance to a ramshackle barn. He shook a pitchfork at the carriage threateningly, looking over our shoulders to a position beyond us.

Since I was invisible, I could not understand what he was looking at, until I turned around and saw a group of tweed-clad women chanting and holding up banners with the slogan "SOPPY – "Save Our Precious Pigs Yard". There was no doubt they were right. The farmyard over the split wood fence was awash in deep and smelly mud, where several very emaciated pigs rooted miserably and lay around. Beyond them, starving cows and a couple of horses leaned weakly against a dilapidated fence. There was no hay in the racks and the situation was, obviously, very serious.

The stout countrywomen advanced slowly, shaking their fists at the farmer, who snarled back at them. The leader, a robust woman in a twin set with pearls, climbed on the fence and shouted at him.

"You ought to be ashamed of yourself! These animals are starving. If you can't feed them, at least give them away to those who can. We're giving you twenty-four hours to get food for them, and if you don't, we'll confiscate them tomorrow. That's a promise."

She gave a cautionary wave of her banner and climbed down. They all marched off in military formation as the old man collapsed onto his knees, weeping bitterly.

I approached more closely, moving around the fence to hear him.

"Why, oh why did my dear wife Emma have to die? She was my greatest helper, feeding the animals and caring for them, churning the butter and baking. Since she was struck down by cholera, I haven't wanted to live, let alone carry on. What is worse, the government has curtailed all the essential farm subsidies I used to get. There was no need to labor in those days, I merely put on the appearance of work when the inspectors came round. Now I have no income and no money to buy food. Woe is me, indeed!"

I could do nothing to aid him, there being no oats or hay available. Instead, I passed an uneasy night by the pigpen, and woke to the sound of harsh cries from the army of women who had gathered, wielding scythes, pitch forks and axes, at the fence. Some of them climbed over and began to lasso the pigs that vainly ran this way and that, shrieking in terror, while other women put halters on the cows and horses and began to lead them away.

The old man went berserk. He ran from one to the other, jabbing them with his pitchfork, grabbing them by their sleeves and trying to drag them away from the hogs, which were becoming hysterical. The scene was a battlefield of churning mud. The honking and snorting of the pigs, the cries of the women as their tweed suits were spattered with mud, and the shouts of rage from the farmer created a immense melee, a mix of pulling and pushing, of lassoing and whipping, of blows with the axe. Pigs were being dragged this way and that as they screamed high pitched cries of terror and fought to escape the lassos that tightened around their trotters.

The women got away with most of the larger animals, and they killed many pigs in the battle. Most of the women fell into the mud and filth, and the word was quickly telegraphed around town, so that all the folks came to see them and laugh. They also took the opportunity of making away with all the dead pigs, and had a magnificent luau the next day, while the old farmer fell on his pitchfork and died."

Again, Paragutt collapsed in a spasm of weeping. I could see he was severely depressed, and I could not blame him. How could people behave like that? Of course, the Black Quarter was ruled over by the Qliphoth. The humans who lived in that land were steeped in their evil influence, and could see no other way of behaving. I felt very sad as Paragutt bravely went on to complete his story.

"The next section I approached with a feeling of trepidation, as the driver chuckled hollowly. "Great! Another example of ignorance. Those women passed judgment without even investigating the real cause of the farmers' problems. That was a perfect case of presumption."

I was witnessing some of the worst behavior I had ever seen. Dread filled my days in the Black Quarter. Whatever would be next? It resolved itself into a giant factory, with the sound of whirring machines, rattling and clanking coming from the building. I found the front door and went inside, where rows upon rows of toiling workers, their faces bent nearsightedly to their tasks, tended shuddering machines that tapped out package after package of cigarettes. The noise was unimaginable.

I moved quietly towards a far corner of the factory, where a small group of workers were gathering surreptitiously, and listened carefully.

"I don't know about you, but I've had enough! We're not going to stand for this any longer." Said a tough looking working man. "It's time to put our foot down. The union hasn't backed us at all – they're pandering to the managers – and we haven't been paid in months."

"We're behind you." Said several voices. "It's time to end this abominable situation."

"Tonight, then, it must be." Their leader announced in a hushed tone. "We'll meet outside the back door with the implements that we need. You know what they are. That was settled at our discussion last month."

"Do we have to go this far?" Questioned a small, scrawny woman. "We'll lose our jobs. I need the money."

"If we're not going to get paid, we might as well be at home. Working for nothing is unacceptable, in my opinion. We've tried to come to terms with the big brass. Now they will see the result of their obstinacy!"

Several of the workers laughed nervously. The group split up and went back to their positions. I made a note to be at the back door of the plant that evening.

When evening came, the group of workers had become a crowd, joined by many people from the surrounding area. Several of them were carrying gasoline cans and boxes, which, it turned out, contained sticks of dynamite. As dusk fell, and the last manager had left, they broke into the plant, pouring gasoline over everything, and laying lines of dynamite that were joined together by fuses. At a signal, everyone left the building and retired some distance away while two men stood, ready to start the conflagration.

I thought it wise to be further away, as I figured their idea was not very sensible. In fact, this proved to be the case as they ignited the fuse. In a few seconds, the place blew sky high in an enormous explosion. I saw, with horror, that the terrible blast had also consumed the crowd who watched. They had destroyed themselves along with their hated factory, and the only survivors were the managers, who had gone home.

There were still three more sections to pass through. I began to understand why the driver snorted approvingly.

"Revenge! It always goes wrong. Revenge is the most unbalanced attitude of all – I love to see how it backfires on the perpetrators."

I could see the cold eyes of the carriage driver sizing up my reactions. I wondered whether I should have tried walking the tightrope in the beginning. Maybe that would have turned out to be the easier way, after all? Anyway, it was too late now, and I soon found myself outside the portico of a large and flashy hotel facing onto a beach walk filled with strolling tourists. It was night, for some flickering lamps sputtered in the breeze. Everything had been dark all the way along – the sun never shone on this place, I reckoned miserably.

I walked into the hotel lobby and went over to the front desk. In a firm voice, I booked a room on the sixth floor, number 66. The clerk heard me but he could not see me. However, he seemed satisfied with my payment, so I went upstairs. Settling down for the night, I heard a fierce argument going on in the room next door.

"You grasping bitch! I did pay you." Came a man's voice. "You're not getting any more for your services. You refused to do what I wanted, anyway. You don't deserve a penny."

"I never promised you anything!" The woman objected. "I don't do that sort of dirty stuff, anyway. Go to someone else next time. You're disgusting!"

"How dare you call me that, you cunt!" The man was in a rage. "You're not going to get away with that. No! you're not. No one saw me come in here with you, and no one will see me leave. They will find you, what's left of you – that's all!"

"No! Put that gun away!" The woman shrieked. "I didn't mean any harm. Just go, I won't mention this to anyone, please."

"Too late, my dear. No bitch calls me disgusting, or any other name. Say your prayers, then kneel down with your back to me."

"For God's sake, no! I haven't done anything to you." Her voice was cut short by a click, as of a silencer on a gun, and a small thump. The door opened and a mans' footsteps hurried away down the corridor.

I was frozen to the spot! I dared not call for help, in case I implicated myself At least, that was my first thought. However, I quickly remembered that I was invisible, and so I dialed 911 on the hotel phone and told them there had been an accident in number 68. I then swiftly left the hotel by the back stairs, hoping that the shot had not proved to be fatal.

The road led ahead, and I was getting tired as I boarded the carriage. It rounded the next bend, the driver, as usual, full of itself.

"Prostitution is such a useful profession. No one has ever been able to get rid of it. Sex is what drives most people – at the lowest level of their possibilities. May it reign forever!" It winked at me lewdly.

An imposing church stood in front of me. People were filing in and the bell was tolling for service, so I decided to sit in one of the back pews and hear the sermon. At least, I thought, nothing bad could happen here. Unfortunately, I was wrong.

The priest appeared in his scarlet and gold robes and genuflected in front of the altar. We prayed and sang some hymns, and then he mounted to the pulpit and opened his Bible at the place for the sermon. Just then, several small boys came out of the sacristy crying and ran to their parents in the congregation. The parents bent over them solicitously, trying to find out what the problem was. There was scuffling amongst the worshippers, and parents were getting up, walking around, and talking to each other in hushed voices. Everyone looked shocked and worried.

The priest came down the pulpit steps, and grabbed one of the boys. "I told you to stay in there." He sounded cross. "I said I'd come back and finish the Sunday school lesson after the service. Go back into the sacristy, now, and don't make a fuss."

"Father, it's too late." The young boy said modestly. "I don't like your lessons and nor do any of the other kids. It was weird and I felt uncomfortable. We decided to tell our parents before you did anything else to us. Please let me go." The boy tugged away from his grasp and ran to his parents.

The priest looked up, to find himself surrounded by a circle of irate people. One of the fathers spoke up. "Now we know what we suspected of you. The boys have told us the truth. You deserve nothing better than lynching! We trusted you with our children, and it's no good us trying to explain to the authorities, because they turn a blind eye. This has happened too many times before. Now we must take this matter into our own hands."

With that, they seized the priest and rushed him outside, where they stoned him to death and left the church well satisfied. The body was never found, as it had been bundled into a mausoleum in the graveyard, and the story was put about that the priest had suddenly left for a sodomite commune in the Middle East.

As usual, the driver had to comment as it eyed me keenly. "Ah! Yes. The Devil himself, who is our Master, wrought child molestation as one of his finest creations. It's all based on sex, of course, since few humans know how to control themselves. And the children are so sweet...." Its voice trailed away and a wistful curve came to its lips.

I turned away, deeply ashamed, yet I felt a sense of relief. There was only one more section left for me to endure. Feelings of horror and disgust at the human race bore heavily on me as I wearily remounted the creaking carriage, which rounded the last bend. Before me stretched a beach of black volcanic sand that led to the ocean. Over to one side of the strand was a small port, with a boatyard next to it where several boats were hauled out for repairs. I walked over and spoke to one of the yard workers.

"Hello. What goes on here? I've been traveling through some terrible situations. I hope that there is nothing to fear here?"

"Well, I don't think so. But very recently a 36' sloop with three filthy ruffians on board washed up on shore here. We managed to get it off the beach and hauled it out. They were very ungrateful, I must say." He gestured towards a battered looking boat in the corner of the yard. "It's over there. They already owe us haulage fees, and they're a no-good lot."

I looked over towards the boat and a flash of recognition shot through me. It was the sloop that the Navigator had set sail in from the Bar, I was certain. Then the three ruffians must be Endevvy, Numbyling and Pompeybou, for sure! I hastened over to the vessel, calling out their names. From a tent under the boat, a face looked out. It was Endevvy, but he was hardly recognizable. His hair had grown long and matted, and he even sported a beard. I held out my hand in greeting, expecting to be welcomed, but a puzzled expression crossed his face and he shrank back into the folds of the tent. Some whispered words passed, and then the other two came out, complaining of the disturbance.

I was shocked! Pompeybou and Numbyling were ragged and filthy. They glared at me, and I hurriedly reminded them. "This is Paragutt – don't you remember me?"

"We don't know you, mister. Don't come here begging for food, for there isn't much left of our stores." They waved their arms, signaling me to leave.

"No! I'm Paragutt. I belong to the Navigator – you know, I was one of the entities, but now, of course, we have all broken away. I was sent by the Navigator to investigate the Black Quarter, and I am now on my way back to the others."

"He's telling us a cock-and bull story, fellers. I didn't know the Navigator had a guy like him. Why, he looks kind of chicken-hearted, don't you think?"

"Maybe we never met." I responded. "I might have been operating through the Navigator at one time, and you were operating at another. Therefore, we don't know each other."

"You're talking a bunch of rubbish! If you don't leave, we'll make you leave." Pompeybou strutted forward menacingly and whacked me hard on my head. I saw stars and fell down, breaking my arm. "If you want any more of that, stick around. Otherwise, get out of here, you scrawny little bastard. Now!"

I made a hasty retreat, the agony from my bruised head and my arm, which I ascertained had a shattered radius, spurring me on. At a safe distance, I stopped, found a paint rag lying on the ground, and used it to make a rough sling. Then I sadly found my way up over the hill to the end of the road. Those that I knew had scorned me and sent me away. It was the final straw.

My story might end here, for I could see the lych gates leading out of the Black Quarter away up the hill in front of me, but I was in too much pain to climb back onto the gun carriage. The driver climbed down, chained me to the back of the cannon, and whipped up its horses, dragging me up the hill. I fell on my knees, rolling and gasping, as the rough gravel on the road tore into my side. I was cradling my broken arm and screaming at the top of my lungs when we reached the top of the hill, and I lay inert on the ground. The driver brought out the prod and gave me a fearsome shock, and I shot upright.

"Well, I hope you enjoyed yourself here. You've been pretty quiet. Taking it all in, I guess. This is how it is in Malkuth, and the Black Quarter holds sway over the entire Island, I'm proud to say." It glanced at me sideways. "Come back soon!"

"I'll never come back here again" I burst out, practically spitting my words. "This is an awful place, and the Navigator must be warned about it."

"Get yerself outta here!" It scowled. "You've seen enough, then! Better not come back. By the way, take that useless person with you, as well."

He pointed to a bundle of blankets by the side of the road. I shuffled over, for it was very painful to stand upright, and pulled back the blanket. A wan face looked up at me. It was the Page of Pentacles, Trid.

"What happened to you?" I asked. "You look dreadful. Can you walk?"

"I'll try." Came the faint response. He struggled to his feet, his clothing torn and in rags, and together we limped towards the gate. But the way out was not so easy. Before us lay a tightrope, strung across the abyss between us and the safety of the other side. We had to cross it somehow. A sonorous voice came to me over the crevasse.

"Ha! I see you're back. Had an accident? Ha! Ha! Ha! Well, you chose the easy way in, but it's very difficult to get out of the Black Quarter, once you have absorbed the evil that lies therein. Only those who are brave enough to fight back the demoniacal influence of the Qliphoth get out of here. Your only hope is to try the tightrope, I'm afraid. Go ahead! After all, you have very little to lose, since you are now aware of the immorality of most people. I wish you luck."

I nerved myself to cross the abyss. It would be especially difficult to balance with one arm in a sling, but I had to try.

Trid shrank back. "I can't make it across." He murmured. "I'll have to stay here."

"Give it a try." I encouraged him. "You'll be able to make it."

"No. I'd rather stay here. I feel I'm needed here, anyway. You go. I wish you the best, and thank you." He stepped back into the shadows.

I was unable to persuade him, so cautiously, step by step, I slid my feet along the cable. Fortunately, my feet were somewhat webbed, from living in a swamp, and so I found it was possible to wrap my toes around the cable to steady myself. Inching along, I made it across without falling, but the broken wires in the cable tore at my feet, and they were bleeding by the time I reached the gate. I did not care. All I wanted was to return to the Navigator.

I rapped on the gate. "Let me out! I have crossed the tightrope. I want to go home."

"Oh! All right, I suppose. You did pass the test. I'm surprised, I didn't think you had it in you." The voice let out a stifled titter, and the gate swung open. I was free!

I limped forward into the light.….."

Paragutt lay back, exhausted with his tale. I mopped his brow thoughtfully. I was sorry to hear about Trid, but maybe his place was there, and he might be able to make some changes. So – our boat was in the Black Quarter. We needed to repair it and launch it - that was clear.

It meant returning to face the malevolent forces that swirled down there. Paragutt should definitely not go back, or he would die. I decided to leave him in the charge of Pullows and take Bazoom with me for protection. The three crew members would recognize me – and I would pull them back into shape without fail.

I took Pullows aside and whispered to her. "Here, I almost forgot. I have a lot more tarot cards to give you. You are still collecting them, aren't you?"

"Oh! Yes." She was delighted. "That is wonderful. Give them to me and I will take good care of them."

"Here are the last few Pips that I encountered after you died as Swollup. I also have all the Court Cards and the four Aces from my time around the Lagoon. I am glad to hand them to you."

"That's amazing! Now, I have 56 cards. I only need the 22 major Arcana cards and the deck will be complete. In return, can I do something for you? Paragutt is too badly wounded to make it on his own. I can give him a piggy back, and meet you on the Path of the Moon, since my talents will not be required on the Path of the Sun. That seems the best idea."

"An excellent plan. I do intend to tackle the Sun first. If we can repair the boat, we can sail the boat around Malkuth to that path. It would be a lot easier than walking."

Pullows hoisted Paragutt onto her back and tucked his legs under her arms. He was quite small and she was a hefty woman, so I was sure she could handle the burden. She waved and walked off towards the East.

I put Bazoom in my pocket and set out swiftly back to the North, reaching it in a couple of days and passing Hecate at the crossroads with an airy wave of my hand. Sure enough, the choice of the two lych gates faced me. I immediately chose the left one, and it swung open to reveal the narrow tightrope.

"You seem very determined." Remarked the sonorous voice from above me. "Made up your mind quickly, eh? The last creature – you could hardly call him a person – who passed here chose the other gate. Boy! Did he ever see trouble! The bad elements were just waiting for him, but he made it through, the little devil. I was astonished."

"That was because he has been awarded the Order of the Non-existent Empire." I said in defense of my little Paragutt. "His character has been honed by misfortune, but now he is truly a brave warrior." I stepped forward, and put my foot on the cable. "I must not waste time. There is much to be done. Farewell, Belvedere. It is you, isn't it?"

"Ha!ha!ha! You caught me out. Yes, I'm your ego. I'll be along to trip you up on your next adventure, too." There was a smothered chuckle, but by then I was darting across the abyss at top speed, Bazoom flying ahead of me to focus my energy on the dangerous crossing.

We made fast time to the boatyard, as my choice of the tightrope enabled me to avoid the first nine sections of the Black Quarter and go straight to the end of the road. We arrived at the boat, and I called quietly to my crew.

"Pompeybou, Numbyling, Endevvy! Come out. It's me, the Navigator. I've found you." I pulled back the tent flap, and recoiled in horror at the shambles inside. The three of them crouched at the back, and from the look in their eyes, I thought at first they had gone mad. I had to restore them to their natural functions as quickly as possible, to stabilize them, so I gave them tasks to perform.

"Pompeybou! Come out here. I need you to help me caulk this boat. It's been out of the water so long, the seams are open, and it would sink if we launched it now." I turned to Endevvy. "Your skilled work is essential. Come with me up on deck, and we will work on the electrics and navigation equipment." I moved towards the rickety ladder resting against the hull. "Numbyling, go and calm down the yard manager. Tell him we want to set a launch date for two weeks from today. Your influence will allay his fears about our finances."

Pompeybou immediately picked up a caulking iron and some oakum, and began hammering, as I climbed the ladder swiftly, followed by Endevvy. The interior of the boat was a mess, of course. They had been without a captain, and I was anxious to hear, eventually, how they had reached the Island of Malkuth. But for now, there was work to do.

Two weeks later, we launched the boat and left a smiling yard manager without paying. Numbyling had done her job well, and he was sure there would be a check in the mail. We set sail around the Island of Malkuth towards the East, heading for the path of the Sun on the SE section. Arriving at the Hodian shore, we found them completely disorganized, and reaching the point of despair. I could not take all of them on the boat with me, but they could launch their fleet again, and we would sail together and set our course for the Path of the Sun.

Path of the SUN

❁

The Hodians crowded around me on the dock while I organized their fleet of boats, moored higgledy-piggledy around us. Each boat would hold ten people, and there were forty boats, so that meant four hundred people could embark. The guard had refused to let them into the Path of the Sun, which would lead them back to their original home in the Island of Hod, so they had fallen into despair and lack of purpose – a fatal mistake in Hod and probably a test the guard set deliberately.

I gave them a talk where I reminded them of their legacy - straight thinking and the resolution of problems by rational means. I warned them that they might be turned away again if they were not absolutely disciplined. They began to pull themselves together, arranging a captain for each boat, and provisioning with food and the necessary safety equipment to make the journey. The Suns' glare shone directly at us down the limpid waters of the Mystic SEA. In view of this, I distributed 405 pairs of Vuarnet sunglasses for them and for the five of us on the sloop. Since there was no evening in the Russet Quarter, we set out immediately, our boat leading and the forty small boats following, their oars splashing haphazardly in the bright water.

As my sunglasses protected me from the brilliant light of the Sun, I was able to look straight at the orb and see something moving about inside. From this distance, it was impossible to make out any details, yet it resembled two faces engaged in a complex discussion. Turning my attention to our fleet, I used my bullhorn to shout orders to the oarsmen who were following us in a long straggle. I reminded them to stay focused on their task and to put down any mutineers who went against the grain, since I knew that tough love was the only way to hold them together.

We reached the Path of the Sun after a few hours on course and disembarked. I positioned the four hundred Hodians in neat lines and marched them ashore. They were beginning to enjoy themselves, but they were nervous about their reception by the guard. I swaggered up to the golden wrought gates of the Path and saluted. The guard seemed pleased.

"Brought back those fallen Hodians, I see." He remarked. "Let's make sure they can pass through this time." He walked up and down the long lines of people, alternately shaking hands, saluting, and patting them on their shoulders as they stood straight, trying not to break ranks. "H'm. They do seem in much better order than before. I can't think why they presented themselves in such an undisciplined manner last time."

"They understand the importance of control over their unruly emotions now." I answered. "That is why they had to leave Hod in the first place. They have promised to day dream neatly in future, in order to connect with the Sphere of Netzach through the Path of Death, for without that transition they cannot balance themselves."

He swung open the gates, and we all marched through. We found ourselves in a dry landscape, made up of sand dunes where cactuses and mesquite grew sparsely. The guard led the Hodians away to a building on my right, to interrogate them before proceeding towards Hod. The five of us, meanwhile, had to decide what to do.

I felt that Numbyling was too apathetic to risk the motivational experience of Hod, and Pompeybou lacked discipline, so I arranged for them to return and stay with the sloop and sail her over to the Path of the Moon, where they would pick up Pullows and Paragutt. I kept Bazoom and Endevvy with me, two rather fierce and very practical entities, who,

I reckoned, would do well in the rational Path of the Sun and the Sphere of Hod.

As we stood there, I saw a shadow behind one of the bushes, which resolved itself into the secretary bird, strutting forward on lanky legs. Its head was adorned with a burst of small black quills behind a reddish eye and a menacing curved beak. This bird harked back to a leftover fossil from the dinosaur age, the only bird that still killed its prey on foot and not on the wing.

Reading my thoughts, the bird made a twittering sound in disgust. "Fossil or not! Here is the parchment I gave you earlier. You dropped it! The Crow brought it to my attention, for, as you know, I am Isa Real Gardy, secretary to the Crow of archaic times. Decipher the sigil on the parchment, for you will need it on the Path of the Sun."

"Just a moment." I said firmly. "You told me that you would meet me with this talisman on the Island of Malkuth. You never showed up, and that idiotic parrot, Arty Weight, took your place, which was very wrong of him, since he is too secretive and won't give sensible answers to questions. It's lucky I managed without your help, and you can thank Paragutt for that, because he undertook to explore the Black Quarter, which is the most harrowing of all."

The bird looked guilty. "Never mind. Sometimes I am late. I get so involved with those magical incantations, you know. I'm writing a book about the Gouden Doorn, and it takes a lot of my time." With that, the bird departed, desultorily stabbing two lizards in the path with the large claw on its foot.

Holding the parchment, I looked at the sigil, not understanding the odd squiggles. Maybe someone here would know the answer. I put the parchment carefully in the hem of my tunic and the three of us moved along, Bazoom buzzing ahead while Endevvy made notes on a small slate. A paved path led among the dunes, and an agama lizard, with its red head raised, scuttled across in front of us. Rounding a bend, we came to a net laid carefully across the path. It was quite large, and a cord led over the nearest dune to an unseen source.

Bazoom immediately managed to entangle two of his spikes in the net during a low swoop across the path. He fought hard to get free, shouting and battering against the strands holding him as the net was quickly reeled in by someone out of sight. I walked up to the top of the dune. There below me, lay a beautiful woman with a garment of deep purple decorated with rivulets of pure mercury. A strange headdress with a pointed cone at the back shimmered on her head, and a book with blank pages lay in front of her. She drew the net in with her prey, and then she looked up as the noose tightened around the frantic Bazoom, who could not stand restraint of any kind.

"Fontanova!" I recognized her instantly. "What are you doing here?"

She answered with her usual rather indignant attitude. "I've been here some time now! I last saw you at the Bar, before you embarked for the Island of Malkuth. You didn't choose me as one of your crew, through." She pouted. "That didn't matter in the end, because, once you were able to become the tiny spot Hadit, and we crossed over on the bridge of Nuit, your circumference, you did not need your entities attached to you any longer. Instead of being projections of your personality, we became free spirits who can roam wherever we will." Fontanova threw back her head and laughed. "It's wonderful to be free at last!"

"I remember being buried alive and beginning to suffocate, and then, in the trance of death, becoming Hadit, the Monad, without ties or attachments. That is how I built the bridge, Nuit, for she was not visible to me before I reached my center, Hadit." I smiled. "It is only from the center that one can see the circumference, Nuit."

"True. Now, I have chosen to come here and study as a day dreamer. This is the opposite of dreaming at night, which takes place in the Island of Yesod, for it is a conscious wish and not part of the unconscious." Fontanova pointed to her book. "I got this little book to write down my day dreams, so that I can connect more fully with the influences in the Path of the Moon, where my beloved Bardogian lies bewitched. Only a monkey guards what is left of his brain, and the tides creep closer." She looked ineffably sad for a moment, then she brightened. "I found my fountain here, though. You know that my name, Fontanova means 'new fountain' don't you? Well, if you look behind me into that garden, you will see a fountain in the shape of Pythagoras' tetractys, the mathematical perfection of the descent of energy into matter. It's pretty, isn't it?"

I had been so absorbed in talking with her, I had not noticed that our path led past a great cross and into a large garden, which was bounded on the far side by a grey brick wall. The fountain stood in a corner, its waters sparkling as the little pottery vessels overflowed from one to another and into a round bowl at the bottom. The garden was divided into twelve sections, in which starry flowers grew in strange patterns. The beauty of the scene enthralled me and I gazed and gazed.

Endevvy shook my elbow. "We need to get Bazoom out of the net," he reminded me, recalling me to more practical matters. I bent down and, excusing myself to Fontanova, disentangled Bazoom from his predicament. "I hope you don't mind. I need to take him with me."

"That's perfectly fine." Fontanova nodded. "He's not the sort of dream I was looking for anyway." She took the net and cast it over the dunes once again. "Let's hope something gentler comes along. I've already caught an agama lizard that was totally unsuitable, and I had to enclose him in a ring of fire before he bit me."

We said goodbye and sauntered along the path and into the large garden. I could see that the circular wall enclosed it on all sides The great ball of the Sun hung above, glowing softly. The heat it emanated was pleasantly gentle, and the two talking faces were visible as two young people who looked amazingly alike, except that one was feminine, and the other masculine.

A quick movement startled me, and a beautiful gazelle brushed past me, leaping in terror from a tiger that was crouched as if to spring. The gazelle ran around in circles, gradually coming closer, and finally stopped right by me and put its head under my arm. I could feel the little creature trembling with fear, so I stroked it quietly. The gazelle wore a blue ribbon around its neck with a little bell attached. Instinctively I wanted to protect the animal from the predator, who watched me fiercely from a bush. I decided to keep the gazelle close to me during my passage through the Sun.

In the far corner of the garden was a small, grey hut, with an old man sitting outside. It must be the gardener, I thought. We walked over to make some enquiries.

I knew he was my Guide immediately. I had expected him to return while we were in Malkuth, but he had not shown himself again. He was late, in my view. The secretary bird had been late, too. There didn't seem to be any notion of Time around here, which was surprising, considering that Time was a very rational way of organizing ones' day under the Sun. Nevertheless, I was delighted to see him as he greeted us.

"Got here in Time, then." He joked. "I dare say you have some questions about the Island of Malkuth. I didn't want to stay there and wait for you – the atmosphere is so negative that it affects my abilities to communicate, so I came here." His eyes glistened as he looked around. "How do you like my garden?"

"It's absolutely beautiful!" I exclaimed. "What are those little sparkling flowers? I've never seen them before." .

"Oh! My. You make me laugh sometimes." He chuckled broadly. "They are not flowers, but stars. What you think is a garden is the Zodiac, and in each section are the star patterns that make up the twelve signs. The Sun organizes this on Earth." He nodded sagely. "These star patterns are visible in the Sun, and the wheel of the Zodiac is situated in Chockmah. It is actually the twelve gates of Jerusalem, as they call it. Each person incarnates through a gate of their choice, and each gate is a discipline, that is why those Christians talk about the twelve disciples. Ha! Ha! They don't understand that the "disciples" are disciplines."

"Wow! That makes perfect sense." I was excited. "What about the four quarters of Malkuth? What did they represent?"

My Guide gestured to a bench close by. "Sit down, and I will explain. All four of the quarters are under the influence of the Ego, as I have told you of the marring of the colors by Black. All the people who inhabit Malkuth believe, without knowing why, that they are living in the wrong place. They would like to be back in their original Spheres, of course. But they don't know how to get back, and we can't tell them. Those in the Russet, Citrine and Olive quarters have hope, and will eventually learn it for themselves." He paused and looked grim. "Now, the Black Quarter is different. Little Paragutt, who is waiting for us on the Path of the Moon, was very brave to adventure into that dangerous area. Fortunately, he is now not only a member of the ONE, but also under the protection of Pullows, who is a very enlightened being."

I interrupted him. "I really feel drawn to Pullows, but I didn't know she was an initiate. How did that happen?"

"Swollup, as she was called during your passage down the river, you knew as a brothel-keeper. She was kind, and made sure everyone got the right partner and was well satisfied. But her efforts wore her out and, as you know, she died tragically." My Guide paused. "She told you she would return, inverted into Pullows – the reverse of her name. That meant she had transcended the Lusts of life and raised her energy to a higher level, so that she abides in the spiritual realm from now on."

"That is wonderful!" I felt a flush of happiness for Pullows. "Will the other entities be able to transcend as well?"

"Alas, no, not all of them. Lust is a natural thing and, as long as it is directed fittingly, can do no harm. But envy, as represented by Covvymor, and greed, by Aquirot, can never become anything other than what they are. So you see, those entities have passed away in some fashion or other. It is only by dropping them from your own personality that you have been able to become centered in Hadit, and make the crossing over Nuit into the Mystic SEA."

"What about the unfortunate people in the Black Quarter?" I asked in a worried tone. "What happens to them?"

"They are trapped in an endless round of errors, and as long as they blame others for their misfortunes and refuse to take responsibility for their mistakes, they will not be able to leave that area. You will have noticed that even the three members of your crew became tainted by their surroundings while they were in the boatyard. Fortunately you rescued them in time, but still Numbyling cheated the manager and he believed her." The old man thought for a moment. "She will have to go, I'm afraid. She is on her way to the Path of the Moon with Pompeybou, but she can't be allowed to enter that path. Apathy, especially in those illusive vibrations, would be fatal. I advise you to tell her to turn back, and I hope she will listen to you."

"Well, Numbyling has been helpful in some ways." I explained. "She was able to calm Fola during her madness and bring her back to sanity. But, it is a drag to have her with us most of the time, because she's not motivated to do anything, and I do disapprove of her relationship with Endevvy, who needs to keep his mind on his job."

"As a matter of fact, Endevvy, being very materialistic, will also become overwhelmed by the difficulties in the Mystic SEA.' The old fellow mused. "I would send him back, too. He can stay in the Castle of Earth, where Little Laboria is living now. Of course, she divorced him after he cut off her arm with the machete, so I don't suppose she would mind if he married Numbyling instead."

Here Endevvy began to raise objections, but I admonished him. "You'll be much more useful to Soyla and the Court there. It will be a good life for you." Smiling, I turned to my Guide and agreed with him. "You have an answer for everything! I must listen carefully to your advice in future. Then I won't get into trouble."

"Oh, yes! I'm afraid you will." My Guide gave a somber grin. "That is why I will remain close to you, and I will grow closer and closer as time goes by, until we reach the Path of the Chariot."

"What will happen there?" I asked in surprise. "Are you going to leave, then?"

"I cannot give you the answer yet. When we are traveling on the Path of the Moon, where we are to save Bardogian, who is in desperate straits, you will learn more. A. Lyster Crow will meet us there."

"Ah! I remember meeting the Crow. He likes clams." I paused. "Whatever is wrong with Bardogian? I know Fontanova is heading in that direction too, and I will be there as soon as I can. I hope my poetic entity will be all right." I dashed a tear from my eye as the old man turned and went into the hut, then we cut diagonally across the garden towards the orb of the Sun.

After I had sent a protesting Endevvy back to the Lagoon, only Bazoom and the gazelle accompanied me as we approached the Sun. Then, from the center of the orb, a set of orange steps folded out, and two lithe figures came down the stairs to greet us. They were Kerry and Kerri, the twins who had advised me about the shark in the great wave during the hurricane in the Seven of Wands. They had performed the ceremony of joining the two flames then, and moving on, had emerged from their fog to help us save Shaman Reeve and his clan from annihilation by the melting glacier during my trial with the Knight of Wands.

"Welcome to the Mystic SEA." They spoke simultaneously with two voices, blended together flawlessly. "We are discussing our final metamorphosis into the Solar Man. He is androgynous, of course, but exemplifies the masculine potential. Very soon, when you reach the Path of the Moon, you will experience the joining of the Moon twins, who will become the Lunar Woman, his consort."

"I don't understand." I puzzled. "You were twins when I met you. You're very alike, almost identical, except that you were boy and girl. Why do you have to become a man, and why do these other twins in the Moon have to become a woman?"

Kerry and Kerri laughed quietly. "When you met us, we were in the material world, where people live with the idea of duality. Of course, duality does not really exist – it is an illusion of the worst kind. Everyone imagines themselves as an 'I' and the other person as a 'U'. That separates them. In fact, there is no separation in the astral world, where we live now."

"Am – I ....." Here I hesitated. "Am I in the astral world now, too? I don't feel any different than before."

"When you were navigating the River and going through your tests in the Lagoon, you were material, but with a dash of spiritual in you.

That is what made you take the journey of the Way of Return in the first place. Now you are astral, but with a sprinkling of material in you. The last vestiges of your bodily form will gradually disappear as you travel the Mystic SEA, and you will complete your journey at the temple of the Archpriestess, where you will make her an offering."

"Who is the Archpriestess? I haven't heard about her."

"She hides behind a thousand veils. It is impossible to know her, unless you have the understanding." The twins paused. "We are inviting you to witness our transformation into the Solar Man now. Will you come this way, please?"

I eagerly went with them up the orange staircase and into the Sun, to find myself in a circular room where the walls pulsed red, then orange, then yellow as flares of gaseous mixtures leapt across the room. I tried dodging a flare as it came at me, but I was too slow, and the lambent flame licked up my body, over my face and directly into my eyes. A brilliant light blinded me, and a soft, burst of energy ran through me. I found I could relax, knowing that the Sun would not burn me, as I had always feared.

Kerry was standing on top of a red, revolving disc that gyrated slowly in the center of the room. Kerri mounted a similar golden disc whose rotation alternated with his and pulsed rhythmically in and out with each revolution of her twin. Gradually the two discs began to move faster, and the two figures moved in unison, as if they were dancing a graceful pavane. I could hear their voices as they vibrated the seven Key Words of the Path. Their discs increased speed as the couple moved as one, edges blurring as the discs spun ever faster and faster. The two figures disappeared in an orange mist and, just as my eyes could take no more, there was a popping sound, and out of their spinning orange globe a thin thread of brilliant red emerged, snaking upwards towards the top of the room. Soon it was possible to see two scarlet arms finding their way out of the thread and fastening onto the top of the ceiling, where they clung for a moment. A head became visible, then a torso, and finally, as the discs slowed down, two legs that reached down to the floor of the room.

The Solar Man stood before me! He was about ten feet tall and of a pure red that did not exist on earth, so luminous was it. The twins had vanished. I knew they were inside this man, or rather, that they were, in fact, the man who stood in front of me. I recalled the prophecy of the priestess on the tripod. She had told them that when the bearer of the second flame appeared, and twin flames united, then the twin beings would dissolve into the eternal flame of the Sun. I had brought the second wand to aid Kerry in his fight against the shark from the sea, and now I was witnessing the fulfillment of the prophecy.

A deep voice that thrilled my whole being spoke to me. "I am Ra, I am Apollo, I am Hunab K'u, and the manifestation of every other solar being on earth. In me dissolves all duality, and if you follow my directions, you will succeed in the Way of Return. First, you must save your Soul that is threatened by demonic forces."

"Where is my Soul? I don't see it anywhere here." I was perplexed.

"It is right there close by your side, huddling under your arm, for it is afraid."

I looked down and met the soft, brown eyes of the gazelle. "The gazelle! She is my Soul?" I was amazed, and stroked the gentle animal as I admired her loveliness.

"Yes, your Soul is fleet of foot and of great beauty. Yet she is fragile, and she can be overtaken by fierce predators. Beware of the evil that lurks in the undergrowth here, in the shape of a tiger, even in the Path of the Sun." The Solar Man bent down and blessed us. "Now, you have not charged the talisman of parchment that Isa Real Gardy gave you. You must do that as soon as possible. Now that you have embarked upon the Way of Return, you need your wits about you, for it is fraught with danger from the underworld."

A squawk interrupted our conversation and the secretary bird stalked up. "Yes! You must charge the talisman, and I will help you with that. You will then know what the sigil represents. Come, now, take the talisman in your hand. We must use the element of Fire, for that is appropriate for the Sun. Concentrate on the talisman and the word of the sigil will come to you. Then, vibrate this chosen word frequently and think red – the color of fire. You will feel your energy pulsing at a higher rate, and that will transfer to the talisman itself." The lanky bird watched as I followed his instructions, keeping the gazelle close by. Now that I knew what she represented, I was going to protect her at all costs.

When the ceremony was complete, Isa Real Gardy bowed and took his leave, strutting back into the mesquite bushes. The gazelle and I moved along the path, Bazoom riding in my pocket. As we walked along slowly, admiring the starry flowers about us and many other wonderful things in the garden, we came to the grey brick wall at the end. I began to walk along the wall, the animal trotting by my side, to look for a gate, so that we could continue on the Path.

Swiftly, with a snarl, the tiger leaped out of the bushes nearby and, before I could turn, the animal was on the back of my gazelle, and she shrieked in terror. The tigers' claws dug deep into her neck and its weight was bearing her down as she struggled to stay on her feet, bleating in agony. Blood began to run down her shoulders, and the tiger raised its head, glaring at me with bloody teeth, and then bit down deep into the gazelles' neck, intending to sever her spinal cord.

At once, I raised the talisman, vibrating a strong current of energy towards the mouth of the animal, and Bazoom flew along this path, hitting the tiger in the teeth with his spikes just before it closed its mouth for the fatal bite. The tiger jerked backwards roaring, its mouth agape, and fell from the sinking gazelle that now lay on the ground, bleeding profusely. Bazoom emerged from the predators' mouth triumphantly as it lay still.

I assumed it was dead, but I approached cautiously to make sure, and bent over it. As I stared at the tigers face, the stripes seemed to blend into a fuzzy blur, and the face began to change. A dark hood appeared behind its ears, and drew over the tigers' head, obscuring its glaring eyes. Then, I knew who it was - the Hoodwinker! The shape-shifter hissed at me, but her energy had been exhausted by the talisman. I turned quickly and picked up the wounded gazelle. I had to save her before it was too late. Frantically I looked around for water to bathe her wounds, and something to bind them and stop the flow of blood.

My eye fell on the fountain, and I ran, with the heavy animal in my arms, to the round basin beneath the flowing water. Gently, I placed the gazelle in the basin of water, and began to bathe her. Blood flowed from her wounds at first. Then, as I carefully sponged her with a corner of my tunic, the wounds became clean and began to close up. Within a few moments, the bright waters began to heal her slashed body, and as I lifted her out, the basin of the fountain ran red with blood, and yet there was not a mark on her.

She raised her brown eyes to me and I began to cry, tears running down my cheeks without stopping. I hugged her close to me, as a familiar voice spoke close by.

"Go now, brave one. You have saved your Soul and I will take care of her for you while you continue on your journey. She will always be close to you, although her life may be threatened again. You must remain strong for her." My Guide smiled and patted me on the back. "The Hoodwinker is vanquished this time, but she will return. Remember, I will be near, and you will also be protected by the Seven Magic Birds, who await you in seven Paths of the Tree of Life, which lies in the Mystic SEA. These Magicians, who were great in their time, know how to handle the horrors of the Seven Shades, who are hiding in the Paths awaiting your entry. You have just met one of them"

"I don't like the idea of that!" I complained. "I thought this was going to be a good trip. After all, I've worked hard and passed all the trials that the Court Cards set me. I should be having an easy time by now, shouldn't I?"

The old man chuckled in his usual irritating manner. "So, you think you have earned an easy passage way? Forget that! Remember, no pain, no gain. That is how it will be from now on. There is no straightforward path on the Way of Return. On the other hand, many do not even succeed in reaching the Bar, for they fail along the way. So be thankful that you have crossed the Bar and now receive the support you need to continue, for it is rare that the Seven Magic Birds will consider helping anyone. They watch the person first, to see if they can manage by themselves." My Guide took the little gazelle in his arms and gestured with his eyes towards the wall. "There is a gate in the wall. Go through it. You cannot enter Hod yet, for you must pass through the Path of the Moon, and then try once more. You will find out."

I stepped through the gate in the grey brick wall, and found myself back on the southeastern shores of the Island of Malkuth.

Path of the MOON

❀

I had to make my way through the Citrine Quarter with Bazoom to reach the shore where we would embark for the Path of the Moon. On our passage, we came upon Semra, Qamra and their followers lying on couches, inhaling the vapors of ether that came up from the vats in polystyrene tubes. There was little communication between us, as they were in a state of trance.

From the southwest corner of the Citrine Quarter, we signaled by Morse code to Pompeybou and Numbyling, who were cruising up and down in our sloop, while Pullows, who had taken Paragutt on board, tended to his needs in the cabin. When the boat docked, I had to send Numbyling back, which was not an easy task, but I was able to convince her that Endevvy awaited her at the Castle of Earth with a beating heart and a large diamond engagement ring. She gave a whoop of joy, which was not like her, and ran off across the Island of Malkuth, forgetting that, at the north end, an irate boatyard manager awaited her missing payment. I don't know how it turned out, as I was more intent on sailing the sloop along the Path of the Moon, which shone silver on the limpid waters ahead of us.

The five of us set out in the boat without delay, the three who had rescued me from the Qliphoth and Pompeybou. I was a little concerned about him, because of his raucous tendencies to relate tall sea stories. This always amused the bar patrons. I was sure that many drinkers, willing to carouse with him, and influenced by the Moons' strong pull on Netzach, might await us.

The crossing was not long, and when we disembarked near some large rocks on the shores of the Moon, I solved my concern regarding Pompeybou by leaving him to look after the sloop with Pullows. Paragutt remained on board until his wounds healed. I arranged for several 12 packs of beer to sustain them while we were gone.

Boulders littered the beach and impeded my progress, while Bazoom rode in my pocket as usual. Fortunately, the tide was out for the next few hours. That was just as well, for ahead of us a lonely figure lay below the high tide line, cushioned by some large rocks, his arm behind his head in a relaxed attitude. A large chimpanzee bent over him, with his hand on the back of the inert figures' head, as if in supplication. We were soon close enough to see that it was Bardogian who lay there, and we hurried up to him. When we tried to wake him, the chimp chattered at us angrily, waving its arms in banishment, and it would not leave. Bardogian was out cold. My heart sank as I saw a hypodermic needle sticking out of his right arm. There was no doubt he was on heroin, and I hoped that he hadn't overdosed, for his poetry was important to me.

A large water beetle was carrying bubbles of air towards my poet and squeezing them into the mouth of a strange vessel on Bardogians' head. I beckoned to the beetle, and it swam over to me.

"What is going on?" I asked in an agonized whisper. "Why are you adding air bubbles to that vessel on Bardogians' head?"

"Oh! My goodness! You scared me. This is the only way to save him. It's pure oxygen, you know." The beetle knotted his brow and leaned closer, his mouth in my ear. "Psst! Don't let the monkey hear us. It was him that stuck your friend. I swear it! The monkey wanted to advance - intellectually, you know. He was going to take away the bards' frontal lobes as soon as the Moon was full. That is, tomorrow." The beetle wiped its antennae with a front leg. "I have been supplying his brain with oxygen to try and wake him before it's too late, like the old crone up there told me."

"Bravo! You may have saved his life. I think we've come in time. We need to wake him, though. That chimp is obstructing us. Could you crawl into his ear and distract him?"

"Of course. Anything to help. I do admire people with frontal lobes, for, as you well know…" Here the beetle hesitated and wept a little. "We don't have any and we just have to keep doing the same thing over and over again. Our kind hasn't advanced in 65 million years. You are indeed fortunate to have ideas for future plans."

"Yes, it's tough on all insects. Never mind - see how useful you can be. While you crawl into the monkeys' ear, I'll go up the path and talk to the crone. I can see her sitting there on the left. Good Luck!"

I set off towards a large black rock that looked vaguely like an ancient woman. Behind me, I heard a shriek from the chimp as he jumped up, wiggling his finger in his ear frantically. I was pleased as I saw him rush off into the surrounding forest, holding his head in both hands and howling.

The lumpy crone was indeed alive, and greeted me with a knowing nod, beckoning me to draw closer. She whispered in my ear. "Only the old know the solutions to the worlds' problems. They have experience. Never belittle old folk – that is a big mistake."

I looked closer at her face in the moonlight. "I've seen you before, I'm sure. Let me see, now. Are you the old carpet seller from the bazaar?"

She cackled loudly. "You don't recognize me, do you? I am Ediug, Tabansis' mother, from the lake. Remember, I gave you the lungfish and what a joy he was – did exactly as he was told and chased away that black goat."

"Ediug! I'm sorry I didn't recognize you!" I was hopping from one foot to the other. "Can you help us revive Bardogian? It's pretty urgent. I'm afraid the monkey might have used an overdose on him, so time is important. What's the best way to wake him?"

"Well, being a bard, he loves the sound of the harp. There is a harp, dedicated to Thoth, the jackal, over there. Bring it to me, and we will make some sweet music."

I went to get the harp. It was a beautiful instrument, but it was dusty and dirty, and hadn't been used in quite some time. I brought it to Ediug, who settled it by her and began to play. To her horror, the chords ran together in a dissonance of sound that grated on the ear. The crone looked down, found that the strings were crossed, and asked me to re-string them. I set to immediately, as I was familiar with harps, and there was no time to lose. I hoped that the beetle was going to sit tight in the monkey's ear, to give me time, as I lovingly sorted through the crossed strings. The carved head of the jackal regarded me intently as I worked. It seemed almost alive.

Eventually I had the strings of the harp in correct order, and Ediug began to play a haunting melody, the like of which I had never heard before. I returned to Bardogians side and watched anxiously. The soft music drifted down the path and over the rocks, settling around us and forming a mist of tiny droplets that gradually coalesced on his body, soaking his orange suit and dripping down onto the pincers of a green crab that had sidled up to us.

Suddenly the crab raised itself up, waving its claws, and pinched Bardogian hard on his right arm below the needle. A shudder ran through his body, and he opened his eyes. I breathed a sigh of relief and bent over him as the crab scuttled away.

"Bardogian, Bardogian! It's me, the Navigator. Wake up!" I shook him lightly and he tried to raise his head, dragging an arm across his eyes and blinking in the moonlight. "Bardogian. You've been drugged! You have to rouse yourself. There is an evil monkey around who did it – he stuck you." I gently pulled the syringe out of his arm. "Look! This is a hypodermic. It probably contained heroin, and that put you into a trance." As I spoke, I felt a splash of water on my foot. "You are in danger from the rising tide. Give me your arm, and I'll help you get up."

Somehow, I got him to his feet and led him out of danger up the path to where the old crone played her melody. "Ah! I see that we have managed to rouse him." She said. "That is good, for the tide around here rises fast, and the tidal bore can be forty feet or more. It's the influence of the Moon, you know. It is very close to us here." She relaxed, taking her hands from the harp strings. "Here you will find the three aspects of feminine power, which lives in the moonshine. In the Moon itself, if you will look up, you will see the twin Virgins, and between them the budding lotus blossom of escape from illusion. On the right of this path is the matriarch, or Mother, with her child." She pointed across the moonlit path to a tall rock that stood slightly bent over a smaller rock, looking remarkably like a little child. They seemed frozen in place and I could discern no movement in the wavering argent light.

"I am the third aspect of woman, the wise old Crone." Ediug continued. "I can move my arms when someone addresses me, and so can she, but we remain rooted in the same place, for we are the two towers that guard the path up to the Moon, and we are the protectors of the Virgins, our daughters and sons."

"Why do you have to stay in one place?" I asked, as Bardogian sat on a rock nearby, blinking slowly. "You can move your arms and speak. Why can't you just get up and go for a walk occasionally?"

"Ah! It is because we are under the spell of the Raven. See! Here he comes!" I looked up, following her gaze, as a sooty black raven spiraled down and settled on the head of the Mother Crone, fluffing its wings. I walked over to the bird.

"Have you put a spell on these women?" I asked indignantly. "That is not really fair. They are stuck here."

The dark bird gave a croak and blinked his eyes, ignoring my question. "You don't remember last September?" He regarded me humorously, his beak stretched into a wry grin. "Do you not recall when I held you in thrall? We met when it was wet, on the grassy mound near the Dark Ground ?"

I racked my brains, but I could not think where I had met a raven before. "No, I did meet a very strange crow that liked eating clams, but not a raven."

"You don't know – I was a crow? I will hark back to that old track." The raven continued. "And where do you go? Now, why so slow?" The bird queried irritatingly.

Now I knew who he was and I recalled his words as he had spoken them so long ago. "See you soon, under the Moon. Where I will show that I am more than just a crow." It was A. Lyster Crow, the magical bird I had met on my first adventure, who had promised me that he would be more than a crow under the Moon. Well, here he was - a Raven. "What is the significance of your change, from one black bird to another?"

"Crows are marauding and very obstreperous. They circle in flocks, attacking passing eagles who are trying to fish for their young eaglets. They are rude and egotistical, and they exploit people. I am none of that, since I metamorphosed." Here A Lyster Crow raised an eyebrow feather. "Now, the Raven is a fine bird and very advanced in magical lore. He is a loner, disdaining the common mob, and he resides in high places, such as the Tower of London, overseeing decapitations, tortures, and the clanking of innumerable prisoners' chains. I always wanted to be a Raven, and here I am. Of course, I had to go through some stiff initiatory rites first." The bird went on. "But, seriously, I can help you during your passage on the Path of the Moon. First, I will take you to meet the two young Virgins that you see crouching in a fetal position in the orb of the Moon. Please come this way."

"What about Bardogian? Can he come too?" I asked, as the bird hopped onto my shoulder circumspectly.

"Let him stay here with Eduig for now. Fontanova will be here soon, for she is in the Path of the Sun, day dreaming their reunion as resolutely as she can. He will be happy to see her and they can then go on their way to the Path of the Lovers, where you will meet them again."

I said goodbye to Eduig and Bardogian, who was fully awake by now. The Sun could not be seen from where we stood, as, of course, it was night time, but he gazed eastwards towards the dawn eagerly, expecting her.

As I stood in front of the Moon with the Raven on my shoulder, a small door opened and a set of silver steps extended silently downwards to my feet. I climbed up, and found myself inside a shimmering globe of silver, with a large lotus bud quivering in the center. On each side, the naked twins stretched their limbs and rose slowly to their feet, embracing me silently.

"You have come at last." They murmured simultaneously. "The Raven said you would be here one day. Now we can unite into the Lunar Woman."

I stared down at them. I had expected that they were both female Virgins, but in fact, one was a male. That made sense, after all, since Kerry and Kerri were male and female twins, too, and they had metamorphosed into the Solar Man. Now I was privileged to witness another transformation.

One of the twins moved to the center of the room and slid the lotus bud aside. Underneath the flower a dark pool of limpid water appeared. The twins stood on each side of the pool, and then knelt down, bending towards the surface of the water, which showed their reflections clearly. They softly whispered the seven Key Words of the Path. Slowly the two reflections moved towards each other over the surface of the water, pausing now and then as they glittered in the moonlight. I was fascinated. The two reflections of the twins came together and touched lightly, then began a dance around each other, weaving gracefully in and out, to merge into one in the center of the pool, while the twins knelt motionless by the edge of the water.From beneath the reflective surface of the water, two sinuous hands reached up, followed by the head of a beautiful woman, who emerged completely naked and stepped to the side of the pool. At the same moment, the bodies of the twins melted into tiny puddles of water on each side of the pool, which drained back into the depths of the lotus basin. The Lunar Woman slid the lotus bud into place again, and it began to open slowly, petal by petal unfurling until a shining white flower with a pale pink heart filled the center of the room. It was the most beautiful thing I had ever seen.

I was distracted from my admiration of the flower by the Raven, however, as he croaked alarmingly into my ear. "Now the metamorphosis must begin. You are the tool that will start this process, for none other can hold the mirror of reflection. Ediug has the mirror ready for you, and she will explain how to use it."

We descended the silver stairs again and went over to the crone, who had set the harp aside. I felt sure the jackal winked at me. Ediug had a small round piece of glass in her hand, with a short dark red handle split into two labia-like forms. She handed it to me. "Take this mirror and turn your back on the Moon, holding the mirror up. You must catch the reflection of the Moon in the exact center. Now, hold this Cup in your other hand directly under the mirrors' handle. That will catch the blood."

I stared at the glass in my hand. "This isn't a mirror. I can see through it! There is no silvering on the other side." I held it up for her to see. "Besides, what's this about blood in the Cup? That sounds rather messy."

"Do as you are told." Came a stern reproof from the crone. "You are a fool to question the secret workings of the Moons' menstrual flow. You have chosen the path of an adept and that is the path of total obedience."

The Raven nodded his head. "Turn away from the Moon and hold up the mirror. You will see the result, but do not spill a drop of the blood, for it must be saved. The Hierophant will want to drink it."

"How disgusting! Who is this besotted Hierophant?" I was asking, when the Raven cawed fiercely. "Pay attention! This is no time for probing the mysteries. Just do it!"

I turned my back on the great orb of the Moon and held up the piece of glass in front of me, with the Cup underneath the handle. To my surprise, the circle of the silver Moon was reflected clearly in the mirror for a brief second. Then the mirror twisted in my hand, uttering a sharp cry of agony, and slow drops of blood began to fall from the labia in the handle. I had difficulty holding the Cup in the right position, for the mirror was squirming and pulsating with pain in my hand, and it moaned and shrieked alternately as blood flowed into the Cup.

"This is the price of the feminine, for she, the receptive one, gives birth to all manner of things." Ediug muttered. "Good. You have done well. Now, give me the Cup of blood, so that the Hierophant may say the mass with it and then drink deep. The mirror must be returned whence it came. Take it up to the Moons' chamber and drop it into the pool, which will calm its torment. Hurry, now."

I climbed the steps to the chamber inside the Moon with the writhing mirror in my hand, and the slim Lunar Woman slid aside the lotus, revealing the deep pool, into which I carefully dropped the tortured glass. Its' refracted image glittered through the green water for a moment, then spiraled slowly down, disappearing in the mysterious depths of the pool. Then she spoke. "I thank you. You have released the feminine spirit after its banishment of three Aeons. By reflecting the Moons' own reflective surface, the double reflection cancelled itself out. Now the full significance of the Moon can be revealed, and I am the one who will take her message to my beloved, the Solar Man, who awaits me in the crystal bed of the Lovers."

The Lunar Woman bade me farewell as I stepped down once more, and Ediug beckoned to me. "You must now go into the forest and find the owl. She waits for the command to fly to the Solar Man with the good news of the Lunar Womans' birth." Eduig paused, looking at me wryly from under her heavy brows. "Now, I have some disturbing news. Bardogian is here anxiously awaiting Fontanova, but she has become stuck in Yesod, the Island of Dreams. Fontanova was progressing well with her daydreams, but unfortunately she made the mistake of falling asleep during a particularly boring dream. Hence she was instantly taken up by the intuitive forces of Yesod, and she must now extricate herself from that influence, which will be difficult. I suggest Bardogian should return to your boat, and await your next passage along the Path of the Universe towards the Island of Yesod. He will then be able to enter Yesod and seek his bride."

"Oh! Am I traveling the Path of the Universe after this? I thought I would be able to pass into the sphere of Netzach from here. The Path of the Moon leads right into it." I voiced my disappointment, in no uncertain terms. "Why can't I get through?"

"It is too dangerous for you to attempt entrance into Netzach before you have followed the correct paths. Your visit to the Moon has destabilized you emotionally. Without the experience of the Passage of the Universe, the affecting chaos in Netzachs' group mind would overwhelm you. I am sorry, but you still have quite a way to go. You must follow the paths in the Mystic SEA in the correct order, or madness would claim you. Do you want that to happen?"

"Of course not! Forgive me, I didn't understand. It seems I'm more ignorant than I thought." I acted the part of contrition easily. "After what I've been through, with the Pips on my river journey and the Court Cards by the Lagoon, I expected my arrival in the Mystic SEA would be straightforward in comparison. I have learned much – why do I need to know more?"

Ediug gave a wheezy laugh. "My, we do think a lot of ourselves, don't we? You do not know what you do not know, alas! Your travels in the Islands of the Mystic SEA will be the most difficult of all, for here you will encounter, in seven Spheres, the Shadow side of yourself as it applies to that state of being. It is represented by the Shade who rules the reverse side of the Sphere, which must be faced and vanquished before you - and the multitude of human kind - can move back up the Way of Return Yet this is not possible in a collective sense, for each individual must battle their own inner turmoil alone."

"So, saving myself will not help anyone else?" I showed my disappointment. "I thought that I could set an example."

The crone cackled obscenely. "That is Ego talk. Belvedere must be beside himself with delight. After all the times you have made mistakes and we have come to save you, how can you imagine that you are free from blame? Now, go and search for the owl. She will be on the topmost branch of a tree somewhere in the forest." Here Ediug bent over with glee. "There are only a few million trees in the forest, so it shouldn't take you long. What is more, that chimp is also wandering in the forest, and he is very angry about the buzzing and scratching in his ear, so do be careful – he might just be hiding behind the very tree that conceals the owl. Goodbye, and good luck."

Annoyed by her cool condemnation, I walked away from the crone rock, Bazoom whirring in my pocket.

"Let me get at her." He gasped, but I squeezed him down to the bottom amongst the crumbs. My attention was on Bardogian, to make sure he took the correct route to return to our sloop. He was very upset, for he had expected Fontanova to arrive at any moment. I told him that it was foolish to have expectations about anything, because one never knew what might happen to change the future. He didn't like that, because it made him feel even more vulnerable then before, being of a weak nature. I worried that, if he and Fontanova gave vent to their mutual attraction, she would end up mothering him, and that would not make for a balanced relationship. Obviously, since they were to meet in the Path of the Lovers, there had to be some serious psychological work ahead for both of them before they got there.

Pushing forward on my path into the deep forest, the full Moon shone overhead, flashing and dipping through the branches of the dense trees. It was hard to see anything and I wished for daylight, but knew the sun would not come up until I had completed this nocturnal Path. After a few hours, I slept fitfully under a spreading bush, alarmed by the noises of the night that pulsed around me. Grunts, squeals, the roars of some guttural animal, the twittering of night birds and the to-and-fro to-whit, to-whooing of many owls filled the night. With so many owls, how was I supposed to find the right one? Then I remembered my search for the right cricket. That had worked out successfully, for I had known instinctively that Joana was the cricket for me.

I must let go of my conscious, reasoning mind and just allow the owl to show up. I had to use my intuition that it would be the correct owl. With that, I fell into a dreamless sleep, and woke refreshed. For several nights I blundered about amongst the great trees, finding sustenance when my hand brushed against the scratchy twigs of blackberries. Then one night I came to a gap in the wood, and glanced up. Against the round, silver fullness of the Moon was the clear silhouette of a large owl. Could this be the one? I called softly, to-whit, to-whoo, and the bird responded. My heart leapt with joy. But then, I had no idea what I was supposed to do once I had found the owl.

Holding out my hand, I hoped that the bird would come down to me, but instead a fierce chattering broke out from the bushes nearby. A dark and muscular form leapt upon my back, bearing me to the ground. I smelt the dreadful monkey smell as the sharp nails of the chimp dug into my neck and forced my head into the mud. The weight of the animal was considerable, and it held me fast with one powerful hand as it turned me onto my back. It was useless to struggle, but I tried to lift my arms to cover my forehead, for I saw immediately what the chimp was after. It desperately wanted my frontal lobes!

I fought with frenzy to keep the chimps' scrabbling claws away from my skull, for if it found the weak spots on my temples, the front of my skull could then be wrenched away and my lobes revealed. Our struggle churned up the muck on the forest floor and disturbed a nest of mice that was hidden under some fallen leaves. I heard a rush of wings, and the owl swooped over my head, snatching up a tiny mouse in its talons. As the bird began to rise with its prey, I grabbed onto one of the scaly legs, and, with a wrench, I was off the ground and swaying high into the air, the chimp falling away below me to a crunching death on the forest floor.

The brindled owl was huge, much bigger than any I had seen before, and seemed scarcely to notice my weight as it soared over the tree tops, landing on a branch close to its nest, where a young one was waiting with open beak. I managed to grasp the surrounding branches to steady myself and jammed my body into a crotch of the tree while the bird fed the mouse to its nestling. After the little ball of fluff had begun to tear open its meal, the owl turned to me.

"That got you out of a jam!" It spoke to me telepathically, for its beak remained closed. "I'm the protector of this forest, and I won't have any monkeying around in my domain. I'm sick of all these insects, reptiles and animals coming here and trying to steal frontal lobes from more intelligent people, such as you. You know, the problem is, everyone who comes here lets down their guard, for the Moons' influence is so strong. Their rational, daily selves are no match for the mysterious persuasion of the Lunar world. It is the proximity of Netzach that causes a dense pressure on the brain of the individual and makes him lose focus, just as one does under the spell of a drug."

I thanked the owl profusely, in thought, for my rescue.

The bird thought back. "Don't thank me. You saved yourself by quick thinking - I just happened to fly by. I suppose you could say that it was synchronicity – your struggles damaged the mouse nest, whereupon I saw my chance for a meal – the young 'un, you know, must be fed. However, since you're here now and the chimp is dead from a bump on his head, I will give you some advice." The owls' thoughts paused cautiously. "The Crone Ediug is inverted. Did you know that? When things are turned back to front, upside down, or inside out, you really don't know where you are with them. Now, I would say that Ediug does her best to be helpful, but she does have a dark side too, so as long as she is with you, rather than that Other One, you must beware, for she should not have told you to enter the forest alone."

"I feel that you protected me, though, and I do have Bazoom in my pocket. So I'm not alone." I pointed out. Then I had a thought. Why hadn't Bazoom come to my aid when I was attacked? I knew the answer straight away. It was because I did not have the intellectual force to be angry, and summon his help. I was under the spell of the Moon and living only in my instincts. I patted my pocket and an answering vibration buzzed under my hand.

"You must leave the forest now, and return to Malkuth, where you will find the entrance to the next Path. It will introduce you to the World Dancer, and by her means you will arrive safely in the Island of Yesod, where Belvedere awaits you." The owl sent her message telepathically. "I will carry you on my back to the shores of the Moon, to keep you safe."

I climbed into the soft, feathery nest between her wings, and we flew under the silver face of the Moon to the boulder strewn shore, where Pompeybou, Pullows, Paragutt and Bardogian awaited me in the boat. Bardogian was deeply worried, for Fontanova had not arrived. Where could she be? Finally, I was able to take Bazoom out of my pocket, and he flew around stretching himself after his long incarceration.

Path of the UNIVERSE

❁

It was a comparatively short trip in our sloop to reach the Citrine Quarter of Malkuth again. I wondered why the three Paths we were investigating all led out of that quarter. Why weren't two of them attached to the Russet Quarter and the Olive Quarter?

I hoped that I would get the answer to my query soon.

Well received by Quamra, Priestess of Nocturnal Hours - since we arrived at night under the full Moon - we found the inhabitants of this quarter far more communicative. They had evidently inhaled a sufficient amount of ether, and they were preparing to leave for the Island of Yesod at last.

"We want to be dreamers for ever." Quamra explained. "The only way to enter the Islands in the Mystic SEA is by using your Intuition. That is why you had to turn back twice Trying to explore the SEA by rational means, as the Path of the Sun suggests, or by emotions, as in the Path of the Moon, leads to a dead end. You must come with us and pass into Yesod through the entrance of the Middle Pillar, the Path of the Universe."

There was the answer to my question. Quamra smiled. "I am able to divine what you are thinking intuitively, without having to use language. The power of speech, developed by our foolish ancestors, the Clan, robbed them of their intuitive abilities, since it was much easier to ask a question out loud than to perceive what was on a persons' mind by focusing on their vibrations." She sighed. "This set the human race back thousands of years, although there were still times when intuition came to the fore. Sadly, these periods have become increasingly brief and will eventually succumb to innate laziness on the part of speakers. Our task is to restore the abilities of perception to the human race, and we must be in Yesod to do that."

"Why is it better to intuit something from a person than to ask a question out loud?" I enquired. "Isn't speech a valuable thing, for we can express many opinions and sentiments through our words."

"Unfortunately, humans have corrupted speech and use it to their advantage for power over other people." Quamra replied. "Do you think that any dictator would have succeeded in persuading the population of his country to believe his dangerous ideas, if he was unable to speak? When we pass ideas through vibrations, they go from one single individual to another. That avoids scenes of mob violence, where a crowd of hundreds would hear the words of a speaker at the same moment and react accordingly. One day the human race may, again, discern the will of each other by silent communication. That is my hope and dream."

During our muted conversation, the fallen Yesodians had gathered by a Path covered by a wide red carpet, which led towards a massive, truncated pyramid. I remembered the pyramids in Fakoors' village that had lost their tops, and how he concealed the golden triangles underground in the lair of the Qliphoth for personal gain. My thoughts then turned towards my crew, who waited silently on the boat.

I decided to take Pullows and Paragutt, who had now recovered from his wounds, with me on the Path of the Universe. Bazoom was a little too inflammatory and Bardogian too laid back, for I felt I had to keep balanced on this Path. Pompeybou was to take the boat and sail with them to our next meeting place on the shores of the Island of Yesod, the place where Fontanova lay in a dreamlike coma, having succumbed to the lure of her day visions. I hoped that Bardogians' presence might restore her to life, for if they were unable to recognize their deep connection, the marriage could never be consummated in the distant crystal bed of the Lovers.

Day was breaking and the exiles were ready to file behind me, so we set out along the red carpet that seemed to stretch on and on without end. As I walked, the land fell away on either side and the path gradually became narrower, until I felt that I was walking on a razors' edge. I could hear scratching and chirping under the path, and I wondered what was making such a noise. The great pyramid seemed no closer, yet a distinct shape was emerging in the center, a stationary blue globe held in the jaws of two immense crocodiles. It resembled a huge eye.

Soon it was difficult to balance on the narrow path, and I was afraid Pullows would fall, so I took Paragutt on my back. Small claws kept appearing along the edge of the path, and furry arms reached out to grab our ankles and upset our balance. We were in danger of falling into the depths below. It was a struggle to keep them away, and soon a little face with enormous eyes appeared over the rim of the carpet. I recognized it as a tarsier from the Citrine Quarter. So, that was the twittering noise I had heard! They had followed us and were trying to pull us off the path. Behind me, as I cast my eyes back, I saw Yesodians falling into the hands of tarsiers as they lost their balance and plummeted screaming into the darkness. It was clear that some of the Yesodians would not reach their goal at the first attempt.

Saddened by their demise, we nevertheless managed to keep going until we came to a shimmering veil across our passageway. I attempted to push it aside, but it did not budge. Had we come all this way, just to have to turn back? I peered through the veil. Behind it, I saw the figure of a beautiful woman who was dancing in the middle of the carpet. She wore a headdress of nine stars from which a yellow chiffon scarf trailed behind her, and carried an infinity circlet made from flowers and herbs.

I watched, fascinated, for the dance was incredibly graceful and the woman, who was nude, resembled the Bride that I had fallen in love with when I met her before. Then a horrible thought struck me! Was this really the Bride of Malkuth? Or - was it the Hoodwinker, shape shifted and disguised, as she had appeared before? If so, we were lost, and unable to continue on this path. The dancer laughed, discerning my predicament, and dropped her fan in enticement close to my feet, and I leaned down and picked it up, folding it carefully and putting it my pocket.

"You laid your hand upon my fan." The woman gave a musical laugh through the veil. "Do you consecrate yourself to the Path of the Tau?"

"Where is this Path?" I asked self-consciously, looking around vaguely.

"You are standing on it. You have noticed that the trail gets narrower as you approach my veil. You are able to balance on this slender path only because you have learned to equalize your psychic forces, otherwise you would fall, as many have done before you. The trials that the Court Cards put you through purified your willpower to some extent. This is called the Middle Path of the Tau, and the Tau cross is the Mark of Cain." She furrowed her brow and looked at me intently. "Do you know what I mean?"

"Cain gave offerings of all the fruit of his labors to the Divine, and he thought that would be enough. His brother Abel only sacrificed a lamb. Divinity favored Abel over Cain because the sacrifice of his symbolic lamb represented the gift of the whole of Abels' essence – his Kundalini force. I believe that to be true."

"That is the right answer. The Divine Universe wanted the whole essence of Cain, but he only gave his material products. Cain jealously killed Abel, and by that deed he also destroyed human potential, the ability to focus one-pointedly on the Divine. You understand the metaphor that lies behind the written words. Now, why would the Tau cross be the Mark of Cain, then?"

"The Tau cross is a t-shaped cross. It is missing the top vertical bar, or circle, as in the ankh of the Egyptians. The top vertical is the ascent beyond the horizon of conscious thought, represented by the horizontal bar. Those who cannot rise above their visible horizon are condemned to remain below the psychic level of enlightenment." I looked anxiously at the dancer, intent on hearing her reply.

"You are correct! Welcome to the Path of the Thirty-Three Secrets that are hidden in the Mystic SEA. You have consecrated your life to the Way of Return. You may enter." She raised her right hand and immediately the veil parted, and we were able to step through and walk towards her.

The gorgeous woman smiled at us and spoke in a low, seductive voice. "I am the World Dancer, and my name is Shekinah, the Bride of Malkuth. Only those who are brave enough to face their own Shadow and look with their hearts can see me, for it is necessary to embrace your Shadow, the Hoodwinker, and become friends with it. There, I see that you have it in your hand now – so you are aware of its tricks." The Bride stopped and pointed rapidly towards my Shadow, which I now saw dangled from my right hand. "Watch out! That little devil has grabbed the tarsiers' ears! Pull it away before the tarsiers drag it under the path. It will be very difficult to get it back, once they have it. Quick, now, pull it up!"

I was surprised. "I didn't notice my Shadow there. I have always kept it inside me. How did it get out?"

"Well, of course it had to come out once it saw me, the World Dancer!" The Bride gave a melodic laugh. "When you step onto the Path up the Middle Pillar, your Shadow can no longer hide, but must show itself. Now, it will be up to you on your future Paths to learn about your Shadow and become friends with it. But, on no account allow it to slip away from you, for it is attracted to the land of the Qliphoth, the demons, and they are always beckoning to it." She continued. "Keep it in your conscious mind always and exercise caution."

"I promise I will. I have met my Shadow before." I assured her, wrapping it more tightly around my arm. "She is called the Hoodwinker, and she can take any shape she chooses. I thought she was bad, but she has very powerful instincts, and has saved me from the dangerous egg, the one that was incubating monsters. Why, she has even pretended that she was you!"

"Maybe I am her!" The Bride smiled. "Now, I will dance for you, and you will see many magical scenes unfolding in my dance" She whirled around, and I saw the long train that she wore behind her, that contained everything in the cosmos from ages past, and the pull of desire swept through me.

I fought and was able to resist the power of her fecundity, but Pullows was swept forward and took her hand, joining in with the dance. I could see that Pullows was in ecstasy, her eyes rolled back in her head and her mouth gently frothing as she leapt and twisted in mad agitation, her head lolling from side to side.

I jumped forward, wrapping my shadow tightly around my wrist, and took her free arm, pulling her back. "No, Pullows, stop it! This dance will distract us from our quest. Don't allow yourself to become captivated by the Bride, for we must press on to Yesod."

I yanked hard to get her away, but to my horror, the strong jerk loosened Paragutts grip around my neck, and he fell off my back and landed on the edge of the Path. Before I could reach him, furry arms lunged up, grabbed him and pulled him below, and, although I knelt down and looked for him, all was swirling gloom under the Path, and the tarsiers had rapidly disappeared with their victim.

This was a serious situation. Pullows was caught up in the dance, and I was powerless to detach her from the Bride, and now I had lost Paragutt as well! I had no choice but to continue on my own, since there was nothing further I could do, keeping my Shadow on my right arm.I had to have faith that both Pullows and Paragutt would be all right. They were no longer part of me, and had their own lives to live. I had relinquished control of them – my Lust and my Fear. Still, I loved them dearly and fought the feelings of guilt that I felt, for I had brought them with me on this Path.

I walked steadily along the narrow path towards the blue globe that hung in the pyramid, keeping my eyes warily on the two crocodiles on either side. As I got closer, I could see the wounds that their teeth had made in the World, for it was bleeding profusely and the red blood ran down the sides of the golden pyramid.

The red-carpeted path ended abruptly, to give way to a bridge that arched across a huge chasm. Over the bridge was a sign that announced "I am the Bronze Bridge. First cross me, if you can." The bridge was, indeed, made of solid bronze, and I set out to traverse it cautiously, looking furtively from side to side.

I was halfway across when a strange figure suddenly vaulted over the parapet of the bridge, shaking a flurry of snow crystals from his dark cloak He seemed to materialize from nowhere. "Just a minute! Where do you think you're going? Abandoning your friends, eh? Not very nice, not nice at all."

The fellow was dressed completely in black and had a sort of halo around his head, consisting of ten tiny sparks of light that circled continuously. In his hand, he carried an hourglass.

"I am Saturn, both planet and tester. I am the metaphor for limitation." The fellow grinned with a wry twist to his mouth. "I have your hourglass here, that is, the limits of your Time on earth and of your own personality fiascos." The black figure raised the hourglass above his head menacingly. "You only have a certain amount of Time, you know, to get everything done. I am going to turn the glass, and from this moment, your Time will begin to run out. Beware!"

"I am not afraid of Time" I said stoutly. "I have Eternity. I learned that after I passed through the veil of the bull and the harp behind the seat of Cosmo, the Guardian of the First Crossing. I have already made that crossing, and I know what lies beyond it."

Saturn shrank back uneasily, his hand on the parapet of the bridge. "You know of Eternity? Then I cannot put you to trial effectively, for it is only when you imagine that you have an end - a termination into oblivion - that I can force you to hurry through my tests." Here, he put on a guileful grin. "But, I am sure you would like to take at least one test, wouldn't you? I can give you a very impressive one."

"Well, OK, then. Tell me what the test is." I felt confident of my powers.

"You see the blue globe of the World ahead, don't you? It is in terrible danger, menaced by the two crocodiles that are called Ignorance and Idolatry. The people of the World have created overpopulation, pollution, greed, and self-seeking behaviors that threaten their own existence. What is more, they have invented a thing they call God, just one of them, and they firmly believe that it exists in the form of a man. In fact, they have created many pictures and statues of this being. But it is only in their mind, which is full of smutty dogma. Your task is to change their attitude and save the World! Can you do that alone with your limitations?" Saturn was snickering to himself now, certain that the test he had just set me was impossible.

"All I can do is try my very hardest." I told him. "The sand in my hourglass will not run out. I have examined the facts, because I am skeptical, and I learned the truth from Destiny, who is the organizer of my life here on Earth. I will go now, to see how I can help the World in some small way."

I walked slowly over the bridge, a little concerned about any further demons that lurked beneath, but there was a breathless stillness below. Did they await me in the World? I had no expectations either way as I finally stood at the base of the great pyramid, gazing upwards.

From below, the globe of the World was placed like a gyroscope in the center of the pyramid, located near the Kings' Chamber. I reasoned that it should be rotating, but it was held fast by the teeth of the crocodiles, which sank into its tender parts. That meant the World was at a standstill and could no longer progress. It must be freed from the jaws of the devouring reptiles. I began to climb the massive stone steps of the pyramid, avoiding the thin streams of blood that came from the pierced globe and dripped slowly from the teeth of the crocodile on my left.

Creeping along the crocodiles' jaw, I attempted to loosen its teeth and pull them out of the Pacific Sea. The beast merely snorted and clamped down tighter. I climbed further up its face, until I was level with the crocodiles' eye, which gleamed darkly in its socket. An idea formed itself in my mind. If I were to pluck out the eye, the reptile would automatically let go, wouldn't it? It was worth a try.

Since the eye was the size of a large beach ball, and very slippery, it was a struggle to yank it free of the socket, but I succeeded in rolling it sideways until there was a slushy pop, and it came free in my hands. I looked down at the thing while a shudder ran through the crocodile, its mouth sagged open and its teeth lost their grip and fell away from the World. In astonishment, I saw the object I held was not an eye, but a gigantic black pearl! At the same moment, a keening wail rose from the black figure of Saturn, who still stood on the bridge, and he turned and flung the hourglass from him into the chasm below, then leapt after it with a gesture of despair.

What had I done? I held the black pearl, remembering its symbolism. The black pearl stood for philosophical thought. That meant I was a "friend of Sophia" or Wisdom. I climbed down the pyramid, carefully carrying the pearl, passing the blind crocodile, who lashed about in fury to find the blue globe again, while the remaining beast roared in anguished sympathy.

"Give me the pearl!" The order rang out, as Saturn leaped back over the parapet of the bridge. "That is mine! Oh! How I have longed for this moment. You have succeeded beyond my wildest hopes, and the Pearl of Understanding is now in your grasp. When I saw what you had done, I was afraid at first, for I believed it would be impossible to stop their desecration of the World, and without that, Saturnine Time cannot exist, for it is the only place that is ruled by Time and Space."

"Why should I give it to you?" I asked petulantly. "I risked my life to get it. Now you want me to just hand it over." I hugged the gleaming object to my breast. "I want to keep it, so pretty."

"Now, take it easy. You will find after a while that it is too heavy. You can't carry it on your journey. I will take care of it for you. Please." Saturns' distorted face was rent with pleading.

"It will be heavy, that's true. I don't really need it right now." I handed the black pearl to him. "You will give it back, won't you?"

"Of course." Came the smooth reply. "Now, do you think you could get the other one? That is the Pearl of Wisdom, and it is even more valuable than the one we have. With both pearls, I can change Time in the World, for I will be able to break both pearls into a trillion pieces, and distribute them. They will charm humanity into learning the attributes of Wisdom and Understanding. It could alter everything and begin a giant leap forward for our population."

"I will try. The other crocodile is raging mad, for he has seen what happened, and he will be on his guard. I do have an advantage, through.

Since his teeth are sunk into the North Atlantic and Brazil, and he won't let go, he can't attack me. I will go now. Saturn, I know you are the Tester. May this be the only test you set for me."

"It will be enough. Go now, and I wish you well."

I walked back along the red carpet and began to climb the right side of the pyramid, struggling over the rough scaly skin of the crocodiles' lower jaw. I could see its eye glaring down at me with a malevolent stare. The eye rolled and followed me as I scrambled up over the back of its neck, and balanced carefully on top of its head. The motion of its crushing jaws, as it chewed on the North Atlantic, caused a major earthquake in the lands to the North. I lay down and inched my way over the bump above the beasts' eye, and reached down, but there was no way to touch the eye from above. I went back to the neck and found a small ridge of scales leading directly to the corner of the eye, which I edged along, taking care not to put a foot wrong. In that position, I leaned forward and, with all my strength, put pressure on the eye. The crocodile roared and tried to move, but could not.

Keeping up the pressure, in a final burst of will power, the eye suddenly slid out and tumbled down into the reptiles open mouth, as it tossed its head back in agony and released its hold on the World. The mouth snapped shut. The eye was trapped inside, and as the crocodile twisted backwards and fell, I was carried down with it, desperately holding on to an outcropping scale. The crash as we hit the ground shook me loose, precipitating me towards the rows of cruel teeth that jutted out from its jaws. They were clamped shut, and I could not open them, although I pushed and pulled mightily.

A short laugh from behind reminded me that Saturn was watching to see whether I was going to succeed in my task. I had to force open the jaws somehow and I hoped the reptile had not swallowed the eye while it was struggling.

"Do you remember me?" A tiny voice spoke close to my left foot, making me look down. Gazing up at me with bright eyes was my friend the rattlesnake, whom I had thought lost when the boat we were traveling in disappeared in a thick mist.

"I think I can help you." The snake announced. "If you recall, I can stiffen myself into a pole, like the pole you used in your punt when we crossed the Lagoon. I have been following you, night and day, but I stayed hidden because I was afraid to show myself in this strange world."

"You are more than welcome." I was delighted, picking up the snake, which coiled himself happily around my waist. "Could you stiffen yourself again? I think a pole would be a useful lever to force open the jaws here."

The snake slithered back to the ground and arranged himself in a straight line, locking his muscles together. I bent down and picked him up, and he was quite rigid. Gingerly inserting his pointed rattle in between the crocodiles' teeth, I prized open its jaws. The eye, a stunning black pearl, lay in the center of its tongue, and I was able to grab it and back out of the opening.

The rattlesnake relaxed. "May I stay with you now?" It asked. "I want to be closer to you. I have seen a very nice nest just above your pelvic girdle, which is guarded from above by your sacrum and right next to your coccyx. I would like to live there."

"You have good energy." I told the snake. "I would like to have you live with me, but how are you going to get in? I don't recommend the rectum route, or, for that matter, the esophageal, since it can be messy and interfere with my normal functions. Do you think you could manage to wriggle through my left ear?"

"It's a tight squeeze, Let me see. I would have to negotiate the intertragic notch, which is rather narrow." The rattlesnake looked doubtful.

"I think that most of your body would get through, but your rattle might catch on something. You may have to abandon it."

"I am willing to do that, if I can be inside you." The snake whispered, the narrow vertical slits of his yellow eyes glistening. "Let me take it off, and I will make the attempt."

He wriggled backwards, turning himself almost inside out, and after making a squirming motion, his rattle lay alone on the ground. I bent down, and the snake softly nudged my left ear. I felt his little nose edging around my concha and down into my ear as his smooth body relaxed and wound around the eustachian tube. I was deaf for several moments until he had moved on beyond my ear and was traveling swiftly down my spinal column towards his nesting place. As he curled up under my spine, I felt a great sense of peace, as if I had come home at last.

I picked up the giant black pearl and went back to the bridge, where I handed it to Saturn, who chuckled with glee. "Now I have the two eyes. What more could I want? I am too lowly ever to see the third eye, but I can work miracles with these." He gazed at me triumphantly. "You have also rescued the World. Let us hope it will not fall into the jaws of death again. Farewell, and may your journey be marked by the acquisition of the third eye." Swiftly he jumped over the bridge parapet with a swirl of his cape and was lost in the murky darkness below.

I sat down to think. The fact that I was sitting on a snake did not bother me, but felt rather comfortable. Before I could move on into Yesod, I had to rescue both Pullows and Paragutt, so I decided to retrace my steps back along the path.

I found Paragutt quite quickly. He was lying in the middle of the narrow path and looked as if he had been chewed over.

"What happened to you?" I asked in concern. Unfortunately, he had only just recovered from his earlier wounds.

"The Qliphoth tried to eat me." He sobbed. "But they spat me out because I didn't taste good. I'm too stringy, and they were really rude about it. It seems they are used to eating maggots and other soft and juicy things."

"Well, I'm glad. That worked to your advantage, then. It was my fault." I added. "I shouldn't have let you fall off my back, but I was taken by surprise."

"Never mind. Please would you piggyback me off this path? Then I can stand on my two feet on solid ground." Paragutt was crouching on his hands and knees. I gave him a leg up and returned to the bridge. "Now, we have to go and find Pullows. There must be a way to distract her from the Dancer."

At this point I remembered the Dancers' fan, which I had put in my pocket. If the fan was able to seduce me in favor of the Dancer, might it not lure Pullows away from her? I realized this was a double standard, and that I should hand the fan back to its owner, but – to lose one of my greatest allies – that was a choice I could not accept. From its inception, this Path had presented me with many difficult decisions. Now, I moved gingerly forward towards the whirling figure of the World Dancer, who was spinning Pullows around by her fingertips. I was afraid she would let go and disappear into space if I didn't hurry.

Unfolding the fan with a purposeful snap, I fluttered it lightly against my chest, bending my gaze upon Pullows as she shot by, her legs trailing in the air, as the Dancer spun round and round. I waved the fan, lowered my eyes modestly and beckoned to her. I saw Pullows' head jerk around to face me, and an anguished look crossed her face. I could see that the Dancer was holding her very lightly. As Pullows whizzed by, I tried to indicate that she should let go just before she reached me. I held my cloak outstretched by my thumb loops and flapped it invitingly, bracing my legs for the inevitable impact. Paragutt was kneeling down behind me, holding me firmly by the ankles, in case I should slip and plunge into the abyss below us.

Pullows saw her chance, and let go of the Dancers' hands just before she reached my position. The centrifugal force of her speed threw her towards me like a rocket. As her body slammed into mine, I faltered and nearly fell, but brave little Paragutt held on, and I was able to wrap Pullows in my cloak and pull her back towards the Bronze Bridge.

The World Dancer stopped and I saw a shadow flit across her face. Hastily, I threw the fan back onto the Path, and she picked it up, glowering at me. As Paragutt, Pullows, and I ran across the bridge, I felt sure I had not seen the last of her, for she would need to vindicate herself from this humiliation at all costs.

As we passed along the red carpeted Path beyond the pyramid, I felt my head weighed down by something heavy. Paragutt pointed upwards. "You've got a hat on. Where did that come from?"

I felt the top of my head and pulled down a small heavy black cap with a point in the center, similar to a French beret. "Well, I don't know where it came from. I'm sure I wasn't wearing a hat before. It's awfully heavy."

"Fool that you are!" Squeaked the hat, as it shuddered in my grasp. "I am the point of the truncated pyramid, of course. But I am not gold, I am lead. Saturn arranged for you to wear me during your progress through the Islands of the Mystic SEA. I will not always be so heavy, for as you move along, I will be able to change into different metals. It is up to you to turn me into gold, and then I can become the tip of your pyramid forever." The hat growled menacingly. "Now, put me back on your head and don't try to take me off again. I will know when the time comes for me to leave and reclaim my pyramid."

I reluctantly replaced the lead beret, although it gave me a crick in my neck, and looked forward to the day when the hat would become titanium, the lightest metal. I also handed three tarot cards to Pullows, the Sun, the Moon and the Universe, with which she was well pleased

A purple glow shone ahead of us as we neared the Island of Yesod, and gathered on the shore were many exiled Yesodians, who had survived the Path of the Universe and were ready to cross over into their dream world at last.

Island of YESOD

A purple glowing mist spread across the sea at the end of the Path of the Universe, as we found our boat waiting for us with Pompeybou and Bazoom aboard. Bardogian had already disembarked on the Island of Yesod and wandered off to look for Fontanova, who was in the throes of a dream somewhere on the island. The boat took us, and the remaining exiles, on board and we had a good sail to the shores of Yesod, although it was a little overcrowded. The Yesodians were not much good at practical things like sailing, and just sat around drinking up our stocks of wine, but I forgave them, for they held the highest degree in Malkuthian capabilities – the art of Intuition.

As we approached the dock, a muscular naked man stepped forward out of the fog to take our lines, smartly catching the flung ropes and securing them with a quick twist around the dock cleats. Must be a sailor, I thought. I wasn't sure whether I was glad to see his nudity or whether I had some reservations about it. In any case, I dropped my eyes modestly as he greeted the crew and handed us each a pair of sandals with foam soles to wear on the island. He escorted the exiled Yesodians to a pinnacled building on my left for testing, to see if they had dreamed often enough, for now they were finally in Yesod, they were to be taught lucid dreaming. This was something I wanted to learn for myself.

In the background, a strange sound, as of a thousand breathing machines, came and went, while people strolled idly to and fro in a dreamlike state. It was odd that these people were, presumably, the workers that ran the machines, for they seemed absolutely incapable of handling such a responsible job. Yesod, in essence, appeared to be an enormous factory, with rows of pigeon holes, presumably for filing items, stretching along the path.

My first task was to find Bardogian and, hopefully, the missing Fontanova. I felt that my allies would be better off remaining on the sloop during my stay in Yesod, for there was an air of menace in the drifting mists that warned me I should continue alone. However it was not for long, since I was happy to see the two Priestesses, Semra and Quamra, wafting through the fog towards me.

"Would you like us to show you around?" Quamra asked. "It's night time here, and quiet. Everyone is dreaming. When the day comes, and Semra takes over, everyone will be intent on running the machinery down in the cauldron and analyzing their dreams."

"I see that you are both together here." I remarked. "Is Semra able to reign at night also?"

"No, but because we both operate in Yesod, it is as if we were bound together, like Siamese twins, and therefore there is no real separation between us."

"I understand, for I saw the same influence with the twins in the Path of the Sun and of the Moon. They became one person, in effect. I wondered if all these sets of twins symbolize duality down here….." I reflected. Then I spoke to them urgently. "I need to find Bardogian, who is searching for Fontanova. Those two sometimes have problems. Although at heart they love each other, they find themselves at odds, and they are often conflicted. Will you help me find them?"

"We can show you the cauldron, if you like, but from there you must continue alone. We never enter the mechanical environment. Bardogian could be anywhere down there, amongst the Machinery of the Universe. In fact, we sincerely hope he has not been cut up and mangled as he wanders about in such a dangerous place."

Quamra led our way along the purple path towards a curved metal wall that rose up high above us. "This is the side of our giant cauldron. You can climb up by using this rope ladder. When you get to the lip of the cauldron, a funicular railway will take you down to the bottom. But, beware, there is a great labyrinth of massive machinery down there, and you will need the thread of Intuition to find your way. You will find locked pigeon holes containing eggs on your left as you reach the bottom. Pick the right egg, that contains your potential, for it has the reel of thread within it. There is one specially made for you -and use it to retrace your steps, as Theseus did when he faced the Minotaur."

I was nervous, but it was important to find Fontanova, for she was my creative, artistic self. My poetic self, Bardogian, was somewhere down there too. What if they had been destroyed by the machinery? Then all my creative thought and effort would go blank - would bring me into a blocked state from which I couldn't recover.

I thanked the Priestesses and started up the rope ladder, which swayed wildly from side to side and banged against the iron walls of the cauldron, stubbing my toes and crushing my fingers as I clung on. I made steady progress in spite of that and reached the top of the ladder, peering downwards. Below me, a boiling purple fog rose out of the depths, wreathing its' way up the dripping walls and foaming over the lip.

From my position, the wall of the cauldron appeared to be straight, not curved, as I had expected, considering it must be a receptive vessel. I realized that it must be so big that I was not able to see the curve, rather as one imagines the horizon on earth to be straight, when it is not. A clanking noise announced the arrival of the funicular, and I was about to step in when I took a look at the driver.

There he stood, a massive figure, about nine feet tall, with a shock of red, curly hair that stirred in the foggy vapor. His huge features were not clear, except for the eyes, which were piercing and seemed to pop out of his head, as the whites were clearly visible all around the iris. I knew instantly who it was – my Ego, Belvedere, dressed in a purple satin suit with lace collar and cuffs and buckled black shoes that were smothered in mud. I never had liked the look of him.

The enormous fellow gave a dull booming laugh like a hollow drum, which reverberated around the cauldron and rattled the door of the funicular. He spoke in a raspy voice. "Your manikins are all over the place! Have you completely lost control of them?" He gave an evil guffaw. "Why, I just took Bardogian down the funicular not half an hour ago. He looked very distraught. Of course, Fontanova was taken down to the machinery room in a dead faint, a few weeks ago. I don't know what's happened to her."

"That's why I'm here. I'm going down to find them. What are you doing here, anyway?"

"Are you crazy? This is where I live, of course. Yesod is the Ego center, and I rule here so that I can receive the emanations from the higher spheres and corrupt them to my own use. It's fun, I can tell you. Personally, I never thought you would make it this far – I'm surprised." He put his finger up in a warning gesture. "Now, don't try getting rid of me like those Buddhist nuts tell you to do. It won't work."

Belvedere always annoyed me because he tried to take control at every opportunity. As long as I wasn't aware of him, I managed very well. But any encounter with him threw me into confusion, because I didn't know what he was going to do next. I felt I would be better off without him, but I didn't know how to get rid of him.

"Step in, now." He gave me a push. "I don't have time to waste on you, little one. Otherwise I'll bring out my pet tarantula again. Ha! Ha! Ha! You didn't like that, did you?"

I hastily stepped into the funicular, and with a grind and a jerk, it started down the unbelievably steep slope, wobbling from side to side so that I had to hold on tight. There was nothing to be seen out of the windows, as the dense purple fog pressed against the glass and the uneven click of the cogs seemed about to falter, leaving us hanging in an indeterminate space. I felt very claustrophobic in the small area with Belvedere manning the controls. I chose to remain silent, to avoid getting into a confrontation with him, which was too easy to do.

After about fifteen minutes, an identical funicular car came up through the fog, and as we passed each other, I was shocked to see a large fellow with a shock of red hair operating the car. I felt a sharp jerk on my right arm from my Shadow, which reached out vainly towards the other funicular, but it was quickly lost in the fog. I turned to Belvedere in surprise.

"Do you have a twin brother?" I asked. "There was someone just like you in the car that just passed us."

Belvedere gave me a knowing look. "No, I don't have any relatives. That is the Shade of Yesod, who is capable of shape shifting. Of course, he might also be my "brother" in a sense, or even my double, the Hoodwinker. I live in the world of duality, and so I can be two people who look exactly the same." He winked at me slyly. "We all have at least two halves or maybe more, you must know that!"

"I don't believe you. To begin with, one can only have two halves. If someone has more than two, they must be thirds, or even quarters." I scoffed. "I know who that was, and she is the other half of you, to be sure. That was the Hoodwinker in one of her disguises. You can't fool me any longer, because I have my Shadow on my arm and it is attached to her I felt it reach out as that car passed us."

"What can I say? You are too clever for me." Belvedere gave me a mock bow and wished me luck. I felt he didn't expect to see me again, for he believed that I would be swallowed in the depths of the cauldron, so I couldn't resist a last stab at him, as the funicular hit bottom with a bump.

"Well, you'd better hope that I return. If I die, you'll die with me. You do realize that, don't you? You would just dissolve into dust and ashes. Remember that. - before you get too confident."

He lost the grin on his face, but parried back. "You can't manage without me either, so there! How would you survive in the material world? I do a lot for you, so don't get snotty with me." He began to laugh again. "I guess we're stuck with each other for good."

I hated him. I wasn't going to respond. Instead I haughtily turned my back and walked over to the pigeon holes on the left. There were millions and millions of them, and one of them contained the correct egg for me. Which was mine? I wondered how I could possibly find it.

Along the rows of pigeon holes there were spaces where cell phones were placed in small boxes,. I picked up one of these phones and dialed my home number. Immediately a stern voice came over the phone. "Where's your basilisk? Get the basilisk! You have to activate your cerebellum. Remember, you are in Yesod, the realm of Foundation, and that is your automatic lower brain, as found in the reptilians."

I was, frankly, surprised. "Do you mean I should go out of my conscious mind? That's hard to do. I certainly don't want the basilisk back in my life. He was horrible. I can do without him, I'm sure."

"Well, you have to forget about your Ego Belvedere for now – he has ruled you for too long. He's in your conscious fore brain and you don't realize how much he controls your ideas and your decisions. Let your instincts be your guide while you are in Yesod. Goodbye, now." The phone went dead.

I sat down and began to meditate. It was hard to tear my mind away from the urgent problem of finding Bardogian, my poetic self. Nevertheless, after a short while I found myself floating along the line of pigeon holes and, feeling a strong pull towards one of them, it flew open on my approach and revealed an egg containing a reel of silver thread. It was only when I picked up the reel that I discovered it was quite securely attached to my navel, and I had never noticed it. With the reel in my hand, I moved cautiously towards the center of the cauldron, placing it on the floor before I went too far, my cares and worries about anyone but myself laid to rest.

Stepping forward as the reel unwound behind me, the first place I found was a great room with many people asleep in simple cots. This room had a hole in the ceiling where a strange orange emanation seeped down into a large basin in the center of the floor. From there, this orange vapor slowly swirled around the room, lapping and whispering over the sleepers in their cots, enveloping them in orange light, at which they would stir and murmur peculiar sounds. I moved hastily on to the succeeding rooms, finding the same system at work, except that the emanating vapor was colored differently, green, yellow and blue, as if a giant rainbow had dissolved and separated into single units. I was puzzled, but found no answer for this phenomenon.

A pounding sound came from somewhere ahead of me, so I walked in that direction. I was careful to leave the reel behind me on the floor as I moved further into the cauldron, so that I might return safely to the funicular. The violent pounding became louder and louder, and the floor seemed to move in unison with the rhythm, so that the whole cauldron appeared to pulsate up and down, and a reddish hue appeared around me. I was now walking on a soft, silky crimson path, and ahead of me I could see a massive bright red pillar that throbbed with life as it shifted up and down in the main room. What could this be?

I passed through the central chamber of the cauldron as a spurt of white foam jutted out from the red pillar. In the foam, thousands of tiny sperm rushed towards eggs that were lined up waiting to be fertilized and form the foundation of a human being, who would become conscious at birth. Around me were many hexagonal cells, which lined the walls of the central room, and in each was a tiny embryo. I watched, fascinated, as the embryos called in their organizers to arrange the sequence of their development, and saw how each cell made its way, without complaint, to the appropriate place in its new body.

Beyond the site of this very basic activity, I came upon private rooms, where, lying upon satin couches, and attended by their servants, lay people who were evidently some sort of royalty, by the way they were treated. I peeped into each room, admiring the crowns, scepters, and other jeweled objects arranged beside the occupants, hoping to find Fontanova, for I felt that she must be among them, but there was no sign of her.

I was sitting down, meditating in order to maintain my out-of-consciousness state, when a shadowy figure ran across the path in front of me. A trail of distinct smoke followed him and I jumped up. That was high quality weed, and that must be Bardogian! I ran after him, to see him disappearing into another chamber that I had missed. Reaching the door, I turned away in embarrassment, for he was stark naked and had just jumped on top of a woman who was lying in an inviting, recumbent position on the bed. It was Fontanova.

I thought it best to leave them for the time being, so I sat a little distance away and waited. After about half an hour, I heard the murmur of voices from their room that gradually reached a high and argumentative pitch. I hesitated, but as soon as I heard the sound of slaps and blows, I rushed into the room and threw myself between them. Fontanovas' face was crimson and the bruise around her eye was already turning blue, while Bardogian nursed some fierce scratches on his neck, cursing softly.

"What do you think you're doing?" I yelled. "For heavens' sake, behave yourselves! We are in Yesod. This is not the time or the place to begin a fight. Calm down now." I stood over Fontanova on the bed and glared at her, while Bardogian tried to creep out of the room, holding a small towel over his vital parts.

"Just a minute! Where are you going? Stay here." He hesitated and I turned back to Fontanova. "I've been concerned about you. What happened? How did you get stuck in your dream, and how are you feeling now? Quite satisfied, I presume." I finished my sentence with a slightly sarcastic tone.

She sounded meek. "I became enmeshed in my dream. It was so wonderful! I dreamed that Bardogian and I were mated, together for ever, and I didn't want to wake up, so I stayed in the dream. Eventually, I believe they brought me here, because they needed the bed for someone else. Bardogian found me here." She paused, sighing softly. "Oh! I was so happy to be woken by him – it was like a dream, but real. We made love, but afterwards we started to fight again, and I was lost. I felt I didn't want to live anymore. We set each other off – I don't know why. My intuition tells me that he is my soulmate, but it doesn't seem to work out for us."

Bardogian, who was still standing holding the little towel, barked out a reply. "It's your fault! You just won't shut up. We make love, and then I want to be silent and poetic, but you must start talking, and that's a fatal mistake. I can't take it any more – your constant need to analyze everything. Why can't you just go with the flow?"

I looked from one to the other. "You both should know by now that you are intended for each other, and that a marriage is, at this very moment, being arranged on the Path of the Lovers in the Mystic SEA. You have until then to work on your relationship, in order to be ready for the Crystal Bed that awaits you there."

"I had no idea!" Bardogian burst out. "Fontanova, we must go into therapy and resolve the issues between us. I have longed for union with you and I know you feel the need, too. Let's try to move beyond our differences and, instead of talking, use our intuition to communicate with each other on a deeper basis. Will you do that?"

She rose from the bed, tossing the damp sheets aside, and stood in her full glory. "I want that more than anything. I will dedicate myself to achieving harmony between us. We need advice and guidance. How can we find the right person to help us?'

I nodded sagely. "I know who will help you to understand yourselves, and I will send you to him. He is my Guide, and I know he lives on the Island of Tiphareth. I will summon our sloop and arrange for the boat to take you there with all speed." I sent a telepathic message to Joana, the cricket on the boat, telling her to arrange a pick up at the shore of Yesod. "Better get your clothes on now. I'll escort you to the shore. It will mean taking the funicular up the cauldron wall. Let's hurry, for I have a feeling there is more work for me here in Yesod."

I was glad that I had the silver thread to find our way back to the funicular, after wending our way between the rooms of sleepers. Belvedere welcomed us with a crafty smile. "Managed to find them, did you then? They look a bit beat up! What happened? Was there a disagreement?" Of course he knew perfectly well of their problems, and was just being sarcastic. I brushed him aside rudely and we stepped into the car. With a jerk, it started up the steep iron wall, passing the other car half way.

I was not surprised when my Shadow tugged violently on my arm and tried to make contact with the person in the other car. I was astonished, though to recognize that the occupant had changed, for the World Dancer, who was also the Bride of Malkuth, stood there at the controls. She gave me a sideways glance, then turned her head away. My Shadow was going crazy, pulling on my arm frantically and reaching its two thin appendages out towards her, but I held on firmly and wrapped it even more tightly around my arm. It was a nuisance, carrying it around, as it restricted my movements and I would have liked to get rid of it, but I didn't know how.

The funicular reached the top rim of the cauldron and we stepped out and climbed down the rope ladder. I safely saw Bardogian and Fontanova on to the boat, noticing that they were holding hands surreptitiously, and gave instructions to the crew to drop them off at the Island of Tiphareth and get in touch with the old man, my Guide. Then I returned to my mission in the cauldron.

Belvedere glared at me as I stepped back into his funicular. "Back again, I see. You'll find things have changed here. When the Moon went down, Quamra, the Priestess of Nocturnal Hours, yielded her position to Semra, who is waiting for you at the bottom of the track." He swallowed hard. "She decided to risk the machinery. Personally, I'd prefer you not to delve into these things. It is dangerous for me, and I feel some control slipping from my fingers already. Just remember, you can't manage without me!"

"That's what you think!" I shot back rudely. "You are simply a nuisance, trying to run the whole show. There are other things in life besides ego, you know."

"But I'm responsible for your survival." Belvedere objected. "Without me, you would have a tough time during your stay in the material world. Look at what happens to geniuses who have forgotten their Egos – they can't manage their lives and they end up having to be looked after by other people. Is that what you want? Do you want to lose your independence?"

"It depends what you mean by that. Is independence only connected to the individual in the material world? You can't answer that question, can you?"

Belvedere looked sad. "That's true. Then, may I stay with you in another capacity? I am your Beautiful View, remember."

"I am working on that. Be patient, we will form an alliance, but it will be a serious transformation for you and I hope you'll be able to handle it. In the meantime, why don't you come along with me, and I'll show you how to understand my intuitive side." I took his great hand in mine and we stepped out of the funicular.

Semra, the Priestess of Diurnal Hours, came up to us at this point. "The Moon, Selene, is asleep at the moment, for day is here. I want to take you around the rooms, for the sleepers are beginning to wake, and we will see how they have transformed their colored emanations. We don't have much time, for the tides change rapidly, and it is not wise to be trapped below the high tide line. Come, now."

"Can Belvedere come too?" I begged. "He needs to know about using his intuition, for he thinks only in my conscious mind."

"I'm sorry, but the shock would be too great for him at this time."
She patted Belvedere on his chest fondly. "You're at the beginning of a
steep learning curve, my dear. You will have to take things slowly. We
will arrange a dreaming course for you tomorrow. For now, stay by your
funicular and relax."

I said goodbye to Belvedere, who was practically in tears, and we
moved swiftly to the series of rooms, where different colored mists had
been undulating during the night, enveloping the sleepers. In the room
with orange light, people were rapidly scribbling down their dreams,
while over in the green room, a group had formed, discussing the idea of a
commune they wanted to form. So it went on. Each color that came from
the different islands in the Mystic SEA was translated into a potential idea,
which would be made manifest in the island of Malkuth. I personally
thought this was a bad arrangement, since, after we had experienced the
evil influences in Malkuth, I feared that these pure emanations would be
corrupted. There was nothing I could do, for I knew that only by purifying
myself could I make any difference in the mundane world.

After we had viewed the various rooms, Semra took me to her bower,
where I rested, for when the Moon rose again, I was to put myself entirely
under the influence of Selenes' illusions. It would be a tricky situation.
Therefore, I lay down to sleep, for I had not rested for many hours.

In my dreams it seemed as if the Priestess of Nocturnal Hours, Quamra,
came to me. She whispered in my ear that I should choose between the
DILD, the MILD and the WILD, because I was ready for lucid dreaming.
My dream-initiated lucid dream included her, of course, and all she had to
do was remind me that I was dreaming. That seemed quite easy, so I asked
her if I could try Mnemonic-Initiated Lucid Dreaming, in which I would
tell myself that I was able to become lucid during the dream.

That woke me up, and I was grumpy through lack of sleep. "Go away,
will you?" I complained, and turned over to face the wall, pulling the
woven silk blanket over my face.

Quamra put her hand on my shoulder. "No. Wait a moment. I want
you to try the WILD dreaming. That is Wake-Initiated Lucid Dreaming."
She paused, looking at me intently. "I feel you are ready for that. You must
focus on my face while you are still awake, but lying comfortably as if ready
for sleep. Can you do that?"

I turned over onto my left side, facing her, and put my left hand on my
right shoulder. My right hand lay inside the curve of my arm and touched

my lips, and my knees were slightly bent. Quamra sat beside the cot and gazed into my eyes, and I focused on her pale and luminous features.

We remained silently in this position until I was conscious of *walking beside her in a strange forest, shafts of light flitting between the branches and making the softly moving trees seem alive. In fact, they were alive, for they reached out towards me with gentle arms, and spoke to me of their pleasure, for they knew I had planted more than 100 trees on the earth plane, and rescued many plants that were sad and in danger. I narrated my thoughts to Quamra, who rested by my side, her face turned towards me. She instructed me to understand that this encounter with the trees was real, and that I would remember it in my conscious state without difficulty, and we walked slowly on, coming to a deep and silent pool, fringed with reeds.*

Out of the pool came many frogs, brown ones, green striped frogs, gold ones, and some with mottled skins. They gathered at my feet, clasping their little hands together, and looked at me with bright eyes. The smallest frog spoke in a faint croak. "We have come to thank you, for making our pond bigger and adding many other ponds for us to spawn in. Now our little ones are bursting with health, and the frog population at this pond has grown quickly, and therefore we sing every spring night to celebrate." I bent down and picked up the tiny frog, cool in my palm, and kissed him. A lump came to my throat. "I love you, too," I cried as a rush of feeling swept over me, knowing that I had saved a tiny fraction of these living beings.

Then we came to a place where hundreds of swallows swooped overhead, darting and wheeling in the clear air over a green meadow. I saw many birdhouses, set on poles, around that meadow, and I knew that I had built them. A small fledgling, barely able to fly, landed on my outstretched hand and chirped brightly. "We are alive and our numbers are increasing because you cared about us, and gave us a safe place to raise our young. All swallows are grateful to you, and when you come before the doors of the Archpriestess between the pillars of Joachin and Boaz, we will be there to aid you." The tiny bird took off, and the swallows circled us, chirping merrily.

Now Quamra gazed at me, and we turned and walked back to the room where my cot was. I lay down, and found myself lying on my left side, with my left arm hugging my right shoulder, and I thought about the dream, which was clear in my head, and then I slept again.

I woke refreshed just as the full Moon was rising over the lip of the cauldron. Quamra sat by my side. She clapped hands in glee and placed before me a delicious breakfast of urchins, who were in a state of ecstasy as they saluted the full Moon. After breakfast, Quamra took me to her bower and arranged a soft couch for me, where I lay down with my head on a little pillow. The space was open to the night sky and the Moon shone with her full radiance, while the dense perfume of incense wafted through the room, lending a mystic impression to my surroundings.

"Gaze at the Moon, and don't take your eyes off her. You will feel wonderful things." Quamra instructed me. "I will return in a few hours, for I have to meet with the Queen of Cups, who controls the tides. She has strong connections to the Island of Yesod through her patron, the Archpriestess, who rules above in the Island of Binah."

I settled back, my eyes on the round brightness of the Moon. After a while, I felt myself drawn towards her, and could no longer think of anything else but her radiance. The cold, clear light bathed me in its brilliance, and I felt a rising undulation in my body, which floated off the couch and rose up through the open ceiling of the room. Soon I was traveling at great speed along a silver path over rippling water, and I saw below me the tides of man, and how they run to and fro, and how they are changed, one moment high, and the next low, and I understood the meaning of perpetual change.

Flying over the Mystic SEA and watching the ebb and flow of the worlds' tides, I understood that I was witnessing a numinous, universal flow of energy that controlled not only the changes in the bodies of men, but also their societies, their countries, and their relationship to each other. Then I felt as I glided on, that my face was wet with tears, for I understood that, until man could grasp the meaning of his sufferings, the world could not change and move ahead on a new path.

I was now close to the Moon, for she had become my destination. I floated down, and my feet touched the fine dust of her surface. All around me, the glow of reflected dust made me shade my eyes. Then, soundlessly, I felt two hands on my shoulders, and I was turned around. A pair of crudely fashioned sunglasses with dark lenses were adjusted on my face, and through them, I gazed upon the source of all this glory, the very Sun itself, pulsating and sending off brilliant flares, and between the two bodies rode the round ball of the Earth, one side illuminated by the Sun, and the other in darkest night. A silver thread ran from the center of my abdomen down towards this earth, fluttering in a light breeze as it disappeared into the dense atmosphere of the planet.

"Do you now understand the Machinery of the Universe?" The pleasant voice of Selene asked me. "Man thinks himself to be the center, but he is only on the periphery, and knows nothing of the grand plan, for he is intent on his little operations. One day the Sun will go out, and, even as we speak, the Moon has moved nine feet further from the earth than the day you were born. Yes, the Moon is gradually escaping earth's influence, and will eventually no longer control the tidal flow, and then all will cease upon the Earth, and all will be dead, in the material body."

I saw all this, and I knew it, and then I was given a little push from behind, and I began floating down to Earth, as the silver cord wound itself back into my fulcrum, and I realized I had been dreaming, for Quamra was there, and a light supper of budding coral polyps was on a tray before me. I ate in a dreamy state, and Quamra was silent.

When I had finished, Quamra explained the illusions that man was subject to. One of these was the idea that the earth was flat, for it appeared to be flat, since everybody was able to stand up on the ground. But the earth was not flat, and people in Australia were actually upside down, looked at from a universal angle. Furthermore, people were convinced that the Sun rose every morning, and went down at night. This was only true from their perspective, since actually the Sun did not move in that way, only the Earth turned around it. The stars and the celestial bodies shone perpetually, yet man could not see them when they were covered by clouds, a thin layer of the earths' atmosphere. Many things Quamra told me, that gave me a new vision of the fragility of humankind, and how the emanations wished for them to succeed, for only they, amongst all that lived, would be capable of grasping the Machinery of the Universe.

As the day approached, Quamra bid me goodbye, and Semra came to escort me to the far shores of Yesod, where I would enter the Path of the Aeon.

My feet were planted on the new path when, suddenly, the ground under my feet undulated and a soft earthquake took place. From a small hole on my left, a tenuous form emerged, taking rapid shape in a figure I knew only too well. The dark cowl of the Hoodwinker concealed her face as she stealthily approached me, and my Shadow gave a cry of delight as the fingers of the repulsive creature caressed it gently. I drew back in horror, the foul smell and the sight of numerous leeches attached to the thin arm, scarred by pock marks and suppurating ulcers, made me throw up immediately over her filthy foot. She snarled and drew back.

"Disgusting! Can you not control your reactions? I have come because I cannot let you leave here yet. The Path of the Aeon lies before you,

and there you must understand the meaning of the Last Judgment."
The Hoodwinker laughed tellingly. "Fools that they are! Their hypocrisy
astonishes me. Millions now believe that, when they die, which is never
soon enough for us, that a god will come to absolve them from their life
work - their destiny - that they consider sinful." The cowl slipped back a
little as the bony head was raised towards me, and I saw the intent gleam
of light on blind eyes, hollow as cataracts.

"What do you mean?" I said nervously. "That is called the Path of the
Aeon. There is no mention of judgment there."

"The Aeon is the judgment, yet it is not the final judgment of an
imaginary god, such as humankind has invented for itself." She paused,
wiping a snotty nose on her sleeve. "No. The judgment is the lasting self-
judgment that every human being must face, in each of their lifetimes. We,
the ones aligned with the Qliphoth, find all sorts of ways to prolong this
judiciary hell, for all are caught up in it, sooner or later, even through they
might deny it a thousand times. The denial itself is a judgment."

Her slack arm fell away from my Shadow, who began to cry in a thin
voice, and she moved away. "I have told you enough. It is a warning. In
time you will find that the warnings that you despise and brush away
become valuable lessons to help you move forward on the Way of Return."
With that, the Hoodwinker backed into the hole and vanished, leaving
me shaken, but determined to press on to the Path of the Aeon, while my
forsaken Shadow sobbed quietly for its maker.

Path of the AEON

❀

A s I left the Island of Yesod, somewhat traumatized by my encounter
with the Hoodwinker, the Path of the Aeon showed itself. A dreary,
flat plain, across which puffs of sulphuric dust drifted aimlessly,
stretched before me. The distant sky was suffused by a red glow and, as
I trod the bare earth, a massive volcano gradually became visible in the
atmosphere ahead. At that very moment, a sudden huge flash of fire lit up
the horizon, and clouds of ash and steam belched forth from the isolated
crater. Fiery rivers ran down the shoulders of the great peak as it erupted -
the distant pounding of these explosions reaching me with a repeated dull
booming sound. The noise seemed to beckon me, for I realized instinctively
that this great volcano was my destination.

The trail before me was getting slippery and I took each step with care
as I crossed a vast area of sludge bordering a large lake, where many strange
cone shaped mud nests were scattered over a wide area. Large flamingoes
sat on these nests incubating their eggs, while flocks of these strange birds

flew over the distant lake and others waded in the shallows, sieving the murky water through their curved beaks in a gobbling motion. The lake was rapidly evaporating, for rivers of red hot lava ran into it, raising great banks of steam that swirled around a distant figure on the far side, sitting in deep thought on a flat block of stone by the lake.

My path ran straight into the muddy waters, and I was soon wading through flocks of flamingoes that curtly ignored me as they squabbled amongst themselves. My hopes that the lake would remain shallow as I progressed were dashed, for I quickly found myself in water up to my chin that rapidly got deeper. I began swimming in long strokes, drawn towards the lonely figure on the far shore. He was dressed in a citrine costume and supported a long wand propped against his shoulder with a flag in the four colors of Malkuth fluttering lazily from it.

Emerging from the muddy lake onto crusty, volcanic ground, I wiped my arm across my wet eyes to see him more clearly. He sat in a relaxed position, one elbow propped on his raised knee, his hand resting thoughtfully on his chin as he gazed into the distance beyond me. He held in his other hand a cord attached to the door of a small cage with an apple inside it. I wondered what he was hoping to catch in it, and then I saw several small jerboas, or jumping rats, hopping around him and sniffing appreciatively at the apple, although they were suspicious of entering the cage.

The flat stone on which he sat resolved itself into the shape of a sarcophagus, made of iridescent blue marble, plain and unadorned. I wondered who might have been buried here, under the volcano. Maybe the young man was mourning a relative? I attempted to attract his attention, but could not rouse him from his trance. Above us, a dark arch rose with a dense mass in the center. Narrowing my eyes against the orange glow of the eruption, I could discern a black panther crouched directly over his head, glaring savagely down at us. I wanted to warn the man, for he was evidently oblivious of the animal that might pounce at any moment.

I waved my arms and pointed up towards the panther with no result. What could I use to rouse the silent man? I felt in my tunic pocket and my hand came up against the small steel triangle given to me by the Bride I pulled it out and struck the bar with the bronze rod. Immediately, a humming noise, as of many bees in a hive, came from the instrument, and the man straightened and turned towards me, blinking as if woken from a dream. His eyes upon me were dark blue and penetrated into my very soul as he spoke.

"Who summons the Memorizer? Who has come into my lonely spot and disturbed my vigil? Who breaks the chain between the dreamland of Yesod and the rational Island of Hod?"

"I am here." I said in a small voice. "I'm the Navigator, who seeks answers on my voyage in the Mystic SEA. What does the Memorizer do here?"

"I am waiting. I have been waiting for many Aeons. I was told to remain here, and that eventually someone would come to relieve me." He looked hopeful. "Are you that person?"

"I'm afraid not. I haven't received any instructions about taking anyone's place. I'm just passing through. I'm traveling on my own, though sometimes I have friends who journey with me." I felt a certain obligation to help him – but I did not want to take his place! I frowned cautiously, looking down at the sarcophagus to distract his attention. "What's in there? Is there a lid that you can open? I would like to see."

"H'm. I never thought of opening it," he said, as he rose and peered at the side to see if there was a crack under the top. "Well, that's astonishing!" He probed with his fingers. "It looks as if there is a lid, but I can't open it."

"Here, let me try." I stepped forward, examining the narrow line of the crack. The tomb was crafted of the finest marble, so the lid would be extremely heavy I walked around it, looking at the corners, and saw a grooved handhold at each one. "This lid is made to lift off. There are handholds, but we need two more people, one of us at each corner. Then perhaps we can move it."

"I'll ask Fight and Flight to come over. It's time they got off that stupid seesaw. The last time I checked on them, it was 7,500 centuries ago and they're still trying to decide which way to react."

He called across to two figures that swung on each end of a plank balanced on a central triangular fulcrum. The wooden see-saw was rocking up and down in a crazy series of jerks as they fought to stay balanced. The person on the left side of the plank was wearing a pale blue shift, which clashed horribly with the reddish color of his body. He contorted his face with rage as he rode the plank, a trident in one hand, while a salamander clung to his right leg. The blue woman on the other end wore a discordant red shift and held a hurricane lamp. The little flame in her lamp seemed to fade and then revive itself as it fluttered with her rocking motion. I felt strongly that they should change clothes with each other, which would make them more harmonious, as I watched them rocking to-and-fro against the perpetual roar of the erupting volcano.

"Excuse me!" I shouted. "What are you doing? You aren't achieving anything! Why don't you both move towards the center and stand above the fulcrum. The seesaw will slow down and you will be able to balance and get off. We need your help over here to lift this lid."

The red man addressed me fiercely. "Why are you here asking stupid questions?

Of course, we can't get off until the Memorizer allows it. He's so lost in thought that we have been waiting for Aeons to resolve our situation." He frowned. "Maybe you can attract his attention and get him into conversation. You are the first person to have come by this lonely spot for many ages. The flamingoes aren't very helpful, they just keep sieving through the mud all day. As for the rats, they are suspicious of the cage and stay outside, although the apple is the most delicious one ever plucked from a tree."

"You're not paying attention." I remonstrated, as I wondered what sort of apple lay in the cage. It looked pretty ordinary to me. "The Memorizer just called you, but you were too wrapped up in your rocking. Get into proper equilibrium and come over here. We need you to lift this lid."

"Lift the lid off the sarcophagus!" Fight gave a yelp of horror. "That has never been done. In fact, they expressly instructed us not to touch it. What has come over the Memorizer?" He edged along the plank towards the center – Flights' end sank down, so she started to move forward as well.

"Whatever happened to us before this moment, now it is time to open the sarcophagus and see if anything is inside." The Memorizer said softly. "We have been hanging around for Aeons, constantly judging ourselves and sifting through our memories, and now this day will mark the end of our sojourn, for the guest we anticipated has finally arrived. Come over here, please."

Looking towards the blue woman, who seemed strangely reluctant to speak at first, I nodded at her encouragingly. She looked at me nervously, speaking in a faint voice as she rocked up and down towards the fulcrum, shivering with fear. "Yes, the Memorizer has to resolve our situation. I am Flight and he is Fight, the basic motivations for human survival. The Memorizer's web has caught us both, for he holds past memories that we cannot resolve. He was fixed in a trance when you arrived, and needed to be awakened somehow."

I watched as they moved gingerly towards the center, until they were standing side by side. "Jump off together." I instructed as I stood holding their hands. "Now!" They landed on the ground simultaneously and the plank leveled out and came to a standstill. They stretched their limbs with relief and hugged each other tremulously.

We joined the Memorizer and each of us grasped a corner of the lid. He gave the word, and we lifted and swung the lid over, laying it on the ground beside the tomb. As it opened, a long shriek burst from within and we hurried over and looked down at the uncovered crypt A series of howls, moans, and wails mingled below us, as a grey mist slowly rose through the opening, separating itself into hundreds of tiny wraithlike figures that drifted around us, crying out with abandon.

The dark sarcophagus mesmerized the four of us. Wraiths continued to emerge in their thousands, crying and shrieking continuously, and wafting here and there. In the tomb itself, we could now see that there was no bottom - only a dark, descending hole from which the hollow plop of dripping water echoed ever upwards.

I straightened my back and looked at the Memorizer. "Who are these faint wraiths that surround us? It seems they were trapped in the sarcophagus, and now they have emerged."

"I recognize them from the beginning of the present Aeon. They are the auras of all those who died suddenly. They left their memories behind by mistake. As you may know, we all carry our memories in our aura, and we must be sure to have them with us when we pass over, or we become lost." He nodded sagely. "Yes, these poor souls must now return to what is left of their bodies and rescue the memories they forgot from their dead brains. That might be difficult. If they succeed, they may move on into the Mystic SEA."

A small group of wraiths was hovering nearby. From them came a keening whisper. "We all belong to a dear Dead lady who lost her mind. She went further and further back into her memories until no recollection remained in her recent lifetime. She tried past life regression, but became lost in a Roman catacomb. Now we are adrift and must find her, our beloved Dead. Otherwise, we can only return as ghosts and do a haunting." They began to sob gently, coiling around each other like a basket of puppies.

"That is really hard for them." I sympathized deeply. "They have no physical power and cannot recover their Dead. What can we do to help? We have let them out – we can't stand by and do nothing." But the Memorizer, who sat on the side of the sarcophagus, seemed unmoved.

Fight answered slowly. "The Memorizer will not help you. He is concerned only with the Akashic Records for everybody. You can't expect him to bother with just a few miserable wraiths that have lost their way."

"Surely, if he holds all the records, their owner must be listed amongst the Dead."

"There is one way for the Memorizer to recover specific records for a Dead. He must experience an unusual and violent act. An Epiphany, as it were." Flight explained. "I don't know how to achieve that."

I glanced back at the Memorizer, who sat motionless on the tomb. As my eyes roved over his figure, I noticed for the first time that he wore a headdress made from a two-dollar bill, with the face of Jefferson in the center. From each side of this headdress there hung descending chains of coins that glittered in the lurid light of the volcano. It was somewhat of a surprise to note his addiction to monetary concerns, a bad habit that I had long since dispensed with. I crept around and cautiously slunk towards him, approaching from behind so that he could not see me, for in any case he had fixed his eyes on a faraway land. Then, raising my arm silently, I quickly snatched at his headdress, pulling it away from his head, the coins clinking as they struck each other. An immense column of orange light, with a bright yellow center, rose from the top of his head as he jerked spontaneously, and spun around to face me, his wand in his hand. He rose to his feet, his body shuddering with the effort, and gazed up at the dark arch above him where the black panther crouched.

"Thank Thou!" He shouted in a terrible voice. "Thou hast sent the one who has released me from material bondage. This is my Epiphany! I have waited many Aeons for someone to rip away my links to the mundane world. Now I see within the lotus flame that is over my head the sign of Mercury, the quintessential spirit!"

He was reeling from the effort of gazing at the flame over his head and I put out a hand to steady him. A shock of electricity ran up my arm and burst in my brain as I touched him, and all went blank as I sank to the ground, powerless.

I regained consciousness to see the two figures of Fight and Flight standing over me anxiously, their seesaw motionless in the background. There was no sign of the Memorizers' head, although his body rested on the edge of the tomb as they helped me to my feet.

"What happened? Where is the Memorizers head?" I mouthed vaguely, struggling to collect my scattered thoughts. "Has he combusted spontaneously?"

The red man Fight laughed. He seemed in a jovial mood and responded calmly. "No. He has gone up the lambent flame to seek the Quintessence of life, and the four Kings are now visible in the dark arch around this fifth essence, for they represent the four essential elements of Earth. You made the mistake of touching him when he was connecting with the Quintessence, and you were shocked by its power."

Flight, who now seemed much more powerful and assertive, smiled in an audacious manner. "The Memorizer knows that he had to put his head in the mouth of the great black panther. This is a test of his spiritual bravery. When the panther, that is the essence of Thou, has absorbed his spirit, all the memories that he has stored over the Aeons will become clear to him, and he will strike the inverted pyramid with his wand and release the trapped experiences that twisted his thoughts. We waited eagerly for the opening of the sarcophagus, to reveal all it contains, for it is truly Pandoras' Box."

"Where is the pyramid?" I was looking around. "I can't see it."

"Look up at his crown chakra. The point of the inverted pyramid is quivering there, embedded in his head. From there his head has risen up through the essence of Mercury to reach the panther." Fight laughed. "His body is down here and his head is up there at the same time."

A frantic chirping behind the tomb diverted our attention. Five jerboas, that chewed and tore at the large apple in the center, had crammed into the little cage while several other jerboas gathered outside hopefully. They were scratching at the closed door, while on every side dozens more jumping rats appeared heading towards the cage, in their anxiety to taste the delicious apple, but not all could reach it.

Above us, perched in the center of the dark arch, the head of the Memorizer rested in between the panthers' paws, as the animal chewed thoughtfully at its skull. The head vibrated inside the cavernous mouth while flames darted forth, and the air shivered with sweet music sounding all around us. Fight and Flight were dancing together in harmony. Their lantern and trident lay on the ground nearby. I wanted to talk to them about their seesaw, yet I decided I would not interrupt their reunion until they were ready.

While I waited, I looked up at the dark arch again. The Memorizers' head had almost disappeared entirely inside the panthers' vast mouth as it slowly closed, saliva dripping from the great jaws. A row of sharp teeth decorated the remaining neck like a primitive choker. The body of the Memorizer, which remained sitting on the edge of the tomb, seemed to be shrinking rapidly.

I wondered whether the ferocious beast was absorbing him. If so, should I reach over and grab his legs, which were still attached by a thin membrane, to pull him back? I chose to leave him to whatever fate developed. He was definitely getting much smaller. I gestured, trying to attract the animals' attention, hoping it would spit him out. The intense power of its yellow gaze turned upon me and I shrank back. At the same time, it bit down, and sucked in a pale, flickering, smoky wraith that hovered around its lips, while the tiny, headless body of the Memorizer fell to the ground in front of me - a flaccid, lifeless heap.

I was shocked! This was not what I had expected at all. I hadn't even had time to get to know the fellow. Now, it appeared that he was already gone. The severed body stunned me as I bent over it. Signs of death were already there, creeping over his shoulders and down the torso like a grey pall. I felt an overwhelming sensation of guilt. My very presence there must have precipitated this dreadful scene! I should never have taken his headdress, for it had protected him from the animal that lay in wait overhead. Over-head! That was not funny. I glared up at the panther that licked its' chops lazily. There was almost a smile on the animals face. I turned away in disgust, knowing that it had imbibed his soul.

Fight walked up and interrupted my remorseful musings. "We are so grateful to you for releasing us from the Memorizers' trance. We don't know how to thank you. We have been working back and forth on that seesaw for Aeons, as you know. Now you have succeeded in breaking the spell that the Memorizer put on us. I am wondering how we can repay you?'

The woman Flight added. "Yes, now we are free to let go of choices, for we can now stand together on the fulcrum, no longer under the dominion of the Memorizer. We are not forced to choose between any action and I am glad that his body is Dead at last." She stirred the limp form with her foot carelessly. "Is there anything we can do for you? We are at your service."

"I have a couple of questions I would like to ask you, if you have the time. Ha! Ha! Of course, you have Aeons of time." I paused, chuckling to myself and looking down at the body, which was turning a vivid green. "First of all, what can we do to restore the Memorizer to life? I feel so guilty about my interference. It caused his death and I'm ashamed of my actions. That would clear my head."

"Oh! Don't worry about him. When he was able to achieve his Epiphany, his head separated from his body anyway. He didn't need the body anymore." Flight explained. "You probably saw the smoky wraith, near the panthers' mouth, didn't you?"

I nodded. "The panther sucked it in with his head."

"That was his aura, his essence. All his memories are carried in his aura, just as they are for you and me, so he hasn't lost anything." Fight elucidated. "When you took off the headdress, which you will recall was formed from mundane concerns, you also allowed him to set aside the worries of his earthly existence, and he was able to gaze up and see the Quintessential spirit at last. Now he is happy, and you should be happy for him. He will truly become the Keeper of the Akashic Records, who enters every memory that has ever happened into an invisible ledger."

"By taking this fateful step, you have healed the rift between us, for we were trapped in a constant choice between the actions of fight and flight – named after us." Fight continued. "When a spirit comes into the world, and assembles a body to live in, it must face the horror of birth. Imagine, traveling down a dark canal that squeezes the very energy out of you, only to emerge into a terrifying world of light, noise and violent human beings. They yank you out of your little tunnel, hold you upside down and slap you, smother you in a scratchy blanket, rush you to a cold table where you are left naked, defenseless and alone, waving your arms and legs frantically in an attempt to return to your warm nest. Well, that's enough to make anyone yell out in fear, don't you think? So we are born in Fear, and that is the very first sensation we have."

"Right from our beginnings, we start to create defenses against that fear." Flight made clear. "We are not yet developed enough to balance delicately in between Fear and Anger, so we vacillate between the two. Anger and rage live in the powerful Island of Geburah, which you will reach during your travels. Fear lives with the Island of Mercy, Chesed. Both these Spheres are very potent and have many excellent qualities. It is the act of knowing and understanding how to get the best out of them that is difficult. You will learn that when you get there. Geburah is strong, yet Chesed, who is born before it on the Lightning Flash, is ever more commanding, for fear is the worst thing that a human being can experience."

A fierce chattering interrupted us. It came from the little cage. The jerboas trapped in the cage were about to attack each other, for the apple was gone, only its core remaining. "We must let them out!" I hurried over to the cage and opened the door. In an instant, the five jerboas inside vanished in a puff of dust, and there was the whole apple, sitting deliciously waiting as five more jerboas crammed themselves into the cage, slamming the door after them.

"What is going on?" I stepped back in confusion. "Where did the jerboas go?"

"Don't worry. You need to understand the meaning of the cage. That apple is the Apple of Knowledge and the jerboas are Random Thoughts from the Island of Hod that jump around inside peoples' heads all day." Fight said. "They must be lured into the cage and eat the Apple, for then they become calm and know the Truth, and they gain understanding of the reason for the Aeon."

"Yes." Flight explained. "The name of the Aeon is also the Last Judgment. Many people think that it means there is a God who will one day pass judgment on everyone and will admit only those who have been virtuous into a place they call heaven. "That is complete rubbish, of course. The real meaning of the Last Judgment is the lasting judgment that we pass on our own actions and those of others. That is why, to be free of the Aeon, we need to heed the words 'judge not, that ye be not judged' in your turn." She sighed. "It is really hard for people to judge their own actions, and therefore they judge other people instead. Although it's important to learn to practice judging your own behavior, you just have to let people be as they are, and accept their modus operandi."

"Oh! That is exactly what the Hoodwinker told me, I thought she was having me on. Now I see. It appears the church turned the meaning of the Last Judgment around, then?" I said. "It was another of those little tricks to keep the congregation under their thumb, eh?"

"Indeed, that is the case. They were able to threaten people with eternal judgment if they didn't believe in their lies. But we, who exist above the lower Spheres, know the real Truth, not the distorted version that the early church preached and that still continues to this day." Flight nodded her head sadly. "I doubt if many will ever learn what we represent." She turned to Fight. "The truth lies between us – at the point of the fulcrum, for there balance is restored between rage and fear."

Fight intervened solemnly. "You will know more of this fact when you meet the Hierophant, who is the self-sacrificed one. His emanation brings opposites into balance. This learning lies ahead of you on your path through the Mystic SEA. For now, we should set out, for we must take you up to the crater of the volcano to search for the lammergeyer, he who extracts the marrow from the bones."

"Lammergeyer – what is that?" I was puzzled. "How can we even draw near to the crater? The volcano is in full-blown eruption!"

"The lammergeyer is a Caucasian vulture." Fight said, leaving it at that. "The current outflow of energy from the mountain resulted from your approach to the Memorizer from afar. The mountain knew who you were, for it had waited Aeons for this day. When the Memorizer became aware of your presence, it was writ in the stars that it would create his Epiphany. Now that he has lost his head, as you might say, you will notice that the volcano is quieter, and by the time we reach the summit, it will be extinct, for its destiny is complete. It will be safe to enter the crater to look for the bird."

"I am ready, then. Lead the way, and I'll follow you"

We set out across the bare, stony foothills of the great volcano, climbing steadily in a zigzag manner up the steep slope, clambering across rough and still-warm lava flows,

wading through deep falls of slithery ash, and avoiding the few remaining boulders that still bounced down the mountain side. When we stopped for a rest, I looked down at the sarcophagus far below, its lid still open. I saw only a dim cavern inside, for the last wraiths were fleeing. The dark arch was disintegrating and at the final moment the black panther, a minute dot barely visible below, jumped from the arch and set off across the arid plain, accompanied by four tiny figures that I recognized as the four Kings. Observing them, I asked my two companions another question.

"I noticed the four Kings' faces mirrored in the dark arch? Why were they there? And - Fight - why were you staring into the eyes of Atmos, the King of Swords? Flight was gazing at King Compos, too."

"Atmos represents the elements Fire of Air, and Compos is Fire of Earth." Fight rejoined. "Atmos drove my Rage, which I express outwardly. When I feel like fighting someone, the fire of my anger flies through the air and hits someone, the same way that you use your entity Bazoom. King Compos, being a Pentacle, is much more repressed. Flight experienced her Fear through passive hostility, which is far more dangerous, because it is hidden underground. The other two Kings, Jetspur of Cups, who is Fire of Water, and Cinarburn of Wands, who is Fire of Fire, are supporters of the fifth King – the Quintessence through which the Memorizer was able to achieve his Epiphany. He who has no name….." His voice trailed away.

"I think I understand." I felt the emotion and glanced at Fight, who fought back tears. "That is a good analogy. Shall we continue up the mountain now?"

"That is a good idea. We are more than halfway to the crater." He pulled himself together. "Look, the eruption has almost ceased and cooling will start now, for I see a lammergeyer soaring above us. Wow! Look out! It's dropping a large bone! Duck and cover!"

Fight leapt aside and we crouched behind a boulder as an enormous femur came crashing down and split apart, the soft marrow escaping from the splintered bone. With a rushing of wings, the great bird landed next to us and began pecking at the marrow, glaring narrowly at us with its red rimmed eye.

I couldn't believe the size of the bone that lay before us. The birds' wingspan was at least nine feet, yet the bone could only be from an elephant or another huge animal. I didn't think this was a suitable environment for elephants. We stayed hidden until the bird had finished eating and flew away, slanting upwards towards the peak.

"There must be huge animals up there." I exclaimed. "That will be very interesting. Maybe we will stumble across a dinosaur or a mammoth. Let's hurry!"

We scrambled to our feet and continued upwards, reaching the edge of the crater some three hours later. Over the lip below us, the boiling lava had completely disappeared, and, except for some threads of steam escaping from fissures, the crater was now covered in a dense layer of incredibly green grass with clumps of trees, across which grazed a large variety of beasts that I knew from experience had long been extinct. Huge brontosaurus, diplodocus and tyrannosaurus roamed about, while giant sloth hung from the trees. How could this be?

"We are gazing at past memories." Flight said sadly. "This must be where they are kept. I always wondered about that, for there are so many trillions of memories. They must be in a repository somewhere. This could be it."

"All these living beings have populated the earth at some time in the past, Aeons ago, yet none remain." Fight mused. "But the memory of them lives on. They are our ancestors."

"I don't see how a giant sloth could be my ancestor." I complained. "There's no similarity between us."

"You are wrong. The sloth has a body with a head and four legs. That numbers five appendages. Count yours! You also have five appendages. That is the meaning of the pentagram, and the five Kings stand for the five points of the pentagram, or Star of the Born. These are your ancestors, and you sprang from them, whatever you may believe."

"Well, I'm not a Creationist! So I do believe in Evolution – creation through evolution. Yes, I suppose they could have evolved into human beings – although it's hard to see the connection."

"Trust us – they all did. We represent the earliest feelings of living beings, namely, Fear that creates the instinct to survive, and Rage, that gives us the means to survive all who attack us. That is how the dinosaurs survived for millions of years. These two basic emotions existed in all human beings from that day to this." Fight insisted. "To prove it, why don't you go back to one of your earliest lives – as a pterodactyl, and find out?"

"That's a good idea. Then I will remember whether I felt fear or anger. Here are the bones that I discovered a while ago. How can we re-enervate the body?"

"Not too difficult. Sit down and meditate, holding the bones. Take yourself back, far back, to the beginning of flying beings. We will wait beside you, for we have all the Time in the world."

I felt my little fingers growing extremely long, and a thin, strong membrane attaching them to my knees. I flapped my arms a little. It was very interesting. After a short while, I was running along the top of a steep cliff. I headed for the edge, and flung myself off fearlessly, gliding down towards a flock of primitive birds that were feeding at the edge of a lake. I was hungry, and looked amongst them for a suitable victim. It would have to be a chick or an older bird that had strayed too far away from the flock. There were a couple of possibilities. I flapped my leathery wings slowly and aimed for one of the birds. Unfortunately, my shadow fell across the flock, and with one accord, they rose into the air, escaping me.

Landing on the ground with difficulty, I rethought my goal – food. I decided to try the lake. Fish were good – I often supplemented my diet with them. I made my way, by using my legs, my wings trailing alongside, to the lake, where I was able to enter the water and float, owing to my very light bones. I managed to snap up some of the smaller fish, but they didn't satisfy my appetite, for I was very large. I returned to the shore and set out to find some reasonable sized dinosaurs.

Coming upon a nest containing some eggs, I snapped up one of them, but it was a mistake. A formidable roar came from the mother, who was close by, and she attacked me before I could eat another egg. At first, I felt very fearful, but then my fear changed to anger, for I was still hungry, and desperate for a decent meal. I backed off, but spread my wings as wide as I could and faced the dinosaur, my sharp teeth clacking as I ground my jaws together to frighten her.

It didn't work. She attacked me and bit a huge hole in my left wing. I limped away, still alive, but sorely wounded. My fear had returned, for how could I fly back to the cliff top with a broken wing? I huddled under a palm tree........

I found my bones there many Aeons later. My two companions were distressed. "I'm sorry that you had to die. But, in the end, all the creatures of that time became extinct. In fact, we must bid you goodbye, for Flight and I will descend into the crater and resume our rightful places amongst the memories of the past, for we are products of the reptile brain." He looked sad. "You will continue to the Island of Hod, the place where dreams do not exist and the rational mind of a logical individual is the key to life itself. Farewell, friend! You released us from bondage and we will never forget that."

The two of them bowed and then began their inevitable descent into the extinct crater of the volcano, while I looked over the plain outside and saw a vast expanse of grey ash stretching to the horizon. From the distant sarcophagus, the remaining wraiths ascended purposefully and floated towards the horizon. I wished them well in their search for the Dead, while I knew that I must reach Hod as soon as possible..

The Island of HOD

Descending to the lower slopes of the volcano, I crossed the intervening ground to the edge of the vast plain. There I found a sand sled, drawn by eight jackals with orange collars, waiting for me, and I stepped in, switching on a small fan beside the seat, as it was quite hot. The driver, a wildcat in dark goggles, shook the reins and hissed at the jackals, and we whirled swiftly over the dunes, the loose sand sizzling under the runners, until we reached the top of a high dune where one of many radio masts stood.

The wildcat pulled up the sled and turned around, my face reflected in its impenetrable goggles. It silently pointed with a whip towards our destination in the next sandy bowl below. My breath escaped in a low murmur of astonishment, for in the great bowl lay a shimmering city of quicksilver, each building moving as if blown by an invisible wind and changing shape constantly. The view was breathtaking! I had been to the Hodian center in the past, but that was merely an outlying post, comparatively small. Here were the structures of the Hodians in their full glory – built of the metal dedicated to Mercury, the deity of intellectual pursuits and courier of the Gods.

We swept down into the city, which was quite large, and entered a wide street between buildings with huge glass windows. Reflected in these windows as they glided past were many small bubbles, moving swiftly along the sidewalks, avoiding each other by some miraculous design. Now and again a bubble floated into the air and hung there for a second, while other bubbles drifted sideways to avoid that spot. At a street crossing, we halted and I was close enough to a crowd of bubbles to see that each of them contained a person, who moved with the bubble as it swayed to-and-fro. An orange light blinked eight times, and the bubbles swarmed across, each one careful to avoid touching the others.

The wildcat was not very communicative, so I kept my questions for a future moment when I hoped to meet someone with useful information. We shortly drew up at a large mansion with quicksilver pillars in the Palladian style, and the cat motioned me to descend. I walked up a silvery path to the front door, made of metal, with a jackals' head emblazoned on it and lifted a jackals' head knocker with the words 'Thoth liveth here' carved into the metal, knocking three times. No-one came to the door. I remembered that the traffic light had blinked eight times, so I knocked again, eight times. Immediately the door swung open, and a valet inside his own sparkling bubble ushered me into a large foyer and then disappeared through some double doors at the end of the room, which was kept cool by the wings of thousands of birds flying overhead.

A metallic voice at my elbow surprised me, for I had not noticed another bubble floating towards me. Encased in the shining bubble was an old man, with a long white beard. "Welcome to the Island of Hod. Allow me to take you to your rooms, which I'm sure you will find very comfortable. There you will be fitted with your own bubble."

I felt glad for some decent accommodations, as things had been pretty rough in the Path of the Aeon. I followed the bubble man to an elevator that took us rapidly up to the eighth floor, where he showed me into my suite.

"We'll have to get you encased quickly." The old man said. "Nobody here goes around without a bubble. It's not safe, for one might lose one's individuality. Other people are always grabbing energy from us, and we are the first to understand what a real individual is. Those jokers, the Netzachians, always live in groups and close communities. They are tied together, for they have never realized their potential as individual human beings and can't think for themselves." He rang a little silver bell eight times and the valet appeared. "Get one of those new bubbles that were delivered from the soap factory yesterday, will you? This person needs protection as soon as possible."

The valet bowed, his bubble swaying about him, and was soon back with a neatly folded bubble, which he shook out carefully and which fitted me exactly.

"Now that you are safely contained, there is only one thing to watch out for, and that is the pricks. These pricks abound in the city and can emerge from almost anywhere. You may have noticed one along the sidewalk.

Before you know it, if they succeed in bursting your bubble, you will become their prey, and they will feast on your knowledge and attempt to take your energy for themselves, for they also want to be individuals like us, but they are not rational enough. So, be cautious and watch out at every turn." The old man motioned me towards a floating bubble bed with a set of headphones. "Take a rest now, and we will have dinner later."

I sank down into a mass of delicious bubbles and reached for the headphones. A sinuous voice came over them. "Rock-a-bye-baby, in the tree tops, open the book and read 'til it stops." As I closed my eyes, the vision of a book descended before me and I could distinctly see the words. As I slept, I began to read, my inner eyes flashing over the words with incredible speed, so that the book was finished in almost no time. The book was lifted up and a second book, equally fascinating, was lowered in front of my sleeping self.

By the time I woke, I remembered clearly that I had read 47 books from cover to cover, and yet I felt fresh and rested, stretching my arms and touching the quivering sides of my bubble. I hoped that I wouldn't encounter any pricks nearby, as I walked to the giant window and looked out at the city. Down the main street of the city, in the distance, a massive statue loomed, and I decided to see it more closely as soon as I was free to do so.

A precise knock came on the door and I turned to see who it was. "Please come in."

The door opened and the valet, dressed neatly in a black tunic with a white bow tie inside his bubble, announced breakfast in the Caduceus Room and escorted me to a large arbor with a statue of Hermes, holding the caduceus, in the center of a huge circular table with 88 chairs placed neatly around it. Most of the chairs were already occupied and more people in bubbles were just sitting down. I wondered how one could eat through a bubble, and my question was soon answered. Numerous valets bent over the plates with bubble mix in their hands and blew through their bubble hoops. Small bubbles formed around each plate of food. These were lifted up and pushed into the faces of the diners, where the small bubbles merged with their larger ones. My plate didn't look very appetizing, since the meal consisted of grated raw carrots mixed with orange peel and decorated with orange nasturtiums, but I ate it anyway.

After breakfast, I was about to walk out into the street to explore, when an arm barred my way at the door. A small hunchbacked White Dwarf with a pale face and pointed chin, in a bubble that was no higher than my waist, was staring up at me. He wore a faded black coat that hung down unevenly, a pair of baggy yellow trousers and a little round cap. On his feet were shoes with the longest pointed toes I had ever seen.

"Just a minute! Don't go out on your own – you're new here. I'm assigned to be your watchman, and my name is Anal. I'll guide you through the city so that you may admire the many wonders we have here. But we must return on time for the conference this afternoon about Prejudice. We are anxious to hear your analysis of Prejudice, since you recently came to us from the Path of the Aeon, which is also the Last Judgment. The Hermaphrodites will be expecting you to answer questions and have rational explanations ready. We have two hours and thirty eight minutes, so now we can go."

He escorted me out of the door, taking care not to trip over his toes, and we headed down the main street of the city towards the great statue. Along the wide street, on both sides, one large building after another reared its head. As we floated in our bubbles, I read the name plaques on each shimmering building. The first was the "Forum of Absolute Biography;" the second "Weird Invention Institute;" the third "Thoth Occupational Oceanography Terminus;" the fourth "Foundation of Experimental Emphasis Technology," and so on. I did not see any houses or residential areas in the city, so I asked my diminutive companion where the people in the city lived.

His answer surprised me. "They reside in the octagons, of course. They are outside the city, to avoid contaminating the city with irrational thoughts." Anal frowned. "Sometimes people receive emotions that filter in from the Island beyond us, Netzach. We try to discourage such erroneous views, and normally these people, when they are discovered, are arrested by our Mental Overseers and incarcerated until they return to a rational way of thinking. This is the only way we can keep our focus on logical opinions."

"So, you don't allow people here to feel emotions?" I asked in dismay. "How can they make rational decisions without considering their emotional state first?"

"The emotional state of man is very primitive. We have moved on from that. After all, there is no sensation in logic or mathematics, and if there were, it would contaminate our procedures and cause chaos." He paused. "The Island of Hod is about organization and development above all other considerations. We have become individuated from the incompetent muddle of group mentality that you will encounter when you visit the Island of Netzach."

As Anal spoke, we were approaching the giant statue I had seen at the end of the main street. In front of me rose up a great silver image of the God Mercury, with winged feet and carrying a dagger, about which was entwined fronds of herbaceous dill and hemp. The statue was not stationary, however, but moved in undulating, sinuous forms caused by an enormous fan that directed the surrounding air towards it, giving the impression that Mercury was actually running. It was a splendid feat of engineering and I was duly impressed.

"This is amazing!" I acknowledged, turning to the Dwarf beside me. "How is it done? We don't have this technology where I come from."

"Ah! That is because you have not examined the properties of quicksilver, or mercury, thoroughly. We are experts in the field of fashioning this volatile metal, for, as you have seen, all our buildings are constructed of mercury, and yet as they move, their windows do not shatter, for they are pliable glass. This technology is not available in Malkuth." Here Anal glanced slyly up at me. "I guess you are a few thousand years behind us, after all."

I resented this remark. The little man evidently caught on, for he warned me not to allow my emotions to color my visit to Hod, for I could be caught by the Mental Overseers and thrown into jail. I gulped and promised him I would try to remain rational.

We returned down the other side of the street, where many universities and institutes with odd names stood side by side. Amongst them was the University of Concrete Rationality, where a large number of students were floating up and down the street in their bubbles, carrying placards with "On Strike – Give us Back our Arts" written on them. A window high up in the building revealed a group of people, obviously administrators, looking down at the scene doubtfully.

"H'm. That doesn't look good." Anal murmured "They have decided to strike, after all. They want Art, Drama and Music restored to the curriculum, and the powers that be have decided those subjects are no longer relevant, since we are now in the scientific age. There'll be trouble, I expect."

"Why can't they study those subjects? They are very important for a well-rounded education. It doesn't matter whether they're going to be scientists, a knowledge of Art and Music is important in their lives."

"Well. We don't think so. A number of logical studies have been done, and they say that those subjects are totally unnecessary. I should know – I am one of the members on the University Board."

I frowned at him. "I don't agree with your decision. But maybe the Netzachians still include dancing, painting and music in their teachings. I will be going there soon."

I wanted to annoy him, and I succeeded. He glared at me.

We were interrupted by a large force of police in bubbles, coming down the street, wielding pricks. They surrounded the strikers and told them to put down their placards and go home. They objected, and continued to move up and down. The cops shifted in closer, and soon a cop used his prick on a recalcitrant student, whose bubble burst with a bang. He fell to the ground and a battle began over him, the police having a distinct advantage, since they had weapons, but the students fought back, bashing them over the head with their placards. A young man, evidently their ringleader, was arrested and handcuffed by the police. Another lunged forward, trying to free him, and the cops beat him back. He fell to the ground, bleeding profusely, his bubble about to collapse.

I thought about getting involved, but I was afraid of bursting my bubble, for I saw how many pricks the police had. I contented myself with shouting from the sidelines to encourage the strikers. The police finally got control and confiscated all the placards. Several of the students were taken off to jail, and the strike collapsed.

I felt really bad about the situation. The dwarf had flounced off, after I had shown him I was not in favor of the university. I walked over to the main doors and spoke to one of the strikers, who were gathered there looking crestfallen.

"I wish I could help." I said. "Why don't you go back to Netzach, if you want to paint and play music. I have heard that they have a great time there."

"We know of Netzach, of course, since we are considered to be a step further advanced. Sometimes I think you are right. However, the Netzachians have absolutely no concept of technology or scientific advances, and we are mostly computer nerds, who are interested in that sort of thing. It would be hard to leave that behind." He shrugged. "I guess life is a compromise – you can't always do everything you want to do. As nerds, we are not into basic fighting, and even this strike took us a long time to put together. With the leaders in jail now, I don't think we're going to try again."

"It sounds as if you have given up." I said, a little scornfully. "I wanted to help, but I can see there's nothing to be done. I wish you the best of luck in your studies."

Out of the corner of my eye I saw the dwarf beckoning me from the end of the street. He was tapping his watch impatiently. I went down to him and, wanting to change the subject, I asked him a question.

"Where are the octagons situated?" I asked Anal. "Is it possible to visit them? I would like to talk to the people."

"You will have to discuss that with the chief Hermaphrodite. We can arrange a meeting with it after the Conference on Prejudice, as it is nearly lunch time." He glanced at an enormous wrist watch. "We have exactly three minutes before lunch."

We floated into the Palladian mansion and sat down to lunch with 86 other people in their bubbles. After a bowl of pumpkin soup, we ate slices of cheddar cheese on orange roughy and finished with sugared mandarin oranges. The scraping of chairs announced the end of the meal and the bubbles, carefully avoiding touching each other, filed neatly into a regimented hall where the chairs were arranged in rectangular groups. I sat down near the front and peered at the closest bubbles hovering on the platform, hoping to decipher the exact shape of the hermaphrodites within, but the shivering reflections on the bubbles prevented me.

A hush fell over the group and a single bubble wafted in from behind a screen and took a position behind a lectern with the design of a Masonic lambskin apron on the front.

"Good afternoon." The speaker announced. The voice did not give a clue to the persons' gender, as it was neither very feminine, nor very deep. "We are privileged to have amongst us the Navigator, who has just arrived on our shores. We are expecting an explanation of Prejudice from this person." It turned towards me and beckoned through the bubble. "Please approach the lectern and I will introduce you."

I maneuvered my bubble cautiously between the chairs, hoping that there were no hidden pricks close by, and reached the lectern, where I was introduced. "Now we will field questions from the audience." The hermaphrodite pointed to a member of the group. "What do you have to say, over there?"

The person rose from their seat and bowed, their bubble slipping down for a moment. "In our world, judgment is very important. What is meant by the term Prejudice?"

I was ready. "Prejudice is considered to be wrong in the material world. It means that one person judges another before the true facts about that person are known. That is pre-judging someone, as it were. .Unfortunately, it is impossible to know the full facts about another person, or why they act in a particular way, since none of those in Malkuth know what the real truth is."

The next person spoke up. "That is very strange. Surely it is easy to discover the real truth behind a persons' actions?"

"Not actually. You would have to know that person intimately, and true intimacy is very rare in our world. People live behind a façade."

"What is a façade? I have never heard of it."

"It is a front, a persona – like your bubble." I tried to explain. "Everyone has a persona, which is to protect them from emotional invasion."

"Ah!" Came a fourth remark. "So people in your world are plagued by their emotions, and they try to hide their real selves from others?"

"It depends what you mean by their real selves. All matter is an illusion, an unreality. Your world is real, but you are also prejudiced, because you despise the Netzachians. It is hard not to be prejudiced, for it creeps unawares into your attitude."

"You are wrong! Hodians are always aware of their opinions. We are not, nor ever have been, prejudiced against anyone. You are trying to undermine our philosophy!" The speaker sat down angrily.

"Your remarks are, indeed, prejudiced against me!" I retorted. "What is more, you have just displayed an emotion. You are angry! Hodians are supposed to be master of their emotions." I continued unabated, unable to resist my next remark, and never believing that it would be so disastrous. "Where are the Mental Overseers? Take this person away!" I joked.

To my horror, two white coated bubbles rushed forward and seized the speaker, dragging him along the row of chairs. Suddenly the bubble between them burst, and blood spattered the shocked audience, who jumped to their feet, bumping into each other in confusion. Several bubbles popped and there was a general panic, as the audience rushed the doors in their dash to get out. The turmoil by the doors was horrible to behold, for bubbles were bursting everywhere and screams of fear shot through the remaining audience, who huddled in a corner.

I gazed at the upturned chairs in the hall, the bloodied floor, and the bodies of those who had been pricked. It was a tragedy of my own making, yet I saw how hollow the attitude of the Hodians had become, for they had quickly succumbed to their emotions after all.

Sneaking from the room, I managed to escape the turmoil around me and make my way back to the bedroom on the eighth floor, where I sat down to think rationally.

Dusk descended but no-one came for a long time. Finally, there was a sharp knock on my door. I shivered in anticipation. What punishment awaited me out there? The rapping came again, urgently. I opened the door a crack, whereupon a potent force from outside pushed the door open, and a dark shadow rushed into the room before I could stop it and threw me back onto the bed, nearly bursting my bubble.

"What are you?" I stuttered feebly, lying through my teeth. "What are you doing here? I have done nothing wrong!"

The wildcat stood before me, ripping off its goggles to reveal evil yellow eyes. "WHAT is right, for that is my call, but beware! I know what you have done. I am here on behalf of the Hoodwinker." The cat chuckled gleefully. "But now you have done a big favor. Welcome to our side of the Island of Hod, the Shadow side. You have caused chaos on the Island, and therefore unwittingly played into our hands. Now we hold you prisoner, for we wish to learn more of your evil ways."

"What are you talking about? I didn't mean to cause a problem." I objected. "I was joking. They took me seriously because they don't have that sort of humor. Please let me go. I will make amends."

"All very well, but after your defiant attacks on us in the past you can hardly expect us to believe you! We are separated by eternity in the Mystic SEA, but we can come together at one location, and one path only. Of course, I will not tell you the name of that path – and it is coming closer, ever closer. Then we will see who is boss."

"Why don't you just leave?" I said petulantly. "I'm tired. I don't like it here and I hope to leave as soon as I can. I'm going to bed now. Please leave – the door is over there."

The wildcat spat at me, but turned and left, promising a future confrontation. I felt certain that this was a Shade who had shape shifted into the cat, so I did not blame the real wildcat, although I felt it was extremely rude.

The following day I was able to get a ride on the sled out of Hod. The White Dwarf accompanied me. I was exhausted as the sled swirled to a stop at the top of a huge dune. The wildcat sulkily ordered us to descend, whipping up the jackals almost before my feet touched the sand. We were at the top of the Hodian world – an enormous dune that rippled in the constant wind and assumed one shape after another, ever shifting. The Dwarf pointed down, and below us the sand stretched towards some dark cliffs, where it petered out into rubble-strewn foothills. I began to descend, believing that my passage towards the Path of Death would turn out to be fairly straightforward. I was wrong!

Anal the Dwarf stopped me. "What are you doing? Wait a moment. You can't leave Hod with your bubble on. We must remove our bubbles, for only Hodians wear them to protect themselves from individuality theft, one of the most serious crimes here." He stepped forward and carefully unzipped my bubble, peeling it off roughly, then removed his own. "There. Now you are ready for transformation and progress up the Tree of Life to Netzach and beyond. The Netzachians know nothing of single-mindedness, for they always operate in a troupe, as your friend Pullows saw when she trained them as actors. We can move down the dune now." He stumped along, putting one pointed foot after another in a rush of sand, and was soon at the bottom, while I stumbled after him.

Path of DEATH

❀

We lurched down the slope, floundering in the soft sand, finding hard ground underneath us at last as we approached the tall cliffs of Death. I was mentally preparing myself for this Path when a dull rumbling ahead made the overhanging crags begin to shake and twist themselves into contorted fissures above us. We turned and ran back, as a cascade of rocks and boulders raced down the shuddering cliffs and thudded around us. After hastening for several moments to outrun the danger, we turned to look back. To my surprise, the ground between the Island of Hod and the Path of Death was slowly separating from the foothills, and a great wave of dark water rushed across the path, obliterating our intended trail. The sea became wider and wider until the cliffs had almost disappeared from our view.

Now the White Dwarf pointed across the raging sea to the far shore where the furrowed cliffs, against which the sea now pounded mercilessly, threw spouts of foam skywards. The coastline looked grim, and since there was no way for us to cross on foot, I knew that I would have to call my crew to pick me up and make the dangerous crossing by boat.

I sent a telepathic message to my cricket Joana, who hung in her cage in the cabin of the boat, telling the crew I needed to be picked up at Hod. I walked down the warm dunes to the seashore and found a suitable inlet, where the water was calmer and the boat might beach for a few minutes as I leapt aboard and pushed off with the boathook. The sloop hove in sight swiftly and I narrowed my eyes to see who was aboard. I was delighted to see Pompeybou at the helm and Bazoom perched on the bow pulpit.

The boat dug her bow into the sand by my feet and I was soon aboard, followed by the White Dwarf, who had amazing jumping powers. Wielding the boathook, I quickly pushed off into the choppy sea, troubled by a gusty force 6 wind that set in from the north. Serious cross seas were kicking up, because the shores of Death were scarred with jagged rocks, and we were all soon soaked as the sloop beat across the channel close hauled, bearing away as we neared the coast, to pass to lee of the danger area and find smoother seas.

We sailed fast on a close reach along the southern coast, but could find no inlet that might allow a landing. Reefs jutted out from the rocky headlands at every turn, and strong gusts of wind blew down crevices in the cliffs, heeling the sloop over on her beam ends, at which Joana fell out of her cage onto the radar and sustained a broken leg. After splinting it with a matchstick, I returned on deck where Pompeybou, the Dwarf and I hung over the windward rail, throwing our weight outboard and spilling some of the wind from the mainsail as Bazoom pressed against the helm.

What if we could find no landing place? The sloop might be dashed to pieces against the rocks, for the surrounding sea was too rough. I reminded myself that the Path of Death lay in front of me, so I had to take the risk, for I must experience Deaths' transformation to reach the Island of Netzach.

We rounded the eastern end of the isle, still finding no break in the cliffs, and, gybing the mainsail, began reaching back towards the north. The cliffs were now getting lower, and in due course a shallow break appeared where a sluggish river dawdled into the sea. The river estuary was choked with rushes, but the mud, as we approached, looked soft enough to beach the boat, so we put her bow onto the shore.

I jumped into the shallow water, followed by the Dwarf Anal. A frantic gurgle erupted from him as he missed his footing and fell from the bow pulpit, disappearing under the murky water. I hastened to search for him. Pompeybou yelled to me to push off the sloop, and he and Bazoom, shouting good luck, sailed off into the distance and were soon lost to view.

I was intent on my search for the Dwarf, scrabbling along the bottom between each wave on my hands and knees, but I could not find him anywhere. What a disaster! He had been a wise companion in Hod and I would now have to face the Path of Death alone and unaided. I continued to search for several hours, but it was as if he had never been. For some time I sat amongst the reeds, feeling forlorn, and even Paragutt did not come, for he had been released from my persona and now led his own life. After a restless night, during which I gave up the Dwarf as lost, I began moving up the river, and soon found myself in a miasmic swamp, where the current slowed down to a crawl and fetid pools, their oily surface left by an earlier flood, spread out on either side of me. Lazy bubbles rose to the surface of the nearest pool as I looked at it with distaste, the foul smell of rotting material assailing my nostrils, and I pulled my cloak over my nose. I moved cautiously forward, as the ground was very unstable, and reminded me of the Dark Ground that my Guide had warned me about many Aeons ago. Where was he now, I wondered?

A ripple caught my eye in one of the pools, and I wondered what lay under the surface. Peering down, I saw the form of a man, red as blood, who was caught in the reeds below the water, struggling to reach the surface. Reaching out my hand, I grabbed his outstretched arm, and with a jerk, pulled him up. He took a great gasp of air as his head broke the surface, his face a mask of fear and his eyeballs rolled back in his head. I held him steady and after a few minutes he was able to crawl out of the stinking pool. My new refugee wore on his head the form of a golden scarab, and in his left hand a seed sprouted. Around him was wound a long sash of pitch, woven tightly, that cut into his skin. I began to remove it cautiously, as his flesh seemed very tender.

"Thank you, thank you. That was very uncomfortable." The man murmured, dashing the water from his eyes. "I saw the clock starfish under the water, and the hands pointed to midnight. I knew my time was up. But I didn't want to die in a filthy swamp where electric eels and sharks make their hunting ground. I still have to pass over, but I felt there must be another way."

"Are you planning to reincarnate immediately, or do you wish to stay in limbo for a while?" I questioned.

"Well, the reason I am so red is that I was burned alive. All my skin has flaked off, and although I am now unconscious in the lower world, tied to a stake, I have not yet given up the ghost."

"That's horrible! I thought people didn't get burned at the stake any more. Are you from a medieval era?"

"All I know is, I am from the time of the Spanish inquisition. I have been condemned to die because the Catholic Church considers me a heretic. I was a healer, using natural herbs to cure people in my local village. The Church arrived, scouring the countryside for anyone who was not going to mass regularly, and someone fingered me. They dragged me to the public square, without a trial, and tied me to the stake with these bonds of pitch that you are removing." He began to weep. "The pain was terrible, but I managed to inhale the smoke and flames, so that I quickly lost consciousness. Now my body is no longer useful to me, but, believe me, I wish to reincarnate as quickly as possible, for there is much work to be done, and I pray that my knowledge of herbs will help mankind in my next life."

"I will help you to seek a way back. I am interested in the Death process, and I would like to examine it further, if they will let me in. Maybe I can sneak in with you."

"I'm open to that. Now I feel my spirit is trying to escape, and it is crying out in anguish. I am anxious to let go." He squeezed my hand slowly.

"Come with me, and we will find another way for you, a way of peace." I took his hand, and we slipped and slid out of the swamp and onto drier ground. Ahead of us, and across a beach of black pebbles, rose a narrow cleft in the surrounding rock face. Two sphinxes sat on either side of this gap, the left one made up of skeletal bones, and the other of plump sprouting seeds. From below the bony pelvis of the left sphinx slithered a cobra, weaving its head from side to side menacingly.

A sibilant sound came from its curving lips. "I am the guardian of the gate of Death. What do you here?"

My companion spoke in an agitated tone. "My time is up, and I must pass over. The clock in the starfish pointed to midnight. I have been burnt at the stake, yet I was innocent. Because I retained angry and resentful thoughts against the Catholic Church as my body lost consciousness, I was cast into that stinking swamp. You can probably smell me, because I haven't had time to cleanse myself. This kind person happened to come by and pulled me out. I wish to cleanse my mind as well as my body, so that

I may pass on in the hope of a productive life for my next reincarnation. Do you have a basin of water and some soap?"

The cobra disappeared and came back with a bowl containing spring water, a little face cloth, towel, and a bar of Dove soap. "Here you are. You asked for it, you got it. All those who don't ask, don't get, and they stay dirty. Enjoy your bath. I will be waiting, and in the meantime, I will summon Death and tell it that there is a spotless candidate who hopes to pass through shortly."

The snake went into the crack and soon reappeared with a ghostly horned shape behind it. This vast vision swirled out of the crack, the folds of its transparent cloak floating around it. I could make out two narrow eyes in the large head as the figure of Death bent over the red man, who was gently patting himself dry.

"Are you ready?" It asked in a hollow but gentle voice. "Now that you are cleansed, do you feel that your conscience is clear and focused, so that we may enter the Crack between the Worlds together?"

The refugee bowed his head. "I do. The cleansing power of your water has banished all thoughts of revenge and anger from my mind and heart. I know now that I carry the seed of my next life already sprouting in my hand, and the sacred scarab is my protector. Please take me up."

Death bent down, placing small fingerlings of its mantle around the red man. As it did so, his blazing color faded gradually and became a deep turquoise. "Now, just relax. You emerged from the water in a dreadful state, not believing in anything, struggling, and confused. I could never have accepted you in that condition." It paused, "However, the Navigator, who begins to understand the passages between the Spheres of our world, or Islands, as you call them, fortunately came to your rescue."

Death looked down on the man, whose body was now limp and relaxed in the folds of its cloak, and gazed upon him ardently. The mans head lay back and his eyes closed gently as Death lifted him up and, with a swish of its mantle, dissolved back into the dark crack behind it, before I could leap forward to accompany them.

I had come to feel sympathy for the dying man, and I was glad that he had cleansed himself. But a question lurked in my mind. Where had Death gone with my unfortunate companion? What lay beyond the Crack between the Worlds? I decided I had to find out, and I stepped forward to the entrance.

A sharp hiss distracted me as the cobra slithered in front of me, blocking the path, its hood fully extended. "Go no further, Navigator! It is not your time. Never try to penetrate the mystery of Death, or you will be condemned to everlasting consciousness. Go away now, for your deed is done at the Gates. There are things to be learned on this Path, but not here." The cobra raised its head, flicking out a tongue towards a narrow set of steps cut in the rock face opposite the Gates. "That is the way you must go now. One day you will return, and then you will know the truth of Death."

I moved sadly away, accidentally knocking against a crystal ball that rested on a stand in front of the Gates. I bent down and picked it up. The clear turquoise ball was heavy, and had untold depths within it. I guessed it was made from pure volcanic ash, fused together in great heat to emerge as glass. Carrying the ball in my hand, I began to climb the narrow steps, wondering what lay beyond. I still foolishly wanted to see behind the mask of Death, but how could I penetrate its mystery?

Reaching the top of the stairs, I found that the cobra had followed me. The sky, which had been extremely gloomy, lightened, and over my head curved a swathe of a million bright stars, forming a bridge that arose in the north of the island and reached over to disappear behind a barrier of boulders to the south. I was fascinated by this diaphanous arch, and gazed at it for some time until I discerned a pulsating section in the middle of the bridge that seemed brighter than the rest. I strained my eyes to see and longed for a telescope. The section was so bright that I lowered my eyes for a moment into the dark, then I caught a glimpse of movement from the south side of the island.

Yes! I could see clearly a brilliant pink form that rose in the sky, moving gently towards the bright spot overhead. Above this figure, and seeming to balance on its outstretched left hand, was a blazing hexagonal star – the Star of David – as it was called by many people. The apparition, which I now recognized as my late companion, rose effortlessly ever upwards, until it was lost to view and absorbed by the spot in the center of the arch of stars. I had rescued this man from the swamp; I had seen him metamorphose in Death's arms and change color. Now I was witnessing him in another transformation. Could this be his spirit, set free at last? And - if so, what did the arch of stars mean, and the central spot to which he was traveling?

"What's that?" The cobras' mind flashed onto another shape. He was sniffing at the ball and his long tongue shot out and gave it a lick.

"It doesn't taste very good. I prefer eggs." He gave me a sly sideways glance then turned back to the crystal. "Oh! I can see something in here. It's me! This thing is just like a mirror, only I don't look like that, I'm sure. I'm distorted! Now, there is something in here that is both behind me and beyond me. What is it?" The cobra peered intently into the crystal ball.

"I'm sure you can't see anything in there except your demented face." I scoffed. I was annoyed with him. His untoward appearance had delayed my investigation of Death, and I resented it.

"Wait! There is something there. I see two fishes, and between them they are supporting a little – Dwarf, I think it is. Yes, they are swimming deep in the sea, and the Dwarf is beating on a little drum. He looks happy, so I guess he must be able to breathe underwater and not drown. Do you want to have a look?"

"Certainly. I thought that the White Dwarf had drowned! I searched everywhere for him." I bent down and focused on the picture in the ball. There indeed was the White Dwarf, Anal, slung in a tiny chariot pulled by two fishes, and making great speed to the south. I assumed that he could not see me peering at his image, but in fact, he caught sight of me, and a brief shadow crossed his face. The ball clouded over, and the vision was gone.

The cobra was disappointed. "I wanted to see where he was going, darn it! Why did you allow him to recognize you? Now we've lost him."

"I'm just relieved that he made it. I thought for sure he had drowned, but I wonder where he's going with those two fishes towing?"

A scurrying behind me revealed a small rat crouched, by my left foot. I turned to see a scorpion stalking him slowly, its tail raised high to strike. The rat could not move fast enough, but I could. Scooping him off the ground, I felt his warm, furry heaviness in my hand, while I kicked the scorpion out of my way.

I didn't realize the terrible mistake I had made as the cobra gave a warning hiss. "Fool that you are! You will pay for this. Did you not know that the scorpion is king here, for he is death itself. Kicking him is very dangerous. Beware, for at some time in your future – I cannot tell when, the scorpion will strike you, and strike again and again - and that will be the end of you!"

I was shocked. I didn't know whether to believe the cobra or not. Was the snake just trying to scare me? The reptile slithered back down the steps as I slipped the wretched rat into my pocket and, brushing off the snakes' warning, I clambered on over the rough terrain, searching for some sort of clue on the island.

After a fruitless day of wandering, I decided to return to the entrance of Death to find an answer. Maybe I could ask one of the sphinxes, although I felt they would never give a straightforward reply. I ran down the steps in my eagerness and arrived outside the Crack between the Worlds again. Here I noticed that both sphinxes were mounted on narrow stands on the edge of the swamp. I approached them cautiously, and turning to the one on the left, I asked it for directions into the back entrance of Death.

The sphinx on the left was made up of assorted bones, having a sort of pelvis, shoulder blade and arm bones. The cobra was curled up in its shadow. The bony face was neither male nor female, but simply a skull, which was appropriate under the circumstances. . But the curious thing was that a half-mask covered the lower part of its face, hiding the mouth and chin. Well, I thought, obviously that one wasn't going to say much, but I was wrong. In a kind of death rattle, it blurted out a riddle.

"No sooner spoken than broken. What is it?"

I scratched my head, considering a possible answer, but could think of nothing.

The sphinx shook its head, the bones rattling mournfully. "Failed! I will remain silent."

Well, that hadn't got me very far. I turned to the other sphinx that seemed friendlier, being fatter and rounded like a plump seed, with a long tail out of which sprouted a large sunflower. "Help me. I need to find my way into Death to discover its secrets. Since I can't get in by the front door, is there a back door I can creep through?"

The sphinx, which had a half-mask covering its eyes and nose, spoke in a guttural whisper. "To unravel me you need a key. No key that was made by locksmiths' hand, but a key that only I will understand. What am I?"

"A key, a key. Not a locksmiths' key. Well, to decipher a code, one needs a key. Is that it? A cipher, I mean." I looked hopeful.

"You are correct. I am the sphinx of Hope and over there is the sphinx of Despair. Death transforms despair into hope, you know. I can give you directions to the back door of Death, but you must go in backwards and on no account turn around while you are in there, or your life will be snuffed out. You must only see what you pass as you walk backwards, and from there, since you are seeing the end before the beginning of the process, you will have to figure it out by inverting your thoughts." The plump sphinx rolled around, laughing in a cracked mumble. "Now, turn to your left and go back up the steps. Take the first turn to your left at the top. Take the first turning to your left after that, and then the next turning you see to your left. The back entrance is there." The sphinx paused. "I must warn you. Watch out for spirits! It is very crowded near the door, as many of them are transforming from the rear of Death and floating up towards the bridge of Art, where they will forge their swords. Then their willpower may take them to the Archpriestess, where they will receive new bodies. Unfortunately, humans are fighting several parallel wars in the mundane world at present, and that means our spirit quarters are crowded with fatalities. Above all, do not try to touch any of the spirits, for it will distract them, and they may focus on you and try to inhabit your body. Go now, with the best of fate."

I turned and retraced my way up the steps, turning to the left at the top. I stumbled over a rock-strewn path for a while and then a branch of the path opened to my left, going down a steep gully towards a narrow cleft, at the bottom of which was a slide of some kind that was angled upwards at about 45 degrees. I reached the slide and began to examine it. It was made of black obsidian, polished to a fine surface by Aeons of wear.

"Look out!" A frantic voice called. "Stand back! The catapult is about to fire, and you're in the way."

At the same time, a roaring noise came from my left and a spurt of fire belched out of a narrow opening in the gully. There was a tremendous whoosh, and a pink spirit shot by me, its head bent back and its nebulous body curved upwards, heading at great speed towards the bright spot in the middle of the arch above.

The catapult fired again, and another pink form went on its way on high. Then there was a pause and a noise of many voices squabbling.

"No, this one is not to go to the Forge! The blacksmith expressly forbids it. I know this spirit is very persuasive, but you must not be taken in by its lies and excuses. This one goes down the other way."

A lot of pushing and shoving took place, and I could see struggling forms just inside the doorway. Finally they seemed to have pushed the offender down another slide. I craned my head to see, but it was too dark to make out anything.

Creeping down the gully away from the entrance and along the side of the catapult, I reached a place where I could slip underneath. It was firing continually and spirits were being shot up the slide in an unceasing sequence. They could be seen gently floating upwards towards the center of the arch overhead where the mysterious Forge was. I was now right under the slide and moving back quietly towards the door. I hoped to slip in while they were distracted by a wayward spirit, and I was fortunate. Another disagreement erupted, and I edged to the doorway, peering in. I could now see the catapult, a massive construction with a leather seat in the center, in which a spirit sat, ready to take off. Several of the workers were trying to pull the spirit down, shouting and complaining that it had to go down the chute instead. After a scuffle, it was removed from the seat, and unceremoniously shoved down a chute that was located in the floor nearby. The chute gulped, and the spirit, flailing its arms in protest, disappeared with a squawk.

I remembered to turn around and managed to back in through the doorway, avoiding the chute and the catapult, but bumping into some of the workers, who did not seem to notice me. From my point of view to the rear of the door, I saw the long slide as it catapulted spirit after spirit into the sky, the noise assailing my ears so that I pressed my hands over them. As I cautiously felt my way backwards, I noticed long lines of ghosts on each side of me jostling each other for position. It seemed that the pink spirits were all headed for the catapult, while those that were colored turquoise were being pushed down the chute in large numbers. Moving further back without touching any spirits, the catapult disappeared from view as I rounded a corner, and I tripped over something that lay across the path. A loud barking erupted and a Black Dog appeared in the dim light and crouched in front of me, snarling. Then the dog recognized me and came forward, sniffing my hand. It wore an orange collar. This dog must belong to the Clan! I thought maybe they were around somewhere.

I knew that Black Dogs were the guardians of the threshold to the underworld. The Romans had created mosaics of Black Dogs just inside their houses. I felt I was moving deeper into Death. I wondered why the spirits had been divided into two groups, and where the chutes led?

The Black Dog was licking my hand. He must have smelt the rat. I pulled it out and set it down, focusing on him to stop myself from turning around to see what lay behind me, thus heeding the sphinx's warning. I could hear a shuffling as of many feet.

"Who is there?" I called out blindly. "Come around and speak to me."

To my delight, a familiar form now appeared before me. It was Shaman Reeve of the Clan, who was naked except for a headdress in the form of a cave bear and an ermine cloak, his hairy body emanating raw masculinity. A strong odor of unwashed bodies and dense smoke invaded the passageway.

"Why are you here, Shaman Reeve? What has happened to the Clan? Are they here in Death too?" I was full of questions, for I respected the fellow tremendously.

"Alas! You must remember that your two warring entities, Fontanova and Bardogian, destroyed the ritual we were performing to rid ourselves of the Seven Shades during the Knight of Wands. As a result, the Shades escaped, and they have returned to the seven alchemical Islands where they hide on the dark side." Reeve paused. "When the message from the last cave bear was brought to us in the maze, I knew that our clan was doomed, in spite of finding the hawk Surohs'egg at the last moment. It turned out to be full of monsters, as you know, and I am thankful that you managed to destroy it before they hatched." The Shaman looked sad. "We did learn Intuition, but the world went into the future too fast for us, and we became extinct. Now we are in limbo in the Path of Death, and nothing can free us save that humankind return to nature and cast off their greedy ways."

I was extremely saddened. "Surohs' egg was brewing evil things. I knew that because Suroh is Horus inverted. The law of inversion creates the opposite of what you experience in the material world. For example, if something terrible happens and many people are killed, that seems bad, but in divine law, that is a good thing, for it frees up more space for other souls who are in a hurry to incarnate. The Earth is crowded these days and it is getting worse. In the world of divinity, thoughts are not divided into good or bad concepts. If the thought occurs, then divinity happily produces it. It's a mind focus." I concluded, regretfully. "It was true, my two entities got out of control at the time and ruined your carefully constructed ritual. Whether that was the powerful influence of the Shades on my entities, I do not know."

The Black Dog, who had vanished, now reappeared, holding a red dish in his mouth. He laid the dish down in front of me and soon returned with his second dish, which shone in golden brilliance. I remembered running back under the collapsing ice cave to retrieve them. The dog pushed the gold dish towards me with his nose, and glanced at me quickly. He seemed to be saying something. I strained my telepathic instincts to receive his message.

"Only you can save my Clan." His message came through faintly. "You are brave enough to make the sacrifice. In the next alcove is a pine coffin.

Walk backwards and lie down in it. We will paint you turquoise and cover you with a reed mat and place food, water and tools beside you. Do not be afraid when we nail down the lid. You must pretend to be dead. That is the only way to cheat Death and avoid total extinction. After a certain length of time, which shall be undefined, you will be removed from the coffin by the workers here."

I interrupted with horror, sending back a mental message. I did not think that was a good plan. What did an undefined length of time mean? I wanted a more precise answer as to how long I would have to remain in the coffin.

The Black Dog rolled his eyes dolefully, but ignored my pleas. "Your color will tell them that you are to go down the chute. Do not resist when they seize you, but stay limp. You must go down the chute. At the bottom you will find the way to redeem us. Please believe me, and do not be frightened. Do as I think, and all will be well." The animal finished, licking his lips pensively.

"What good is that going to do anyone?" I protested to Shaman Reeve, who was intuiting our conversation. "There must be a better way – something active that I can do, to make up for spoiling your ritual."

"Do not give way to your cowardice. You are now traversing the Mystic SEA. Cast aside concerns about your physical body. Focus ever more keenly on your progress along the Way of Return." The Shaman was serious. "There is no way out. Step back towards the coffin now." He made a small move towards me, his bearded apelike face a hairsbreadth from mine. I stepped backwards, my heart in my mouth, until I felt the rasp of raw wood on the back of my knees.

The Clan were now milling into the passage in front of me. They removed my clothing. In the faint light, one of the Clan carried a small palm frond that he dipped into an earthen pot, where a juicy mix of ground turquoise powder and animal glue was simmering. Another stood back, carrying a stone knife, spear point and a reed mat, while a third held a bowl of mashed grains and a small skin water bottle. The primitive people crowded around me, swiping at my body with the warm paint mixture, spreading the mix over me and pawing my private parts with glee. They pressed in so closely that I lost my balance and fell backwards into the pine coffin, scraping my elbows on the narrow sides in panic.

The coffin was a tight fit, which terrified me, and I struggled to rise, but could not get my arms under me to move. The Clan pressed over me, their pungent odor stifling me as I struggled for breath. I felt an arm pressing down beside me, and the dropped rattle of the stone knife jolted me back into a moment of clarity, I fought wildly, but soon the food offerings were wedged in and the reed matting was suffocating me. All was black and I lost consciousness.

I never heard the sounds of their stone hammers, as the wooden nails forced my coffin shut. I woke in unfathomable blackness to feel – what was it? – a strange body lying very close beside me. A hand stole over my face comfortingly and a soft voice spoke. I trembled.

"Who are you?" I stuttered through clenched teeth.

"Don't you remember me? I am the Prince you saw in the Nine of Wands. You came to the vault in the desert where I was buried in my round coffin within the square cubicle, and you stole my nose. It was a precious possession, my quicksilver nose, and sacred to the God Mercury. But it was useless without the rest of my Mask, - the obsidian eyes and the iron mouth with bloodstone teeth. Over the course of time, they also were taken from me."

"I remember. That nose rose from your face and came to me, snuggling into my hand. It was a strange sensation, at once cool, and heavy, and again almost like a small animal in its movements. I put it in my pocket." I frowned, trying to remember what had happened to the valuable nose. "Oh, yes! I swapped the nose for a camel, Lemig. I needed a camel to get across the desert. It was essential. The camel driver Mablevi took the nose, and he seemed very pleased with it."

I racked my brains to remember what occurred next. "I was traversing the White Pyramid. I was with Liquilim, the Ace of Cups, and she set me a task. I had to find Mablevi, who was hiding in the center of a great maze, wearing the Mask. He had obtained the obsidian eyes and the bloodstone teeth from somewhere to complete the illusion. Fortunately, he had to come down to Anahitas' pool to get water. She is the Goddess of Water. I morphed into a newt and ambushed him and after a fight, he drowned, and let go of the Mask. My Guide told me that Mablevi didn't really exist – he was merely a form of the Hoodwinker, who is able to shape-shift." I thought for a moment. "Yes! I left the Mask in Anahitas underwater cave, where it must be still, for I trust her."

"Never trust a Goddess!" The Prince laughed. "They are very devious. I hope that you'll be able to track down the Mask, for without that, I cannot leave the realm of the undead and rise to my assigned position above the Sun. Be patient, for you will leave here soon and experience your ride down the chute, and at the bottom, I am sure you will be able to find what you need." He stifled a yawn. "Now, I am going back to sleep. I will meet up with you in the Path of Fortune. Make sure you have the Mask."

There was no further sound from him, and as I wriggled around in my tight spot, I could no longer distinguish another body beside mine. I felt a little reassured, although I now apparently held both the fate of the Clan and that of the Prince in my hands. I wondered what lay at the bottom of the chute, but I was exhausted, and drifted into a dreamless sleep.

The coffin was bouncing now, as I woke. It was being carried by several people, as it rocked from side to side, and was then put down with a thump. I was disturbed by a creaking sound above me, and a thin sliver of light entered as the lid was forced off by a bone lever. I remembered to appear dead, and managed to stay limp as hands lifted my body and carried me, dropping me feet first into a cold, metal shaft. I began to slide, and swiftly reached warp speed. The feeling of rapid skidding seemed to go on forever, and I felt I must have traveled for miles. I landed hard, my eyes flitting over the dusty ground in front of me. Oh! My God! There was a large scorpion scuttling towards me, the poison bladder at the end of its tail pointed straight at my foot! Before I could move, the scorpion struck fiercely. A sharp burning sensation made me wince and I felt the poison immediately coursing up my leg and through my body. I was about to kill the scorpion when a voice spoke behind me, and I recognized my Guides' presence.

"Stay calm. This will not kill you. Remember, you kicked the scorpion, and this is payback time, for it is the symbol of Death and its presence is very important here. Do not slay it, for if you do, a dozen more will attack, and their combined stings would destroy you. Just let it go under a rock. Now, you will feel tingling and maybe have blurry vision. Come into my hut, and I will care for you." A hand reached out to me as my vision faded, and I was led into his familiar hut. I had not seen my Guide for a long time. Now he was here to save me from the grip of Death, which I had stupidly entered voluntarily.

I lay down on a bunk at the back of the hut. My Guide wrapped my foot in a cool wet rag and calmed me. Then he spoke seriously to me. "You are handling the Path of Death very poorly. You must realize that this is part of the Second Crossing, called The Making of the Rose Diamond on the Way of Return. You are not centered. Your will is scattered in many different directions, and you have allowed your curiosity about what lies beyond the Crack between the Worlds to overcome vigilance. Now we arc here, down In the depths of Death, and I have to get you up again, because you are not yet a fully developed soul. I am still in charge of your gazelle!" He frowned thoughtfully. "You saw the Path of Art high above you. That is the Diamond Bridge over Death, where the souls that have committed themselves to their spiritual quest go to overcome physical death and obtain their swords of willpower. However, you cannot enter the Path of Art until you have reached the Island of Netzach, and from there you must experience the Path of the Devil to bring you to the entrance of the blacksmiths' forge where lies the true meaning of Art."

The pain in my foot prevented me from probing his statement, though I managed to squeak out a short response. "I saw pink souls heading up to the Diamond Bridge. Is the forge up there? I saw a bright spot in the center of the bridge."

"Yes, you saw the fires in the blacksmiths' forge. With their great heat, and the trough of water into which the swords are plunged, the smith, who we call the Demiurge, fashions the sword of willpower for each soul as it alights in the forge. I can tell you no more, but you will find out when you get there." My Guide paused. "Now, we have to get you up again as soon as possible, and on your way to Netzach."

"I understand what you are saying. I realize I made a mistake by spurning the scorpion." I concentrated on the present situation. "So, how am I going to get out of here?" I knotted my brows in despair. "What about the Prince? He is waiting for me to bring him the Mask."

"You must go back the way you came, out of the rear door of Death. It should be easier since you will be walking forwards. But, climbing up the chute will be impossible. It is too steep, and besides, it is crowded with souls who are coming down here all the time in terrible disorder. They are unaware of their Kundalini force, which lies at the base of their spine waiting to rise."

"Oh! I have a rattlesnake down there myself! He entered my left ear a short while ago, and is curled up happily, I believe." I felt my backside gingerly and an answering thump came from my perineum. "Yes, he is responding."

"Ah! That is excellent. Then he is the answer to our problem. Do you feel able to sit up yet?" The old man asked. "We can meditate together, and if Kundalini chooses to move up a little to your next chakra, I'm sure we will get out of here quickly."

"I am ready to try anything." I assured him. I rose stiffly, putting as little pressure on my stung foot as possible, and took a lotus position on the floor of the hut, with my Guide opposite me. Together we went into a deep meditation. At first, I was not aware of any movement from Kundalini, but after a while I felt the rosy warmth rising from my coccyx and spreading upwards towards my genitals. From there, it was not too difficult to engage the feminine parts of myself along with the masculine. I hovered between the two genitalia during my mediation, and when it ended with a gentle reminder from the old fellow, I found myself sitting outside the abode of Death on a large, flat rock by the lapping sea.

I rose to my feet, noting that the pain from the scorpion sting had subsided, and, being careful to hold the rattlesnake Kundalini in its new position, I walked slowly down to the swamp where I had entered Death, and sent my thoughts towards my cricket Joana, who received them and informed the crew on the sloop of my intentions. They were to pick me up and take me to the shores of Netzach without delay.

The Island of NETZACH

Our sturdy sloop, crewed by Pompeybou and Bazoom, hove into view, tacking briskly against a sharp breeze from the SW. I rose from my flat rock and strode down to the waters' edge, where I quickly swung myself up on the bow and pushed off. I was delighted to find that Joanas' broken leg had healed as I opened her cage and she jumped happily onto my finger. Pompeybou swung the boat through the wind and set off on a broad reach towards the eastern section of the Mystic SEA. The breeze was a steady 15 knots, but gradually began to weaken, and the horizon faded as fingers of fog crept in. Soon we were ghosting along in a world where the faint sounds of sea birds echoed strangely from somewhere close by. It was eerily humid, and, if not for the compass, we would have questioned our direction. However, we stuck to the course set, and after three days, saw a low and rather marshy coast arising out of the mist ahead.

Fortunately, there was a dock running out from the low land, and a figure stood there, ready to take our lines. It was a beautiful naked woman, wearing only a thigh girdle around her left leg, who caught the rope skillfully and made a quick bowline around a bollard. Scarcely had I stepped off the sloop, than I saw there was a large crowd of people awaiting me at the end of the dock, carrying bouquets of roses. Leading the crowd was a small three-legged chicken, wearing a bedraggled kilt, who strutted about as if he owned the place. Several of the crowd stepped forward, showering me with rose petals as their laughter chimed out.

Personally I thought the chicken looked silly as he spoke, because I knew who it was – that wretched McSmother Feathers, who had challenged me to chop off his leg during my travels in the Six of Pentacles, and who I had to obey through some force not of my own making.

"I am on a visit here from Scotland." The chicken clucked. "I came here to meet you on this part of your quest and to give you this ring."

"I'm sorry. I don't understand. I already have the yellow plastic ring you gave me. I have no idea what it is for, but I have kept it."

"Yes, you are right." His beak stretched into a wry smile. "I was fooling you. The ring I now wear is merely a plastic replica of the original plastic ring. However, only those who obey my commands without question are sufficiently advanced to be candidates for the Work. That is why you must be tested ad infinitum. Now, do you remember what the ring is for?"

"Yes, I do. It is one missing link in a golden chain that will join that chain together. I have not yet found the other links, though." I felt a little ashamed.

"Don't you worry - the other links are forming around you as we speak. You are now voyaging in the Mystic SEA." McSmother Feathers nodded slowly, his red comb waggling. "Each Island or Path that you travel through is a link in the golden chain. Now you have arrived at the Island of Netzach. I like it here, for there is a close group mentality that helps people to work together. It's not like those individualists on the Island of Hod, with their stupid bubbles. They are constantly warding off pricks and shun the sense of touch, for fear that their bubbles will burst. They never experience the closeness of other human bodies."

I agreed "I must admit they did seem to spend a lot of time avoiding each other."

"Yes. It is essential for them to realize their individuality, but once that is done, they must allow themselves to reach out to others, and not to be so mistrustful." The chicken McSmother turned and beckoned me to follow him. The disheveled crowd filed in behind us, giggling amongst themselves, pushing and punching each other in a friendly way.

The unpredictable fog had lifted somewhat, but the air was still very humid, and I noticed many fumaroles were adding their steam to the moist atmosphere of Netzach, as we made our way to a pleasant village set in a green meadow by a rapidly flowing river. Their small round houses were untidy, yet I was immensely attracted by the casual atmosphere of the people. They led me to a large domed building that looked like a renaissance cathedral, but it was not for religious purposes, for there was none of the usual rigmarole.

Since there were no selected speakers, several of the people spoke in chorus. "This is our Imagination Station. This building has moveable imaginary scenes that can be set up by thought forms, in order to enhance a musical composition, poetry reading, art exhibition, or a stage play. Each person in our group is specialized in a particular manifestation. You won't see the backdrops, for they are, of course, imaginary, but you can conceive of your own setting if you have something creative you want to produce for our pleasure."

"That sounds like a wonderful idea. It is so hard to get anyone to use their imagination in the mundane world nowadays. Everyone is supplied with manufactured images through the TV and news media." I sighed. "The sad thing is that they survive on this type of brain food, and never fend for themselves, so they know no other diet and can no longer think outside the boxes they have unwittingly created."

"We know there is great danger in that, for the human race has submitted, for the sake of comfort, to be influenced by a few who set themselves up, by wealth or by wiles, to govern them. They call this Society. It is a misnomer, for although they are led to believe they can make choices - after all, they are a "democracy" and that means government by the people, doesn't it? – in fact they are virtually powerless." The chorus continued. "Those who are voted into office have the mind of the masses, and the masses believe their vote counts. That, of course, is where the whole system breaks down."

"What can be done?" I asked in a forlorn voice. "It has ever been that way, as far as I know. Malkuth is a terrible Island, for life is so unfair there."

"You will see when you reach the Path of Fortune that each person makes the ultimate choices that he confronts in his life. Whether these choices are pre-ordained by Destiny, or subject to free will, you must decide for yourself when you travel that passage. For now, let us go down to Anahitas' pool by the river, where we can bathe and play."

"Oh! Is the goddess Anahita here, then? There's something urgent I need to do at the pool." I did not want to elaborate further, until I had secured the Mask and returned it to the Prince.

"Of course she is. This is Anahitas' territory, for she is the Goddess of Water, and Netzach is sacred to Venus and holds the magical Cup as its weapon. Here we are at the pool now. My group tells me they want to swim in the river, so we'll see you soon."

I sat down by the pool, which was covered by green algae, so that one could not see into its depths. I wondered how I was going to recover the Mask, which lay hidden in Anahitas' underwater cave. My ruminations were brusquely interrupted by a loud and persistent croaking. Oh no! Did I recognize that sound? I hoped not, but sure enough, it was Oojo, the toad that had bothered me during much of my earlier progress, and he was staring at me with his round eyes from under a nearby rock. I had last seen Oojo when I imprisoned him in the little bag that I kept with my belongings on the boat. He had come to my aid during the battle with the Shades outside the badgers' burrow, when he diverted the attention of the Shades and sent them off after the red monkey during my passage of the Page of Wands. Although that had been one of his finer moments, I still didn't trust him, for he had played some dirty tricks on my friends, and he had also tried to eat Joana, my cricket, but had found her totally indigestible.

"What are you doing here?" I asked peevishly. "I thought I was done with you. I put you away. How did such a lowly creature as you gain entrance into the Islands of the Mystic SEA? I left you in the bag. "

"You must treat me nicely." Oojo protested, batting his eyelids. "I only came to help. The battle with the Shades set my adrenaline afire and I struggled to escape from the bag, which you had left hanging next to the spinnaker in the foc'sle. It was dry and scratchy, and you know I like cool and wet, that's why I broke out, followed you, and came to Netzach, for it is never arid and uncomfortable here. How about yourself?"

"Well, I'm not sure what I'm doing here." I relented. "This Path is very confusing. The other experiences have been clearer – Hod, for example, is very narrow- minded and logical. It's about individualism, and that seems to stultify people. This place doesn't yield any useful information like that. Everything seems very vague – hazy, as it were."

He ignored my answer, regarding me with a piercing glare. "Where is Joana? You took her with you, didn't you? You left me behind deliberately. I know it!"

The toad fastened his stern gaze on me and I felt guilty. Maybe he wasn't so bad, after all. Should I give him another chance, I wondered, as I replied. "No, you were both on the boat, but her cage hangs over the chart table, for she is the weather prophet. I put up with that even when she shits on the charts occasionally. Unfortunately, while crawling over the radar, she slipped and broke her second leg on the right during rough weather. I splinted the leg and now she has completed physical therapy and is hopping well."

A soft giggle interrupted me and I looked up Anahita was sitting on the side of the pool, dangling her feet in the water. "I know why you're here. You can't have it, you know – the Mask. I have it hidden in my collection. Now and again, I like to wear it and I'll be going to Mardi Gras soon. I need the Mask to complete my Venusian costume, which I've been sewing since the New Year." She scowled. "If you try to enter my underwater cave, you will drown. You will never get the Mask, I warn you." With a scowl, Anahita slid back into the water and disappeared below the surface.

In spite of her warning, Oojo and I sat on the bank, enjoying the warm sun, for we were chilled after our experiences and somewhat confused. I was angry with Anahita and wondered how I could get down to retrieve the Mask. I knew where the underwater cave was, for I had been down there before. That was with the help of the Goddess, but she had turned against me and now she was denying me access. I knew why. I had witnessed her tryst with King Jetspur.

Oojo looked up at me. "I will go! I am small enough that she will not see me sneak in. I can breathe through my skin underwater, long enough to find the Mask. I will bring it back to you!" Before I could stop him, Oojo leapt bravely into the water, breaking the surface algae, which floated to the sides of the pool. I bent forward to see him swimming downwards, his powerful short legs thrusting out behind him. I hoped he would succeed, for I could do nothing to stop him now.

I began to wonder whether I had really left the Passage of Death. Was I still experiencing it? Events and fast changes were precipitating me from one scenario to another. I had gone into the rear door of Death backwards, then been pushed into a coffin. It was very confusing. Was this all really happening? Or was it just an illusion of my mind? The presence of the Prince in my coffin had reassured me. Now I waited to see if Oojo would be successful in recovering the Mask, for I was anxious to free the Prince from his confinement.

I sat by the pool for several hours, but Oojo did not return, and I became increasingly concerned. He was always a nuisance, but in a way I loved him. I hoped that nothing bad had happened to him. Night fell, and I slept uneasily, nightmares chasing themselves through my mind. In the morning I woke and rolled over on the grassy bank, rubbing my eyes to waken.

A small flat form lay spread out on the grass in front of me. I was stunned to recognize the shape of a toad. A shudder of horror shot through me. It was Oojos' skin! He must have been caught, flayed, and then possibly eaten by the Goddess. I picked up his dangling remains, which drooped from my hand. There was his little face with the wide mouth, his warty bumps, his small legs hanging down, all perfect and untouched, complete. But the body inside had gone…..

A little laugh made me look up. Anahita sat on the other side of the pool with a dish of stew in her hand. She was eating voraciously, thrusting spoonful after spoonful into her mouth and smiling the while.

"Your toad is delicious!" She sputtered, throwing back her head in glee. "He was hard to catch, but I was guarding the Mask. I expected you would make an attempt to get it. Well, you've failed, and now Oojo is gone for good." With that, she scraped the last morsel of toad stew into her ravenous mouth and threw down the dish.

I reacted with revulsion and extreme rage, but my angry entity Bazoom did not come. I threw Oojos' skin into the pool and ran and ran, I knew not where, but I had to get away. Sorrow for my toad erupted and I cried as I ran, tears streaming down my face, and rising to a shriek as I collapsed onto a patch of marshy ground, unable to control my grief. I cried myself out and my sobs gradually subsided. Being a practical person, I soon sat up determinedly and wiped my eyes. Oojo had died bravely, in the Princes' service. I must look forward, not back. I hated Anahita. There must be a way to get revenge for her cruel act. I would brood over the predicament and find a method to obtain the Mask.

I left the pool next day, saddened by this tragedy and missing the annoying toad, which was strange, since he had been a great nuisance to me. The group came to meet me, pulling me excitedly towards the Imagination Station.

"We have a special performer here. She is about to stage a one-person show, which has been billed for some time. We would like you to meet her after the show. Her name is Pullows – and she used to run a very special parlor in her youth, which pleasured many people who visited it."

"I know Pullows! She was headed here with Paragutt from the Path of the Universe. I wonder where he is? She was my lustful entity, Swollup, and I visited her parlor myself many times." The remembrance of my dark-eyed lover came before me and I brushed the thought hastily away. "I would like to see her perform before you take me backstage. I want to keep my presence here a secret, so as not to startle her."

They sat me down in a comfortable place that was not a chair, but had soft, floating cushions that seemed to mold themselves to my body, gently massaging me as I settled back to watch the show. The heavy satin curtains swirled aside and Pullows stood in the center of the stage in her full glory. She wore what appeared to be a large, plumed hat that curved low over her brow, so that one eye was hidden, while the other, darkened with kohl, seemed full of a glorious vehemence that swept over the rapt audience. Her body was completely naked except for several large, tinkling anklets that curled around her lower legs. But what astonished me more than her nudity was her amazing figure, which had become young and curvaceous once more and which she shifted from side to side, her breasts bouncing with glee, to amuse the audience. Of course, they loved it, and, shouting, they rose to their feet with loud applause.

I was not so sure. The Island of Netzach was definitely very different from Hod, where nobody would have dared put on such a show! Those people all wore clothes inside their bubbles and kept to themselves. Nevertheless, I put aside my prejudice and waited to see what she would do next. Reaching for a silken cord above her, she pulled down a small cloud, waving her arms gracefully before it. The mist parted and a hand appeared, holding an Orphic lyre that she began to strum. Each note came out singly and hung in the air above her. As more and more notes joined them, they formed themselves into a beautiful melody and the essence of it stole around the theatre, enchanting everyone. The notes, which were entirely visible, changed form gradually and became tiny fairylike figures that twined and twisted to the music, shifting form from human to tree - to bird; to animal; to rock; to fish - continually so that one could not tell exactly what was there. All the while, the atmosphere around us undulated constantly through a myriad of sounds and light effects.

Pullows then let go of the lyre, and picked up a large paintbrush, with which she made expansive gestures in the air. From the end of the brush appeared dazzling colors that wove themselves into rapt patterns and scenes of glory that made the audience gasp. Then she produced a long tube of parchment which she unrolled, reading in a sensitive and discerning manner a poem that was not quite – something that either rhymed or set to meter - yet it wafted into the ear and left a profound meaning behind it. The curtains then fell for the interval.

By this time, the audience was lulled and relaxed as they waited for her next act. The curtains rose on a white statue of the goddess Venus, holding a long copper pole in its right hand. A large lamp hung at the top of this pole. The statue moved, bringing a second copper pole close to the first one, whereupon a flash of brilliant light leapt between the two poles, and a ball of St. Elmos' Fire ran up towards the lamp, which took the light and glowed, giving forth fluctuating waves of light. As soon as the audience saw the lamp afire, they jumped to their feet, shouting and clamoring loudly.

"The Lamp! The Blessed Lamp! Our spirits rise towards the Sacred Fire!" With that, they all joined hands and began to dance, slowly at first and then with more and more abandon. The soft cushions were hurled aside and the ardent crowd filled the entire auditorium, as the dance grew more frenzied and vigorous. Men and women threw off their gauzy robes and pressed close together. I turned to leave, as couples rushed towards the cushions and sank down onto them, fornicating wildly.

I hastened from the building, overwhelmed by the magnetic force behind their celebrations. Running along, I bumped into a tall person, who took me by the shoulders and shook me. I looked, and saw the face of my lover, plain as day. There was no need to speak. We held hands and found a secluded spot, where we sank into each others arms. The night fled, and morning came, to find us separate again. But this time we had made a promise. We would meet again, if not before, then in the Path of the Lovers, and our troth would be pledged there forever.

Dreamily, I found Pullows surrounded by an animated crowd the following morning and quietly handed her two more cards, the Aeon and Death. The group was full of her performance the night before and how it had energized them. Of course, nobody had thought of making breakfast, or even washing the piles of dirty dishes that cluttered the sinks. I pushed my way through the throng, recognizing a small figure standing close to Pullows. To my delight, it was Paragutt, and he was clapping his hands with glee and sending familiar glances towards a rather shapely Netzachian woman, who returned them warmly.

I had never thought of Paragutt as manly. He always seemed more of a nerd, and yet, there had been many times when he had stepped forward bravely to protect me, and he had been awarded the Order of the Nonexistent Empire by the Knight of Wands, which made him a ONE. Could a ONE become a two?

Paragutt came over and gave me a high five. "I've been watching you. You're surprised to see how I'm behaving, aren't you?" He laughed, his large ears pricked eagerly forward as I had never seen them before. "Coming to Netzach really allowed me to contact my inner essence – and

I discovered who I really am! I am Fear itself, the archetype of fear through the ages, the force that has come down through mankind for aeons, and was manifest in you, also, for you are a being. Netzach taught me that, for it is the Island of archetypes in their volatile state, ever ready to inhabit the human imagination. You gave me my freedom, for now you have no fear, and here I am."

McSmother Feathers, who I had not seen at the previous nights' celebrations, came sauntering towards me. "Good marnin'. I'd like to show you the Museum of Archetypes this morning. My wife Moaner is the curator. Would you enjoy that?"

"I certainly would. So, you actually keep archetypes in a museum here? I had heard they were only thought forms."

"Everything here is a thought – more of a force than a form, since the Hodians are the ones who use form to express themselves – more concrete, you know." McSmother Feathers smiled. "One can do so much more with the forces. They are more fluid. Once they take form, they become like the Hodians themselves – too rigid and separated from their source."

He ushered me through the door of a vast, rounded structure that reminded me of a troglodyte palace, all lumps and curious bumps. A woman stepped forward. "This is my wife, Moaner. She is extremely knowledgeable."

Moaner ducked her head bashfully. "I don't think I know as much as you do, dear."

"You are too modest, my love. Let us go and examine the dioramas in the museum while we have time. Everyone is still keyed up over Pullows performance out there."

We walked into a huge thoughtorium, around which were uncounted numbers of dioramas, each of which showed one, two or three archetypes engaged in their normal pursuits. I walked over to a large diorama, set up as a desert with a small, grey hut in the middle. Sitting on a stool by the hut was a very old man with a long white beard. He seemed incredibly lifelike, and I turned to ask McSmothers who he was.

"This is the archetype of the Old, Wise Man, of course. Are you interested in renting him out? Maybe you could use him."

"No, actually, I already have one very similar to this. In fact, I would almost say that this is the very fellow, he looks so like him." At this, the old man rose to his feet and winked at me. It was, in fact, my Guide, and this was not the first time he had placed himself in a window setting. I was delighted to see him, and we embraced.

The chicken, however, was anxious to move on. "Come, there are so many more I want to show you. Look, here is the nagging Mother-in-Law in a diorama with her daughter-in-law. That is a tricky relationship, I can tell you, with lots of yelling. Look over here – the Suckling Child and the exhausted mother. You can activate them, you know, just as you did with the old man. Just give them a thought."

I focused my attention on the diorama and thought about sleepless nights. The figures, which included an irritated father, began to move and the whole scene came alive. The baby screamed, the mother rose from her bed, and the father thrashed about in the blankets, cursing and trying to get some sleep.

"That is really effective." I agreed as we moved on to another exhibit. This was obviously a Rebellious Teenager, shouting at his parents. A fourth diorama showed the archetype of a horrendous crone, bending over a large cauldron.

"Here is the Witchy Woman." McSmother remarked with pride. "We created them all ourselves, you know."

"How did you do that?" I was astounded. "Is there a method?"

"We practice magical rituals, of course. We are experts in the field. It's not difficult to invoke them, once you use the correct method." He sighed. "The difficulty is to retain them and set them in place, for, being thought forms, they are always anxious to escape."

We strolled on through the anteroom, admiring the painstaking work that he and his wife had created. Finally we came to the last diorama. A drunken man, carrying a burden that was half-woman, half snake, was staggering down a set of steps towards a deep pit, in which a donkey swam. The animal was braying loudly in fear, yet the man paid no attention to it as he slipped and fell into the water, disappearing under the surface. The snake-woman sat on the brink, stroking her tail and smiling in an evil manner.

"That's really horrible." I shook my head. "What is this diorama?"

"This is the diorama of the Devil. We have taken the archetype of the Devil and split it up into its component parts for effect. He is known also as Satan and sometimes as Lucifer, although that is a misnomer. Lucifer, the light-bearer, was not an evil person."

"This is absolutely fascinating." I leaned forward to examine the characters. "Would it be possible to rent out the Devil? I would like to know more about him. I'd like to rent the snake-woman too."

"We only allow one archetype to be rented at a time, but, since she is part of his diorama, we could allow two. Otherwise the renter would find themselves out of their depth, as it were." The chicken clucked loudly with amusement. "Yes, I recall one day, we made the mistake of renting out the archetype of the Brave Warrior at the same time as the archetype of the Cowardly Nerd. The poor nerd had the shit beat out of him, but he came back to us and betrayed the warrior, who ended up in an execution scene where he was beheaded for overacting his part." McSmother frowned. "These archetypes, as you are aware, are hard to pin down, and we can't afford to lose them like that. It took some time before another Brave Warrior was willing to materialize for us."

"Oh, I see, that could be a problem. Well, what about just renting out the Devil to me? I would only need him for a short time."

McSmother shot me a long look under his red comb. "I don't think that is a good idea. The Passage of the Devil is very close by here, and he might be able to escape, taking you with him. No, I would rather rent you a friendlier archetype – the Happy Camper, for example – or the Lazy Vacationer. They are easier to deal with."

I was obdurate, for I was, unfortunately, completely free from fear and wanted to interact with the Devil – just briefly, of course – to get to know his tricks. "Please, please let me have him, just for a few hours." I begged.

McSmother Feathers and his wife stepped back and conferred in whispers. "All right. You can have him for 6 hours, 6 minutes and 6 seconds. We will time it. I'll collect the rent money later – if you are still here." They passed a secret smile between them as they took a net on a long pole and fished the Devil out of his pit, dripping wet, and handed him over to me.

The Devil was clad in purple and, balanced on his head, an empty wine skin drooped over his right eye. The snake woman trailed along behind us. I thanked them and led him away by a small leash that hung from his neck. Little did I realize that my pride was to put me in terrible jeopardy, and that events would move so fast that I would have no time to think, for, once I left the building, the Devil had me in his power, and whisked me away from the Island of Netzach into his own domain without delay.

Path of the DEVIL

❀

The Devil clutched my hand tightly as he bounded down the slimy spiral staircase to his quarters. Round and round we whirled, until I was dizzily unaware of my surroundings. I sank to my knees, begging him to stop, but he cackled horribly and continued to drag me, bumping and bouncing, down the narrow stairs. I soon passed out from the bruising pain.

I opened my eyes on an unforgettable scene. We were at the bottom of a great abyss, whose walls rose up perpendicularly on either side, except at the top I could discern a splinter of daylight. Reaching across this chasm high above me was a curved bridge that shone lapis lazuli blue in the filtered sunlight. The bridge was an unusual shape, having curves on the underside that did not seem to fit a normal engineering design. Below the bridge, and falling down each wall, were myriads of black figures that shrieked and moaned as they attempted to clutch onto outlying ledges to stop their fall. Each ledge had a motto written over it, but I was too far away to read them.

I saw the Devil calling upstairs to someone named Melusina. Nursing my agonizing bruises, I fervently regretted my decision to rent my tormenter – even for 6 hours, 6 minutes and 6 seconds. I hoped the time would pass quickly, so that I could hand him back and pay McSmother Feathers. Then I remembered I had no money! Damn. The chicken must have known that. If I couldn't pay, maybe he would refuse to take him back. The thought sent me into a violent fit of shivers, but I could not feel fear, since I had dismissed Paragutt. That was a bad decision, too. Being afraid of the Devil would have prevented me from the idea of renting him. However, I could do nothing to change my situation, so I started to think of a way out in my usual manner.

The Devil was muttering to himself. "Where is that woman? Melusina! Come down here! I need to copulate with you. For heavens' sake, it has been at least ten minutes since we last did it. I can't hold out any longer. Melusina, come back now!"

He sounded pretty desperate, and I didn't want to be around as a witness. Enough already! Since I had gotten myself into this mess, I decided to take a good look at my surroundings, which I assumed was the place they called Hell. There was, indeed a fire burning in a large furnace up in the right hand corner of the area. In front of the fire, one of the black figures who had evidently fallen down to the bottom was now doing a shoulder stand right in front of the furnace. He had taken up a Y-shape, and his backside must be burning, I decided.

Turning to the other side of this filthy spot, the low entrance to a glittering ice cave beckoned., the overhang decorated with some pretty icicles. I bent my head to go in and explore. Immediately a great wailing arose and a freezing blast of air smacked me in the face, as a large vampire bat with red undersides to its wings brushed past my head, nearly becoming tangled in my hair. I put my hands up defensively to make sure it had gone, by patting my hair, which was now soaking wet. The icicles were rapidly melting and cold drops now ran down my cheeks and neck onto my tunic. Wild screeches from the interior of the cave deafened me and a foul odor assailed my nostrils as a civet scuttled under my nose, voiding itself in fright. I backed away from the cave, nearly falling into a large well behind me, which stank of sewage. Looking back at the cave entrance, I noticed that the icicles had gone, but that there were five black and red bats still hanging there – at least they looked like bats at first – but then I saw they were malevolent faces, faces that looked like the Witchy Woman up in the Museum I had just seen. I stared back at them, forcing them to take off in a flock, flapping their bats' wings and slanting up towards the darkening sky.

The Devil had gone back upstairs, calling out repeatedly for Melusina. From above the ice cave, a poignant melody now cleft the air, and the sound of pagan pipes called out to me. I quickly climbed up the small hill and found the piper sitting on a rock, composing a tune that sent thrills down my spine and roused my basic instincts. I sat down at his feet and listened to him play for a long time, and I was soothed.

He finally put down his pan pipes and spoke. "What are you doing here, of all people? I thought you would have had more sense than to come down here, but now you're here, I'm glad. I get lonely sometimes, for people are forbidden to dance or make merry here. The Devil doesn't like it. He does sometimes dance with Melusina, but only if she has proved that she has not completed a project. She is the goddess of unfinished projects, you know, and that's why she is so popular with the Devil."

I looked up at him. Here was a man clad in goatskin pantaloons, with a little horned cap on his head. He had a friendly grin, so I decided to make a guess. "Are you Pan? You know, the pagan god? You look as if you might be."

"I am. I'm only down here temporarily, until people remember me and start putting up their maypoles again. They've forgotten me, you know. They don't dance together any more, except in Netzach, and they are the worst fornicators, by gum! No, the old thread of the dance is gone, and instead of weaving in and out, bodies are jerking, jumping, jabbing, jittering in all sorts of ugly ways. But they like it that way - for now. Dance, you know - it mirrors the hidden essence of society. Dancers are acting the way people feel. When it is restless and demanding, the dance shows that society is in a turmoil, and cannot find its smooth, relaxed center any more. It is very sad. So I came down here, because, basically, I was kicked out of the forest by rude priests, who took my ideas and made them their own."

"I know some of them." I replied softly. "I'm on your side. If it makes you feel any better, I've eaten the red monkey. You know who that was, don't you?"

"You did that! You! I'm delighted. The news had come to me through the grapevine – I do love a bag of wine, as you know – and I could hardly believe it. But I did not know who had the courage to take the Father down."

"It was a combined effort, in a way." I didn't want to take all the credit for myself. "Many people helped. We also raided the Fathers' library and got away with some very important books. Did you hear about that?"

"No! That is even better." He bent down and gave me a little punch. "Of course, a lot of the pagan books were burnt during the sack of Alexandria, which is a crying shame. But there are those who have carried on the oral tradition, and the ancient secrets may not have written words, but they are known, and a time will come when they will be revealed again."

"Indeed, that is true. My intellectual entity, Einerline, has the books from the library and he is working on modern translations. Of course, this will take some time, but a few years are as nothing compared to the urgent necessity of relieving the ignorance that humans wallow in. Why, even now, after years of wisdom have been passed in front of their eyes, they don't see it."

"That's true." Said Pan. "That's why the situation here in the Path of the Devil is so interesting. Do you see, over there, emerging from the rocks above the furnace, the letter 'I' ?"

"Oh, Yes! There's a goat with a saddle standing on top of it. That's where the blue bridge ends – the arch that is just behind you. What is that?"

Pan smiled. "The letter 'I' stands for the Ego, which is born from the furnace of desire. The goat, being originally part of the Devil, is now the scapegoat. That is the one who is blamed for everything. Did you know that, in my time, vagrants would come into the villages to get something to devour. In exchange, they would agree to become a scapegoat and take on the sins of the villagers, and then they would vanish into the forest. That way, the villagers felt they could really get up to all sorts of mischief before the next vagrant blew in. As long as they filled their wooden bowls – nobody had to be responsible for anything."

"That sounds like a false pardon! Why is the goat wearing a saddle, though?" I was curious. "And what about the bridge?"

"OK, OK, take it easy! Give me a moment. The goat that represents our lower instincts is saddled awaiting the Christian saint, who will overpower his lower nature and jump aboard, riding off into the sunset. Ha! Ha! I don't think so." Pan chortled. "The supposed saint will be carted off into the forest, and the goat will dump him, bump him and jump him, and then leave. He will become the vagrant who wanders there evermore. Ha! Ha! Ha!" He bent over, holding his sides with mirth.

"Tell me about the bridge, then. It looks very strange, kind of lumpy and bumpy – but not dumpy. Ha! Ha!" I was also choking with laughter.

"OK, OK, calm down. Yes, the bridge. Well, she is the goddess Nuit, the circumference of the Monads' circle, and the center is Hadit. Hadit is the little spot in the middle of the circle. He can be very, very small, so small you could never see him, but he is there. He is inside you, and inside me, and inside the Devil too. But in this place, he is the little hole at the end of the Devils' penis. Ha! Ha! He hides inside Melusina as often as he can, so he never even sees Nuit, his beautiful circumference."

"What are you implying by a little spot and a circumference? I had to contact my Hadit to make a bridge. That was Nuit."

"That is how the Magi describe a person. You are activated by the spot Hadit, and you see your own prescribed horizon, the circumference bounding your material life. In order to return to nature, you have to move towards Nuit, who is your circumference, and pass through her, or over her, whichever you like. Then you will be outside your own self, and you will see marvelous things. That is where I came from." Pan sighed. "One day I will return."

"So that is not a bridge, then. It is a woman named Nuit who is a horizon. Is the little spot Hadit then a male?"

"Well, if you have to describe them in terms of duality, yes. Hadit is the projectile, the energizing power, and Nuit is the receptacle, since she is the boundaries of the circle around each person. You must know the symbol of the cross, which the Christians use. That symbol was originally the path that Hadit must take upwards to pass through his own horizon, which is the bar across the upright – Nuit, in other words. Above the bar, we have the Egyptian ankh shape, whereas that has disappeared in modern times. However, if you look carefully at some of those crucifixions, you will see that the head of the Christ figure is above the cross bar. That means he has attained enlightenment. This is where the ignorance of the masses in modern day religion completely misses the point. Alas!"

"H'm, I see." I was about to ask more, when a great scuffling arose and the Devil came into view, staggering down the steps towards the pit, clasping Melusina very close to him. She had her tail wound around his leg, and it looked as if she was trying to trip him up, for as they passed, I could see her mean little face with its sly eyes and tight lips. Then there was a great splash and a loud braying as they both stumbled into the fetid well water, right on top of an unfortunate donkey that was swimming around underneath them.

Melusina came up first, spluttering. "You......idiot! What do you think you're doing? You're the one that faces forward and you're supposed to be looking where you're going. I'm facing backwards so that I can see what a shambles we have managed to create. Too much wine again, I suppose."

"I face forward but I don't really know where I'm going." The Devil confessed. "People keep calling out to me, and it is very perplexing I am hearing these voices – What the devil is that? What the devil are you doing? The devil take it! Devil may care! Where the devil have you been? I keep running after them because they are calling me. They say if they are going to dine with me, they need a long spoon. What is that supposed to mean? I can't help tripping up sometimes."

"Well, you're an ignorant fool! I'm the one who has to leave unfinished all the projects that you start, for you always think you can do more than you're capable of - isn't that the truth?" Snapped Melusina.

"Oh! Stop your nagging. Here, your headdress has fallen off." The Devil held up a spiky crown with a fire horn on top and a bunch of purple grapes hanging down the back. "It's soaking wet. Put it on top of the furnace to dry it out."

"That goat will eat it." Melusina was pulling herself out of the well inch by inch, swearing under her breath. "You can get out yourself – I'm not here to help you." She sat over the water with her hands on her hips, watching the Devil swimming round and round in despair. Finally the ass picked him up in his yellow teeth and tossed him on to the steps, where he lay yelping like a kicked dog under her tail.

I had always admired the Devil, in a way. He seemed strong and master of many worlds. Now he lay, pussy-whipped, at the feet of a raging snake-woman, weak and humiliated. I was profoundly disappointed. It was a waste of time renting him, as he was obviously not capable of performing anything really evil. I had arranged, when I reached the Path of the Devil, to read through the catalog of outrages against my person. I felt it was time to pay back and I had a list of people ready to give him, so that he could put a decent, vengeful hex on them, but now I doubted he had the power.

Melusina pulled him to his feet and pushed him in front of her up the steps. "I suppose I'll have to make it up to you with another copulation." She complained bitterly. "That's the only thing you're interested in."

I turned to Pan, who had watched the whole scene with concealed amusement. "Well, the Devil turned out to be extremely inadequate. He couldn't fend her off, because she has him by the balls. As long as she agrees to copulate, he will do what it takes to keep on her sweet side – not that she has one – because he always bows down to his lower nature."

"He is lower nature itself, so how can he change that?" I puzzled. Even his name means division – Devil, to divide. Divinity does not want division. They say there is no separation, and so I wonder how separation happened in the first place?"

"I cannot tell you the answer to that, but you will learn it when you reach the Island of Da'ath, which is still far away. The truth lies there. But the Devil has other names, too. He is known as Satan, or Saturn, the tester. The planet Saturn has many rings, and an initiate has to pass through those rings to reach enlightenment. Each ring is a stage, just as you find in traversing the Mystic SEA and its many Islands and Paths."

"I know the Devil is also called Lucifer. That has always puzzled me, for Lucifer means the light-bearer, and the Devil is dark natured. How can there be any connection?" I paused a moment to think. "The story is well-known, of course. Lucifer fell from heaven because he set himself up as a god, equal to divinity. But when he fell, he also brought with him the Emerald Tablet of Hermes, that which has a brilliant green stone in it. I always wondered why he managed to take an emerald from the divine, and why that particular jewel? After all, both the diamond and the ruby are equally beautiful."

Pan looked grave. "The emerald represents eternal youth – the green of renewed spring, which never withers away in the everlasting light. When the emerald was taken from the upper regions, the one who brought it down destroyed eternal youth, and condemned all who live down in Malkuth to eventual death. You have seen Death in his kingdom and you know he comes when he chooses. But he gives to those who aspire to greater knowledge, the opportunity to seek the Passage of Art, where they will experience rebirth and forge the Sword of Willpower."

"So that is why some of the spirits were being catapulted up to the bridge of Art! They made the choice to overcome Death."

"Indeed. That choice must be made during a persons' lifetime. Once you are dead, it is too late, and then you must experience reincarnation over again, until you abide by that choice." Pan sighed. "These continual lives are very exhausting. Personally, I am glad I don't have to go through that, for I am already an established God."

I chuckled at his proud statement, looking over at the white goat. "I'm going to take a ride on that goat. I don't believe it will dump me, for I'm no saint. I want to give it a try."

"I advise against that. The goat is more potent than it looks, and you may not succeed. But, of course, I can't stop you if that is your chosen path."

"Well, it is. But thanks for the warning. I'll be back shortly." Standing up, I walked over to the furnace, where I began to climb to the top of the little hill. The hand and footholds were burning hot, like molten lava, so I went very swiftly, arriving on top of the letter 'I' with blisters on my hands. Grasping the goats' lead rope, I leapt into the saddle, and the animal bounded nimbly down the hill and took off at a gallop with me sliding about in the saddle, with no stirrups to center myself. I held onto its long, curving horns as the animal ran with its head raised, not looking where it was going. Soon we entered the outskirts of a dark forest, and my heart sank. This was not good. I had hoped to keep the goat out in the open, where I could handle it more easily.

The goat took a nosedive into the dense trees, trying to brush me off. Twigs whipped past my face, stinging me as they snapped back, while brambles tore at my exposed legs. My hands were so blistered, it was hard to hold on, but I did my best by crouching low over the animals' back, shielding my face with my arms. By now the forest was pitch black and nothing was visible. The goat slowed down, picking its way carefully around the larger trees, as it seemed to be heading in a specific direction. After a while, the animal stopped at a bubbling spring that gave off a faint yellow light. The pool stank of sulfur, its noxious smell pervading the air and making me feel quite sick. I slipped out of the saddle and the goat began to graze quietly. It all seemed rather odd, so I sat down a little way from the pool to avoid its stench, and waited to see what would happen.

After a couple of hours I heard a shuffling sound coming from the undergrowth, and a head poked through the bushes. I could just make out that this person was on his hands and knees. He came crawling out of the bushes, making slow and awkward headway, as his left arm was shackled to his right leg by a short chain. He saw me and inched over towards me, where he immediately began to cry piteously, now and again pausing to eye me for my reaction.

"Please free me. The Devil put me in chains so that he could keep me close to him, for he admires my abilities. But I don't want to be a part of it any more. I'm tired of talking behind peoples' backs, for this is what he has made me do. I am the Slanderer, who spreads malicious gossip, often without foundation, and I am very good at bending the truth – whatever that may be, for we don't have any truth down here."

"If I break your bonds, will you do me a favor?" I asked, meaningfully. "I have a list here of all the people who have upset me during my lifetime, and I want revenge for their insults and enmity. I didn't deserve to get such a bad reputation. I'm a good person. Please use your skills to start some nefarious gossip about them. That would make me feel better."

The Slanderer grinned. He had sharp front teeth, capable, I felt, of biting through anything that resembled truth. "Free me, and I will do this for you. But it must be the last time. I am your slave until then, and afterwards, I can be the kind person I long to become." He indicated the lock that held his shackles. "There is no key to this lock. Do you know the combination?"

I thought for a while, and decided to try 666, since it seemed an obvious choice. The lock snapped open and the Slanderer rose to his feet. Standing up, he was amazingly tall, probably six feet, six inches and six-sixteenths of an inch. He threw back his head and laughed. "I'm free, I'm free! Now I can have the influence I desire, for none ever knew the real truth, and malicious rumor hides the truth and leads people astray, so that they know not what to think. I will only speak the truth in future, and if I don't know it, I will remain silent."

I gave him my list. "That will be very nice for you, I'm sure. Now, please start with this person." I indicated my ex-spouse. "Then I would like you to attack my son-in-law, who has never finished a project, and then the noisy tenant upstairs who has disturbed my sleep so many times. When you have done those, you can continue down the list as you like."

"I'll really screw them up, I assure you." He paused. "Incidentally, a promise made down here in the Devils' lair is always kept. Promises that are made in the real world are often put on the back burner and forgotten. People are flakey, especially in this day and age. There is no loyalty among thieves. Do you want a hex as well?"

"Yes, you can do a hex on each of them – they deserve it for treating me so badly. Go ahead, and I wish you luck on your mission."

The Slanderer leapt off through the dawning forest with my list. I lay back to catch some late sleep, as the goat was also lying down by the stinking sulfur pool. I wondered how the animal could stand the stench, but goats were extremely smelly themselves, so I suppose he was used to it. I settled down, my head on a soft mossy bank, and slept.

"Yahrrrhhh!" I jerked awake after a hideous nightmare. In the dream, *I saw my ex spouse standing in front of the Slanderer, who flung out a pointed finger towards the left eye of my lately beloved. This person shrank back, trying to protect the eye, but too late, as the mouth opened in an agonized shriek. "No! I have only one eye! Do not blind me! I beg of you, by all the saints." Yet, when that person turned towards me, I could see that both eyes were totally blind.* No! How awful! I could not let that happen, but I had already set the Slanderer in motion. I lay down again in a quandary, hoping that the dream was not a precognition.

I tossed and turned for a while, but I was tired, so I went into an uneasy slumber again, only to be woken again, shaking in terror, as I dreamed *my son-in-law was lying groaning in a hospice bed fighting a losing battle with hepatitis.* This dream scene quickly changed to *a bent man, moving very slowly with a walker across the parking lot of a building. My upstairs tenant looked frail and worn out, and had deteriorated rapidly since I last saw him.* The Slanderer was rubbing his hands in glee, for now he had completed my requests, and could go on down the list I had given him, and instead of feeling relief and delight at the downfall of my enemies, a wave of unbearable compassion overtook me.

What had I done? True, it was only a series of dreams. But, suppose these events had actually happened? I must find the Slanderer to stop him, before it was too late. I didn't really want these people to suffer. I could forgive them their behavior if I looked into their lives in truth and saw who they really were. I jumped to my feet and set off into the forest, now lit by the rising sun, to find the Slanderer.

I spent several hours, exhausted from lack of sleep, searching the forest for the Slanderer. I found him peacefully asleep in a little clearing, and shook him awake. "Have you really done it?" I cried in despair. "I mean, did you put the hex on those people last night? I had horrible nightmares about it."

He sat up and patted the grassy bank besides him. "You have been taught a lesson by the Devil. He is the most experienced teacher of all." He looked thoughtful. "No, I did not do your bidding, for, if you remember, you took away my bonds and freed me from being a Slanderer. Instead, I sent those dreams to you as a warning – that seeking revenge for past hurts is never a good idea. Why perpetuate the evil? The Devil does not want evil – he only places evil in your path so that you can make choices. If you choose evil, you will pay for it, and it will be more expensive than the rental you will not be able to pay for the Devil archetype."

Of course! I owed money to McSmother Feathers, yet I couldn't describe how relieved I was! I now wished only the best for my former enemies. I understood perfectly how I would feel in their place, probably not knowing why they had been struck down, for most hurtful behavior had no intention behind it. People could not help themselves, but I could, for now I was aware of the consequences. The Devil had shown me that through his henchman. I thanked the Slanderer profusely and said goodbye, returning to where I had left the goat.

The animal was waiting patiently for me to mount him, and he trotted obediently back to the lair of the Devil. Pan saw us coming, and raised his pointed brows in surprise. "You're OK after all? I'm glad, for I was worried about you. What happened?"

I lowered my eyes. "I learned a hard lesson. I was able to ride the goat, and didn't get thrown off. I met the Slanderer in the forest, and tried to persuade him to put a hex on my enemies. But he sent me bad dreams, and I understood that this was not what I really wanted. Fortunately the hex was not true - and was only a dream. The Slanderer, the slave of the Devil, has taught me a lesson about choices, and now he is free. Now I must return with the Devil to McSmother Feathers, who is waiting for him in the Museum of Archetypes."

"I will be sad to see you go." Pan looked downcast. "Will you put up a maypole somewhere for me? If we can bring people back to nature, then I can return as their King."

I promised Pan I would tell people about him, and they would begin to understand. Then I went looking for the Devil.

He was in bed with Melusina again, humping busily. I averted my eyes and said in a loud voice. "Time to go! Get it over and done with now. You can copulate again in the Museum when we get there. Get up! No, I don't mean like that. Rouse yourself! No, I don't mean like that….."

Melusina glared at me from under the sheets. I ignored her, grabbing at the Devils leash and yanking on it with force. He slid out of the bed, still attached to her, and I bundled them both up the stairs.

We reached the Museum of Archetypes shortly afterwards. McSmother Feathers was waiting impatiently for me. "This is disgraceful! Your rental time is up – you have been gone for six hours, six minutes and seven seconds. That means an added interest cost on your rental."

I handed him the Devils leash, and they rearranged them in the diorama in a full copulating position. Melusina gave me a wink. But I was more concerned about the rent I had to pay.

I had to confess. "I don't carry any money. I haven't been traveling with cash, and my credit card was lost a long time ago. I will have to pay you in kind somehow. What can I do to work it off?"

McSmother smiled faintly. "I was expecting that. I won't be really mean and make you keep the Devil, for he and Melusina are a big draw for us in the Museum. People like to watch them. No, you will have to sweep the floors here for six hours, six days and six months. Then you can leave – and don't let it happen again!"

And that is exactly what I had to do.

Path of ART - Calcination

When I had completed my six months of forced labor for the chicken McSmother Feathers, he came to me. "You must now leave the Island of Netzach and continue on your quest by the Path of Art. You have learned much, especially during the two passages of Death and the Devil, which are very challenging."

"Yes, I've been brought down a peg or two." I laughed. "I'm always taking the risk, because I imagine that I'm all powerful. After all, I have reached the Mystic SEA unaided."

"Unaided? Indeed? What about all those who have been by your side, fought for you and befriended you? Overweening pride in your accomplishments can be your downfall." The chicken warned. "Just remain simple and humble, like every decent chicken."

"You're right - I must remember that. Now, how do I get to Art from here?" I asked petulantly. "There are three Paths leading from Netzach. I have already traveled the Path of the Moon, and that of the Devil. Should I go up the Path of Fortune next?"

"That won't lead you in the right direction, for it's on the Pillar of Mercy. As far as possible, you need to stick to the Path of Art on the Middle Pillar, if you want to progress faster. Fortune can wait her turn. Fortunately…" Here he gave a little grin… "I've trained some very fine flying chickens just for this purpose. Come this way, and I'll show you."

We left the Museum of Archetypes and walked some distance to a large group of free range pens, where chickens of different colors were scratching happily in the dirt.

"Here, chicky-chick, come to Daddy." He called, holding out some corn. Some of the birds that had been perching high up took off and sailed over to his outstretched hand. Their wings were huge, with glossy feathers and strong flight quills.

"How did you do that? Chickens can't fly." I objected. "That's how they foolishly got entrapped years ago, when men found them in the forest, for they were originally flightless jungle fowl. Now they have come to serve man and, I'm sorry to say, are grossly exploited by humans."

"We know that, and we are working through human emotions to relieve their lot. It has begun, for now people often refuse to buy cage laid eggs. My idea is to remind chickens that they used to be able to fly, and they can learn again, then they can escape this cruelty." McSmother stroked the soft feathers of the bird he held, then he gently put it down. "That's what we do here."

"I'm not sure what these flying chickens have to do with my journey to Art." I said.

"Well, of course, you will fly there! You will soar over the paths you have traveled. The chicken I pick for you will be extremely powerful, for he has been invoked by magical means. Here, in this special pen."

McSmother opened a gate and an enormous chicken came running towards him, cackling loudly. He held out a pot full of corn and the bird pecked eagerly. "This bird will be your steed until you reach the forge of the blacksmith Demiurge, who is, even now, shoeing the dun mare for your journey to the Fortress of Time." As he spoke, he placed a little saddle cloth on the bird's back and attached a rein to its beak. "Jump up, now, for it is past time for you to leave."

I mounted the chicken and settled down in its soft feathers. I had never felt so comfortable, so I lay back, holding the rein lightly. McSmother let the bird have its head, and it began to run across the field, gradually picking up speed until it took off, gliding up and up on outstretched wings.

The flight did not last long enough, which disappointed me. From my perch on the chicken, I looked down on the roiling Mystic SEA and the passages I had already undertaken. I could see the Path of the Devil. It was empty, save for the donkey, the goat and the bat, that looked downcast in the absence of their master. Further to the south, the Path of Death was plainly visible, although I could no longer make out the long line of pink spirits floating ever upwards towards Art. Over the Island of Yesod, vaguely visible through a purple mist, the chicken banked to the right and I saw the bright bridge of Art stretching over Death in front of me.

The bird slowed its speed by lowering aero foils at the rear of its wings, and we came smoothly in to a small runway that led directly into the double doors of a forge. The area was flat and sandy with no living tree to be seen. I dismounted and bade goodbye to the chicken as it took off on its return journey.

A blast of heat struck me from the furnace at the back of the forge as I entered. At the rear of the building, a huge set of bellows pumped fiercely, the fire roaring. On a rack above dangled a row of horseshoes, and an old lute, whose strings had long since vanished, hung on the wall. But my attention was soon drawn to the blacksmith himself, who was busy filing the hind hoof of a pretty dun mare. He was a squat, tough fellow clad all in red and he wore a leather apron. The horse was already saddled English–style, but had no bridle. Instead, a fine smothering-cloth was draped from its poll.

I stood behind a large anvil where a double-headed hammer and a pair of tongs awaited the blacksmith's hand. The red hot shoe would soon be taken out of the furnace with the tongs, plunged into a vat of water to cool it, and then hammered into the correct shape for the hoof. During the shoeing, the blacksmith would frequently take the hot shoe over to the mare and press it down upon her hoof, to make sure that it was a good fit. Then the shoe would be laid aside to cool down and wait for the nailing.

The mare whickered softly, and I went up to her head. I frowned as I petted her. She seemed familiar, and suddenly the memory came back to me. I had already ridden this mare! It was during my travels in the Three of Wands, when the Hoodwinker had tied me on a pale horse and sent me galloping towards a steep cliff overlooking the ocean. Faith in my Guide had saved me from certain death when the mare plunged over that cliff, for he had held out his hand and caught us both. Later, I had formed a close friendship with the mare and often brought her tidbits. I wondered if she was to be my steed – I hoped so, for I would need a friend on the difficult journey ahead – but, could I trust this mare? I was certain that she was a real horse, but the Hoodwinker had used her body to shape-shift before, so I wasn't sure.

I could already discern, through a veiled doorway, the distant Fortress of Time high on a rock in the encircling desert. The vision drew me towards it, but the blacksmith interrupted, taking me by the arm and leading me towards the furnace.

He spoke to me sternly. "The Path of Art is the first stage on the sevenfold alchemical states around the Island of Tiphareth, allowing you to discover your higher self during this section of the Way of Return. The Shade of Art will stay beside you during the process."

"I don't really want to meet the Shade. We have had a lot of trouble with them." I felt grim. " I would prefer my Guide, but he only appears when he wants to."

"Doesn't your Guide often come when you need the most help? I have noticed, for I am the Demiurge, that he is always there for you when you are wounded or threatened. To attract his attention, therefore, you must begin the process of breaking away the crystallized notions in your attitude. That can only be accomplished under great heat. My furnace is not only used for heating steel to make swords and horseshoes, but also as a crucible. Those who wish to be adepts must step into it and experience calcination." He indicated the roaring furnace, and gave an extra pump on the bellows to emphasize his meaning.

My stomach sank to my knees. I was to be burnt alive! So, all my journeys and trials were for naught, they would end here, when the Truth I sought was still far ahead. I would never reach the Fortress of Time, or experience the other marvels that awaited me. I felt a numbness in my head and my legs gave way as I fell to the floor in a dead faint.

The Shade of Art revived me with a kick. "It is not you or your Soul that will die in the crucible, you fool – it is the first blow of seven blows to Belvedere, your Ego. He must be brought under control." It leered at me. "I promise you will feel a different person after you have entered the crucible. Come, now, are you a coward? Be brave, for this process is inevitable if you wish to proceed on the journey you began so long ago."

"This isn't going to work! I shouted. "I don't want to go through this process. I would rather keep the faults that I have. I will go back to square one again. I can't face this!"

"As the Shade of Art, I represent your lack of willpower, which you are now exhibiting. Are you going to shame yourself before me? After all, you have fought all seven of us many times. Why give up now?"

He led me ever closer to the raging fire. Faint from fear, I felt the terrible heat searing my face. I drew back, fighting to stay away from the fire, but he was insistent, and pushed me gently through the furnace door. All I could feel was burning, scorching flames, and then I saw myself through other eyes, and before me stood my Guide, In a vision, I saw Belvedere cursing and stamping as he fought the flames, and whirling past his head, all the illusions I had believed in my whole life. I saw through them to their depths, and knew that they were all false, every one of them, and had been created by him. He was truly my enemy. I slowly slid to the bottom of the furnace and passed out, feeling myself reduced to a pile of ashes.

Regaining consciousness, I lay on the floor outside the crucible. I saw the Shade of Art far above me, wielding a large broom, which it swept towards me, its' bristles pressing against my side hard and sharp. I felt myself being moved towards a large dustpan, into which I slid. This was carried outside the forge door, and I was dumped onto the ground. However, a little breeze that was blowing threw me up in the air, and I had a hard job to hold onto my totality.

The Shade was looking down at me. "Don't worry. You have courage and you did well. You will feel different now – lighter. You will get up in a moment when you feel better, and rest a little by the blacksmiths' anvil, for he must now begin to forge a sword for you." It helped me up. "My task is done now, for I am only necessary to take you through your first process. Come now and I will introduce you to a lady the blacksmith is expecting shortly."

The blacksmith looked up as a door slammed at the back of the forge, and a tall, handsome woman strode in. She wore a striped cape and patterned Capri pants, which fit her like a glove, and bore a bearskin cap on her head. Slung over one shoulder was a quiver full of arrows, although she was not carrying a bow.

"Demiurge!" She had a commanding tone. "Is my sword ready yet? I have left my bow at home in the Moon, for I will no longer be chasing the stag or the boar, but hunting the elusive quarry of Time, and for that I need the sword that you have fashioned." She cast around her with a large flashlight, shining it into the dark corners of the forge to look for her sword.

"I have it ready." The blacksmith replied deferentially. "We just have to do a final test on it, to make sure that the temperance is correct, for if it is too flexible, it will not cut straight, and if it is too stiff, it will not cleave the air for you to pass."

"I know the temper of my sword is very important. The Japanese have perfected that. It is a Zen thing. I will verify the quality of the sword once it is in my hand." She looked ahead, her eyes fastened narrowly on the round exit from the forge, whence an arrow-straight path led towards the Fortress of Time in the distance. "I have shot many an arrow from my bow, but this quest is a challenge for me, even though I am the goddess Artemis, known as Diana by the Romans."

I was a little overawed by her majesty, for she certainly had a royal air about her. I ventured a question. "Why have you decided to undertake this quest? I would have thought you were happier in the moonlit forest, hunting the deer and the bear."

She looked down at me, for she was a head taller than I, the eyes of her bear cap glinting in the light of the furnace. "If you know hunters, and you should, for you are one yourself, you would understand that there is ever a desire for unattainable quarry – that which presents itself too easily to your drawn arrow loses its savor." She tossed her head. "I have long known the moment would come that I would finally confront my ultimate prey – the essence of Time. If I can overtake Time and kill it, I will be free forever from its grip, and I will embrace eternity. That is why I am here."

The blacksmith came over to us with a long, glittering sword in his hand, which he presented to her. "This is your sword – may it bring you Willpower everlasting and be a true weapon in your hand. Test it now."

He stepped back, motioning to a pig carcass that hung from a hook at the back of the forge. She placed the sword hilt on the ground and, with her finger on the tip of the weapon, lightly bent it. The sword quivered under her pressure, but remained steadfast. She then settled the hilt in her hand and, feinting towards the pig, drew back her sword arm to its fullest extent, swung the weapon through the air and cut the carcass neatly in half, without a drop of blood spilling.

"It is good." Was all the goddess said.

An Abyssinian cat, lean and brindled, came creeping into the forge. I bent down to stroke it. I had been so intent on watching Artemis, it was only now I remembered the pink spirits that should be floating up from Death to obtain their swords. I turned to Demiurge, the blacksmith. "I saw many spirits catapulted into the air from the Path of Death. They seemed to be coming in this direction, but I don't see any of them here. Where are they?"

The blacksmith motioned me to follow him. Leaving Artemis to prepare for her journey, we went through a side door into another forge, and from there, another and another. In each forge the furnaces were blazing and piles of swords lay ready to be distributed, but no-one was there. We traversed many forges, but still all was emptiness.

"Where are the spirits?" I was puzzled, when we reached the last one. "I saw them leaving Death, but they are not here now."

"They are here. You can't see them, for they are spirits, remember?" The blacksmith replied. "When you were in Death yourself, they were plain to see, but once you leave, they become invisible. Be still, and you will feel them." He raised a hand for silence.

A faint rushing sensation was present in the room, and the warm air stirred lightly. A peaceful sensation wafted around me, and I knew from whence it came. Then I saw that the pile of swords was dwindling, as invisible hands picked up each one, tested it, and moved towards the door of the forge, ready to depart.

"Where do they go from here?" I asked. "Are they all heading in the same direction?"

"Not necessarily. It is easy to lose your way up here. Some will make it to the Island of Tiphareth eventually, and be received by the Child, but most will not. It depends on the quality of their swords, for the sword represents each spirits' will power. Some are stronger than others, but many are led astray onto the Pillar of Severity, or the Pillar of Mercy, and cannot maintain their central balance."

"The Way ahead is not so easy, then. Even armed with the Sword of Willpower, one can still miss the mark. Why is that?"

"Many swords are made, but few are wielded correctly." The Demiurge replied. "In fact, when you reach the Island of Geburah, you will see that many people use their swords to conquer others, for they have allowed pride to hold sway over them, and consider themselves as good as gods. That is the final trial set by Saturn, the tester, who abides both in the Path of the Universe and in the black Island of Binah."

"Why does Saturns' influence rule in two places?" I asked.

"The Island of Binah is the root of the tree that flourishes in Malkuth, the lower world of matter. Saturn, who is also the God Chronos, sets time limits on human lives, and all who inhabit Malkuth must eventually pass through the Crack between the Worlds, leaving their transient physical bodies behind. Now, when they reach Binah, they will understand the meaning of Time."

"Well, we are soon traveling to the Fortress of Time. I can see it through the round exit of the forge. It is not so far away. Surely, when we enter it, we will understand the extent of Time. I want to get beyond it.
"

"I cannot elucidate on that matter. You must see for yourself. Undertake the journey, and that will give you the answer." The blacksmith turned away, his eyes lowered, as we returned to the first forge. "I want to complete the shoeing of your mare, so she is ready for you. I see that Artemis is impatient to be gone, for she is already standing by the exit, ready to break the veil of the hymen."

I looked at Artemis, who was flexing her sword, and realized that I still had no sword. The blacksmith had made her a sword, and all the spirits were given swords. Why was I left out?

"Where is my sword?" I asked plaintively. "You have not given it to me."

The blacksmith stared at me gravely. "Artemis ordered her sword months ago. Besides, she is a goddess, and that means she gets first priority. As for the spirits, they have already courageously passed through Death, and therefore I prepare the swords for them. In your case, you are neither theoretically dead nor a god figure. That means you have to forge your own sword. Didn't you realize that?" He shrugged his shoulders. "Better get started!"

I was at a loss, for it appeared he was not going to help me. I had some knowledge of sword making, because I had watched the brothers Yevgeny and Yaroslav in their forge during my time in the Ten of Swords. I picked up a length of iron and placed it on the fire, giving an extra push with the bellows. When it was red hot, I reached for it, but forgot to use the tongs. I burnt my hand on the metal and gave a shriek.

"Better make sure you can handle hot subjects." The blacksmith muttered darkly. "Now, cool it in the vat of baptismal water."

I plunged the metal bar into the water, using the tongs. Great clouds of steam arose, and then I took it to the anvil to beat on it, returning it to the furnace to heat it again and again.

I won't distress anyone by recounting the number of times, and the different metals, that I had to weld to my sword. It was a long learning process, and I toiled between the furnace and the cooling vat many times. Artemis became impatient and gave up waiting for me, and she rent the veil with her sword and flounced out of the round door, setting off across the plain by herself with long strides towards the Fortress.

Frustrated at being left behind, I continued to work with my sword. The blacksmith was inspecting the weapon at intervals, but I could not get it right His testing booth was somewhat like a shooting gallery, and consisted of problems that popped up like rabbits, which one had to sever quickly to solve. Sometimes my sword was too blunt, and unable to cut through the problems, which indicated I had not approached them correctly, while on several occasions it was too brittle, and shattered. That meant I had allowed them to overcome my resolve. I had to remake my Sword of Willpower many times.

After much Time had passed, I had a reasonable Sword, which I showed to the blacksmith. He nodded, and passed it favorably. "Now you may set out. I will complete the shoeing of your steed."

His hammer rang out as he formed the shoe on the anvil, turning it this way and that, giving the iron little taps to make it fit perfectly. He did this with all four shoes, nailed them in place with seven nails, and then the dun mare stood ready for me to mount. I still had so many questions.

"The mare has no bridle, only a cloth draped over her nose. How am I supposed to control her?"

"She will control you, for she is born of me, the Demiurge, and that means the desire to move on, to evolve form, to turn, finally, and seek the Grail."

"I see. I know your name Demiurge means the urge to become one of the people – the urge to come into manifestation as a human being. Is that right?"

"You are on the right track. Now, no more questions. It's time for you to go."

"What happened to Artemis? She had no horse." I picked up the Abyssinian cat, holding her gently. "May I take the cat with me?"

"By all means. The cat will be a good companion for you. Don't worry about Artemis. She travels swiftly on foot, and she awaits you at the end of the hunt. Urge your mare forward towards the exit of the forge, which is the womb in which you have been conceived, ready for your second birth. Remember, do not stray from the marked path, or you will find yourself in trouble."

I slid my sword into its sheath by my right side, for I was to wield it left handedly, and rode the mare up to the round doorway, settling the cat on the saddle in front of me and expecting to be able to pass through the veil of the hymen easily. I sought to brush the gauzy stuff aside, but it was not as simple as I thought, and it resisted with extraordinary strength and flexibility. After a struggle, pushing my horse forward bit by bit, the cat managed to tear a small slit in it with her claws, and then it gave way. With a rush of breaking water from the cooling vat, we were outside in the endless desert, marked only by the narrow path pointing arrow-straight to the rock where the Fortress of Time awaited us.

Three days into the journey, and sharing my water bottles sparingly with the two animals in the dry heat, the Fortress seemed no nearer, but shimmered before me like a mirage. It was on the morning of the fourth day that I noticed a large cloud of dust gathering to my right and slowly rolling towards me across the plain. Soon the figures of galloping horsemen were visible through the haze, and in front of them ran a pack of great hounds, that bayed loudly as they bunched together and turned, following their prey, which was still unseen.

The hunt grew closer and I stopped, hoping the riders would not sweep us aside, for the path on which we trod was narrow. The hounds rushed past, their noses to the ground, leaping forward as if the quarry was just ahead, but I could see nothing. Maybe they were following the scent and had not yet caught up. Meanwhile, the horsemen arrived and swirled around us, their steeds blowing heavily and dripping sweat. I saw that Artemis was leading them on foot. A man in a Celtic breastplate rode at their head, and he dismounted, bowing to me, and sweeping off his helmet in a gesture of friendship. Artemis stepped forward and turned to face him.

"Arthur! Do not waste time. Remember who is leading you! How are you faring on this hunt? Do not stop now. Your prey is not far ahead." She smiled faintly. "Don't allow hounds to outdistance you, or they may be lost."

Arthur ignored her, being more interested in my sudden appearance. "Why don't you join us? There is a fat armadillo not far away, and he carries the Page of Wands on his back. We are rapidly overtaking them, and hounds will have them in their clutches without delay. Come, ride with us." Arthur remounted, whirled his horse, and set off at a gallop with his troop closely bunched together.

I turned to Artemis in horror. "They are chasing Ripskin, the Page of Wands! He might be killed, and that would harm Intuition. I must ride to the rescue. Will you be beside me?" I swung the mares' head around and, without thinking, sent her at full speed off my marked path, gazing ahead of me to try to distinguish the armadillo and its rider. Managing to cut across by a faster track, while hounds were delayed by a false scent, I reached the armadillo and, swinging out my arm, gathered Ripskin onto my horse behind me, where he clung on wildly. The armadillo immediately began to dig, and soon disappeared down a hole in the ground, filling it in with sand behind, so that nothing could be seen.

Now I had Ripskin riding behind me. He was the most advanced of the four Pages, being capable of the art of Intuition. But, here was Artemis, striding up, and her face was a mask of anger.

"Fool! You galloped off the path, and I had to follow you. Now we're lost! We'll have to wait for Arthur to catch up, and then accompany him to his own castle. But that was not our goal." She began to weep. "How will I ever find the Fortress of Time again? We have been led astray yet again by the desire to hunt. It is hard to learn to ignore the hunt, for we are the accursed hunters. Nevertheless, I will think of a way to find the path again." She straightened her shoulders. "Follow me."

Her attitude was a little strange, as I knew she had already been following the hunt with Arthur. She must have stepped off the path herself, and now she was blaming me. I resented that, and made up my mind to treat her with less deference.

Ripskin clung onto my shoulders, but although I had rescued him, I did not really want him along. He was too spacey and intuitive, having shed many skins and lost his sense of Ego, which might have been all right if we had already passed the Island of Tiphareth, but we had not, and still had an infinity to travel.

"We had better ride to Arthurs' castle with him." I muttered under my breath to Artemis. "Ripskin is too scatterbrained to accompany us. We must leave him with the King. He will find a use for the Page."

Arthur rode up shortly, and seemed annoyed. "Hounds lost the scent and the armadillo has disappeared." He pulled a large pocket watch out of his chain mail. "It is getting late and quite time to return to the castle. We can hunt again tomorrow." He turned his horse. "Come with me, and I will give you all you may desire. We will have feasting, dancing and many games, and you will take pleasure in all I have to offer." He gave me a wink. "Why, you may even want to stay with us forever."

I had no choice but to join him and his followers, since Artemis and I had lost the path. Arthur and his court turned out to be a motley group, all bent on pleasure and the desire to perpetuate it. Once we reached the castle, we were swept up in constant merriment, with the most excellent dishes of food set in front of us, and Artemis was even chased by a fellow dressed in a hairy stag suit, with six-pointed horns on his head. I do not know what became of her, since they were last seen leaping over the distant hills, and never reached the Fortress of Time.

As for me, I gave Ripskin the Page of Wands to Arthur as a jester, and he amused the court for many years afterwards, because of the daft things he said, but I knew he was really far out and that he would reach his goal on the Way of Return before me.

A considerable amount of Time must have passed while I was at King Arthurs' court, and I had not marked it, for I was really enjoying myself. I had become a much-vaunted performer and acted in masked plays and mimes for the courts' pleasure.

Then came a day I fell into great grief, for the Abyssinian cat I loved so well became sick, and I was anxious to heal her. I begged audience of the King, and he told me that the cat could only be healed if I made a sacrifice to the gods. The victim would have to be my dun mare. She already had her smothering cloth draped over her nose.

I did not like that idea, for the mare had carried me safely on my travels on several previous occasions, and the cat was merely a recent acquisition. I, of course, protested to the King. I did not want to sacrifice the mare for a mere cat! He raised his eyebrows and looked at me quizzically. "That mare is obviously of great value to you. Why is that?"

"Sire, I need the mare to carry me to the Fortress of Time when I find the path. The cat is very sweet, but not essential for my journey."

He began to laugh. "You are still expecting to reach the Fortress! After all I have offered you for your enjoyment? I am astonished. You should remain here and live with us permanently, and I will give you the Order of the Unified Tribes, which will mean you are OUT of the running." Here he roared with laughter.

"No, sire, I wish to continue on my quest. I have spent a great deal of time fashioning my sword. If I sacrifice the cat, may I keep the horse and be on my way, for I am exhausted with revelry, and wish for peace and silence once more."

"Well, it is your decision. Will it be the cat or the horse? Think hard – for there may be more to this question than you imagine."

The King allowed me an hour to decide, and my little cat grew weaker. I made the hard decision to sacrifice the mare that I loved dearly, for the Abyssinian cat had a mystery about her that I could not define, which drew me to her. I led my horse to the sacrificial block, where she was duly smothered and went down on her knees, rolling onto her side and breathing her last. Immediately a great cheer of victory rose from the assembled crowd. I was taken aback and held the cat closely to me, mourning the loss of my valuable mare.

The little cat already seemed better, and soon leaped from my arms and sat in front of me on the ground. Its tiny mouth, with pink tongue and sharp teeth, opened, and from it came a puff of sand, that formed itself into two tiny horses. The little sculptures grew and grew, until they were full sized, and there was my dead mare and beside her, an identical mare carrying a pack of stores for the journey. The two horses nuzzled my hand, and I felt the living softness of their velvety noses. The mare was alive again, and brought with her a twin mare for my journey. When I looked, the cat had vanished, and nothing remained of her save a patch of brindled sand, yet a tiny voice echoed in my ear.

"You sacrificed that which was dearest to you, and therefore it has been returned in double measure. Be on your way!" I said farewell to King Arthur and his knights, and they drank a toast in their finest wine to my journey.

With the two horses, I made rapid progress, traveling at 90 degrees across the plain in order to intersect with the path of the Arrow that led to the Fortress. Coming to the path and turning towards my destination, the noon sun struck my eyes so that I had to shield them from its blazing rays. My dun mare and her identical twin trotted along the narrow path, and after several days, we arrived at the foot of the great triangular rock from which the Fortress of Time rose. Discovering as I got closer that the rock had an arch through which the arrow led, I entered its dim interior.

As I rode in, the massive cave echoed around me. I was hoping to find a trail that led upwards. I soon reached a blank wall where I could go no further so I tethered the two mares and fed them from the generous pack supplies the King had given me. I then explored the walls, going around carefully in a circle in the dim light, feeling my way, looking for a door or a staircase, but there was none. I was directly under the Fortress, but there seemed to be no way up to reach it.

I settled the horses for the night and slept close to them. In the morning, I decided to ride around the base of the rock. I didn't want to leave the packhorse behind, so I saddled up and took both of them. I began by leaving the cave entrance and turning to the right, jogging slowly along and searching the steep rock walls for any sign of an entrance. I circled the entire rock, which took most of the day, and returned to the cave, where I spent the next night. I had not seen a single stair or foothold in the sheer rock.

The following day I set out again to circle the rock, this time turning to my left as I came out of the cave. I assumed the angle of the light must have caused me to miss a narrow cleft or some steps. I was three-quarters of the way around when I noticed that the rock on one side seemed to have become flatter, and there was a distinct zigzag path leading up towards the Fortress. I scratched my head. I was sure that it had not been there the day before. But here it was, so I set my mares' head towards the summit, the pack horse following closely. Up and up we went, plodding slowly in the heat, and reached the walls of the Fortress at midday.

To my utmost astonishment, the walls were covered with clocks of all shapes and sizes, and since it was midday, they all began to chime. Huge grandfather clocks boomed out their twelve strokes, mixed with the calls of cuckoo clocks; chiming mantle clocks; kitchen clocks; and gold pocket watches, causing a frightful din. The dun mare reared up under me in fright and I had no time to save myself. I fell from her back, loosing the rein, and she made off down the path at a gallop, towing the packhorse behind her. I held my breath, fearful that they would miss their footing in their mad descent, but they reached the bottom of the rock and made off over the plain in a cloud of dust.

This was rather a disaster. All my stores were in the packs, so now I had only the clothes I was wearing and the items I always carried in my pockets. The Fortress still seemed impregnable, but I began to circle around the walls to find an opening. I came upon an arrow, lying on the ground and picked it up, holding it by the shaft. The arrowhead twisted on the shaft, pointing towards an old door in the wall. The arrow fitted itself into the keyhole of the locked door and opened it, so that I could squeeze through. I was in a small courtyard, similar to the castles I had visited, but silent without the usual bustle of grooms, washerwomen and fowlers. There was one person prowling around the courtyard, however, with a bunch of keys swinging from his belt. It was Belvedere, my tiresome Ego.

"Fancy finding you here!" I exclaimed in mock pleasure. "Are you the janitor of the Fortress?"

"How dare you suggest such an idea! Why, I am the owner of the Fortress of Time, and I control all the clocks that are on the outside walls. I am the one who manages your time and how you spend it – without me, you would just sit around and have someone combing your hair. That doesn't make sense – for you have to learn to hurry along and not waste time doing nothing."

"So that's your opinion! I'll have you know that you are not the dictator of my time. You don't even belong here." I walked up to him. "Give me the keys now. Hand them over."

Belvedere shrank back. "No! I won't give them back. Without the keys I won't have control of your time. I need to have control always." He backed up and tried to turn and run up the narrow stone steps towards the battlements, but I tripped him and he fell heavily, the keys landing in the dust. I picked them up. Belvedere seemed to shrivel a little. He hung his head. "All right then, you win. But I'll get even with you next time, you watch out!"

He turned and slowly climbed the steps to the battlements. I watched him leave, resolute anger in my heart. A voice interrupted my brooding.

"I'm glad you managed to get rid of him." There, in the center of the precinct, was a small hut made of grey, shimmering material with an old man sitting outside the door. He opened his arms to me – it was my Guide!

"I waited here for you, to dissuade you from learning the secrets of Time, for the land beyond Time would bewitch you and carry you away from your purpose, which is to tread the Way of Return. Nevertheless, I can at least show you the operation of Time from a distance."

He got up slowly, hands pressing on knees, and walked across to the inner bastion of the Fortress, which soared up some seventy feet above me, its round walls built of an unknown substance that clicked to and fro constantly like the pendulum of a huge clock. We entered a small door in the wall and climbed to the top, where we stepped onto the battlements. There was no sign of Belvedere until I looked over the steep walls and saw him stiffly descending a rope ladder, that hung from one of the turret windows.

Beyond his defeated figure, the dreary plain I had just crossed was transformed into a brightly colored kaleidoscope of simultaneous events that wove in and out sinuously. I could not believe the sight as I brushed my hand across my eyes, for incidents, procedures, battles and treaties through the years were in continuous motion, forming and reforming side by side - yet I knew from history that these events had happened in separate eras. This expansive pattern wove in and out, with figures running across the surface like shadows, to appear and disappear endlessly.

"I know these events happened at different times. How is it that they are all happening at once?" I asked my Guide. "What am I witnessing?"

"This is the absence of Time – the state of parallel universes." My Guide explained. "Humankind invented Time, as it were. Being upon the Earth, which rotates at – what you would call the present rate – they were not satisfied to merely exist in the moment, but had to divide everything up into years, months, weeks and days. Then, they insisted on splitting days into hours, minutes and even seconds. This has helped them to measure their idea of the Universe. Yet we of the higher source know that they are still struggling to understand the notion of no Time. For every moment of life, there exist parallel universes, and people step from one to the other continuously during their lifetime, but they do not know it. The answer lies in the Path of Fortune, where you will learn more about personal choices."

"That is amazing! So every choice I make is, in a way, arbitrary. At any moment of my life I am presented with parallel existences, alongside my own." I said seriously.

"Yes, that is correct. Now, let me show you inside the bastion." He led the way down some stone steps into a chamber that had a narrow gallery around the inner wall. In the center was a massive glass container in which a Cube was suspended, four brightly colored Trees of Life inside it. The trees were shown in three dimensions, and the four of them fitted into each corner inside the Cube perfectly, each sphere having its own space with a cross inside it. There were many other geometric designs in the fabulous Cube, including the signs of the Zodiac, but my Guide drew me reluctantly away, and we descended to the courtyard.

"That is the Cube of Space, made up from the knowledge of Sacred Geometry. You have seen as much as it is prudent for you to know at this time." Here he gave a wry smile. "I know. It is difficult to converse with humans without raising the question of Time, for they know nothing else, and 'nothing else' holds many mysteries." He patted me on the shoulder. "Now it is time for you to upgrade to another boat. When you leave the Fortress, you will find yourself surrounded by water, and your new cruising ketch, moored nearby waiting for you, with faithful Pompeybou at the helm. Come, let us go and meet him." The old man opened the door and we stepped outside the Fortress of Time. He was right, the plain had disappeared, and in its place the Mystic SEA lapped against the rock quietly.

The boat was a beauty. It was a 50 ft ketch, with a center cockpit and a stern cabin for privacy. Indeed, a vast improvement on the much smaller sloop we had been using when it was necessary to sail from one place to another. I went below to settle in to the boat. There didn't seem to be anyone except Pompeybou on board. The foc'sle was filled with new sails neatly hung in bags on either side, while coils of rope stood ready. A pipe cot was raised along one side and a small "head" with a roll of toilet paper was in the center. The saloon was extremely pleasant, with a good sized chart table, over which swung Joana the cricket in her cage, and an array of modern electronics completed the area. Bunks supplied with sensible lee cloths were on either side of the central folding table, and opposite the chart table, the galley boasted a gimbaled cooking stove and canvas support band for rough weather.

As I climbed aboard happily, my Guide gave me a word of warning. "The Path of Art leads directly to the Island of Tiphareth. However, you cannot enter the presence of the Child until you have completed the journey of the Infinity Symbol, which is the weaving of the figure of eight between the sevenfold alchemical processes that encircle Tiphareth. The experiences on these paths will prepare you for the high energy in Tiphareth, which you will glimpse many times as you pass that Island, sometimes Above, sometimes Below, and sometimes Beside it. Now, the next Path is that of the Tower, an enigmatic path, but one that is indispensable for you. It will change your state of mind, believe me, for you will find yourself separated."

He waved goodbye, and we cast off and set the jib and mizzen sails until we were clear of land, and then raised the mainsail. The ketch took off at a swift pace as we headed southeast, towards the Path of the Tower.

Path of the TOWER - Separation

A s we rounded the Island of Tiphareth, leaving it on our port beam, we shortened sail and came onto a beam reach. Some gusts from the pinnacles on the island made us hang on as the ketch heeled over, yet it was a fast and trouble free crossing to the Tower. I was in for a surprise, however, as I was creeping through the narrow passage beside the engine room. I emerged in the master cabin at the stern. The bed looked very lumpy, so I prodded the blanketed forms. To my horror, two figures sat up, giggling and embarrassed. It was Krackenwergle and Festerbash! What an unfortunate combination this was! Krackenwergle was my trickster entity, and Festerbash my hedonistic self. They had both smuggled themselves aboard the ketch.

I raised myself to my full height. I had to remember that they were both free from my influence now, since all my entities were redeemed when I sailed into the Mystic SEA. That did not mean they had gone away, though. I addressed them sternly as they crumpled together into a heap of mirth. "What are you doing here? This is not the place for either of you. Where are some of my reliable entities?" I was angry. "I suppose you think you can do what you like, now you're free?"

Festerbash was completely convulsed with laughter and could not answer, but Krackenwergle spoke up. "Er-hem, twit, we – er-hem – came along because we wanted to climb the Tower. It looks, er – decidedly interesting, hmmmm." He gave me his engaging grin, which I could never resist. "By the way, er- what is our position here?"

I knew he was trying to change the subject. There was no way to get them off the boat until we reached the Path of the Tower, anyway. "I suppose, since you're here, we'll have to put up with you both. But don't get started on any trickery or pranks while we're on board. Sailing is a serious business and we must follow our course."

Festerbash found his voice. "You won't regret it. We're really great company. Why, it's St. Patricks Day tomorrow. We can celebrate! Let's have a little party! I'll make up some green costumes."

"No, Festerbash, you can't party on the boat. You might fall overboard – and I won't turn back to rescue you." I announced severely. "You stay on board under certain conditions – mine. Now, get up on deck and tend to the sails, the wind is rising and we need to take in a reef." I pulled the blanket off them and they jumped up through the after hatch, giggling again.

This was a real nuisance. I didn't seriously think that I could control them, and I remembered only too well the drunken chaos Krackenwergle had caused on the last occasion in the Queen of Cups, when we attempted to rescue Jafar, who had been turned into a cuscus. The combination of Festerbash with him was a deadly mixture. I would have to hide the booze somewhere.

While they were on deck, I decided to pour all the drink down the head in the foc'sle. It seemed a criminal waste, but I feared the alternative. I opened bottle after bottle, pumping away at the head until all was gone, and then heaved a sigh of relief. They couldn't get drunk now, I felt sure.

The following day, Festerbash had made some green costumes for St Patricks' Day out of seaweed he had collected. They were very fetching - Pompeybou in dark green kelp, with a baby sea otter on his shoulder; Krackenwergle wearing green spongeweed, in which tiny guppies were swimming; Festerbash dressed in green algae, on which a leatherback turtle was feasting, and my costume being green sea lettuce with an entwined batfish over one ear.

It was a sunny day and the ketch was under full sail. There was no sign of land yet. We sat on deck, and exchanged jokes and frivolities. Then the moment came when Krackenwergle looked around him. "Where's the booze, twit, - hmmmm? I know, er-hem, there was plenty on board. I er-hem, counted the bottles. Let's bring some up – the sun is almost under the yardarm, hmmmm."

I cringed. They were going to be mad when they found out it was all gone. Festerbash went below, and he was gone for a while. Then he handed up a huge bowl of punch, which smelt so strongly of alcohol it almost knocked me over.

"Where did you get that?" I exclaimed in alarm.

Krackenwergle, already scooping punch into a tin cup, swallowed a great gulp as Festerbash came up the companionway with a full bota bag, which he poured rapidly into his gullet. They were choking with laughter. Finally, Krackenwergle was able to speak.

"Ahh! Er-hem. We knew when you – er – came on board that you would try to pour the booze away, er-hem, when you found us. Since – er-hem – you sent us up on deck, we knew you couldn't pour the bottles overboard, for we would have stopped you, hmmmm. So the only alternative for you was the er-hem, head!" Here he took another swig and broke into guffaws. "We rigged the head with a tube leading to a rubber water tank in the bilges. You pumped all the booze into that. Now – er-hem, we have a fine mix, hmmm, of every different kind of liquor on the boat. Cheers!" Grinning, he displayed a brimming cup of punch.

They had outwitted me. In secret, I was rather proud of them, and I reckoned if I couldn't beat them, I would join them. Might as well, I thought, as I dipped my cup into the bowl of punch. Pompeybou was drinking, too, as the boat swung into the wind, her sails flapping. I was soon unable to stand up and reach the helm. We drifted for several hours while we continued drinking and partying until the two jokers collapsed in a heap on the foredeck, thereby blocking access to the genoa jib. Pompeybou, who was used to alcohol, wandered unsteadily to the wheel and trimmed the boat, gybing the mainsail to get back on course. I felt sick and dashed to the lifelines. Leaning over, I threw up violently. Clinging to the lines, I retched again and again. When I staggered back, weakened, I had at least cleared my body of some alcohol and could think clearly once more.

I spoke feebly to Pompeybou. "We'll have to sail the boat, just the two of us without them. I can't have any more of this, so I'm going to tie Krackenwergle and Festerbash up. Stay on your course. I'll be back."

I made my way to the foredeck and tied up their recumbent forms with some stout rope, which I attached to the mast, and then I laid the wrapped bodies out on the cabin top under the boom, to make room for any change of foresails we might have to make. I sprinkled them with a mixture of sulfur and iron filings that I felt would separate their energies and save a lot of trouble. Fortunately the wind was steady from the northwest. Night came, and Pompeybou and I sobered up and did three-hour watches each. On my watch I observed, through the binoculars, spurts of fire on the horizon that was not lightning. It was still and warm. The morning brought promise of a hot day that revealed a group of small volcanic islands. The largest cone was in continuous eruption, and our planned course led towards it. But another night passed before we neared it, during which Krackenwergle and Festerbash slept off their binge and, to begin with, seemed meek and compliant. They busied themselves around the boat, tidying up and trimming the sails, now and again casting lowered glances towards me that I pretended to ignore.

The following morning, we were right under the volcanic isle, and hot ashes were drifting on the wind and landing on our deck. We altered course to get to windward of the volcano and put in at a narrow inlet, where we dropped anchor and sent out a stern line to some rocks. The Tower should be somewhere on this island, so we planned an expedition around the island to find it. That would be dangerous, for soot and pumice cascaded from the skies and red hot lava crept down the slopes in some places. I left Pompeybou to guard the ketch and took the two jokers in the new dinghy, rowing in to a beach of fine black sand.

To split them up, I insisted that Festerbash stay with me, while Krackenwergle was savvy enough to manage on his own. We took separate sides of the island, putting on steel construction helmets as protection from the falling pumice. Krackenwergle was to take the north side and report to me at the far end of the island, which was quite small, probably only a couple of miles wide. He saluted insolently and made off at his usual lope. We began our trek along the south side, trying to stay as far away from the lava flows as possible, which meant adding distance to our search.

Halfway along the south side we came to a level plain of black sand that was considerably wider than the beach, and here we found a person, clad in orange, sitting in despair, with his leg chained to a small post in the ground. Near him a boar stood, with its foot caught in a crown that must have fallen from somewhere. I looked at the figure and was about to speak to him when a clap of thunder sounded from the mountain. The skies had grown unnaturally dark and thick black clouds were covering the slopes and rolling towards us, obliterating the volcano, and the reek of burning undergrowth filled our nostrils. Under the clouds, a tongue of flame appeared, licking downwards. Soon there was a wall of fire between the volcano and us, but fortunately the fire had nothing to burn on the black sand, and so its advance towards us was halted.

I breathed a sigh of relief and looked towards Festerbash. All the intemperance had drained out of him and he looked as white as a sheet. He was keeping a safe distance between him and the boar that snorted and tossed its heavy head vigorously. I bent towards the seated person, who was curled into a fetal position, his head down and his arms closely hugging his knees.

"Excuse me. Are you by chance a Hodian?" I knew by his color that he must be connected to the Island of Hod. "Where is your bubble? It's not safe for you here without it."

A broken cry came from the figure. "I was caught in a stampede some months ago during the Conference on Prejudice in the city of Hod. Several people were trampled, and what is worse, their bubbles were broken. I tried to save my own bubble, but it got caught on a fellows' belt buckle and popped." He sniffed loudly. "You may know that Hodians without bubbles are ostracized, if they survive, and placed under special orders. I went to court and my probation was to spend eight months on this Island, in order to understand the meaning of the Tower, but I have not achieved anything except a few dozen burns on my arms and legs."

"I don't see the Tower." I remarked. "Where is it?"

"It's around the next corner. Just follow those stepping stones set in the black sand. The Netzachian went that way too, but I am chained here by my rational thoughts and cannot see the Tower clearly, for it is a very disturbing location, since its energy comes from the direction of Netzach."

Festerbash and I were glad to get away from the miserable Hodian, who was trying to review his Shadow self, its terrors revealed by his lost bubble of safety, that had enclosed him since birth. We followed the stepping stones, which crossed the plain to the next bluff, avoiding some steaming mud baths, and peered around the corner of the rock. There, in the middle of the plain, rose a huge Tower of grey concrete, built in a very modern architectural style, with nooks, crannies, steps, ladders and even a suicide platform with a rope, from which dangled a disconsolate corpse. A rancid smell pervaded the air and a wall of flames rose up behind the great Tower. Heading towards this building was a weeping figure in green – evidently the Netzachian, with a trailing rebozo hanging from his shoulders that muffled his intense sobs. We caught up with him and I laid a hand on his shoulder.

"Where are you going?" I asked. "Have you had a quarrel with the Hodian?"

"Yes, of course. We can never agree. I'm just too emotional for him. I don't understand his cold and practical approach." He sneezed into the rebozo. "He's in a foul temper because he lost his bubble – whatever that is. It's supposed to protect him and keep him separate from other people. He doesn't like to touch them very much."

"I understand. I am aware of the Hodian attitude. I have traveled in both Netzach and Hod, his Path. I know the Netzachians are very warm, friendly people and like to gather in groups. But sometimes they are not very sensible and don't make good decisions. They are led astray by their passions, and the Hodians don't approve of that. In fact, they specifically go after addicts and people who stray from their way of thinking, condemning them. It is one of the problems that constitutes their Towers."

"Oh! I wondered why the Tower was here, and why I feel I must follow the stepping stones towards it and climb it. I am trying to reclaim the rejected parts of my personality." He looked up, wiping his eyes. "It looks as if it's made of concrete blocks. It's an evil looking thing, and I see there are people up there – two of them are fighting at the very top. Look! Do you see them?" He pointed to a narrow ledge high up on the right side of the Tower, where one figure was lunging towards another, about to push it off the ledge.

They must be Fight and Flight, I realized. I had better hurry and climb the Tower to find out before there was an accident. "Excuse me. Let us go in front of you on the path, please. I need to dash. You have pointed out a problem at the top of the Tower." I politely moved past him, Festerbash following me reluctantly. "Come on!" I urged him. "Don't get left behind – stick with me." I rushed the first wide flight of stairs up the Tower.

The steps wound up and up, getting narrower all the time. I passed a splendid black omphalos, resting in an inverted triangular alcove, the red glow of the raging fire behind outlining it somberly. I made a mental note to come back and collect it. At the level of the suicide platform I stepped aside to make sure the victim was dead, and then cut him down with a quick slash of my knife. I didn't know who had hung themselves, but I sincerely hoped the suicide was for a worthy cause, such as complete and utter dejection. The body plummeted down and landed almost on top of a small lamb that bleated raucously and ran for its life. I continued up the stairway to another alcove that resembled the eye of a snake, and from there to the left of the Tower, where I paused for a moment, brandishing my sword, to wait for Festerbash, but he was not behind me. Peering over the edge of the platform, which had a long ladder leading above it, I couldn't see where Festerbash might be. My concern for him grew greater when I saw the dark clouds massing lower and lower, and a roll of thunder coming in on the gusty wind. Oh, well, it was no good waiting for him – I had to reach Fight and Flight quickly, so I pushed on, arriving on their platform in time to grab Flight, who was perilously near the edge and about to fall.

"What are you doing to her?" I yelled angrily at Fight as I pulled her back from the drop.

He stood in a daze, as if he had lost his senses. "I – I don't know. We got here, and she couldn't speak my language any more. We had settled our differences on the Path of the Aeon, and we were getting along fine, but when we saw the Tower, it seemed to have an evil influence on us, and we began to speak in separate languages, so we didn't understand each other, and that set us off."

"The Tower will do that to a relationship." I explained quickly. "It's like the Tower of Babel – nobody understands anyone else because they don't speak the same language. That language is the language of Truth, and none of us know the exact truth."

"Did the Tower warp our thinking, then?" Flight stepped forward. "That isn't what we were expecting when we came here."

"We all see one Tower, which we have now climbed. But in reality the one Tower is many towers, for each of us constructs our own separate Tower from our egotistical behavior. That's why the Tower is built of grey concrete blocks. The grey matter of our brain creates the solid blocks that we have developed over our lifetimes, and each Tower gets higher and higher, as we build on our false beliefs and habits – unless we have the courage to tear it down." I looked up at the gathering storm. "Or unless it is demolished for us by a sudden event like a lightning strike."

I hurried them down from the high platform to a safer place lower on the Tower. Returning to the bottom of the ladder, I looked upwards, noting the spaces between the rungs got wider and wider near the top. I couldn't imagine how anyone could climb it. Someone tapped me on the shoulder. I turned, and saw a dark figure, the cowl of its hood pulled low over its eyes. I shuddered, knowing it must be the Shade of the Tower.

"You must go down immediately! Don't stay up here, for the Tower that you have built is secure. I am looking after it, to make sure that it stays in place and doesn't get damaged."

"Oh! Well, I was thinking of rebuilding it. I have a new design for a tower, and I intend to demolish it, bit by bit, and reconstruct it."

The Shade was not pleased. "No, leave it the way it is. It is fine, and it will see you through. After all, Belvedere is here, and he thinks he built it. Don't embarrass him."

"I disagree. I'm trying to get rid of Belvedere. I don't need him as much as I did. I'll build another tower, whether you like it or not!"

The Shade made a lunge towards me, but I stepped to one side, and he fell over the edge of that level. I didn't bother to look, for I felt he had probably perished. Instead, I narrowed my eyes at a slight movement in the increasing deluge. There was someone up the ladder, perching on the third rung uncertainly. The storm swept around me and a blast of hail struck me hard, soaking me. I dashed the ice from my eyes and looked again. There was a figure up there, who peered down at me silently, possessing a very large face crowned with a shock of curly red hair that whipped soaked fronds across it in the violence of the gale. I saw he was wearing a drenched purple suit with a lace collar and cuffs, and filthy buckled black shoes, It was the dirty shoes that finally made me wince. I knew that figure. Clinging to the ladder above me was my Ego, Belvedere. The thunder crashed right overhead, but I dared not flinch.

I yelled above the storm. "Come down here! I know who you are. Belvedere! What are you doing up there?" The wind whipped around me as I clung to the bottom of the ladder. I had to get him down – the rungs were too far apart for him to climb any further, and he might fall and be lost to me.

He shouted down to me. "I'm not coming down. This is my Tower! I've spent years helping you to build it. I want to climb to the top." He began to take another step up, but fortunately the rung was too high, and he split his satin trousers. This was very embarrassing for him, and he hastily came down, looking abashed and holding his torn pants.

"I told you that you can't climb that ladder. Now, I have to insist that you go down to the plain, because I fear that this Tower may shortly be demolished." I took his arm, looking up at him as the rain streamed down my face. "Go now. For once, do my bidding – you will not regret it."

He turned mutely and began to lumber down the steps, sniffling to himself. I waited until he reached the bottom. This was my trial – I had to demolish my Tower alone, and if I fell with it, I would meet death as bravely as I could, but my Ego, who fancied he had built it, must be saved for future use if I survived.

The storm grew worse. I let go of the ladder for fear it would act as a lightning rod. The Tower shuddered as the gusts of wind grew stronger, and I felt myself sliding on the wet concrete. I clung to an outcropping block, but as I did so, a terrifying blast of fire seared the far side of the Tower, accompanied by a tremendous clap of thunder, and below me, concrete blocks exploded out of the building like an avalanche and fell rumbling to the plain below. The entire top of the Tower tilted to one side as it collapsed and my feet slid out from under me. I lost my handhold and fell, turning over and over, with the crash of the ruptured Tower pounding in my ears.

I woke to utter darkness, my mouth full of dust. I couldn't move, as my right leg was pinned under a large object, and struggle as I might, I was unable to free it. It felt numb. Reaching down was extremely difficult and painful, and I soon understood that my left forearm was broken, for it flopped uselessly when I tried to move it. I was lying on my left side, with my left leg folded under me, but free, and I could just move my head. All around me dust still rose from the fallen concrete blocks, some of which had been blown to pieces by the blast. My hair and face were covered with debris, and I attempted to spit some of the dry flakes out of my mouth, which told me I was facing downwards. There was absolute silence except for a faint moan coming from somewhere under the rubble. I couldn't place it, and I didn't know how deeply I was buried myself. With the force of the storm overhead, water was trickling down between the blocks, so I was able to wet my dry mouth and drink a little. I gathered my strength and began to yell.

"Is anybody there! Hello! Help! HELP! Please help me! Hello! HELLO!" Then I stopped to listen. I kept up my appeals for several hours, taking sips of water in between. The pain from my broken arm was intense, but I was more alarmed by my right leg, which had no feeling at all. There was nothing I could do, and I began to think I might die there. It would serve me right! I had deliberately stayed at the top of the Tower, when I could have saved myself when I saw the storm coming. I didn't really expect the Tower to be struck by lightning – I had, instead, planned to begin taking it apart block by block, so that I could control the rate of demolition myself from the top.

I don't know to this day how I survived the fall, but eventually I heard scrabbling overhead and voices arguing. "No! Letsh's move thish one first, otherwis' that one will schlide over thish way and block ush."

"You - fool! Tha' one ish balanched on the edge of thish one, 'n if we move th' one over there, it'll fall on ush." Between the raised voices, I heard the clink of bottles striking the rubble.

"Over here! Help me! I'm under here!" I kept up a running commentary. They were gradually digging down to me. Two or three hours passed – I had lost track of time – until a chink of light shone above me which rapidly got wider, and Festerbashs' head appeared in the hole.

"Ole! There you 're! Sschtill alive, then? Thatsh's good." I could see him taking a quick swig from a beer bottle before he again bent to the task of freeing me. They cleared enough space to get down to me, and then unpinned my leg and splinted my arm with a piece of wood. I screamed loudly as they dragged me out of my prison. Realizing I was lucky to be alive after the top of the Tower was blown off by the lightning strike, I asked after Fight and Flight. They had perished in the wreckage, along with some tourists who had been visiting the Tower to gain a view over the surrounding countryside, when the entire building collapsed on top of itself

Festerbash was my hero. I thanked him for saving me as I lay on a rough litter they made. Three burly men who looked like construction workers gathered around me and shook my good hand. They seemed rather drunk, so I asked Festerbash where he had been.

He shuffled his feet in the dust and looked sideways. "Climbin' th' Tower wash too hard. I deshided to stay 'n wait for you at th' bottom. Then thesh guys invited m' over for a beer, sho we had a few drinkshs and start' partyin'. Over there." He pointed to a large walled pen in which several boars were milling around, snorting. "They're buildin' a new 'unting lodge for th' King of Pentaclesh. I'm afrai' we got quite drunksh. I was sh-shocked when the Tower was schtruck. I thoug' you wash a goner, for shure." Here he took another swig of beer and wiped his mouth with his sleeve.

For once, I was glad he had decided to party instead of staying with me. Now, we had to find out more about my injuries, and whether my right leg was seriously damaged, before we could proceed, for the rebuilding, I felt, must start immediately and I was full of new ideas for the design of my new Tower.

"Not so fast, my friends!" An old, cracked voice sounded near us. "Before any of you can begin to build, you must clear away the debris. Every sign of the old Tower must go, and you should be left with a flat plain, clear of rubble, and uncontaminated. I will take the Navigator to my hut and tend to these wounds. Start work now – here are four wheelbarrows. The wreckage can be dumped over there." My Guide, for it was he, pointed to a large crevasse in the plain about a hundred yards away.

"Wait a minute!" I cried, raising myself on one elbow. "The black omphalos is somewhere in that rubble. I must find it." I attempted to get up, but my right leg was too weak, and I sank back. "Festerbash! Would you look for the omphalos while you're clearing the debris? It must be in there somewhere."

Festerbash gave a mock curtsey. "Of coursh. I'm shure we c'n find it. I'll bring it t' you when we do." He pushed his wheelbarrow tentatively over to the mountain of debris and began shoveling the broken blocks into it, moving backward and forward in a measured but unnatural rhythm. My Guide directed the workers to carry my litter into his shimmering grey hut, which had appeared from nowhere. One of them scratched his ear. "I don't remember that being here a minute ago. Where did it come from?"

I was in no mood to answer questions, as the old man, who seemed to have inhaled some dust, for he was coughing, settled me on a bunk at the back of the hut and checked the splint on my forearm, which he seemed to find satisfactory. "A clean break, I think, and the bone has not surfaced through the skin. That is your sword arm, so it will take a while to be strong again. Now, let's look at your leg."

He examined my right leg thoroughly, pressing down in various places, and finally taking a pin and prodding my foot with it, at which I winced. "Ah! Good! You can feel something. Your leg was numbed by the weight of the block on top of it. I believe the nerves will gradually recover. I will brew some herbs and poultice it. Then, give it a few days, and you should be able to walk again." He got up and threw a handful of dried herbs from a leather bag into a pot on the fire.

The working party, with a sobered Festerbash in charge, took three weeks to clear the rubble of the Tower. They found the omphalos at the very bottom, dusted it off and carefully brought it to me in the hut. I pressed the heavy stone to my center fervidly, feeling the sunny warmth of it. I had thought it was black, but when I gazed at it, I could discern flecks of gold in the material that became more numerous as I fondled it. Within a few moments, it had turned to a bright golden color, and almost all the black had disappeared. I lay back contentedly, the stone on my stomach, feeling every restraint leaving my conscious mind. I was floating, far away – in one hand holding a sieve, through which I was pouring my own essence, and I knew I must keep the specks of gold that were left behind. I relaxed and drifted with the currents of air which puffed gently around me as I separated myself.

Festerbash and his crew swept the area where the Tower had been, removing all traces of the foundations, and the dust settled as if the building had never existed. The next day I sat in front of the hut, the flat, level plain stretching in front of me. The construction workers went back to their job of building King Compos' hunting lodge, but one day the gate to the boars' enclosure was mistakenly left open, and a number of them escaped. They trotted off in all directions, and we only caught one, that had somehow managed to get his leg caught in a crown.

We held him down while we removed the crown. It was a tawdry looking thing as I twirled it in my hand – made of some sort of cheap metal and with fake jewels in it. I took it over to the old fellow to ask him about it.

"I wonder where this came from. Somebody must have dropped it. I know it doesn't belong to King Compos. Are there some other Kings around here?"

"That is the crown that fell from Belvederes' head when he ran away – in that direction." My Guide pointed towards the south. "He seemed very upset when I saw him. Of course, he was under the impression the Tower belonged to him. After all, he had mainly built it for you. When you sent him away, he began to realize that his control over you was slipping, and that may be why he looked so distraught. I hope he won't cause trouble in the future, as he needs to know his place."

I knotted my brows. "It's true, I sent him down to the ground, and he obeyed me. I've been having a lot of trouble with him, though I think he is learning respect. The Tower was struck by lightning very suddenly. I had planned to dismantle it myself. I knew I had to change some ways of thinking that had harmed others in the past. I want to build a new Tower now. Can we get started soon?"

"Hold your horses! Before you begin a new Tower, consider this." He looked at me with a long stare. "First, you must experience the emptiness of the plain without a Tower. Then you have to ask yourself, do you really need a Tower at all now that you have separated yourself from it?"

"Well, I had naturally assumed that I couldn't operate successfully without one. How would I manage without my usual defenses?"

"Why, you would remain on the open plain without preconceived ideas and suspicions. After all, how many of those concrete blocks were of any real value? They merely stopped you from seeing life through other peoples' eyes, and when they tried to explain their point of view, your Tower made it sound like a foreign language. It was impossible to communicate with them at any depth, for most people live on the surface of their own Towers, and many forget why they built blocks lower down, because they are focusing on relentless construction at the top." He smiled a little. "No, the whole thing has to come down at once, and there is nothing better than a sudden shock to achieve that, as we have seen."

"So you feel that I should carry on across the plain on the Path of the Tower, without raising another building." I pondered as I walked up and down exercising my right leg, which had almost returned to normal. "I'll do that, then. A few more days should see my sword arm healed. I'll take my sword of willpower and journey with that alone. Should I take Festerbash with me? And where is Krackenwergle? I haven't seen him for weeks."

"Krackenwergle is his own master, you know. He is on a good path, and will always come and go. He has great knowledge, although he does not always use it for the best purposes and it is hidden from you. As for Festerbash, he has worked hard, for once, and deserves a rest. I'm sure you will see him again at the next party!"

My wounds from the collapse of the Tower finally healed under my Guides' expert care, and I had completed the process of separation that would take me through the seven paths surrounding the Island of Tiphareth. I would only be able to enter Tiphareth after finishing these paths, and they were long and intricate. I left my Guide sadly as I set off, for the more time I spent with the old man, the more I longed to stay with him for ever, but that was not yet possible, as he explained gently. I shouldered a small pack of food and thanked the old fellow profoundly, for the respite with him had renewed my determination to complete the Way of Return. Setting off across the plain of black sand, I left myself completely open to new experiences, without making any preconceived plans.

Path of SUSPENSION - Dissolution

I walked for several days across the empty plain where the Tower previously stood, devoid of either human construction or animal life, and reached a bleak shore on the fourth morning. There I knew a long passage lay between the Tower and the Path of Suspension to the east, but I needed the ketch, for there was no road joining the two. Pompeybou had become very worried, for I had been missing a considerable time while my wounds healed. He had anchored the boat nearby in a deep and narrow cleft in some rocks, rowing lines ashore with the dinghy. I was able to reach him on my cell phone, and soon the ketch hove into view to pick me up. We were to set our course due south towards the Path of Suspension, and after the debacle with the drunkards, Krackenwergle and Festerbash, we decided the two of us could handle the ketch alone, rather than take on crew that might prove to be more of a burden than a help.

My sevenfold travels had begun in the Path of Art with my calcination, and my next step had been the Path of the Tower, where I achieved separation It was a long passage to the east across the Mystic SEA, passing Tiphareth on our starboard side and crossing two other Paths on the way. We sailed for several days on the same course, with the weather becoming increasingly sunny and bright. As we drew abeam of the Island of Tiphareth, I could see it shining in the distance, its high golden pinnacles just visible across the horizon. We were forbidden to stop there, but had to press on, having plenty of stores on board, and taking four hour watch-on-watch alternately. I made a mental note to try to buy a self-steering vane at our next stop, which would relieve us of helming all the time.

The wind started to pick up as we left Tiphareth astern, and veered around to head us. We shortened sail and began to tack, as the gale became stronger and more violent, heeling us well over, so that the lee rail was awash. We decided to reef, and later that evening, put in a second reef and doused the mizzen and jib, raising a storm jib instead. The gusts were hot, as if coming from a boiling cauldron, and the air steamy. We sighted the Path of Suspension after two days of hard sailing and pulled in to a very small island with a willow tree, to which we moored the boat after putting out a stern anchor.

Suspension was a watery path, and the island the only land visible, while to the southeast we could see the red flickering light of Geburah, the Island ruled over by Mars. I shrank from the thought of that visit, and hoped that I would do well when I reached Geburah after passing the remaining five alchemical processes. Surrounding the little island where we had moored, the water was calm, and reflected the reddish sky, while white lotuses floated on the surface and huge dragonflies flitted to-and-fro. I was surprised to see a couple of loons, thinking them to be a northern bird and more acclimatized to cool waters.

The loons were diving for fish, bobbing up alternately and uttering their mournful cries. Close to the island, two yellow poles stuck out of the water, joined together by a thin cable. There was something attached to this cable, so I took the dinghy across to have a look. In the center of the cable a loop disappeared under the water, but, to my surprise, there was a foot suspended in it. I gazed into the water and saw a green man, hanging by his foot from the cable, wearing a pair of tight swim trunks. He had an underwater lamp on his head that shone directly on a large open oyster on the shallow sea bed below him, revealing a large pearl. He was desperately trying to reach the pearl, and grabbed for it repeatedly, but each time he stretched out his hand, the oyster shrank back mysteriously. I soon saw why. Two little seahorses had their tails wrapped around the oyster, as if in protection, and they were obviously controlling it, tweaking it this way and that to frustrate the diver on purpose.

I rowed back to the ketch, and Pompeybou broke out a couple of beers. It wasn't exactly clear what I was supposed to do here, so I waited patiently for the diver to surface. He must have extraordinary lungs, I thought, for he had been underwater for a long time, and I hadn't noticed any bubbles coming from his mouth. I wondered if he had some sort of hidden breathing apparatus.

After a long while, two arms came out of the water and grasped the cable as he pulled himself up, untied his foot, and swam to the little island, hauling himself out on shore close beside the boat. We looked down from the deck and offered him a beer.

"Thanks, but I only drink nectar. I am a God, you see, and my name is Osiris. I am the green man, who heralds the return of spring. But, what is spring without the floods of winter?" He raised his weed-filled eyebrows and sighed. "It's all about water, you know. I wish Isis was around, but she is busy sailing her copper boat across the sky in the Path of the Star. While I await her, I am trying to reach the pearl of existence, but the hippocampii are keeping the pearl away from me, cheating me."

"Who are the hippocampii? Why are they guarding the pearl?" I questioned as I knocked back my fifth beer. Pompeybou had gone below to sleep it off.

"They are seahorses, but also parts of the brain and there they guard the precious things that lie at the heart of the brain. Heart of the brain…. Sounds silly, doesn't it? But that's where the treasure is." He trailed off, looking morose.

"Maybe I can help you get the pearl. I did manage to get two other pearls that were masquerading as crocodiles' eyes. They wept tears when they lost them, I can tell you." I gave a swift snort of laughter. "Yes, I am a pearl gatherer myself."

"Well, that's good." Osiris was pleased. "How long can you breathe underwater? We may have to go far to find the pearl, for the seahorses have made off with it again."

I hesitated. "I'm not that good underwater – I can hold my breath maybe for a minute - unless, of course, you could manage to bewitch me. When I am out of my senses I can last quite a long time."

"It might be worth trying." He said. "Come, let's dive together. I can do a quick bewitching, as I'm a God, you recall. With a companion, I will be more grounded, which is hard for a God anyway. I won't have to hang from the cable, either, and that will give me a lot more scope."

We dived together into the cool water. At only ten feet we were swimming close to the sandy bottom until we reached a ledge where the sea floor plunged downwards, vanishing into dark space while swirling currents rushed by us.

I opened my mouth to remind him. "You..uu haven't bewitch....uggeh ! I protested, but he dragged me down swiftly. I had to take a great gulp of water, and my head spun as I gasped for air. Breaking away from his clutches, I quickly surfaced and coughed up the liquid I had swallowed. I thrashed around on the surface for a bit, and then took a breath and made a shallow dive. I couldn't see Osiris anywhere, so I floated along to the edge of the cliff, where I saw some disturbance in the water below.

To my horror, Osiris was engaged in an underwater battle with a very large lamprey that had wound itself around his body. The lamprey had its head in his groin. Osiris jerked back suddenly, as lood spouted from between his legs. The lamprey had something in its mouth. Oh, My God! It was his penis! He held his groin and swam slowly back to shore, trailing blood. I hoped there were no sharks around as I swam back and helped him out of the water.

"Lie down here, my friend. I will stanch the blood flow. You have lost an important part of yourself. I should have been with you, but you forgot to bewitch me and I ran out of air. Now we need to find your missing part." I called mournfully to the two loons, and they paddled over. "Can you catch lampreys? Being very primitive, they don't swim that fast."

The loons nodded. They both dove into the water and swam off at great speed. Within a few moments, they returned with a lamprey, which they tossed onto the shore. I picked it up. The animal had Osiris' penis in his mouth, and was sucking on it, draining the blood. It gave me a sly look. I was shocked! At this rate, the penis might be ineffectual in the future, thus meaning that Isis would be disappointed and Horus would never be born. I shook the lamprey, and it reluctantly dropped the dying phallus.

Osiris picked it up. It was rather flaccid. "Not too good. I can reattach it, however. After all, I am a God and I can replace missing parts of myself." He stuck it back where it belonged, holding it for a moment, and the penis seemed to have some life in it still. The lamprey, meanwhile, looked at me dolefully with his big eyes and sighed. "I've waited for this tasty morsel for

360 million years, and you stole it from me." He whispered, through his sucking teeth. "That is really mean. Put me back in the water, for I have no legs. You are a nasty person and I'll never speak to you again."

"I'm terribly sorry, but we need this penis desperately. It is the channel for a very important God. Maybe you can find another one? I advise something more mundane – if you like penises, maybe one from someone less important, like a serial killer." I threw the lamprey back in the sea without feeling any mercy, and he swam away.

As he was a God, Osiris' wound healed swiftly and we decided to go on another expedition to find the missing oyster. I wanted the pearl as much as he did, although I felt it would not be in my best interests to take it from a God. But, then again, why didn't he have his own pearl? Most Gods did. Maybe he had lost it earlier in life. After all, being torn into 14 pieces was no joke. The two of us set off the next morning. This time Osiris remembered to breathe into my mouth the breath of a God, and I found that I could easily stay underwater for several hours. This saved time, as we could go quite deep without having to return to the surface. He swam fast, and it was hard to keep up, so he towed me behind him on a length of seaweed. We were over the depths and getting deeper, until we hit a rising bottom at about 60 feet. We began to see oysters scattered about, some open or half-open, some shut. We tried not to stir up the sand for fear of frightening them. A few of the open oysters we looked at had small pearls in them, but none of a great size. Osiris turned them down. We were looking for large pearls, of course.

We filled a small net bag with about twenty oysters that had good sized pearls in them, and swam back to the island. The oysters were reluctant to open, but we coaxed them with tidbits, and extracted the pearls, putting them in a bowl from the boats' galley. Osiris tested each pearl, gently nibbling it with his teeth, but from each one, little flakes began to fall, and he threw it away in disgust.

"These are fake! They aren't even cultured pearls, but plastic Chinese replicas! We must get some more oysters and try again." We took the oysters back to their spawning ground, where they bid us an ungrateful goodbye, being annoyed at losing their pearls. But we told them that they had been fooled, and that they had to learn to grow their own pearls, for someone was coming by and persuading them that the fake pearls were real, and they could nurse them cheaply and without effort. I suspected that it might be the Shade of Suspension, and I wondered if I would meet up with it before long.

We continued in this manner, selecting the biggest oysters with pearls, and testing them, but not one was real. Osiris became very distressed. "I had always heard that there was only one pearl – the Pearl of Great Price – but I did not believe the sages. Now I know it to be true – there is only one real pearl out there, and maybe it isn't even here, but I think it might be near the Island of Binah, for they cultivate fine pearls there."

"I can't go to Binah yet." I explained sadly, for I liked him. "I'm on the sevenfold path, and must complete it before I can travel to these distant islands. This Path is where I must learn to dissolve myself, and if you can explain that, I would be grateful."

"I'm afraid I don't know anything about dissolution. I am already dissolved, you might say, and I can't remember how I did it. I wish you luck, but I am going to leave for Binah now. Thanks for your help and I'm sure we will meet again." He lowered his headlamp and swam away from the island in a southeasterly direction.

I returned to the ketch, where Pompeybou broke out a couple of beers. As we drank, we discussed the Path of Suspension. It did not seem very interesting, and it was all underwater, which was a distinct disadvantage. Maybe it was time to leave, although it would be shortening the Path. But, as I pointed out to him, I was supposed to be processing dissolution here. I didn't know where to begin and there was no-one left to instruct me. Losing faith, and becoming impatient, we decided to press on to the next Path. I untied the ketch from the willow tree and jumped on board, while Pompeybou was pulling in the stern anchor. The chain came in steadily until it was directly under us, and then it snagged on something underwater, maybe a rock. This was really annoying. We pulled and pulled, reversing the boat, paying out more chain, and heading her forward to try and clear the obstacle, but nothing worked. I would have to dive down and see what the problem was, but this time I used my scuba tanks, as Osiris had gone, and I needed air to breathe.

Rolling backwards into the water, holding my mask and ventilator steady, I paddled swiftly downwards. I reached the bottom at about twenty feet and could see the anchor chain pulled taut. Our anchor had snagged, and was stuck under a large monolith that stood upright at the bottom of the sea. The stone was intricately made and about six feet tall, and consisted of a hollow frame in which an anchor hung, with a triangle attached to the bottom of it. The top of the anchor resembled a beautifully carved Egyptian ankh.

I tried to free the chain, but somehow our anchor was solidly embedded under the monolith. The only way we could free ourselves was to cut the chain, leaving our valuable anchor behind, or try to raise the monolith, in which case we could leave it on the island. I swam back to the boat and we swung the boom around and took a block with several purchases of rope down to the monolith, where I hooked it onto a convenient eye at the top of the structure. Back on board, I removed my scuba gear and we both began to winch in the line. It came in surprisingly easily, and soon we saw the top of the monolith rising above the water. We swung the boat around, letting out some more chain, and hauled the boom over with the monolith swinging from it. Leaping on shore, I directed the stone to the center of the island, and then signaled Pombeybou to lower it onto firm ground.

At the very moment the great stone touched the ground, the sea behind us began to churn, and a whirlpool appeared that swung the ketch around abruptly. It was fortunate that our anchor was still holding ground, for the whirlpool grew bigger and bigger, until we could see down into it to the sea floor, and a small trapdoor opened in the sandy bottom, revealing two seahorses on either side of it, beckoning to us. This was very surprising, and we looked at each other. We had drunk quite a few beers, and that gave us the reckless courage to descend towards the trap door, to see what was there.

We jumped into the center of the whirlpool and landed by the trapdoor. The two seahorses bent towards us, ushering us through the door, where we entered a large underwater hall filled with hundreds of rainbow colored seahorses, and they were dancing in a long chain, each one hooked to the other by its curving tail. A strange melody pervaded the hall, which was hung with draped loops of seaweed that glittered in a flickering turquoise light. On the far side of this hall, another door hung open to a darker passageway. The music stirred us, and the seahorses invited us to join the chain, so we hooked our fingers into their tails and danced along with them. The chain wound around the hall and then began rolling into the passageway beyond, and we followed it. The path wound in and out, and the dance drifted along, until we came to the bottom of a pool with a white, sandy floor. Here the seahorses left us alone. We continued to float along a narrow passage lined with beautiful rock formations – draperies, stalactites, soda straws, columns, all there – and amongst these marvels danced thousands of tiny bubbles, forming a multicolored pattern that was quite entrancing.

A short while later the passage opened up into a stunning underwater palace – but my heart began to thump in my chest as I recognized with dismay where we were. I let go of Pompeybou's hand quickly and urged him to return to the surface, for we were in grave danger. I had seen the throne of Anahita in the center of this palace, and she was my enemy, for she had devoured the toad Oojo in front of my eyes, and had laid his skin beside me.

Pompeybou, being obedient as all true sailors are, made for the surface of the pool without further delay, leaving me facing the opalescent water goddess Anahita, who narrowed her eyes and clasped me to her damp breast. "So, you are here! Come to steal the Mask, are you? Don't worry, I have it well hidden. You will never find it." She fixed me with a liquid gaze. However, there is one way that you can obtain the Mask, which I would then give freely, for I know the Prince lies enchanted, and his spell cannot be broken without it." She paused, looking deeply into my eyes, but I turned from her.

"You murdered Oojo, my toad!" I exploded in horror. "You made him into a stew and ate him. I can never forgive you for that, and I don't trust you." I was shaking with emotion.

"You do not understand." She said gently. "Oojo was under a curse, and although he sometimes seemed to be helpful, he could not shake free from the evil that surrounded him. It was only by making the supreme sacrifice that he knew he would be free. When he jumped into my pool and swam down to steal the Mask, he was aware that he would not succeed. However, he was willing to give himself up to me, and he knew that to lift the curse, I would be forced to eat him." Anahita looked wistful. "I didn't want to, but I had to, and I had to pretend to you that I was doing it from evil motives, so that you would blame me."

"You mean that he willingly let himself be immolated? I didn't realize that he was so brave and good." I began to cry, the tears mixing with the fresh water around my face so that it became quite salty.

"He is free now. You must not worry about him anymore. It is good that you are sad, for I can now help you with your dissolution process. Remember, I told you to take on the Optimistic Attitude, didn't I?" She led me to a couch in the corner of the great palace. "Lie down here, for the dissolution is exhausting. It is easier to go through it underwater."

Anahita brought out a large mirror and instructed me to look into it. I saw my tearful reflection, which made me sadder than ever. I saw in the mirror all the parts of myself that I had rejected, all the sadness I had repressed; all the buried feelings I had failed to acknowledge. I gazed at my drooping, convulsed mouth, and the floodgates opened in me, releasing a load of pent up inhibitions and prejudices against those that I felt had harmed me. After a while, Anahita lowered the mirror and gently laid me back on the cushions, where I immediately dropped to sleep.

I dreamed that the Shade of Suspension came to me, and told me to hang on to my feelings, for if I let go of them, I wouldn't be able to survive in the mundane world. It told me that I would find my thoughts of revenge and vindication very useful, but I did not agree with that.

When I awoke, Anahita was floating by the couch, and in her hand was the Mask, which she offered to me. I was astonished. "The Mask! You said I could never have it! Why are you giving it to me now?"

"You remember I said there was only one way you could achieve the Mask? Well, that was by experiencing dissolution. You have now been through that, and vanquished the Shade. If you focus for a moment, I think you will find that you have moved beyond the notions of past pain that were embedded in your Soul, and you are released from that illusion." She pressed the Mask into my hands. "Go now, and take this Mask on your travels until you come to the sepulcher where the Prince lies, and place it on his face, and he will wake. He lies in the gyroscopic clock in the Path of Fortune, and you will reach that Path before too long."

I thanked her profusely, and swam to the top of the pool, where I pulled myself out of the water to find faithful Pompeybou sitting waiting there. We were on the little island with the monolith, and the ketch bobbed gently on the sea nearby.

"Time to move on, I feel." I jumped onto the boat and carefully placed the Mask in a hidden locker in the focs'le, then went on deck and set the genoa jib. Pompeybou pulled up the anchor, which was now free, but to our surprise the boat remained in position and the jib backed, causing her to swing around rapidly and ground on the island.

What had gone wrong? I soon found out when I saw the length of line that was made fast to a stern cleat on deck, and at the other end was Belvedere, who had tied the line to the monolith.

"What are you up to now?" I said, gruffly. "That was a stupid thing to do. The boat has gone aground. Fortunately, it is soft sand. Now, let go that line and help us by pushing her off."

"No, I won't." Belvedere sneered. "I think we should take the monolith with us. I can load it onto the foredeck. It looks as if it might be worth something in the Atlantis museum."

"How dare you defy me!" I shrieked. "Neither you nor that useless monolith is coming on board. The ketch would sink under it." I jumped off the boat and strode over to him. This time I lost my temper completely and punched him in the stomach. He gave a short gasp and sat down, then began to cry.

"You aren't going to leave me behind again, are you?" He wiped his nose on his sleeve. "Why, for years you have relied on me, even though at first you didn't realize the influence I had over you. Just lately you have been acting strange. I can't understand it. You aren't trying to get rid of me, are you?" He burst into another fit of sobbing.

Irritated beyond measure, I answered him abruptly. "That is exactly it. I don't want you any more. You have blinded me to the real world and created an illusion that you called "reality", and it wasn't true. Now I have seen a glimpse of a different reality, and that's what I'm aiming for. I want you out of my life." I shot out one final blow. "You are not welcome around me any more."

With that, I loosed the line Belvedere had tied, pushed off the ketch and jumped aboard, while he sat alone by the monolith, his head in his arms, silent. Brushing aside any feelings of guilt, I focused on our next stop, which would be the Path of the Lovers, a path I had been anticipating, due west of us. We would again skirt the Island of Tiphareth and pass over three other Paths to reach the Lovers.

There was a gentle breeze from the south, so we set off with the wind on our port quarter and the sails pulling well across the Mystic SEA to our next destination.

Path of the LOVERS - Conjunction

The weather proved calm and misty, with the ketch slipping quietly through the water at about three knots on a close reach. After four days, we could see a faint line of very high mountains in the distance, and as we drew nearer, the entrance to a large fjord. We ghosted in, surrounded on all sides by sheer cliffs thousands of feet high. The buildings of a small port appeared to our left, and we looked forward to replenishing our stores, but as we drew closer, we found that the harbor had been abandoned, and the whole town lay in desolation. There was no sign of anyone.

We tied up to a broken down dock and walked into the town. A pale light shone through the morning mist that rose from the fjord. The population had left very recently and abruptly, for shop doors were swinging open; donkeys and their carts wandered about; fishing boats had not finished unloading their catch; and meals lay on restaurant tables on the sidewalk, the chairs scattered, as if a sudden disaster had occurred. A number of discarded helmets were upside down in the streets, and several turtles wandered to-and-fro. Behind the ruined town, the furthest houses were overshadowed by a vertical cliff wall, but we could see no sign of any rock fall. We walked back to the harbor thoughtfully. What could have occurred to scare everyone away from the little port?

We soon found out as we sat on a bench overlooking the harbor. A vast ripple in the water began out in the fjord, about a mile from us, and something under the water began to move in our direction. Curious, we watched tensely as the top of a large, jellylike head passed through the entrance to the port, trailing a tremendous wave of water behind it. It stopped below us, at the foot of the harbor wall, and began to rise out of the water. Two octopus-like arms reached out and grasped the jetty in front of us as the thing pulled itself up slowly.

"Quick!" I grabbed Pompeybou and ran with him away from the jetty as the hideous head rose up and a mouth full of sharp teeth snapped at us. "It's a Medusa! They're extremely poisonous, and I've never seen such a big one." I was shaking all over as we hid around the corner of a ruined building. "That must be what has frightened the townsfolk. They have fled into the hills."

By this time, the monster had climbed over the jetty and was heading towards us rather like a large spider, moving each of its eight tentacles alternately and making rapid progress. We did not hesitate, but ran to the cliff wall, and found a narrow set of steps cut into the rock that led upwards, which we began to climb feverishly. Glancing back, we saw that the Medusa had stopped below us and was looking up with a single narrowed eye.

"Don't look at it!" I put my hand in front of Pompeybous' face and pulled him back against the rock wall. "Its glance is deadly. I don't think it can climb up here, though. We escaped just in time. Let's go on and see if we can find someone from the town. "

We climbed upwards until we reached the top of the cliffs, and then set out across rock strewn ground towards a line of high mountains. The port lay far below us, and we saw the frustrated Medusa slipping back into the water and swimming off to the fjord. I caught a movement in the rocks ahead of us, so we hailed the laggard, who stopped and waited for us.

He was an old, stooped fisherman, wearing a rusty helmet and carrying a pet turtle. "Did the Medusa attack again?" He asked breathlessly. "All the townsfolk are evacuating up there."

He pointed to the mountains ahead, and then I saw an amazing sight. Perched on top of a pass through the peaks was a large globe that glittered like crystal in the hazy light. The top of it was an open slot, rather like an astronomical observatory. A thin line of figures was inching toward the pass, zigzagging up the mountainside.

"I can see everyone up there. They're fleeing from the Medusa, aren't they? What's happening here, and why have you abandoned the port?"

"Yes, again they are escaping from the town, and they have had enough of it. This has been going on now for several generations. That's why you see the town in shambles – there is never time to rebuild, for the monster comes back regularly and has caught and eaten several of our best people, including the mayor, and the attorney who ventured to start a lawsuit and got too close." The old man shook his head. "That was no loss, but I don't know what we're going to do. There is only one way to get rid of the Medusa, and that is if the Solar Man and the Lunar Woman can meet and marry, for that union would produce the Genius, and the Medusa cannot face such power."

"Where are the Solar Man and the Lunar Woman? I witnessed their birth, you know, on the Path of the Sun and of the Moon. Are they supposed to be here?"

"They were expected many months ago, but they must have got lost and wandered off to another galaxy. We built the crystal observatory for them to conjunct. It took us seven years, seven months and seven days, and we expected them to arrive when we had finished it. But even with our telescope sweeping the heavens, we see neither the Sun nor the Moon, for the Medusa has extinguished them." He sighed. "Our lavender crops are failing through lack of sunlight and the catch is very poor, for no moon rises to thrill the fishes anymore."

"We'll have to find them, then." I announced firmly. "We'll walk with you to the observatory, and then I can look at your telescope to see if it is correctly focused. That may be the reason you can't see them."

We continued to climb the narrow, winding path towards the observatory, where quite a crowd had now gathered under its walls. We joined the townsfolk, who pushed us towards the front of the crowd where two people were standing on a small stage, making an announcement.

"People of the town! We have come here from far away to officiate at the wedding of the Solar Man and the Lunar Woman. The wedding feast is ready, and the bridal gown hangs in the closet, but our loving couple has not arrived. We are also harassed by the monster Medusa, who will not

leave us alone, although we have asked the heavens to send us some relief."
The woman stepped forward and, with a shock, I recognized Isleta, of the
Four of Wands, and behind her stood her consort Galeno. I quickly went
up to the stage and signaled to them.

Isleta spotted me. "Look, Galeno! It's the Navigator! That's amazing!
Maybe that's the answer to our dilemma, and we can now receive help."
She turned back to me. "I'm so pleased to see you. It's the right moment,
for I'm sure you have the power to resolve our difficulties. Come up on the
stage." She bent down and pulled me up with her. "Here's the answer to
our entreaties! This is our friend the Navigator, who has come in the nick
of time to help us."

I stepped forward and raised my hand in greeting, and the crowd
roared their response, but I spoke gravely. "I don't know whether I can
resolve your issues, but let's look at the telescope in the observatory first to
see if it's focusing properly." I stepped down from the stage and, with a few
people following me, went into the observatory, where the giant telescope
reached upwards to the sky.

The observatory assistant came to meet us. He explained that something
had happened to the mechanism and it was out of focus. He had tried
everything, but could not see a single astronomical body through it, as it
had fogged over. I asked him to take me up the winding spiral stairs to
the top of the instrument, where I peered into it and saw the lens. It was
covered by a large, hunched up figure that sobbed quietly, trapped inside
the telescope, its dirty purple suit in tatters around it. In its arms was a tiny
creature clad in gauzy garments that spread out and obscured the lens. I
stepped down, calling everyone around me.

"I know what the problem is." I explained gently. "There are living
objects in the telescope that are hiding there and covering the lens. I'm
pretty sure who they are." Here I paused, and an expectant hush ran
through the crowd. "Inside the telescope is my Ego, Belvedere, who has
been dogging me unmercifully. He has kidnapped the Genius and holds
it in his grip, for he doesn't want it to be born. He tried to meddle again
and fix the telescope the way he wants it, and now he is trapped in there
until the wedding takes place."

A murmur ran through the group. "If he is obscuring the lens, how
can we see through it to find the Sun and the Moon? And, if the Sun and
the Moon are not found, the Genius can't be saved!" A hollow gasp went
around the crowd. "That is true. We are caught in a vicious circle, and
nothing can break it!" They began to disperse, some openly weeping, for

they had now lost hope. I had to break this circle, and the first thing to do was to block the harbor so that the Medusa could not get in and terrorize the town. I sent Pompeybou back down with several stout fishermen, and they maneuvered our ketch and several other fishing boats into the harbor mouth to defend it. They were not to shoot the monster, and on no account to look it in the face, but they could use sledgehammers to squash its tentacles if it tried to get on any of the boats. At this, the townsfolk began returning to the port with some hope that their problems could be resolved.

I didn't want to disappoint them. I arranged the town athletes into pairs, and put them to sculling up and down the fjord. At the first sign of a ripple, they were to pour perfume into the water around the Medusa. The strong liquid would temporarily blind it, so that it would retire to its lair under the cliffs at the other end of the fjord. This would buy us some time. Now there had to be a way to lure Belvedere to give up his hold on the Genius and come out of the telescope, and I thought I knew how to do it. I called the assistant and explained to him that we must reverse the telescope.

"But, there is no mechanism to do that." He complained.

"Then we must manhandle it. Get six strong people and begin loosening the holding screws. At my signal, we will lift it, upend it, and replace it in position. Belvedere will fall out of the end, and the lens will be clear."

With a great struggle, we managed to invert the telescope, but Belvedere clung on high up out of our reach, and refused to come down. He was stubbornly declining any enticements. What was worse, since the telescope was now upside down, we only had an enlarged view of the floor of the observatory. I thought again. Maybe the Solar Man and the Lunar Woman could not come until all was prepared. What had we forgotten? Was everything ready for their arrival? There was a magnificent crystal bed in an adjoining stateroom, covered with a diamond studded bedspread and real feather pillows; the feast was prepared in the fridge; the decorations were up; the cake was on the banquet table; the dress hanging in the closet with the jewelry; and a hairdresser and make up artist were in attendance.

Ah! They needed something to sit on for the ceremony. The Man would, of course, sit on the Sun, and the Lady on the Moon. If we could get the Sun to shine, that would solve half the problem. But the Moon should definitely be in a comfortable spot underwater, probably not a full moon, but a nice crescent would be fitting. Of course, this raised the problem of the Medusa, but now that the fjord was being patrolled by the paired rowers in the sculls, I thought we could safely arrange the crescent seat in the harbor itself, and with that in mind, I organized a party to do that.

With the telescope still out of action, I went on board the ketch and fetched a pair of very powerful binoculars. I climbed back to the observatory and looked through them, sweeping the sky. I thought I saw a tiny planet a few million miles away. Could that be the Sun? I looked again. Yes! It was, and it was coming towards me at the speed of light. I quickly lowered the binoculars for fear of being blinded, before the Solar Man landed lightly beside me next to the observatory. He was burning hot, yet I welcomed him warmly, explaining that the marriage feast was ready, and he went to get changed into his red wedding suit.

Now, I had to search for the Lunar Woman. That should be easier, as the Moon was much closer and would not require great magnification. I quickly picked out the Moon as it lay, close to the horizon, shimmering in a pale pink suit. I beckoned and the full Moon came cautiously closer and closer until a smiling and beautiful Lunar Woman alighted close to me. I shook her hand and told her that her attendants were waiting to dress her, and she ran inside joyfully. I followed her into the observatory, to note that Belvedere was still holed up in the telescope. I knew he would probably not come out until the ceremony was completed, but I wondered how I could get the Genius out of his clutches.

The actual ceremony was to take place in the harbor, as it required a great deal of reflection, and then the merry crowd would come back up to the crystal observatory for the reception and the introduction to the marriage bed. The bride and bridegroom floated down to the harbor while I remained up at the pass, guarding Belvedere in case he escaped and meddled with the ceremony. Through the judiciously placed binoculars, I could see the Lunar Woman daintily settling herself in the crescent seat, just underwater. Above her, the Solar Man gazed down into the surface of the water, as he hung upside down from the solar globe. The crowd pressed around the harbor in awe, for this was a splendid sight.

I watched through the binoculars as the Solar Man pressed his face against the surface of the water. Under the water, I could see the Lunar Woman coming up to greet him. He put his hand tentatively on the reflective surface, and she matched his gesture from below. Then their lips met through the gleaming surface, and from each of them a circular sword pierced their breasts, meeting in front of them in a circlet of yellow flowers that floated close by them. They remained thus for some moments, and then I heard a scratching, slithering noise coming from the telescope behind me, and a tiny homunculus clad in gauzy raiment emerged from the telescope, ran outside and took off with a swish of its tail, sweeping rapidly down towards the couple. It was the Genius joining them, alighting inside their circle to greet them, then picking a single yellow flower from the bouquet, which it carried into the air as it took off like a puff of smoke, hovering above them as the married pair became unified.

The townsfolk were delighted. They took the pair and their Genius and ran with them up to the observatory, where the wedding feast was prepared. Everyone sat down and enjoyed the feast, which consisted of several different kinds of paired delicacies, such as ice cream and chocolate syrup, and sausages and mash with gravy that always went together. Afterwards, the couple cut their cake and toasted everyone with champagne.

The moment then came for them to enter the stateroom and lie in the crystal bed. Because they were a very important couple, several people had to remain in the room, to make sure that the marriage was consummated, as in the state of a King and Queen. Before we entered the stateroom, we had to draw straws, to see who would be chosen to accompany them. The straws were ready in a jar on a table next to the door. Isleta was about to pick up the jar, when it was snatched from her by a furtive figure in a long cloak.

She stepped back in surprise. "Who's this? Let go of the straws, if you don't mind."

"No! I won't. I don't want the Solar Man and the Lunar Woman to be together. They are separate beings, and can only rarely see each other at the same time. They should remain like that." It was the Shade of the Lovers speaking. "It would cause a permanent eclipse if they were united, and that would mean everyone on earth would die."

"Well, we don't want to die." I said, trying to calm the Shade. "I think it's important for them to be together. May I offer myself as an alternative? I would be happy to take their place as a separate being."

"Pshaw! That would not work. You are a separate being anyway and you can't fool me. Do you have a lover? I've never seen one." The Shade laughed. "You're alone, aren't you?"

"I do have a lover, but I don't know where that person is. I could go and find them."

"Why don't you do just that? You'll be out of the way, then. I don't want your conjunction either, since you must stay down in the world of duality. How can you expect to make choices if you don't have alternatives?"

"That is true. But I will make a bargain with you. I will go and find my lover. If I succeed, you must allow the Sun and the Moon to unite. We will hold back in exchange, and we promise never to copulate while you're around." I was fishing for an excuse, for I didn't want to give up the excitement of sex with my beloved, however rare it was. I had to get rid of the Shade somehow.

"Why don't you come down to the port with me in a moment?" I suggested blandly. "There's something down there I'd like to show you. It will really turn you on. But you must give back the jar of straws first."

"OK, then. I'll come down. It had better be pretty exciting." The Shade handed back the jar of straws and we left the stateroom. I hoped that some worthwhile people were able to pick the right straws.

Belvedere was still stuck in the telescope, and I wanted to know how he had lost control of the Genius. I looked up the inverted telescope and told him firmly to come out, for the ceremony had been completed without him anyway. He slid down, looking very miserable. "I failed to hang on to the Genius. It bit me hard on my thigh, and I let it go."

"That's OK. It was meant to leave. When the ceremony was complete, it had to be with them." I explained. "But there is another who waits for you, down in the harbor. We are going down there. Why don't you come with us?"

He agreed, and the three of us returned to the port together, leaving the happy crowd to celebrate the conjunction of the Sun and the Moon.

On our arrival, a violent uprising of water took place in the fjord, and everyone gasped and looked out to see what was happening. A tall fountain of water was boiling at the far end of the fjord, and in it, rising to the top, was the Medusa, her dying shrieks and howls echoing from the distant hills as she writhed and twisted, ripping her tentacles to shreds. The crowd stood transfixed then, and saw her give a last frenzied scream before she fell dead into the depths of the fjord. What had killed her, I wondered? Then I realized it must have been the copulation of the Sun and the Moon, which had finally taken place and created the perfect hermaphrodite.

Of course, they didn't now expect any action, since there was only one person there, which was very disappointing to them, as they didn't understand the significance of it, but I was astonished to see a familiar figure step forward from the shadows of the port wall.

It was my poetic entity Bardogian, and with him was my creative entity Fontanova. I wondered what they were doing here, and then remembered that they had wanted to get married themselves. Bardogian came up to me, smoking a joint in one hand, with a grin on his face.

"I'm glad you're here. Me and Fontanova, we've been engaged for a long time. We were too afraid to get married before, but since you have all the trappings for a wedding here, this would be a good time for us to pledge our troth. Can we go up to the observatory and celebrate our wedding? It would be a pity to waste the food. Let's have a party - I've got the munchies!.

The townsfolk, who had been anticipating a wedding, and had been a little perplexed by the amalgamation of the Sun and the Moon, were all in favor of another. , Fontanova was dressed in the wedding gown, and her hair and make up done by the artistes, while Bardogian brushed off his rather dirty hippie jeans and stood waiting at the end of the aisle formed by the crowd. Leaving the Shade to look after Belvedere, I took Fontanovas' hand and gave her away, and Isleta and Galeno, the officiating priests, guided them in their vows. Then the dancing and festivities began, and the townsfolk were celebrating merrily all night until the dawn came. They crowded eagerly around the marriage bed, and the couple gave them an excellent show, but I wandered sadly out to look down from the pass, for I was alone and could not find my lover.

The following day, with the festivities cleared away, I bade goodbye to Bardogian and Fontanova, for they were now pledged as a couple. I was happy with the idea that my poetical self and my creative, artistic self would now work together, and yet there was still something missing from my life, and I knew what it was. I needed my own Conjunction.

I returned to the ketch and helped Pompeybou fend off the bouncing fishing boats and moor her by the jetty. The fishermen were singing and crowding onto their boats, their nets at the ready, and their lugsails set for the fishing grounds, now that the terrible Medusa was dead. I went below and opened the cage of my cricket Joana, and she hopped onto my hand. I stroked her thoughtfully. A telepathic message came to me from the cricket.

"I know that my enemy Oojo died bravely. I'm so sorry for your loss, but I'm rather relieved that I won't be swallowed again. I had to tread on eggshells when he was around. Now, I know why you're sad, and you must cheer up, because I have a message from your friend Pullows, who has just arrived from the Island of Netzach. She gave a magnificent performance there, you know."

"Indeed, I was there to watch her." I thought back to the cricket. "The Netzachians were well satisfied, in more ways than one. But, what is the message that you have received from Pullows?"

The thought came from Joana. "She is on her way up the pass, and she has a friend of yours with her. They are expected there shortly, and they want to meet you up at the observatory."

"Oh, I wonder who her friend is?" I mused. "Maybe it's one of the Netzachians, or the chicken McSmothers."

"No, it's someone that you met at her parlor, many Aeons ago. This person seeks you directly, and has asked Pullows to find you." The cricket looked a little smug. "You'll see."

Well, that was interesting. I set Joana back in her cage and gave her a piece of apple. I didn't like the thought of having to climb all the way back to the observatory, but there was still the telescope to be reverted into its correct position, anyway, and I should do that. I set off on the arduous scramble up the cliff once more, yet my heart was glad, for I dared to hope that the friend who awaited me was the one person I desired.

Arriving at the observatory, the attendant led me inside. Pullows and my friend had not appeared yet, so we set about reversing the telescope and putting it in its right position. I then made sure that the lens was clean and well focused. Placing my eye to the end, I searched the ascent for any sign of the approaching pair. A small fuzzy area caught my eye, which did not seem to fit in with the view, so I concentrated on it as it got bigger. The mist gradually cleared and there was a nursemaid floating down towards us, holding a small child by the hand. They came right up to the front of the telescope and then disappeared suddenly, as if they had been swallowed up by the instrument. I was perplexed.

At this moment, Pullows and my friend arrived. I need hardly say that I was overcome with joy, for it was the tall, dark haired person I had met before, dressed in flowing chiffon and silk robes which partially revealed the body, but hid the gender. This person had a shaved head, except for fore- and earlocks, gentle brown eyes, a lean nose and sensuous mouth. I stepped forward and we joined hands, moving, as if in a dream, towards the crystal bed, where a thick curtain fell behind us.

Our wedding night was then consummated and we were joined forever in conjunction, the nurse later presenting the child to us for our approval. She joked. "He is called Rocky, for he is really a Lesser Stone, you know, and his parents are your soul and your spirit, who nurtured him together, and gave him birth."

Then my partner and I looked into each others eyes without speaking, and we knew what she meant, for he was our genius.

Path of the STAR – Fermentation

❀

My lover and I were anxious to spend time together after so many Aeons apart, so we remained with the townsfolk for a while to celebrate their release from bondage by the Medusa, and to enjoy the freedom we now experienced. We were absolutely equal in masculine and feminine polarities and operated as a single being, our thoughts shared without words and our physical selves bonded without restraint. We were joined in our nuptial celebrations by Isleta and Galeno, who danced the Minuet of the Unicorn for us. Galeno shape-shifted into the animal and Isleta rode on his back around the town, her long hair hiding her bare breasts. Bardogian and Fontanova, who had also married, were now an incredibly creative force together and performed a stage play for us, written by Bardogian and sung in iambic meter with costumes and backdrop envisioned by Fontanova. They still argued affectionately, but the tension between them led to greater innovative efforts.

Now I was finally with my beloved, but I still had to complete my voyage through the Mystic SEA, and the three remaining transformations that surrounded the Island of Tiphareth were my next challenge. We wanted to present ourselves to the Child in Tiphareth completed, and give him our Lesser Stone, so we traveled together as a single being, our love lifting us high in the clouds above that Island, whose brilliant peaks shone below us. We landed safely on the Path of the Star, a shore made up of low, rolling hills. It was dark, and would remain so during my time in the Star, for the night itself would reveal the fire of inspiration I sought.

Standing on the lonely shore as a unified being, I waited until the star Sirius rose above the eastern horizon. Beneath the great star, its twin, Sirius B appeared to dart across the heavens. Its faint light reflected on a green lake, covered with duckweed, while in the distance more gentle hills curved. At my feet grew masses of lilies of the valley, and an empty earthen pot stood close by. The sound of a double flute came faintly through the sweet night air, and a large chestnut colored dog bounded up to me. The dog wore a blue collar with the sign of Mercury dangling from it, and a small saddlecloth with "Godog" embroidered on the side. Following the dog was a tall woman, playing the flute softly, with a headdress symbolic of Hathor. Her eyes were covered, and I wondered why. She must know her way about instinctively, even though her eyes were darkened by the blindfold.

"Who are you?" I ventured to ask. "Is this your dog?"

She lowered the flute for a moment, not seeming surprised, and removed the blindfold. "I am Nepthys, sister of the goddess Isis, and I expect her to arrive here shortly." Nepthys looked down and her dog playfully jumped up for a caress. "This is my pharaoh hound, latest of a long line of Egyptian dogs dedicated to the star Sirius, and his name is Anubis." She looked into the sky, where Sirius blazed bright, as a copper boat bearing the goddess Isis came into view. "Here is my sister, arriving in her boat."

Nepthys lit a censer that she took out of the pot and hung it in a tree nearby. In the dense rising incense, the image of Isis, clad in green draperies, rippled sinuously as if performing a graceful dance in her Egyptian funeral boat. As her copper vessel slowly drifted across the sky, I saw that Isis was pouring a white liquid from a large jar on her shoulder into the lake. Nepthys explained that they used the lake for fermentation, and that the milk would become food for a singular fish that would be brought to the lake. That fish would convert the celestial milk into pure water for a plant that would grow out of the pot beside her.

Fixing my gaze inexorably on the stream of white liquid, I began to move towards the shore of the lake. I stepped out, my intent clear, to drink from the flowing milk. I progressed rapidly over the lake, treading lightly on the green duckweed, and held out my palm. The milk of Hathor, the cow, spilled into my hand, and I drank greedily. Thanking Isis for her gift, I observed that the water was holding up my body, for I had not sunk under the surface. That was curious! I wondered whether I still had any physical weight.

Nepthys began to play quietly again, and the dog Anubis stood listening. The copper boat moved slowly, almost imperceptibly, across the face of the Star, and I became entranced. I gazed at the figure of Isis, and she returned my glance. She had given me sustenance when I was in the grip of the Qliphoth, and I felt my veneration for her course through me. I sank to my knees, my palms uplifted in the gesture of devotion, and bowed my head.

The voice of Isis purred reassuringly. "You seek the moistness, the slippery mouth which leads into the vastness of the depths. This mouth may not speak, for it has become the mouth of a fish." Her voice was low, humming. "Sit down now, relax and slip into meditation. Long ago I told you that I was the Star, and I would wait for you. Trust me and my sister Nepthys to deliver you safely, and remember, I agreed to take your greedy self, Aquirot, to rid you of your material desires. That has been a great godsend to you."

I sensed her copper boat drifting away slightly and I found myself pulled rapidly backwards, as if through a vortex. With my head whirling, I dropped into a seated lotus position on the surface of the water, my hands held lightly, palm upwards, in my lap, with the thumb and forefinger touching. Before my eyes closed, I observed, as if in a dream, the funerary vessel slowly drifting across the sky above me. Behind the boat, Sirius glimmered warmly, and my lids dropped. In the dark redness of my closed eyes, I felt pressure in my forehead as my conscious self slid away and my mind moved out into the cosmos.

I was aware in my deepest self of a long, snakelike column rising from the pot beside the shore, higher and higher, until it stretched far above Nepthys and ended in a rattlesnake head holding a small lamp in its mouth. A brown nightingale flew over, landed on the column, and burst into a sweet song. Entranced, I listened to the bird, and time took wing. The melodious tones chimed repeatedly in my mind, following the song of the bird, its trills and warbles rising through the night in ever increasing vibrations, until I felt I must swoon.

Nepthys put down her double flute, and her voice came vaguely to me through a thick mist from the shore. "Now, gently begin to come back, just very slowly, bring yourself back and open your eyes."

As I blinked and returned to tranquil consciousness, I found myself back on the shore, watching Nepthys as she moved over to an area of thick reeds by the lake. Bending down, she parted the reeds and drew forth a large cradle, woven of rushes, and set it down beside me. From the interior of the cradle, she brought a water pipe, and filled it with the purest hashish, which she lit from a small taper, taking a deep puff. She offered me the tube from the pipe, and I accepted. After I had inhaled, she indicated the cradle.

"Oh! Am I supposed to pass this on to the baby?" I questioned in surprise. Without speaking, Nepthys nodded, so I peered into the dark cradle to find the baby. There was a stirring, and a little figure in a top hat sat up, grabbing eagerly at the tube and sucking deep on the calming smoke. Then the strange baby lowered the tube and handed it to Nepthys. This gave me a chance to take a good look at the little creature. It very much resembled a baby I heard about before – especially with the top hat, for there was only one baby that was dressed like that. I leaned forward and took off the hat – and there were the two horns that had sprouted from Princess Maalis' child after he was born.

"Reficul! I never met you before now, but I know it's you. I'm the person who rescued your mother from the ledge in the Three of Swords, before you were born. I see you still have the pearl necklace your mother gave you. I am wearing the matching bracelet myself." Here I showed the baby my wrist, and he chuckled gleefully, fingering the pearl bracelet.

"See. They are a match. You must have the bracelet." I took off the bracelet and put it on his wrist, which was not so tiny. He gurgled and smiled. I wondered if he was able to speak, and then I knew the answer. I had seen in the American newspapers that at three years old, he had questioned the motives of Prince Amgodovich, who was arrested in Miami for disseminating false doctrines. Reficul had called out from the crowd, wanting proof of what he claimed. The boy was a child genius who wore a top hat, a visitor from the Caucasus and a descendant of an obscure Gnostic hierarchy. I was excited to meet him here on the Path of the Star, although I had little respect for his mother, Princess Maali.

Reficul stood up in the cradle and began to climb out. He was not wearing a harness, so I asked Nepthys if that was all right. She assured me that he was very well behaved, and that he would want to go over to the pot and retrieve his little lamp when the rattlesnake descended again. The snake was already sinking down, curling itself up inside the pot, and the baby politely took the lamp from its mouth, waving it around his head in delight. To my astonishment, he then put the lamp into his mouth, swallowing it, and turned upside down, standing on his head. The budding horns proved to be very useful in this position, as they provided a stable base for his performance.

After a short while, Reficul somersaulted onto his feet again, looking refreshed. "Where is the fish! Do you have the fish? It was in your care last time I saw it, for it chased me out into the lagoon when I was metamorphosed into a black goat. Where is the lungfish?" He cried out.

"Oh! Yes, I have him. What shall I do with him?" I turned out one of my pockets and retrieved the hardened mud ball that contained the hibernating lungfish. There was a small hole at the top of the ball, and I put it to my mouth and softly blew into it to revive him. The ball started to shudder and cracks appeared across its surface, then the mud broke apart, and I held the lungfish in my hands. He looked quite rested, for he had been in his mud ball for a long time.

Reficul took the fish gently, holding him in his little hands, and spoke tenderly to him. "Welcome, my Lord. The censer is lit, the holy smoke burns, and the draught of celestial milk awaits you. The Navigator will carry you into the lake, so that you may receive sustenance from the milk of Isis." He returned the lungfish, who had taken on a greenish glow, to me, and I took him to the shores of the lake and walked out on the water.

Carrying the lungfish tenderly, I was still able to tread on water as I gingerly stepped to the center of the lake where Isis was poised in her boat. I placed the fish carefully on the duckweed, directly under her stream of milk, and he drank eagerly. As he finished, licking his broad lips, his body started to sink below the surface of the weed, and I felt myself sinking at the same time. Soon I was below the surface, the fish in front of me. He opened his moist and gaping mouth and I became mesmerized, forgetting that I was underwater. A long, dark tunnel through his mouth appeared and I dived eagerly into it, following its curved passages. I came out into a large chamber, where the sound of bubbling liquid arose from many vats that stood in neat rows, tended by strange beings that looked like the Shades. I strolled towards one of the vats with an open top. One of the figures was stirring the mixture. I couldn't quite see over the edge of the vat properly, so I asked the attendant, who wore a dark cape, to give me a leg up.

The next moment, I was tumbled over the edge and plunged into the vat, completely submerged. I came up gasping and attempted to grab the top rim of the vat, but it was too high, so I swam around in circles in the bubbling liquid. It was warm and not unpleasant, giving off a scent of lilies of the valley, and shimmered in a greenish yellow glow. A mysterious froth rose to the surface all around me, and I felt myself passing into another state of consciousness, the light pulsating throughout the entire vat, which was a lot bigger than I thought when I first saw it. In fact, the sides of the vat seemed to be getting further and further away as I swam around.

The liquid in which I was suspended sloshed into my mouth as I swam, and I began to swallow it. It tasted good, so I drank some more. Then I felt tired, so I turned onto my back and floated for a while, the frothy liquid bearing me up. Overhead I saw the heavens clashing together in my imagination, and a great battle was being fought. I saw Reficul leap forward, fighting hand to hand with a shrouded foe, then the scene changed, and a white figure was walking, carrying a dead child, and laying the naked child on an altar, where he left it. The form of the child began to melt as I watched, the body disintegrating and the flesh falling from the bones, as a million maggots swarmed over the corpse, destroying any remnants of flesh and leaving only the shining white bones.

This vision was quite upsetting, but I couldn't tear my eyes away. I remained focused on the tiny skeleton, and I thought it moved. Maybe it was just a trick of the atmosphere, which was alternately dimming and brightening in waves. The skeleton child sat up, though, and got off the altar, toddling away from me. I strained my eyes to try and see. Was it Reficul, clothed in flesh again? The vision had gone, leaving me without a clear answer. I turned over and began to swim again, wondering whether it was real or only my imagination.

At last I landed on a fair shore on the other side of the vat, and shook the froth off my tunic. A swinging yellow door in front of me broke the line of a high wall, which I pushed through, revealing a grassy meadow where many peacocks were strutting about. I moved among them, petting first one, and then the other, remarking that the friendly birds were much gentler than those I remembered. Several hens were bunched in front of me, pecking corn, and a large male bird began to raise his tail, showing his wonderful display of colors. I stared at the metallic turquoise, intense blues and purples in his tail that engulfed me, as a myriad of rainbow colors flashed past my eyes. The intensity and speed of the swirling, flashing colors flitted all around me, and I turned this way and that, trying to catch one color, then another, but they darted out of my reach. Then the colors rapidly began to fade, and I found myself facing the lungfish again, suspended underwater in the middle of the lake.

The fish took a last penetrating glance at me and, with a flick of his tail, vanished into the surrounding gloom, leaving me to surface and strike out to shore through the dense weed. It was a long swim, and I wondered why I had lost the power to walk on the water. That ability must have come from the lungfish, which was surely a magical creature. I mentally thanked the crone Ediug again for giving me the fish, and hoped that he had reached his rightful home in the lake at last.

Stumbling onto the shore I collapsed, exhausted. Nepthys was still there, playing her double flute. She lowered it and smiled. "Congratulations on your Fermentation. You did well. Now, remember that, although you are passing through these alchemical processes for the first time, they will repeat themselves over and over again, and you will understand more deeply during their repetitions."

I thanked her profoundly and asked. "Where is Reficul? I thought I saw him, dead, and then he was just a heap of bones. I hope he hasn't met an early death, because I was hoping to ask him some questions."

"He will be back." She assured me.

"I know the Shades only too well, and I made a commitment to fight with each of them when I met them, in the hope of winning. So far, I have fought with four Shades, and have conquered them. But they are insidious, and creep back into my mind constantly, so that I have to pay attention." I went on. "There is one thing I don't understand, Nepthys. Who is Reficul really? I know there is something special about him. He's a genius, isn't he!"

"You will soon see Reficul as he really is. Can you guess?" Nepthys gave a little smile. "The law of Inversion works in powerful ways in the Mystic SEA. Invert his name, and you get – Lucifer!"

"Ah! The Light Bearer, no less. Most people believe that Lucifer is a bad angel. Yet I saw him myself in a vision, fighting with the Shadow. Why do humans condemn him?"

"You will remember that, when Lucifer is the baby Reficul, he is a genius who displays a great understanding of ethics. After all, he brought down the Prince Amgodovich, and revealed him as a false preacher in front of thousands of his followers. He was only three years old at the time. The Prince was disgraced – I expect you have worked out that his name 'Am-God-ovich" indicates that he thought he was divine, like many of these misguided priests. That is a great disgrace to Lucifer, who once knew what it was to be divine, and he knows the Prince could never reach those sublime heights. However, many people believed the Prince, for he set himself up as a great prophet. It was Lucifer's duty to expose him, to save their souls from believing in falsehood." Nepthys paused. "I am the sister and earthly double of Isis, and I have seen the evil perpetrated by many groups on earth who call themselves churches, and who profane the Truth to suit themselves. That is what Lucifer came to earth to eliminate – even though many call him Satan, the Devil, and other names that the church wrongly bestowed upon him."

"I understand what you're saying. Lucifer brought the light of divinity down to earth, and that is what his little lamp is. It is not nearly as powerful as the astral light, but it is a tiny proof of its existence above." I remarked.

"Yes, Lucifer has other names, too. He is Dionysus – the god of spiritual wine, and he is the one they call Jesus, who carries a little lamp - and they call him the Light of the World." She looked sad. "They say history repeats itself, and in your world today, human behavior has not changed one whit for thousands of years. The greedy take advantage of others; the lustful cannot control their urges; the weak have no courage. I ask myself - where will it all end up?" She sighed deeply, but perked up suddenly with a firm order for me. "Well, there is nothing I can do. Now it's time for you to visit the Pup and see what's up."

Nepthys played a shrill and unusual tune on her double flute. It was music I had never heard before, without harmony, rhythm or chords, just a collection of mixed up sounds that were unfamiliar and irritating to my ears. I sat and tried to meditate, looking up at the stars and focusing on the faint Sirius B. A jet of brighter light shot out from this dying star and separated into a trail of sparks, with an object at the head of it coming rapidly closer. Within minutes, a large circular machine was hovering overhead, and a set of steps swiftly came down from the center, landing on the grass in front of me.

From an open vent in the underneath of the craft, three small figures appeared and hopped down towards me. They flickered in a greenish yellow glow, moving in jerky zigzag motions, their long tails whipping out behind them to keep their balance. Then three kangaroo rats stood before me, their great bulbous eyes trained intently on mine and their little arms outstretched in greeting.

"Come, it is time for you to be subjected to the penultimate experience. We are the emissaries of Sirius B, for we have partaken of the Apple of Knowledge that was in the cage of the Memorizer, and we have retained all knowledge. In order for you to understand the Universe, you must be processed."

I rose from my position in one liquid, dreamlike motion and accompanied them up the steps. The dog Anubis followed me as the vent door thudded softly shut behind us, and I felt the acceleration of the craft as it spun away from earth. In minutes we were docked on Sirius B, and they led me up a ramp into a bare room that smelt of embalming perfumes, and laid me, unresisting, on a table.

One of the rats, wearing a long cloak, bent over me, explaining in a sharp, clicking tone. "This is the mummifying chamber. Here you will receive Anubis, who will perform the necessary sacrifice by cutting out your heart, and then you will be wrapped in cloths soaked in coconut milk, and left to dry out for several days. Then we will return to see what is left of you."

I struggled to sit up. This must be a bad dream. The rat was wearing a cloak exactly like the Shades. They were planning to murder me! How could I have allowed myself to be taken in such a compliant manner? It was almost as if I had wanted this, welcomed it. But now it was too late, for they held me down as the dog Anubis, now clad in sumptuous robes, sharpened a gleaming scalpel, a look of amusement on his thin lips.

"No!" My voice rose to a shriek. "I need my heart to survive! Don't do this! I have not finished my journey of discovery. I need to complete the Way of Return. Please, please have mercy. Give me more time, I beg you." I fell back on the table, weak from fear, as Anubis approached me, grinning sardonically.

"You have not used your heart properly. I have seen only twenty-five percent compassion emanating from it during your tests. You have shown arrogance, pretentiousness and an overriding sense of superiority in your dealings with others. Your heart must be removed, and a better one put in its place." Anubis came closer, the scalpel held in one paw, and bent over my chest. I wriggled from side to side, trying to escape the knife and hysterically calling out to Belvedere, my Ego, to save me.

Instantly Belvedere was there, grappling with Anubis, and being very tall, he overpowered the dog at first and wrested the scalpel from him, holding it up for me to see. With the other hand, he had Anubis by the scruff of his neck, yelping miserably. Unfortunately, he let go, and the dog escaped, running into a side room. He returned with a sword, and removed my own sword from its' sheath at my side, handing it to Belvedere.

Striking his sword on the ground and then throwing down a gauntlet, Anubis spoke sternly to Belvedere. "I challenge you to a duel. Prepare and choose your seconds. The winner will have the right to the heart of the Navigator, whether it is for good or ill." He feinted at Belvedere, who stood unmoving in disbelief, as two kangaroo rats volunteered for seconds on each side.

The combatants faced each other, as I lay, propped on my elbows, watching them with keen eyes, my heart thudding at breakneck speed in my breast. Belvedere must win! I felt I could not survive otherwise. I didn't believe Anubis. He had no intention of replacing my heart – probably just meant to kill me and be done with it. Dogs can be hypocritical sometimes and jackals, from whom he was descended, are decidedly tricky.

Anubis circled lightly on his feet, darting and slashing at Belvedere, as he clumsily turned around, swiping with my sword and attempting to deflect the blows. My Ego had the advantage of being much taller, so he could try for a complete skull cleavage if he chose the right moment. The fight went on for some time, for Anubis seemed to be taunting the big fellow, and sweat showed on Belvederes' purple velvet suit. He raised my sword and slashed down with all his might as the dog passed, but Anubis was too quick for him, and caught the blow, riposting with a low lunge that forced his sword into Belvederes' side. A stream of dark blood flowed from the wound and Belvedere dropped my sword, clapping his hand to the wound and sinking to the floor on his knees.

Gasping, he begged Anubis not to deliver the final blow, and swore that he would stand by while the heart surgery was completed, and not attempt to interfere. The rats quickly brought in a small trolley with ER equipment on it and commenced to bind his wound, which was near the liver on his right side. I was fascinated and horrified at the same time, for Anubis had won, and I now knew that I faced certain death with the removal of my heart. I lay back, weak with terror.

Anubis bent over me, his eyes gleaming. "Your Ego cannot defend you at this height on the Tree of Life, he is too big and too weak. You have relied on Belvedere too long, for you are stupid enough to think that survival of your physical body is the most important thing. That is not true." He pressed his nose close to my ear, whispering. "You must have faith, faith that I will replace your heart with a better one. Belvedere must accept this for your spiritual growth. Do not worry. You will not feel a thing. Lie still, now."

I fixed my eyes on the ceiling while Belvedere sobbed quietly in a corner and Anubis murmured a soft prayer. In a flash, the scalpel came down and sliced through my breast bone; Anubis dipped in his paw and pulled out my dripping heart; and severed it neatly from the blood vessels, throwing it into a kidney dish. A kangaroo rat stepped forward with a small cooler, which he opened. Anubis took out a magnificent heart, already beating, and thrust it into my chest, neatly suturing the vessels into position. Passing his paws over me, he muttered a further incantation, and a greenish yellow glow spread upwards from my solar plexus, hovering in the air between us.

"It is done. You may rise now." The dog smiled, showing his white teeth. "You didn't feel a thing, did you?"

I sat up. My new heart was beating with a strong pulse and seemed to fill my chest, like a fluttering bird trying to escape. And yet, I felt a glowing sensation and a great feeling of love for both Anubis and Belvedere. I drew them to me and blessed them fervently. Belvedere fell on his knees, suppliant and thankful, and the rats – or were they Shades? - all gathered around and hugged each other.

"Now it's time for your mummification." They announced, and I saw that they were dipping lengths of linen into a large cauldron of coconut milk. They came towards me and I lay down again. This time, I was confident that I would not be harmed, and I allowed them to bind my limbs tightly in the cloths, winding them round and over very neatly and finishing with a nice reef knot. Then everyone trooped from the room and I lay on the table alone, feeling the drying bonds getting tighter and tighter, until I felt I might suffocate.

I don't know whether I passed out or whether I slept the sleep of exhaustion, but I did not awake for three days, which is what they told me when they came to remove the mummification cloths. As I was unwrapped, I looked down and screamed with horror. There was no flesh on my bones! I was a skeleton. They had removed my flesh with the wrappings and I had also been eviscerated, my organs placed in a large glass jar by the table. I recognized my liver, my stomach and the large beating heart that seemed to be still operating, as if it was inside my body.

What was I to do? I still felt alive, but how could I continue my journey with no flesh or internal organs? Anubis approached the table.

"How are you feeling?" He enquired solicitously. "A little lighter, more ossified, as it were? Don't worry. You have done well. You have proved that you can suffer bodily sacrifice and still have your faith, even through it is a rather unnerving process. Now, rats, I want everything put back, so that the Navigator looks just the same as before, even though profound changes have occurred internally." To me he said. "I will meet you outside, for we will shortly take off for the Path of the Star again, and Nepthys awaits us."

The kangaroo rats bustled around, putting back my internal organs and then draping my missing skin over my body and squeezing it into its proper contours, so that I resumed my original shape. Yet there was no doubt, I felt different, freer, and as if I was walking on air which, of course, was true, since the gas inside the space craft was helium.

Thanking them in a squeaky voice, I joined Anubis and a chastened Belvedere, and we took the ride back to the edge of the green lake, where we were greeted by Nepthys. She called to her graceful dog. "Anubis! Come here, my love. It is time to say farewell to our friend, who has successfully been Fermented. The Navigator will now progress to the Path of Fortune."

The Star had been a pleasant path that had become unpleasant. I was so relieved to get away from the Shades that I was ready to face anything on the Path of Fortune.

Path of FORTUNE – Distllation

S tanding on the shore with Nepthys, her dog Anubis and my somewhat humbled Ego, Belvedere, the sister goddess of Isis gave me some discouraging information that I did not want to hear. Briefly, I was to dig a tunnel under the Mystic SEA in order to reach the Path of Fortune, my next destination. Contact with Tiphareth had to be avoided at all costs, and we had already taken a risk by flying over and past it several times. I could only approach Tiphareth when I had completed the seven alchemical processes. There were still two left - Distillation and Coagulation - and the first of these would take place in the Path of Fortune.

Nepthys disappeared into the woods nearby and returned driving a giant backhoe. I clapped my hands in glee, for I had yearned to handle a big machine like this for years. I jumped up and began operating the controls, while the others watched me break ground in a west-south-west direction. The wound Belvedere had received from Anubis during their duel had not yet healed, but it was important for him to join me in Fortune as soon as he was well enough. He could follow me through once I had finished digging the tunnel, and that would give him a few weeks to recuperate.

Riding the backhoe like a wild mustang, I dug furiously, sinking lower and lower into my tunnel until the others were lost to view in the Star. The damp smell of earth was all around me, and I resolved to dig deeper, making sure that I missed the bottom of the Island of Tiphareth, for I did not want a mining disaster there. I would have been much happier sailing over in my ketch, yet I trusted Pompeybou to follow me and keep a close eye on my travels between beers, making sure the boat was always ready for my needs. Joana the cricket watched the weather in her cage over the chart table and sang happily all day, now that she knew her arch enemy Oojo, the toad, had been eaten.

I knew enough about tunneling to recall that I should shore up the tunnel behind as I dug, but I was in a hurry and did not intend to return the same way, so I merely pushed the loose earth behind the backhoe, with the result that I was working in an enclosed space all the time, the moist earth close around me. Nepthys had given me a long tube that I could extend through the earth above my head, and that allowed enough air to seep through. I slept only when I had to, and ate little, keeping time with the LCD clock on the backhoe. I also still had my underground sonar GPS, which gave me my position at the end of each days digging, and my progress was swift.

When the GPS announced my position directly under Tiphareth, I knew that I was almost half way across. I could faintly hear angelic music coming down from the Island, and longed to stop and dig my way straight up, for I was tired. It would be so easy just to go straight there, to relax in that beautiful land and partake of the pleasures that must await me, but I was afraid the doorkeepers might turn me away, for they would know I had tried to cut my journey short, and I would arrive unprepared. I sighed, withstood the temptation, and dug on.

After three weeks of tunneling, the GPS showed that I was directly under the Path of Fortune, and I began to slant upwards with the backhoe. One day I broke ground and, looking around, heard a fierce struggle going on with grunting and roaring coming from a dark, tarry region nearby. I wished that I hadn't chosen that particular spot,. I got off the backhoe, forgetting to put on the brakes, and the machine slid back into the sink hole I had dug, disappearing under a ton of mud. I was now trapped on the Path of Fortune, and this was not good fortune for me, although it meant that Belvedere could not follow me. Furthermore, two enormous dinosaurs were fighting to the death close by me, both of them sinking into a pitch-like substance from which they could never escape. I recognized the two equal opponents as they battled for supremacy. They were a Triceratops and a Tyrannosaurus Rex, sworn enemies in prehistoric times. I was looking into the distant Past, which was a part of Fortune, and somewhere on the Island must be the foreseeable Future. I did not want to become involved in the dinosaur fight as their shared victim, so I melted quietly away across the stony desert that gave way to high ridges of ancient sand, frozen rock-hard into wave like formations. Climbing over the top of one of these, I found what I was looking for – a row of satellite dishes that were revolving steadily, facing the sky, looking for any sign of life above them. This must be the Future, and between the Past and the Future was the Present, where there should be a rainbow that I could ascend.

Knowing that the end of that rainbow must be somewhere near, I began to search closely for the leprechaun with the pot of gold. He must be dressed in green, and probably have an Irish accent. I stumbled along the top of the ridge, which had several caves bored into the rocks, until I heard a faint, rollicking song borne on the wind. That must be the leprechaun! It was definitely an old Irish ballad, and I made for the sound as fast as I could over the rough ground. Rounding a craggy outcrop, I found the leprechaun dancing in the center of a vast pile of gold coins, more than I could possibly count. I ran down the slope and was about to pick some up and stuff them in my pockets, when I remembered that I had abandoned my greedy self, Aquirot, and allowed Isis to take her away. I was able to resist the temptation, drew myself up and walked stiffly towards the leprechaun, an enigmatic grin on my face. The little fellow wore a bright green outfit with a tiny pointed hat, and his grip was firm, dry and rather rough as he shook my hand.

"And what may you be doing here, my friend?" He chortled as he looked up at me. "It's a long way from Tipperary! You are Irish, by the set of your face."

"Yes, indeed, half Irish. I'm the Navigator, and I'm on a long journey. The Path of Fortune is my next stop. I see that you have amassed quite a fortune here. Is this your hoard?"

"Aye, and I'm still collecting funds. You see, I live under the stock market – Wall Street, it's called, I think. They throw so much money around that some of it gets dropped, and slips through the cracks of the exchange into my domain. There I have my pickings, while above me the foolish chatter of the world economy goes on and on without end." He bent down and picked up some coins. "Would you like some? I have more than enough."

"No, I won't just yet. I recently overcame my desire for money and material goods, and I hope to resist the temptation." I looked askance. "I hope you understand?"

"Well, really, I dinna. Gold is good – why not fill your pockets with it? That's what they do on Wall Street, and the other stock markets, too." He looked a little puzzled.

"I suppose, since I'm on the Path of Fortune, that there must be a partiality towards money here. However, that's not what I'm looking for. Rather, I search for the gyroscopic clock, for I've heard that there is a Prince concealed inside it. Do you know anything of that?"

"Why, yes! The Prince was buried here many years ago, along with his grave necessities – you know, pots, jewelry and things to accompany him in the afterlife. But there was one thing missing from the grave goods. That thing had been lost and there is a suspicion that it has been broken up into three parts. It is the Princes' Mask, and it has two obsidian eyes, a quicksilver nose and an iron mouth with bloodstone teeth. Have you ever heard of it?"

"I have it!" I blurted out without thinking. "I found the three separate parts in different places, and put them together. I've had a hard job keeping hold of it, for it was stolen several times, but it's hidden in a safe place now, I assure you."

"That's wonderful! When the Prince can put on his Mask again, all the fairies, elves and other little pagan folk will be released from bondage, and the Prince will reign over us once again and there will be harmony on the earth, and people will not suck oil and dig coal out of the earth, for Gaia does not like that."

"That's right. But I don't understand one thing. I have looked on the face of the sleeping Prince, and he is fair as the Sun. Why would he want to wear a Mask?"

"That is precisely it." Nodded the leprechaun. "He is so beautiful, that merely to look on him would burn out the eyes of most people, so he hides his face in deference to them. They can still feel his presence, you know." He looked at me keenly. "You say you have looked upon him? That is amazing! Your eyes were not damaged, then?"

"No." I affirmed. "When I found his tomb in the desert vault, I did not know of his power, and therefore I gazed upon him without fear. I loved him instantly and he did me no harm, for he was sleeping."

"So, you have the Mask. Is it handy? I would like to see it." He looked a little too eager, so I was cautious in my reply.

"It's in a safe place. I have orders not to allow anyone to touch it until the Prince wears it once again and has risen from his sepulcher." I put on a sad look. "I am sure that you will be able to see it eventually, especially if you can tell me where the gyroscopic clock is, in this godforsaken desert."

"OK. I will help you, for I love the Prince too. First we must slide up the rainbow, which will be here soon, as I see a shower of rain approaching us. You must move fast, for when the rain stops, the rainbow disappears, and then you would fall out of the sky, and it is a long way up to the clock. Do you see that black pole over there? The clock revolves on that pole. You can just glimpse the bottom of the clock above you. See how it gyrates?"

I peered up. There was indeed a dark green disc revolving slowly around the pole, keeping absolutely level. I wondered what the face of the clock looked like, and whether there was anyone up there. My ruminations were interrupted by a spot of rain, and the leprechaun took my arm and hastened me to the middle of the pile of coins, where he insisted that I put on a pair of skis. The rain increased, yet the sun shone behind us and slowly a magnificent rainbow formed in the falling raindrops. In the center of the path up the bow was a simple ski lift on a moving rope, of the meat hook type, with little supports for the backside. We edged up to the rope and timed our movements to grab the rope and coincide with the moving seats without falling off. The leprechaun was expert at this and I managed to hang on, although one ski slid over towards the side of the rainbow. However, the rain kept falling and the rope tow took us rapidly up to the arch of the bow, where we were level with the top of the clock and I was able to step off and remove my skis, while the leprechaun continued at a furious pace, slaloming down the other side of the rainbow.

A bright light illuminated the top of the clock, and there was the planet Jupiter, ruler of Fortune, hanging in the sky. The horizontal face of the clock was divided into the usual system of twelve hours invented by man, and three figures were evenly spaced around the clock, as if to keep it in balance. On my left, at the number three, a naked, skinny beggar was motionless in a yoga headstand, a small tin begging bowl set out in front of him, while on the far side, at the number seven, a fool in a motley costume balanced on a unicycle; and at the number eleven, a strange, grey woman, carrying a thyrsus, was standing, looking somewhat hesitant and frightened. The clock was steady until the fool began to move his unicycle forward, at which time it began to tip to the left, and the beggar was forced to get up and resume his position at the number two. The grey woman began to step off the clock onto the arch, which was still shimmering below her. The clock tilted further to the left and began to wobble alarmingly as she cautiously put her foot out towards the rainbow.

Waving at the fool, I urged him to back up towards the number eight, for the beggar was at number two and the woman with the thyrsus had now shifted her weight off the clock completely, leaving a small goatskin bag of coins behind. The two managed to balance the clock and it leveled out. I watched as the woman sat and slid down the disappearing rainbow, noticing my own weight on the clock did not affect it at all, which was strange.

"Ah! She chose to get off the clock just in time, at the eleventh hour." It was the fool who spoke, balancing expertly on his unicycle. "I was worried about her. She threatened suicide, you know - seemed very depressed. I tried to talk to her, tell her to put a smile on her face hoping she would feel better. I even did some little tricks for her, but it didn't change her underlying mood."

"Why was she so melancholy?" I asked. "She had the thyrsus and the baboon headdress. It looked as though she was ready to shift."

"Well, she was fed up with life on the clock and wanted to go down and meditate in one of those caves by herself. Daft, I call it. She would have been much better staying up here and going from the number nine to the number five every day, in my opinion. It's all the baboons' fault."

"Why is it the baboons' fault? And what was the thyrsus for? I'm not familiar with the symbolism."

"The baboon is Thoth - it's his symbol. He is the god of Thought. She got it into her head that she would meet Thoth in a vision if she went into the caves. I personally doubt it. He's not that easy to pin down. Shape shifts, you know, and always goes by different names, like Hermes and so on." The fool still moved back and forth a little on the unicycle while he spoke. "The thyrsus she carries is a symbolic staff attributed to Bacchus, the god of wine. It is in the form of a pine cone, which represents the sacred eye of the ancients, the abode of mans' spirit. The pine cone is also used to sprinkle holy water on the initiate, and it has a deeper meaning which I cannot tell you yet." He shook his head sadly. "In this world, we don't have many people lining up for initiation, you know. Most people have been thoroughly brainwashed."

"I can guess who did the brainwashing. I have observed that many times on my journey." I sighed. "You can only expect one or two people to make the right decision. That's the meaning of Fortune – determining which direction to go in. It's the personal choices you make while you exist in space time."

"Yes. Now, I will show you how each personal choice alters your path, so that you slip into different parallel universes. You won't realize that you are in a different universe, for the change is seamless, but it means you are, in fact, changing direction slightly. That can happen hundreds of times in one day, for example. That's why we have the clock, for your choices are based on your daily, material life, ruled by Chronos, the god of time."

"So, do you mean I have already made choices since I got onto this clock?" I was surprised. "I've only been here a few minutes."

"You have, though." The fool nodded his head, on which he wore a cone shaped hat with a bell. "For one thing, you decided to get off the rainbow when you got level with the clock. You decided to remove your skis. You observed changes happening on the clock once you were here – the grey woman, whose name, by the way is Partita, finally got off and that changed the balance on the clock, so that we had to move our positions. Then, you chose to talk to me. From that you gained information. Next, you will start wondering about the beggar, I can tell. You will ask his name and that will give you a shock."

"I see. So, I could have decided not to get off the rainbow. I could have decided not to remove my skis, and that might have meant that I skidded off the clock, or maybe bumped into you and knocked you off. Then, I could have talked to the beggar before I talked to you – that would have changed things, because he might have told me who you were. Now you have aroused my curiosity as to who the beggar is." I looked towards the tin bowl. "Whoever he is, he has fallen on hard times, I fear."

The fool fell silent, gazing at me with mournful eyes. I now understood that every single choice I made on the Path of Fortune was going to change my direction without me realizing it. I wondered how many millions of similar hidden changes I had already made in my lifetime. Why, if I had made the appropriate choices, I might be captain of a mega yacht by now. But, then I thought that some choices were denied to me by outside circumstances that could not be overcome. For example, how could a person who was born with one leg compete in a two-legged race? Obtaining a prosthetic leg would be a choice, but if the program said the legs had to be real ones, there was no way around that.

My interest aroused, but assuring myself I would be wary of all my choices in the future, I turned to the beggar. "Good morning. May I ask who you are?"

I knew the beggar had the choice of answering, or not. He chose the former, flipping onto his feet and standing up on skinny legs in front of me, his ribs sticking out of an indrawn stomach and the bones of his face thrusting through the thin layer of skin so that I hardly recognized the artist Julian from the Seven of Cups.

"Julian! My God! What has happened to you?" Horrified, I reached forward to touch him sympathetically, but he drew back. "How did you get into this state?"

Julian lowered his hollow eyes and spoke in a raspy voice. "I fell on ill fortune through your choices, unfortunately. Although Fontanova did her best, she was your entity, and so that influenced me. You chose not to contact the galleries and try to market my paintings, and I was thrown out of my lodgings and have been living on the street ever since."

"Oh! My God! I didn't think. I mean, I'm so sorry. I kept putting off the marketing, telling myself I should only be creating, and that someone would eventually show up and buy my work. I just didn't consider your side of me." I burst into tears, at which the fool commented dryly about my decision to pity myself.

"Julian!" I sobbed. "I will do whatever I can to change things and make better choices. You must come with me, I will find somewhere for you to live and make sure you have food and a studio to work in." I tried to persuade him, but a sinking sensation told me it would not work.

"No, it is too late." He seemed calm. "I have abandoned painting, for I realized every picture I created was an Ego trip. I am happy now, for I don't seek to push my talent forward any longer, and I have seen the reality beyond reality. I wish to stay as I am and hope to overcome this world of illusions." He looked at me poignantly. "Your choice affected me, but it was for the best. I have committed myself to the life of a simple beggar, just as Buddha did, and I know fortune will provide me with my essential needs."

I was desperate! This was not good. My artistic entity Fontanova had been in charge of Julian since we met him. I had made the wrong choices, and therefore so had Fontanova. Instead of focusing on her creative muse, she had thought only of Bardogian, of life with him, for she was in love. Now she was married to him and leading a different life. Did this mean that I could no longer live as an artist myself?

I watched sadly as Julian resumed his headstand. I picked up the bag of coins and poured its contents into his tin bowl. The fool laughed. "See how your choices affect other people? The whole universe is a web, a set of vibrating energy, so that your thoughts make an impression on others, even on those who cannot speak, the animals and trees, rocks and seas. All are interconnected. Beware of your decisions in the material world, for you will be held accountable for them by the one who writes the Akashic Records."

I knew he was right, but just then I heard someone calling me from below, so I dried my eyes and walked to the edge of the clock and looked down. It was disappointing to see Belvedere waving his arms and signaling that he wanted to come up. Darn it! How did he get here? I didn't want him up here. It might upset the clock again, and the Prince inside his sarcophagus would be tossed to and fro. Maybe some of his pottery jars would get broken, too. I would have to go down to Belvedere, but how? The rain had stopped and the rainbow had dissolved, although the ground was awash with mud. There was no visible way down except by the pole. My thoughts whirled. There was another important thing, too. The Prince was entombed in the clock and needed the Mask, so that he could be restored. The Mask was in a locker on my ketch, which was sailing offshore with Pompeybou at the helm. I had to make a decision.

I squeezed myself down a small gap in the center of the clock, making sure I did not touch the hands and thus alter world time, and slid down the pole to the mired and soggy ground. There Belvedere met me and drew me up in a gigantic hug. He was filthy and covered in mud.

"Here I am! I'm all better now, and I dug myself here all the way through your blinking tunnel. I wish you'd left it open. Boy! That Anubis is a fierce fighter. I won't take him on again. What's happening here?" He dropped his huge hands from my shoulders and stood waiting for my reply as I brushed off the dirt on my tunic, hoping that it would not rain again for a while.

"This is the Path of Fortune, and I have to be careful about my choices here. Don't try to influence me, or it will be the worse for both of us." I drew in my breath carefully. "There is something you can do for me right now. Go to the coast and signal to Pompeybou on the ketch. He will bring the boat in to shore. Ask him to give you the Mask which is hidden in the foc'sle locker, and then bring it to me quickly. Beware, for you will be carrying a valuable object, and there are those who may try to steal it from you. Guard it well. Be gone, now."

To my surprise, Belvedere saluted and set off at a trot in the direction of the coast. I had never observed him doing anything I asked before without objecting strongly. Was he having a change of heart? I would see what happened in the future and, for now, hope that he could bring back the Mask safely, for then we could rouse the Prince. In the meantime, I decided to investigate the caves, to see where Partita had gone, and whether Thoth had actually appeared, so I made my way past the leprechaun, who was busy counting his money, and entered the nearest cave.

Fumbling around in the dark, I brushed against a seated figure, who gave an echoing scream. "Look out! You just frightened Thoth away! He was approaching me from that corner, with his baboon headdress and all." Partita gave a gasp of irritation. "Now I have to conjure him up again. What are you doing, bumbling about in here, anyway?"

"I'm sorry. My curiosity overcame me. I wanted to see Thoth, too. He wrote the book I'm writing, but I never met him. Do you mind if I sit down and meditate beside you?"

"Oh, all right, I suppose so. I got off the clock, putting myself at risk by leaving a life of imagined security, to get away from people like you. Is there no peace? Sit down and shut up, for heavens' sake."

I lowered myself into the lotus position in the dark and we sat motionless. I couldn't get her rudeness out of my mind. She seemed obsessed with leaving everyday existence and separating herself from the crowd, but I knew that was not possible, nor was it wise. I managed to clear this pointless frustration from my mind and went into a deep trance. The silence was intense, and whispered thoughts flitted through my mind constantly, but I did not allow them to stay. Then came a faint chattering, which became louder and louder, and in my minds' eye a large a ferocious troop of white baboons came into the cave. They seized Partita, who seemed to be asleep, and carried her away, ignoring me.

This was very disturbing, and I came out of trance and put out my hand to feel Partitas' leg. She had really gone! Now I was fully awake, feeling around with my hands and calling her, but the silence was complete and a vile monkey odor hung in the air. It was not a vision! I had actually observed the baboons kidnapping her. Were they taking her to their leader, Thoth? I did not have time to worry, for I heard Belvedere's voice outside the cave, calling me.

"I'm in here. Just a minute, I'm coming out." I responded, stumbling out of the dark and rubbing my eyes, to see Belvedere holding up the Mask in excitement. I quickly told him to keep it hidden, but the leprechauns' sharp eye had already spotted it, and he came scampering up. Too late, Belvedere hid it inside the lapel of his velvet jacket, but the little man jumped up and down, trying to see it and tearing the buttons off Belvederes' jacket in his efforts.

"Get away, you horrible little dwarf! You're ruining my best jacket." Belvedere slapped the leprechaun down.

"Please! Calm down, here. You must know the Mask is not for public view, until it is replaced on the Princes' face. Then all may look upon it. By itself, it's dangerous, for it carries great power, and many would want to wear it." I pushed the leprechaun back. "You are in danger, I warn you. Do not try to touch it."

"You claim it's dangerous. Well, I know of its magic." He protested. "My magic is just as powerful, for I am rich. Look at my gold, lying there in heaps. I have enough money to buy the Mask! You can't stop me, either."

Belvedere looked interested by the mention of gold, and he was about to reveal the Mask, when I leapt at him, reaching up into his jacket, and tore it from his grasp, twisting around to avoid the grabbing leprechaun and running towards the pole. But there I was stuck, for I could not climb it. I put the Mask in one of my pockets and drew my sword, brandishing it fiercely.

"Don't try to get it! I'll defend it with my life." Panting, I had my back to the pole. Now I longed for rain, when a little while before I had wished for sun. But the sky was clear without a cloud in sight.

Fortunately, the whistling noise of my sharp sword as it cut the air stopped Belvedere in his tracks, and the leprechaun shrugged his shoulders and went off in a huff. Obviously neither of them was willing to face a sword fight for the Mask. I sat down by the pole. I would have to wait for rain, now, to get another rainbow. I wished fervently for rain, canceling my previous wish that it should be dry, and hoped for the best. In the meantime, I wondered what had happened to Partita and whether the baboons had torn her to pieces.

With the leprechaun sulking and Belvedere sitting disconsolately on a rock, picking at his missing buttonholes, I thought it best to remove myself from sight, so I slunk quietly back into the cave, muttering something about searching for Partita. The monkey odor was stronger than ever, coming from a dark passageway to my left. I moved cautiously down the passage, feeling my way, until a gleam of light appeared at the end. I came out upon a wide heath, bounded at the far side by a great wall which swept around a large enclosed area. Etched on this wall was a series of crosses of different types, from the Celtic cross to more elaborate and jeweled crosses that spoke of Orthodoxy.

On a small mound outside the wall a strange figure hung on a larger cross, its eyes fixed upon me with an unnerving blank stare. It was a doll-like figure, similar to the popular Cabbage Patch doll that had swept the western world by storm some years before. I began walking towards this apparition, when a ladder was suddenly flung over the wall from inside the enclosure, and Partita, looking scared and disheveled, climbed rapidly down. I ran over and helped her off the ladder, laying her down on the ground, for she could barely stand, ruptured by grief. To my surprise, she looked pregnant and about to give birth. When I saw her a few hours ago, she had been slim almost to the point of starvation. I bent down, giving her a drink of water and mopping her brow.

"What's going on? Your clothes are all torn and there is blood on your face and hands." I asked her.

A great sob shook her. "He raped me! Thoth! There are dozens of them in there. They held me down. They were – laughing. No, it was not laughter, but a vile screeching sound. He had me by my ears, banging my head on the earth and shouting. He said I was the perfect vessel for his emissions. Oh! My God! I became pregnant right away, and now I feel my labor pains are starting." She threw herself back in convulsions as I held her.

We were at the foot of the wall, and I could see faces at the top, looking over at us. They were not the faces of humans, but of white baboons, and they were beginning to climb down the ladder. I raised Partita to her feet, and quickly led her away, my arm around her shaking shoulders. We had to leave this awful place and return to the cave before she gave birth.

As soon as we reached the cave mouth, Partita sank to her knees again and gave a loud cry. I propped her against a rock, her legs spread, and waited with my knife ready to cut the umbilical cord of the babe that would soon arrive. I encouraged her to push, but she did not seem to be straining at all. Then, with a loud scream, a tiny white creature burst from her womb, followed by another and another. The little baboons immediately jumped to their feet and began milling around, and all the time, more and more were being born, until there was a endless stream of them that filled the cave and the surrounding area.

The leprechaun gave a shout of horror, for they had already reached his hoard of gold and were picking up the coins as fast as they could.

Each tiny baboon was able to carry several coins, and they hurried back down the passageway at the left of the cave, gabbling and muttering. The leprechaun ran from one group to another, trying to grab his money out of their clutching arms, and weeping, while Belvedere, rooted to stone on his rock, stared blankly at the scene.

At last the birthing was over and Partita sank back, exhausted. I had lost count of the number of baby baboons that she had borne, but there must have been hundreds, and, sadly, they had completely stripped the leprechauns' pot of gold and taken every last coin away. The little man sat in abject misery, cursing Partita and blaming her for the loss of his fortune.

"Cheer up!" I joked. "Fortunes come and go, you know. Now you have plenty of time and space to start collecting gold again. But I advise you to consider a different kind of gold."

He looked at me in bewilderment. "What do you mean? I have lost everything."

"You still have yourself. Instead of spending your time making money, spend it making your journey to your Higher Self, for even little people have souls, and you haven't been paying attention to that, have you?"

Partita interrupted. "What happened to me? Thoth raped me. I was expecting a baby, but why were there so many of them? Why did they take the leprechauns gold away?"

"Thoth did not give you a real baby. He inseminated you with hundreds of thoughts. After all, he is the god of Thought. The baby baboons were thoughts, and most of those thoughts that came through you manifested as money grabbers, because you are not yet purified and willing to give up material wealth."

Partita frowned and glared at me. "That is not true! When I stepped off the nine to five clock, I left behind a bag of gold coins. I felt I had given up my thoughts of material concerns then. You are wrongly accusing me of harboring those horrible creatures."

"Partita." I looked solicitous "Your mind still retained some desire for material goods, even though you felt you had conquered it. That remnant was enough to turn Thoths' seed into desire for the gold you saw spread out in front of you. It is not so easy to dismiss worries about our material survival, for we retain vestiges of our ego that crop up constantly, persuading us that we cannot manage in life without stability, stability that is represented by money in the bank."

"That is true." She replied sadly. "I did leave the money bag behind, but I had regrets about it. I began to worry that I had made a bad decision. I thought about going back, but the rainbow had gone. My thoughts, when I was meditating, led me towards Thoth, and now he has taught me a lesson I won't forget."

The sky darkened and a steady rain began to fall. I had to wait until the rain passed before a gleam of sun revealed the rainbow I needed. Strapping on a pair of skis, I grabbed the rope tow and was soon back on top of the clock. The beggar Julian had disappeared, taking with him his tin bowl and the bag of money that Partita had left. I hoped that he would put it to good use by buying more canvases and oil paints.

The fool greeted me joyfully. I explained that I had to find the entrance to the interior of the clock, where a certain person was interred.

"Oh! I know who that is." The fool laughed. "It's the Prince, isn't it? Of course, he can't come out. He has lost his Mask, and he knows that without it, no-one can look upon his face, for they would go blind. Why do you want to go down there? There is no point."

Avoiding a direct answer, for I didn't want to tell him I had the Mask, I said that I was interested in discovering the era of the burial by examining the pottery that had been placed in the sepulcher. The fool showed me a small indent in the face of the clock and produced a key.

"Here you are, then. I use this key to wind up the clock every week, otherwise it wouldn't run any more. That's the job for fools, winding clocks to keep time. The keyhole also gives access to the interior chamber. From there, you will have to find your way. Do you have a lamp?"

"No. I didn't bring one. But I'm used to feeling my way around in the dark." I knew that once I pushed back the lid of the sarcophagus, illumination from the Princes' face would shine out and light up the entire chamber. I hoped that it would not blind me, but I trusted the fact that I had gazed upon his face before without harm.

The fool shrugged his shoulders and gave me the key. I turned it three times, and a small trap door opened in the face of the clock, with dusty steps leading down into the sepulcher. Cautiously I went down, closing the trap door behind me.

A close, musty smell pervaded the interior of the clock, as I felt my way around, stumbling occasionally over grave goods and bumping up against large pottery jars. I felt along the rounded inner wall for some moments, hoping to find the cold marble of the sarcophagus, but I made a complete circle and came up with nothing. Then I remembered the musical triangle which the Bride had given me, so I took it out and struck a few notes, running up and down the scale. As the note of C-minor sounded, a rumbling sound began and the inner wall of the clock started to roll back, the sudden brilliant light revealing a magnificent round coffin in the center of a small cubicle.

The square room was lined with yellow silk, and the coffin itself was of gold, and from it the rays of a bright sun flashed and rippled as if it were alive. The room was furnace-like and I began to sweat. I locked my fingers under the projecting lid of the coffin, giving it a push. The lid moved smoothly to one side and intense golden light flooded the chamber, making every item in it luminous, as if with an inner glow. There lay the most stunning Prince, clad in costly garments, and with his hands folded around a scintillating wand. The face was fresh and young – in no way touched by death.

I leaned over the coffin with reverence, drawing the Mask from my tunic, and gently fitted it over the Princes' face. The brilliant light went dim, and at the same time, the Prince began to stir, at first fluttering a finger, then twitching a leg, and then slowly sitting up, turning his head from side to side as if entranced.

I went down on my knees and spoke. "Lord! Allow me, your humble servant, to return the Mask that you must wear, so that all may gaze upon your majesty without losing their sight, until they have learned to understand the truth of your presence within them."

As I knelt, the Prince rose up out of the coffin and addressed me. "I have been locked in the aspect of space and time inside this clock, for Aeons. Now, with the restoration of my Mask, I can achieve material manifestation, and come again into the world, where I am greatly needed."

I bowed my head and he blessed me silently. My tears ran down like a river, and yet they were tears of joy.

Path of DESTINY - Coagulation

The tears I shed during the Path of Fortune had sufficiently Distilled my imperfect essence, so that I could continue to Destiny and there complete my coagulation. I therefore prepared to leave Fortune, but again I had to work out a way to get across the Mystic SEA to Destiny without getting too close to Tiphareth.

I had crossed the Mystic SEA by Air, by Water and by Earth. I would now find a way to cross by Fire, so I sat down and worked out a method. I needed to be totally enveloped by fire, and therefore I would need a fireproof suit. Where could I find some asbestos for the suit? If I had that, a few gallons of gasoline and the correct cannon would do the rest.

I consulted with the leprechaun, who told me that there was an old castle, Fort Une, at the top of a hill a couple of miles away. There were discarded cannon at the castle, where many crusaders had stopped in olden times while seeking their fortune. As for the asbestos, when Belvedere heard of my problem, he stepped forward, looking embarrassed.

"I know where you can find an asbestos suit." He announced. "I didn't want to tell you, but I wear asbestos undergarments. You've never seen them, because I don't change my clothes very often."

I agreed wholeheartedly about that, as I stared in horror while he ripped open the last couple of buttons on his jacket to reveal a thick layer of asbestos beneath it. "I have to wear this as a survival tool." He explained, as he removed his filthy shoes and purple velvet pants. "This material is impervious to most cruel and vengeful jibes, therefore I can survive in the material world in safety."

I turned my head in shame as he began taking off the sleeved underwear and the long legs of his protective garment. I hoped he was wearing boxers underneath, but a short gasp and a cackle of laughter from the leprechaun told me he was not. Belvedere put on his purple suit again and handed me the asbestos underwear. Of course, it was too big, since he was seven feet tall. The leprechaun had some safety pins and made sure that some pleats in the back would give me a reasonable fit, but the stench of his unwashed garments nauseated me.

Thanking Belvedere for his kind offer, I determined I would have to get used to his odor, as he and the leprechaun accompanied me on our short hike to the castle of Fort Une. We found some rusty cannon scattered about, one of which seemed to have a reasonably clean barrel, except for a nest of salamanders. A bag of gunpowder and a gallon of gasoline remaining from the previous occupants, a group of terrorists, were stored in the castle ramparts. Setting up the cannon to face due east – the direction of Destiny – the leprechaun packed gunpowder into the cannon and put in a fuse, while Belvedere stood by with the gasoline. He was to douse me at the same moment that the leprechaun lit the fuse with his matches, setting me on fire as I rose rapidly into the air.

Rolling me up into a ball, my feet around my ears, Belvedere forced me down the mouth of the cannon and then threw the gasoline over me. I could scarcely breathe for the fumes. At the same time, the leprechaun set a match to the fuse, and with a loud explosion, I shot into the air, soaring up skywards until the earth below seemed far away and streaming a cloud of gasoline behind me.

Unfortunately, Belvedere had not lit his match, and I was not on fire. I halted my flight in mid air, back peddling with my hands and feet frantically, and fell in a shallow sky dive to earth, where I could see Belvedere running to catch me. Landing safely in his arms, I berated him soundly.

"Why didn't you follow directions? You have to do as you're told!"

"I couldn't set you on fire!" He moaned. "Suppose you had burnt up? That would have been the death of me!" He shook his head. "I need you and I can't let myself go – it wouldn't be right. We are dependent on each other."

I bared my teeth. "Will you never understand, you idiot? You must follow the path I decide on, not the other way around. Try not to worry – I am looking out for your interests, but mine come first now. It's time for you to finally submit to my will power. Now, we'll reload me and you will strike the match and set me on fire. Is that clear?"

"Yes, Master. I will do it." Belvedere hung his head as he carried me, soaking in gasoline, back to the castle and squeezed me into the barrel of the cannon.

This time all went well, and the rushing air as the cannon fired made the flames around my asbestos suit roar fiercely. I whistled through the air rapidly, with a G-force quite equal to any rocket, seeing below me Tiphareth in all her glory, where maidens clad in flowers danced around a gigantic maypole. The glorious sight was rapidly gone and very soon I was touching down in Destiny, where I found myself standing in front of a massive flight of steps that led up to an empty throne. By a miracle, I had avoided getting burned, although my hair was somewhat singed. I was glad to cast off the uncomfortable asbestos suit, which smelt even worse than before.

On each side of the staircase two elephants stood guard. One was an Asian elephant, easily identified by the twin bumps on his forehead, and the other an African elephant, flapping her big ears back and forth. The animals were both gorgeously clad in trappings of gold cloth, interwoven with jewels, and each elephant carried a howdah on its back, surmounted by a round parasol. Their tusks were neatly lopped off and capped by red velvet covers. The sense of stability that emanated from the elephants calmed me after my hectic flight as I took in my new surroundings. There was nobody around except a brown owl that flapped aimlessly in circles, its great eyes searching everywhere. The bird carried a rolled up blueprint that it dropped while landing on the lowest step. It began to preen. I walked over and picked up the blueprint, but I couldn't make head or tail of it, since it was written in Enochian language with strange angelic designs. Flinging it aside, I walked up a steep slope beside the steps, hoping to find a sign of human life, and, sure enough, a young and athletic looking woman appeared, driving a pair of oxen who pulled a plough behind them, the blade sunk deep in the earth. She was dressed in a skintight black and white suit with white ostrich plumes waving from her black cap. Halting the pair, she moved gracefully towards me, holding her hand out in greeting.

"Ah! You have arrived at last. I have prepared the furrows for you to sow your seeds. Did you bring them?"

"What? I don't know anything about seeds! Nobody gave me any to bring here. I don't know what you're talking about." I found myself backed into a corner and trying to defend myself. Should I feel to blame for some reason? I secretly hoped that Belvedere was not going to show up again with his guilt trip – maybe that was mean of me, but this was an increasing problem. The woman and I walked down the slope together to the bottom of the steps.

"No seeds? Well, it's not the first time. So many people show up here without their seeds – I get pretty tired of it." She shrugged. "I guess we'll have to send off for them – they must be held up in the mail somewhere. The Post Office around here needs some attention before it drives someone else mad."

She bent down and picked up the discarded blueprint, looking closely at it. "This is the blueprint for your current life. The owl must have left this behind for us. I see that you are constructing your life in accordance with this plan, except for a few minor mistakes you have made along the way." She laughed softly, and then she looked at the parchment again, turning it over. "Ah! Here are the seeds, after all. Look!" She handed the parchment to me and I saw a small package of seeds stapled to it. These were no ordinary seeds, being multi-colored and patterned in all sorts of different designs, some striped like tigers, some paisley, some donkey brown and some spotted like woodpeckers.

"They are beautiful." I breathed. "What sort of plants are they from? I'll be happy to sow them now, if that's what you would like. I wonder what fruit they will bear."

"They bear strange fruits, as you will find out when they appear. It is a good idea to sow them now, but, before we go up to scatter them, I want to tell you what they are. These are the seeds for your next life, which you are sowing during your present life. Everything you do in this life prepares you for your next reincarnation, so that each choice you made in the Passage of Fortune, which represented your present life, is like a symbolic seed of karma for your next life." She smiled gently. "You have some very interesting seeds there! Let's get them into the ground so that they can mature."

We ascended to the two oxen that waited patiently at the top of the slope, carrying the packet of seeds. I gave the animals a cursory glance, but looked again with a jolt of surprise. There were two beasts, and two oxen should have eight legs – four each. I could only count six. The animals had a pair of forelegs each, but their back legs were fused together. They were Siamese conjoined twins! I felt immensely sorry for them – or was it him? Were there two or one?

A tinkling laugh from the woman interrupted my musings. "You are surprised, aren't you?" She put her hand on the wooden yoke that joined the animals together. "This yoke represents the discipline of yoga, which brings two into one, and I am in control of these animals just as I control your human life." She held up a pointed ox goad in her right hand. "See this goad that I carry with me at all times. It represents the goad of your Destiny - to encourage your lower body to stay on the right path, and to move along without stopping to graze."

"Who are you, then?" I enquired. "You are dressed like a Harlequin in the colors of duality, black and white."

"I am Destiny. I am the adjudicator of every life on earth, which is inevitably lived in duality. I wear the dual white feathers of Ma'at, the goddess of Truth, for we must live in truth if we want to follow our blueprint to the letter. I represent Justice, whose throne at the top of my staircase is empty, for true Justice cannot be found on earth, but only in the Passage of the Archpriestess, who rules over the Law and who examines each dead wraith that comes to her before she allows them to be born again."

"I haven't reached her Passage yet, but I have been trying to follow the Law as I best know it. Sadly, it is extremely difficult to know the exact truth about any experience. In fact, even my memory of past events in my life is flawed. It comes to me in fractured pieces, and I have to fill in the blanks the way I think a particular event happened, and when I compare it to others' memories of the event, they are never the same."

"That is because our brain can only hold so much information, and it is selective." Destiny nodded sagely. "A major event such as an assassination or a tsunami which kills many people is held more clearly in our memory, because of its emotional impact, whereas small daily events are forgotten. Mind remembers everything, but we normally do not have access to that knowledge through brain until we cast off our bodies. Only those who are enlightened remember experiences exactly, and therefore they are the only people who speak the absolute Truth."

"I understand that the knowledge of Truth is important, yet it seems a veil is drawn between us and Truth itself. Why is it that we cannot find truth on earth?"

"To know the Truth about everything would be an overload on the human brain. Our brains only deal with truths as they concern us – Belvedere, your Ego, is blind to many aspects of life, and that is why you must move beyond him soon. His ideas are extremely limited, since he cannot know the real truth about anything."

"I have been trying to distance myself from his views, but he won't listen. How can I get rid of him, and what will happen if he dies?"

"Don't worry – he will not die as long as your bodily survival needs him. But he must be brought to submit to your Higher Self, whom you know as your Guide."

"I haven't seen my Guide lately. I can't understand why he isn't here for me during these challenging times."

"He is waiting on the sidelines to help in an emergency. He is watching, along with my two witnesses, whom you will meet when we have sown your seeds." Destiny then moved to the first furrow. "Come now, and make sure the seeds are spaced out and not lying on top of each other or you will have sudden episodes in your next life that get very confusing. While you place the seeds in the furrow, I will rake the moist earth over them, and then they will be ready for your future existence."

When the seeds were all safely lying in their furrows, covered over by the damp, nurturing earth, we descended the steps. Suddenly Destiny gave a gasp of horror. I saw what had disturbed her. Seated on the back of the African elephant, lounging comfortably in the howdah and twirling the parasol, was Belvedere. That, however, was not what had shocked her the most.

Pointing at the colorful trappings the elephants were wearing, she whispered faintly. "The trappings! Someone has changed the trappings. The African elephant is wearing African designs, and look, over there, the Asian elephant is wearing Asian designs. That person up there...." Her she indicated Belvedere... "... Must have meddled with my distribution. I know who that is. He has been dogging you during your alchemical transformation, causing endless troubles and distractions. How do you put up with a lunatic like that?"

I glared up at Belvedere, who gave a significant smirk as I replied. "As you are aware, since you oversee my Destiny, he is the fellow who was attached to me at birth, and for years I was not even conscious of his influence over me, for I thought I was always the one who made the decisions. I have discovered, during my travels in the Mystic SEA, that he is an interloper that must be banished, for his ways are not my ways any more." I sighed. "As for the elephants' trappings, they are on the right elephants now, aren't they? So why worry about it? They must have been muddled up before Belvedere changed them."

"Well, you are mistaken. Sometimes things in the material world seem to be wrong, but there is a lesson to that. It is meddlesome to try to put everything right. When humans judge what is going on around them, they see experiences as either good or bad, on the material plane. However, what appears to be bad may actually be beneficial on the spiritual plane. One has to see past ones' automatic initial response."

She shook her head. "Let me give you an example. Once upon a time humans relied on substances that they found under the earth, and they drilled and dug deeper and deeper, damaging the core of Mother Earth, and she became angry and struck back with great power. She blew out an underwater oil well with such force that the rig exploded and sank, killing many workers and leaving a plume of oil that soiled the waters around it and destroyed thousands of living beings from the deep ocean. The people who were dependent on fishing for their livelihood were in despair, and so it remained for many years, but other forces were at work, too. It was a big learning curve, which taught humans how ignorant and greedy they were. When they finally stopped the flow of oil, after hundreds of people came forward with ideas, they had learned many things, as it is always a tragedy that teaches us the most." Destiny nodded to herself. "They learned how to clean up the mess, and learned to survive by adapting their lives to different occupations, and they learned to make a cleaner, more efficient supply of energy for their future. If they had continued to rely on oil, they would never have made the great leap forward in technology that has been the result of the spill."

"I remember the spill. It was one of the great disasters. So, that was a lesson from Mother Earth, like her earthquakes that cause houses that have been foolishly built on the edge of a cliff to slip down, or houses that have been built on flood plains that become inundated by water."

I realized that people thought they were omniscient – able to withstand the forces of Nature – yet in reality utterly vulnerable to those forces, which

Seatime 273

could, in a few moments, completely destroy their way of life and kill many of them. "Is that part of Destiny?" I asked her.

"A persons' Destiny is, of course, woven into the fabric of the environment, both as to conception of the fetus and as to the family it is born into. One must also take into account the geographical position and ecological facts of the birth, and the astrological assembly of planets. This is all carefully chosen by the Society of Enochian Anchorites before conception, after they have inspected the plants for the future life that grew from the seeds sown by the previous life, for remember, those seeds were formed by karmic choices and acts in that life."

While we were discussing these issues, Belvedere was listening intently as he lounged in the howdah above us. Now he gave a snort of disgust and shouted out. "What a bunch of crap! I'm not staying here to listen to this any more. I'm off to find out more about the Viceroy of Muckabad, for I have discovered his initials embroidered into the cushions up here. Incidentally, look at this!" He held up a gold velvet cushion with red tassels.

I jumped at the sight. "Give that to me immediately!" I shouted. "That is the missing cushion belonging to Himself. I need to return it to him."

"No, I won't! See if you can catch me!" Belvedere prodded his African elephant with a stick and it lumbered away rapidly, disappearing behind a barred gate under the steps that had rolled back unexpectedly.

"Quick! Get onto the Asian elephant and ride through the gates before they close." Destiny instructed. "I will wait for you here. You need to get that cushion back, for it is an offering you must make to Himself."

"Aren't you coming with me?" I cried in desperation as I bade the elephant kneel and leapt into the howdah.

"I cannot come with you. I am bound to remain at the empty seat of Justice, for there are others who need my guidance." She raised her arm and a small white owl landed on her wrist, carrying a new roll of parchment. "Here is the current life of a child, who will die young, but achieve great things in its next incarnation. I must help the innocent ones."

I had no time to argue, for the gates began to rumble back into position. Spurring my elephant, I was just able to squeeze him through before the gates closed, leaving some tufts of tail hair behind.

The Asian elephant made great strides across a vast, desiccated plain with rolling hills and pockets of greenery, through which ran a broad river. Ahead of me, I could see the African elephant, with Belvedere on her back, heading towards a large group of people clad in the most colorful garments. Behind them rose a brightly lit mansion on the bank of the river, ready for a festival. As I approached, I saw Belvedere slip from the back of his kneeling elephant and greet the noisy crowd, who rushed up to him in excitement. They were deep in conversation for a moment, and then several of them turned to look at me, for I was getting closer, and then ran off in different directions.

I came up to a flat, green sward laid out as if for a tournament. A stand built at the back of the mansion was crowded with people, while flags and banners flew from the roof of the mansion and the dozens of flagpoles that encompassed the jousting area. Bidding my Asian elephant to kneel, I slid off, and I was immediately surrounded by a crowd of people who led the elephant off towards a paddock, followed by Belvederes' mount. I walked over to the paddock and found Belvedere talking with a hooded, bent figure that I recognized instantly.

It was the Hoodwinker! Oh, horrors! They were in league with each other, I was certain. But no! Apparently not. The Hoodwinker thrust her gnarly face close under his nose and shook her fist at him, shouting angrily. He pushed her away roughly, yelling back at her. She flew at him, burying her face in his neck and he screeched aloud as blood spurted from her fanged bite. An official separated them, bidding them calm down and wait until the jousting began, for then they could do battle with each other legally.

The Hoodwinker ran off and disappeared into the shadows behind a large barn. The officials, who swarmed around Belvedere in horror at the attack, were soothing him and treating his nasty neck wound. Then a chorus of trumpets sounded and the ugly Viceroy of Muckabad strode into the stands and took his place in the center seat. The tournament was about to begin.

Not wishing to waste my valuable time watching the ensuing fights between Kings and Queens mounted on dolphins, ostriches and armadillos, I spent some time around the elephants, climbing up into the howdah of the African elephant in search of the gold cushion, but it was not there. I searched around the paddock, but eventually came back to the stands, for the two elephants were preparing for the fierce battle between the Hoodwinker, my Shadow, and Belvedere, my Ego.

The great figure of Belvedere was immediately recognizable as the African beast strode into the arena, clad in purple chain mail with a flaunting cavaliers' hat on his head. The Shadow figure, in black armor, was riding the Asian elephant. I hadn't given permission for the Hoodwinker to use the animal, and I thought it was a bit of a cheek for her to have appropriated him, but it was too late to challenge her. They stood at each end of the jousting arena, both armed with a pitchfork and a laser gun. The Viceroy rose from his seat to give the signal, and, to my horror, I saw that he was sitting on the missing gold velvet cushion! I would have to sneak behind the first row of seats and get it back quickly.

Although I was anxious to see which rider would be the winner of the elephant joust, for my survival depended on Belvederes' success, I felt the distraction of the joust would be a suitable moment for me to crawl behind the Viceroys' seat and, when he rose again in his excitement, pull the cushion out from under him. I wriggled my way under the feet of the onlookers, who were clapping and cheering as the two elephants came together in the center of the arena. The clash of pitchforks, followed by sharp flashes from their laser guns, meant they were fully engaged in a fierce fight. I tried to stay calm, crouched behind the front row of seats. Then there was a gasp of dismay, and the Viceroy jumped up, shouting to the Hoodwinker to deal the final blow.

I grabbed the cushion and began quickly making my way back to the edge of the arena. I could hide it behind the barn for now, until things had quieted down. I still had to find Himself, and I didn't know where he was or what he looked like, which made things a little perplexing. After secreting the cushion in the straw of a pigsty, I switched my attention to the result of the joust, seeing, only too well, that Belvedere was down, his elephant on its knees. The black shrouded figure of the Hoodwinker stood over him, her laser gun pointed straight at his heart, while she pinned down his legs with the pitchfork.

I held my breath in dismay. My Shadow figure would hold me in her grip forever if she killed Belvedere, for he held the balance between us. Rigid with terror, I watched closely to see her strike the final blow, but the Hoodwinker lifted her pitchfork suddenly and backed away from Belvedere. A ghastly groan rent the crowd, for they were disappointed in blood lust. The Hoodwinker dropped her pitchfork, released the straps and lifted off her helmet. To my astonishment, it was not the hooded, dark woman of my nightmares who hid there, but an old, bearded man. It was my Guide!

I ran into the arena, waving my arms to greet him, but before I could speak, the African elephant rose up, screaming, and charged at me in a fury. I tried to dodge out of the way, but her blunt tusks caught me up and tossed into me the air like a rag doll. I landed hard on my back as she lunged upon me, rooting with her tusks in the ground and trying to trample me with her feet. I rolled from side to side in an attempt to avoid her, while all the time the crowd shouted and howled with excitement at this new entertainment. Then the elephant picked me up with her trunk, swinging me up and down until I was dizzy and longed for it to be over.

Now there came a thundering of heavy feet and a vicious thump on her side, and she dropped me immediately and turned to face her new opponent – the Asian elephant. He had lumbered forward to draw her attention away from me, and I was able to roll out of range. Now the two elephants locked together in a furious battle, their tusks entwined, pushing and shoving over the arena, each trying to gain the advantage. Meanwhile, Belvedere was watching from the paddock, where he crouched in a cowardly fashion. The crowd was enjoying the elephant fight, which was becoming bloody, and fears for the survival of the elephants arose, so the old man walked towards them, raising his hand in peace and chanting unintelligible words. The animals immediately raised their heads and separated, standing quietly while my Guide calmed them and whispered something in their ears.

From the edge of the arena I watched, badly bruised, as the old fellow made an announcement. He addressed the crowd sternly. "Your blood lust disgusts me! You think you have just witnessed an ordinary joust between two riders on elephants. What you do not understand is that this battle is not just an entertainment, but mirrors the conflict between opposing forces in your own nature, between your Ego and your Shadow. This battle is also between your primal instincts, symbolized by the African elephant, and your spiritual desires, represented by the Asian elephant, for it was first in Asia that man began to understand the forces of the divine world. May you now leave this arena, and think about what you have witnessed in truth and in my words, and remember each of you must become aware of your personal Destiny and abide by it."

The old man turned as the crowd began filing out of the stands. He was about to speak when a scuffle broke out in the front row. The Viceroy of Muckabad had one of the people in the crowd by the scruff of his neck, beating him and cursing. "Where is my cushion, damn you? Stealing it right from under me, you scurvy knave!"

The man swore he hadn't touched the cushion, and I kept a low profile. As I watched, the Viceroy had him arrested and he was dragged off to jail, protesting loudly.

My Guide regarded me with a stern eye. "I see you didn't want to step forward and own up! Now an innocent person is going to suffer for your theft of the cushion. Your mind has been become defiled by contact with these people, at the very moment you should be exhibiting more purity. Come with me, because you are in a very vulnerable state, being on the point of Coagulation, and subject to evil outside influences. We must immediately return the gold cushion to Himself, and end this unresolved problem. I know you have hidden it in the pig sty."

"Where is Himself, though? I have been trying to find him." This was not strictly true, for I hadn't been thinking about the cushion until I saw it in the howdah.

"You are lying. I can read your thoughts. You just let the matter drop, although you knew it was important. Now we will go to find Himself. Once he has the cushion, we must make sure that the innocent bystander is released from jail." He led me over to the pig sty and I remorsefully picked up the cushion, hiding it under my tunic.

We mounted the Asian elephant and returned across the plain and through the gates under the throne of Justice, where we found Destiny waiting for us. She was now clad in a silvery grey gown embroidered with purple stars, and the symbol of the moon rose behind her headdress. My Guide spoke with her out of earshot, and they nodded their heads in agreement. Turning to me, Destiny told me that I had fallen off the Path, for I had been untruthful, and that I must make amends in order to continue towards my coagulation. She pointed to an elevator door just inside the gates, and pressed the button. The doors slid open and I stepped inside, but my Guide did not follow. Instead, I saw him ripping off his outer garments to reveal a strange old woman in the guise of a crone, and before my eyes, Ediug, for it was she, crouched low, sprouting a distinct hump on her back that morphed into three whirling blades and opening a zipper that ran from top to bottom of her solar plexus. She now resembled some sort of flying object. I had no time to speculate on this, or to wonder where the old man had gone.

"Ediug! Where have you been? Aren't you coming with me?" I cried, as the doors rumbled closed and the elevator spun downwards rapidly at such a pace that my breath left me for an instant. I knew we were deep in the earth by the time the elevator stopped and the doors slid open again. I stepped out, holding the cushion tightly, into a large underground vault with a single seat at a rough wooden table, where dozens of McDonalds' hamburger wrappers littered the floor. When I saw the wrappers I knew, my gaze riveted on the person seated at the table munching a large pickle, with a grin on his face. It was my trickster entity, Kracklewergen!

"Hey, twit! Er-hem. How come you're here again?" He laughed. "You are-er, looking for Himself – yes? Indeed, hmmmm, I am Himself – the er-trickster in you. You thought, hmm, that Himself was someone else, didn't you? So, twit, I'm here to-er, receive the gold velvet cushion, hmmm, with the red er-tassels that you, hem, have hidden under your er-tunic, hmmm." He suddenly rose to his full height and yelled at me, which gave me a fright. "Give it back now!!! I'm er-sick of playing with you, hmmm." He sat down again and gnawed restlessly on a chicken nugget. "That's enough, already."

I was reluctant to hand over the cushion, but fed up with it, as it had been appearing and disappearing over and over again during my journey, so I took it out, somewhat the worse for being in the pigsty, and handed it over.

"Phew! Stinky. Hmmm. What on earth er-have you done with it? You twit! It's been er-near the pigs, hasn't it? Filthy habits you have. Now, I'll er-see you, hmmm, when you reach the lair of the White Dwarf. He's my homunculus. Er-beats the drum, you know, so I can er-perform. You can leave now, hmmm." He unwrapped another hamburger and bit into it, tomato sauce and mayonnaise squirting all over the table.

I didn't know what a homunculus was, but I had seen the White Dwarf making off underwater, slung in a little chariot pulled by two fishes, at the time I reached the Path of Death. I backed into the elevator thankfully and pressed the top button. It shot up with such force that I felt my feet sink into the floor and I sat down with a bump. Reaching the top, I stepped out and Destiny met me, holding in her left hand a steadily burning candle, while each side of her stood two figures with dark green cloaks, one of them carrying a long staff.

"I am glad that's over. Now, listen to me carefully. This candle represents your life, which is steadily burning down, if you will observe the hourglass at my feet as the sand runs through it. Everyone needs three witnesses to their life, so I have asked these kind people to join me as witnesses. They are from the seven watchers in the Path of Strength above us, and they came down as soon as I called for them. They had to pass through the Island of Geburah to get here, but they braved its extreme dangers. I hope, therefore, that you will appreciate their presence at your coagulation." She paused. "You must go again – for you have been before in the Three of Cups – to the Viceroy of Muckabad, to tell him that you are the cushion thief and that you have given it back to Himself. Did you get a receipt for it?"

"No, Himself did not give me one. But I did pick up this, to prove that I was with him." I produced a McDonalds chicken nugget bucket. "Will this do?"

"Yes, that is certainly proof of your meeting. Nobody else eats that rubbish on this plane of existence! Here is the Asian elephant to take you back to the Viceroys' mansion. Hurry, now, and get this ordeal over. We will wait for you, which will not be difficult as we are no longer subject to earthly time."

I mounted the kneeling elephant and we lumbered off through the gates and back to the mansion. Leaving the elephant in the now deserted paddock, I walked past the pig sty to the dreadful Viceroys' mansion, and knocked at the door. A footman opened it and asked me to wait in the foyer. There was not a trace of the jousting event, and the crowds had disappeared. An upper door on a balcony opened and a figure came out and leaned over the railing. My heart started to pound.

"Hello! I understand you wanted to speak with me? How can I help you?" The light was behind the speaker, but as he turned, I saw the charismatic face of my dream lover, he that I met during my sojourn in the Three of Swords.

"I am the Viceroy of Muckabad. Do you need money? I can arrange for my footman to give you what you require."

"Thank you, but no, that is not what I came for. This is for you." I held out the chicken nugget bucket, in which I had placed a half-eaten pickle with the distinct imprints of Himselfs' dental plan on it. The footman took the bucket from me distastefully and mounted the stairs, handing it to the Viceroy.

"I am the thief who stole the gold velvet cushion from beneath you. I was under an obligation to return it to Himself, for it really belongs to him. I hope that is OK with you. I have brought this bucket as proof that I was actually with Himself recently. See – the pickle is still fresh."

"It does look like the rubbish Himself eats." The Viceroy peered into the bucket and thought for a moment. "If you are the thief, then I have arrested the wrong man. I will free him immediately and give him a pardon. Thank you for telling me the truth, and good night to you." He waved and disappeared into a backlit bedroom.

I was momentarily disappointed, as I had hoped for further audience with him, but at least I had done the right thing. I left the mansion and mounted the Asian elephant, and we quickly returned to Destiny and the two witnesses. Now I had exonerated the wronged man, I was ready for my coagulation.

Destiny and the two other witnesses now stood at the foot of the empty seat of Justice on a heart shaped red stone. They drew me into their center between the two hourglasses, which were on each side of the stone. Destiny pointed to the hourglass on my right, in which the sand was rapidly running out. She then pointed to the left hand hourglass, which she turned, so that it was empty to receive the first trickle of sand. "You have extended your span in eternity, although you will be going in and out of different lives as you progress. Now accept this body of solidified light, which is the Stone of the Philosophers, for your alchemical work is complete."

She handed me a dazzling silver rounded stone that scintillated with reflected light from every angle. I held it and felt a powerful energy vibrating from the Stone. My blood seemed to slow down in my veins and stop for a second.

Destiny continued. "From here you will be in the world of Soul, as you remember your gazelle is now inside you. Those who will meet you there can lead you into the realm of pure Spirit that lies beyond." The two witnesses nodded as a light breeze caused the candle flame to flicker.

At this point, the crone Ediug stepped forward. "It is now time for you to visit the Island of Tiphareth, for you are ready to experience the Longing Forces that lie within the Six Peaks. For your convenience, I have shape shifted into a flying object to take you there, for you cannot reach Tiphareth through the powers of Earth, neither those of Water, Fire or Air, but only by connection with your Higher Self, namely, me." She unzipped her solar plexus, revealing a comfortable padded chamber just big enough for one person.

I grasped her hand. "I have missed you, Ediug. I haven't seen you since you played the harp so sweetly in the Passage of the Moon. Shall I step into your little chamber?" Then I remembered the owls warning – that Ediug, like most women, had a dark side. I must watch out for that, I decided, as I stuffed that sinister thought.

"Indeed, yes! I will give you a soaring ride across the Mystic SEA to Tiphareth." She beckoned to me, and with some misgivings, I stepped into her protective space and closed the zipper. The air inside was stifling. I could barely breathe and I realized, too late, that there was no ventilation in the chamber, as she rose into the air vertically and then, adjusting her blades, swept forward at a 45 degree angle, heading due west.

Island of TIPHARETH

Hurtling along in the confined and stifling darkness inside Ediug, I curled up into a fetal position and slowed my breathing to one exhalation a minute. Thus, I was able to conserve what little air there was, hoping that the journey would not be too long. Fortunately, she begin to level out and slant downwards after a short while, so I prepared myself by strapping on a small parachute I had found in the chamber, for I suspected she was going to dump me unceremoniously.

There was a cackle of laughter from Ediug and the zipper under me shot open, revealing an incredible view below. Six giant golden peaks jutted out of the center of the vast island of Tiphareth. The strong flow of air pulled me out of the chamber and I couldn't hold on any longer so, leaping from the belly of the descending crone, I went into a skydiving position, hoping that the parachute would open when I needed it. I zoomed downwards, finding that any slight movement of my body steered me, and at the correct altitude, I yanked on the parachute cord, sighing with relief as it spread out above me with a jerk and slowed my fall to a gentle descent. Now, scanning the Island below, I searched for a suitable landing place, and saw a field with some cows grazing in it so, steering in that direction, I hoped to avoid landing amongst the peaks.

At the last moment, a gust of wind lifted me up again and I crashed feet first into a large Christmas tree, hung with all kinds of lights, bells and whistles. My parachute ripped as it caught on the sharp wing of the angel at the top of the tree, so I divested myself of it and swung down from one branch to another, rather like a chimpanzee. Landing at the bottom of the tree, somewhat scratched, I felt springy grass under my feet and, as I stepped forward, discovered that I could bound into the air and travel several yards at a time. In this manner, I rapidly covered the distance between the Christmas tree and a small grey hut beside a pile of natural boulders that shimmered vaguely in the center of the grassy plain. An old fellow sat beside it, watching a beautiful gazelle as it grazed peacefully nearby. The gazelle, startled, abruptly raised its head as I approached and drew back. The old man said a few quiet words to the animal and it relaxed, then turned and came trotting towards me, putting its sleek head under my arm. I felt its quivering warmth walking close to me as I approached the hut.

"Here you are, then." My Guide smiled. "I told you that I would bring the gazelle, your Soul, to greet you. So take this fleeting opportunity to combine with her before you move on. The gazelle will stay with you while you are on this Island." His face fell as I caressed the gentle animal. "But alas! By the time you leave Tiphareth, she will become old, for when you leave here, only your Spirit must remain to carry you forward into the Chariot of your Higher Self. You may not know that Tiphareth, along with the two Islands of Yesod and Malkuth, suffered a catastrophic fall at the beginning of Time. These three Islands sank down below their correct level, and they have remained in that position. They can be restored to their rightful positions on the Tree of Life only when human kind has raised its vibrations sufficiently. At that time, Tiphareth will once again join with Da'ath."

I began to weep, and the grief of years fell from my eyes in rivulets. I kept the gazelle close to me, stroking it and wishing I could absorb its beauty into my body. The old fellow invited me to a plate of roast meat that turned slowly on a spit over the fire. I soon cheered up, as I was ravenous, drying my eyes and eating heartily while he told me I must journey into the mountains and define the meaning of the six peaks, and then I would meet the Child that lived in the center of the Island.

"Tiphareth is a wonderful place, but it will lure you into staying here, for it is lovely, yet deceptive." He warned me. "You must resist the temptation to remain here, among those unfortunates who have been seduced by religious rubbish. Your Ego nature, Belvedere, will submit to you in the Passage of the Chariot – provided the forces that swirl around the abyss do not turn you to stone in the narrow defile that leads to the Sea of Sorrow. Before you reach the Chariot - the Merkabah - you must pass through your initiation." He paused. "By now you must know that the crone Ediug and I are one, and that she is merely myself inverted, for I contain both male and female polarities – an attribute of all Magians, who live between Wisdom and Understanding. The missing sphere, Da'ath, contains all Knowledge, but because it has been eliminated by the Fall of Tiphareth, the knowledge is hidden." He laid his hand on my arm. "Now, the first Knight will be here shortly to accompany you on your first test, and after that the other three will come in their turn." "Take care of your gazelle, for I must bid you farewell until we meet in the Passage of the Chariot. "The essence of the gazelle is now inside you – she is no longer a separate part of you, but you have integrated her into your belief in yourself, which has been changed in the process you have just experienced. You will always be conscious of her, but soon you will not see her with your outer eyes as a gazelle. Instead, you will know her in your deepest being." He pressed my arm and, with a puff of wind, he was gone, leaving me standing beside the gazelle that bleated and shivered plaintively.

We were not alone for long, for the sound of galloping hooves came on the breeze and a rider appeared, thundering heavily across the grassy plain. As he pulled up, I saw the familiar face of Terramud, the Knight of Pentacles, clad in full armor and mounted on his horse Claydung. His nightjar slept around his neck and he led a spare horse for me.

Terramud greeted me gruffly, handing me a small bridle for the gazelle, whose swift flight could easily keep up with a horse. "Your first task on the Island of Tiphareth awaits you. I will accompany you to the lion cages, where you must seek the Solar Lion of Strength and free it, so that it may subdue its natural instincts in homage to Strength, the omniscient woman. Pinpointing the correct lion amongst so many, for there are thousands of lions that are associated with the Sun deity in Tiphareth, will not be easy." Terramud gave a short laugh. "However, you were very successful in finding Joana, the correct soft cricket amongst millions, during your visit to the Seven of Pentacles, and so this should be a lot easier. Bridle your gazelle and mount the dun horse I have brought for you, and we will ride to the Solar Animal Park."

I jumped into the saddle of the dun mare, gathering up her reins and tying the gazelles bridle rein to the pommel, gave the mare my heels, and we were on our way at a steady trot. Terramud, being an Earthly Pentacle, was weighted down with much material armor and traveled much more slowly than the other Knights. Seated firmly in his saddle, he did not rise to the trot but bumped along in a relaxed slouch. Nevertheless, we covered the ground comfortably, the gazelle trotting confidently alongside on a loose rein.

We traveled steadily and were soon entering a narrow cleft between the soaring peaks that rose up to six thousand feet straight from the flat plain. Turning right, we arrived at the gates of a large zoo, and my blood curdled, as I smelt the raw scent and heard the roaring of many lions. We dismounted and the gatekeeper agreed to feed my gazelle while I looked for the correct lion, as her tender flesh might prove to be a distraction to the beasts. Leaving our horses tied up at the gate, Terramud and I walked along the cages where the lions padded up and down, each more magnificent than the last, with splendid manes and lashing tails. Personally, I disapproved of caged beasts and wonder why the authorities in Tiphareth had not thought of a more humane way of sheltering the lions. Terramud slogged along beside me, refusing to take off his armor although I pointed out that he was likely to get heat stroke, for the sun was surprisingly warm.

We walked for several miles amongst the cages, and there were still more lions to check out. The sun was glancing off the golden peaks, and the reflected rays heated the path to boiling point. I could see that Terramud was sweating profusely and I urged him to loosen his stiff gauntlets and take them off, but he refused. He began to stagger and suddenly keeled over and fell to the ground in a heap, gasping like a caught fish as he passed out. Quickly I removed his helmet and loosened his throat guard, then eased his bronze cuirass and massaged his chest, but he remained limp and unresponsive. I hurried to a water fountain and filled my skin bottle, pouring the water over his flushed face and torso, and he began to come round. Gently insistent, I bade him remove the rest of his armor and throw it to one side, explaining why.

"Your armor consists of psychic defenses that you have built up in the material world. You cannot survive in Tiphareth unless you drop these defenses, which are past rejections, hurts and repressions. Come now, walk free in your simple cotton undergarments and help me to find the correct lion."

Alas, my pleas fell on deaf ears, for Terramud did not feel comfortable without his armor. He pushed me away and began to put on his greaves again. Annoyed, I rose to my feet, shrugging my shoulders. "I'm sorry you are so insistent. I hoped you would come with me, but you are slowing me down. I'll leave you here and come back with the lion." I frowned. "I must find the correct lion soon, for there is much to be done here, and the three other Knights await me."

Terramud was too busy armoring himself to reply, so I strode on, examining each lion closely. Several miles further on, I found myself instinctively halting at an ordinary looking cage. The lion inside was quite large, obviously a fully mature male who glared at me fiercely, his mane spiking aggressively. I held his yellow gaze as the mane rose around his head in a golden aura, giving off scintillating sparks. I could feel the heat emanating from the glowing mane as sparks gave way to bright solar flares that burst out all around him. His eyes became liquid gold, and still they held mine. In a trance, I opened his cage and he walked out, pacing by my side calmly as I headed back towards the zoo gates. I was sure I had found the correct lion. The gatekeeper congratulated me, as this lion was the chosen one to draw the chariot of the King.

At the gates the Knight of Swords, Typhona, with her horse Swirl, her albatross perched on her shoulder, greeted me hastily as I mounted the dun mare, took the bridle of my gazelle, and followed her towards the next path through the peaks. We soon entered a gully, which grew narrower as we progressed. I began to feel hemmed in and panicky. I wanted reassurance from Typhona, but she kicked her horse into a slanting jump, whirled around, and disappeared with great speed up out of the gully. Alone, I rode on nervously until I noticed the bright light from Tiphareths' sun fading rapidly. Twilight settled in and I thought it must be evening. I stopped and dismounted, tethering the mare and the gazelle near a patch of thin grass to feed. I was settling down for the night when I looked above me and saw a dark grey mass with a black dot in the center floating down. This cloud was settling over the gazelle, and I ran over to push it away. To my horror, the clinging envelope of a thick cobweb brushed against my face, and a monstrous spider crawled from the web and settled onto the back of my gazelle, its mandibles ready to bite into her neck.

A piercing fear shot through me and my hair prickled on my head as adrenalin raced through my veins. I must battle the thing I dreaded most, a giant spider, before it destroyed my very Soul! Drawing the sword of my willpower from its sheath, I slashed at the clinging web and fought my way towards the spider, the clutching cobweb smearing itself over my face and body. The spider watched me closely, darting this way and that as I distracted it from its prey. The gazelle was motionless in terror, its eyes rolled back in its head and its legs giving way under it. I shouted to the animal to react, encouraging it to master its instinct to surrender, and to fight back. At the same time, I reached the spider and cut through the web surrounding it, isolating it so that it could not hide from me. It reached out towards me with two hairy legs, its mandibles wiggling furtively, and

I leveled my sword, cutting off the nearest leg, which fell writhing to the ground. Cautiously getting closer, I slashed at the other leg and soon it fell, severed. The spider backed away on six legs, avoiding me, but it had nowhere to run.

The gazelle straightened up and gave a little buck, which unbalanced the spider, and it slipped off the animals' back and fell at my feet, its remaining legs in a tangle. Swiftly I thrust my sword into its exposed belly, holding the horrible creature down as it went into its last struggles. Soon it was lying, legs neatly folded, silent in death, as disgusting as ever but at least unmoving. I stepped over it carefully, not wanting to touch it, and embraced the gazelle, who nuzzled me in relief as I led her away from the hideous scene. Exhausted, we slept together until light came again with the descent of Typhona, lightly cantering down from the edge of the gully.

"Where were you when I needed help?" I asked angrily. "You are as useless as that wretched Terramud is. He passed out when I needed him, too."

"I am sorry, but you cannot rely on the Knights during your time on the Island of Tiphareth. We are only here as guides, to show you where to go and what you must do. We cannot do it for you." She pointed to her legs, from which the armor was falling. "You see, your influence is far more powerful than we are – and you are here to help us let go of our armor, which we have worn since the beginning of time. By releasing our armor, we open ourselves to the rays of Tiphareths' sun and we bathe in its light."

"The sun was too hot for Terramud, though." I remarked. "He got heat stroke and passed out."

"That is because he is only a Pentacle, dwelling in Earth. He lives on the plane of sensation and cannot rationalize the thought to cool himself off. As a Sword, I am at least able to use the logical powers of Air to free myself from some of my restricting armor, but not all. That process continues with the other two knights." Typhona reached into a small scabbard on her left side. "I have brought a gift for the Child. The King of Swords and his consort wish to acknowledge your feats of endurance by allowing you to present Reficul with the Emerald Sword, which you wrested from the grasp of the Seven Shades and left with us for safe keeping. That will please him greatly." She handed the brilliant little sword to me before leading the way out of the gully, and I bade her goodbye as the third rider, preceded by a swiftly moving stormy petrel, galloped into view. The Knight of Cups, Surgey, pulled Catarack up and he reared high above my head. He did not hesitate, but took a different path through the six peaks, the golden light still radiating from their smooth sides. As we rode, he explained. "The Child, our Lord Reficul, awaits you in the Hall of Initiation. While we are traveling there, fix your gaze on the six peaks and endeavor to extract their secret, for entrance to the Hall is only granted to those who have the right answer."

I had little time to think as we rode along, although I noted that Surgey had lost his arm and leg armor, and had on only a cuirass and a helmet. Six peaks. What else had six points? I ran the thought through my mind as, rounding a bend in the path we came upon an open space, where a vast mirror set in the ground reflected a distant light that was so bright I hid my eyes. With my eyes closed, I could still see the light in the mirror in my mind, and I saw the six peaks reflected in it. Slowly the peaks moved around and rearranged themselves into two triangles, their points touching in the center. The upper triangle moved slowly downwards and the lower one rose to greet it, forming a six-pointed golden star. I knew it for the Star of David, the hexagram, the secret of Tiphareth, and felt my heart lift.

We dismounted, the great gates of the Hall ahead of us, handing our horses and the gazelle to the doorkeeper. I told him the six peaks represented the six points of the hexagram that ruled over Tiphareth, and he nodded warmly, allowing us to pass. Surgey accompanied me as we walked in, the vast ceiling above us vibrating with a hollow echo to our steps. The Hall was empty save for a large cradle, woven of rushes and caulked with pitch, with a hookah beside it. Puffs of smoke rose from the cradle as the Child pulled thoughtfully on the pipe. The goddess Nepthys sat in attendance and we greeted her as we bent over the cradle. The little figure sat up, pulling off his harness. He raised his top hat in greeting and stepped out of the cradle, smiling seductively at us. Sweeping off the hat, he revealed the two small but distinct horns on his head.

Seeing Reficul emerge, Surgey backed away, shielding his eyes and giving a gasp of fear, as the babe did a quick somersault and then stood on his head for a few moments. I could see something was about to happen, as Surgey hurried out of the Hall in a panic. The upside down baby was growing rapidly bigger, his trunk, arms and legs were already developing into adult size, and his little face became leaner and sprouted a small pointed beard. Then he somersaulted to his feet.

Nepthys laughed aloud. "Welcome, my Lord Lucifer! I would like you to meet the Navigator, who has heard of your inverted self, and wishes to know you better."

I bowed down before the transformed Child, holding the Emerald Sword, at which he gasped with delight. "Where did you find this? I lost this many years ago! I believed the Seven Shades may have stolen it." Lucifers' stag horns were rapidly growing into an impressive nine-point rack with a tuft of bright red hair sprouting in between on his forehead.

"Yes, you're right. They persuaded Damalis to steal it from the armory and give it to them in the Seven of Swords. I managed to get it back and conceal it at the Castle of Air. The Knight, Typhona, brought it to me. Here, it's yours."

He took the sword and plucked the great Emerald from it, raising it in his hand and holding it out for me to see. "I am extremely grateful to you for recovering the Sword. I can now tell you the secret of my Emerald. You met me on the Passage of the Star. I was then a Child in a cradle. The pearl bracelet you wore matched the necklace that my mother placed around my neck at birth, therefore I knew that you were the right person to hear the secret of the Emerald Tablet. I will now tell you the story. First, I am giving back the pearl necklace and the bracelet. You have earned them by your dedication to the Way. Instead, Nepthys will adorn me with the Celtic torc. She had hidden it in her earthen pot."

Nepthys here produced a magnificent golden torc, which she entwined around Lucifers' neck, and we completed the exchange of jewelry as I put on the pearl necklace and bracelet. Then we moved out of the Hall of Initiation and sat down by a beautiful waterfall in the garden outside. Lucifer told us that his name meant the Light Bearer, for he carried a lantern to show people the way to find Tiphareth. His strength was such that it rivaled that of divine power, and he wanted man to have access to that strength. He decided to depart from the sphere of Da'ath in the higher regions and take with him the Emerald Tablet, as a gift to humans. When he arrived on Earth, the people who saw him did not recognize who he was, and rudely spurned him, calling him bad names. They would not even look at the Tablet, although he tried to show them, and they pushed it away, thinking it rubbish. Saddened, he decided that, since they were so ignorant, and had refused the gift of the Tablet, which meant eternal youth, that they must, therefore, perish. He set a limit on each humans' life, so that when death occurred, they might return to the cosmos and receive knowledge of what they had lost, in order to begin again with a new life.

Dismayed by his tale, I understood that, as a result, each person must find their lost youth, and that might take many reincarnations. What was the real meaning of eternal youth, anyway? It meant being born again, in spirit, beyond the powers of entropy, which was the inevitable end to everything subject to gravitation. His confession was a revelation to me, and I felt a great affinity with him, for he had suffered rejection, as I had during my time on Earth. Since the Emerald Tablet was now within my grasp, I asked Lucifer if I could see it, and he handed me a small bone fragment - a copy of it that he kept in his pocket. I read the words, written in an elegant hand, with reverence, and they fled into my heart.

He spoke softly. "Many people wonder why the Tablet is Emerald, whose brilliant green symbolizes spring. That is the time of renewal and hope. It is associated with the Green Man of the Celts and with Osiris, consort of Isis, who is the resurrected God. The Tablet speaks the Truth – for those who have the wits to understand it. In order to be perfect, one must return to Earth many times. The Archpriestess will tell you that. For the ignorant, who have not received this gnosis – well, they are not ready. They don't know how to make the ultimate sacrifice." Lucifer looked at me gravely. "You are now both man and woman, unified by the celestial marriage of the Sun and the Moon, and your own union with your beloved. You will spread the Word. When you have completed your journey on the Way of Return, are you then willing to take on this task?" His piercing green eyes sought mine. "Tell me, in this moment, will you do the bidding of the Universe?"

I met his eyes unflinchingly. "I have made a commitment from the first day of my voyage of initiation, which began when I collected the Tarot cards, one by one. Pullows, my earthly devotee, is keeping the cards safe and she is waiting patiently for the rest of the deck. I will do what is commanded of me, for the sake of all those who remain in ignorance, for I have committed myself to the Great Work."

Lucifer tossed his head back, as a stag would, and bellowed to the Sun, a haunting, powerful sound that reverberated through the golden peaks around us, echoing long after the utterance of the first note. Then he lowered his head and spoke urgently.

"The time has come! You must translate your energy from one form to another. The Knight of Wands, Ignitia, will take you on your final mission here. Free the phoenix from her prison. When the bird is free, take your gazelle into your solar plexus, the resting place of the Soul. She will bond with you in complete union. You will then have absorbed the influence of your Soul on your dual nature. Your masculine and feminine polarities were married in the Path of the Lovers. However, while I wait here for the successful outcome of your quest, I am in great danger. Your Ego self, Belvedere, has been stalking me for many moons. He plans to kidnap me. This I know, because I know all things. I have passed through the hidden Island of Da'ath on my way down here." Lucifer gripped my arm tightly. "Do not fail to release the phoenix, the emblem of rebirth, or I am lost."

I felt the desperation in his words, and I resolved to find the bird and give her liberty, no matter how difficult it might be. Leaving the gazelle, I jumped on the dun mare and joined Ignitia on her mount Smokey, and we rose in a great jump away from the garden and into a lush, green landscape filled with incredible plants that spread their varied foliage to the bright sun. The peaks had vanished, converted now into the sign of Tiphareth, the hexagram, and all around us fresh greenery glistened, its chlorophyll throbbing in the sunlight.

We soon came to a small forest, riding rapidly through the sparse undergrowth, so that one could see a considerable distance. I glimpsed a shadowy form slinking from tree to tree some distance away, so we spurred our horses and gave chase, only to find that it was merely a flitting shadow. New forms began to populate the forest, some leaping, others crawling or climbing trees, and all proved to be images of our minds and came to nothing. As the trees gave way to a clearing of soft moss, we paused to rest. In the center of the clearing was a large standing stone that I decided to investigate, for I saw a dark opening beneath it. Pushing it aside, I sprang back in revulsion as a nest of slithering copperhead snakes came to view. There must have been hundreds of them, and they began to pour out of the nest and swarm over the clearing. Ignitia jumped onto Smokey and made off at a gallop, for she was afraid of snakes. I stood my ground, however. I had vanquished the spider, and I was not afraid of snakes, even though copperheads were venomous.

Carefully avoiding the escaping snakes, I looked into the hole again. Something under the snakes was fluttering wildly. I glimpsed a reddish feather, and then a beady eye glared up at me. It was a bird. Quickly I grasped the last snake behind its head and threw it from the nest, my heart beating fervently. A golden red bird was evidently trapped under the snakes, its wings held down by two heavy stones. Carefully I lifted off the stones and the bird began to climb out, chattering fiercely so that I drew back a little distance from the nest. It looked like the phoenix I was searching for as it stood on the edge of the nest and stretched its wings, then, with a little run, it took off and spiraled upwards, vanishing over the top of the nearest trees.

There was something else in the hole, hidden under the bird. I knelt down and lifted out a little vial, with the word Vitriol written on the label. I unscrewed the stopper and sniffed the liquid, which smelt good, so I drank it in one gulp. A burning fire shot through me and I dropped the vial. I felt myself lifted off the springy turf and shooting into the air like a rocket, my head full of a myriad thoughts and sensations. I saw my entire quest from the Island of Malkuth before me in a flash, and I knew that I had reached a point of no return, yet I had further to go. I leveled out and flew low over the trees. I saw, galloping below on foam-covered Smokey, Ignitias' armor falling off her so that she wore only a green helmet. Above her, two hawks were flying, so I swooped down to join them. They were Suroh and Horus, who came together in a mating grasp and then separated. A peregrine falcon, dressed in a blue bonnet and cloak, then appeared and the three birds and I flew on for some distance, watching Smokey stumble and finally collapse under the Knight, who managed to jump free in time. We continued our wild flight, zooming back towards the Hall of Initiation, where I hoped Lucifer was waiting. I touched down on the ground, feeling distinctly light headed, and the falcon landed on my outstretched arm, eyeing me astutely and addressing me in penetrating tones as it tossed back its blue cloak.

"I expected to find you here." It said firmly. "This is the right place and the right time. I am Hawkley P. Mann, and if you remember, I gave you a barred feather way back at the crusader castle in the Eight of Swords. I have been watching Belvedere. He is totally out of control. Hasten into the Hall, for he has kidnapped Lucifer. I will stand by."

Exhausted by my flight, I wobbled unsteadily into the Hall. There was an air of panic and people were scurrying in all directions. Someone was shouting. They were saying that he had gone in that direction, no, this way, no, he was over there, no – someone had seen him streaking through the garden towards the waterfall - carrying a struggling object wrapped tightly in a parcel under his arm. I ran towards the waterfall and squeezed into the space behind it that opened out into a small cave. A tall familiar figure was digging in the earth at the back of the cave, while a bundle on the ground wriggled frantically. I rushed to the bundle and began to untie it. Belvedere turned and began to shout. His purple suit was filthy and his shoes covered in mud. He threw aside his spade and lunged towards me as I lifted the last piece of brown paper off the bundle, and Lucifer appeared, panting for breath and ready to fight.

Belvedere backed away cannily, looking for an opening and shouting at Lucifer. "I have come a long way to meet you. I have gained great experience and knowledge during that time. Now, do you think I am afraid of you? Certainly not, for I am more powerful than you are." He beat his breast as he planned to attack.

I was thinking quickly. Should I allow my Ego to fight the Light Bearer? Was it up to me to stop Belvedere, or should I stand back and merely observe? I decided on the latter course, and stepped back to the cave wall. The two redheaded contestants faced each other, fists clenched, their breath coming in heavy gasps. Circling, circling, each sought the chance to strike a blow. Belvedere saw his moment and his fist came out, flying through the air, but instead of finding its mark, Lucifer caught his wrist and quickly clapped on a pair of handcuffs. He whistled, and two maenads tiptoed forward and dragged my Ego away with them.

Lucifer smiled and turned to me. "Sorry about that. Had to lead him on, you know. It's part of the game. He's proud and it's very hard for him to give up control. It isn't always something you are aware of. Bit of a loose cannon, I would say. He'll have plenty of time to alter his attitude in Purgatory Jail." Lucifer patted my shoulder. "Don't worry. He'll be set free in time for future Paths. By then, he'll finally understand his position."

Hawkley fluttered down to my shoulder, his blue cloak floating behind him. "I will stand by you while you go through your final phase in Tiphareth, for the Hoodwinker awaits you. See if you can outwit her, now that Belvedere is incarcerated."

The thoughtful hawk flew in front of me as we made our way from the garden, through a narrow gate and onto a rustic suspension bridge made of ropes. Far below the swinging bridge, a torrent rushed ever onwards over tossing rocks. In the center of the bridge a dark, hooded shape was squatting, turning its head this way and that.

I knew it was the Hoodwinker. Personally, I was quite pleased with my progress, since my arrival in Tiphareth would not have been possible without my success in the previous seven tests, where I had encountered the Seven Shades. I knew my Guide well and could count on him to back me up and keep me out of trouble. I had little to fear and the road ahead seemed to present few problems, for I felt I had advanced far along the Way of Return.

I strode onto the bridge, nimbly keeping my balance on the swaying structure, which was about sixty feet above the cataract. Drawing my sword of willpower from its sheath at my belt, I advanced boldly. "Do not bar my path, Hoodwinker, for you cannot hope to prevail over my power." I said as I gestured scornfully with the sword, lunging towards her as she rose to her feet, imagining her hidden scowl. A foul stink wafted from her and several lice and spiders fell from her cloak as she shook it menacingly.

She stood her ground as I warily pressed on, my sword flashing in the dim light, for it had grown dark. I glanced back, but a thick mist had arisen, concealing the hawks' ghostly shape, and I felt its cold fingers touch my neck, and shivered. The Hoodwinker seemed bigger than I thought. She was unmoving in the center of the swaying bridge, and the rush of the torrent seemed much louder.

I hesitated. Why was I crossing this river, anyway? Was it the correct way to go towards the Abyss? Surely not, for the river was running at right angles to me. I should be following the current down to the Sea of Sorrow, which lay straight ahead beyond the Passage of the Chariot. Should I turn back? No! I had fought the Shades before, in their own den. I would go forward, conquer the Hoodwinker, and see what lay on the other side. With that, I began moving towards the foul creature again, and soon we were face to face - although her drooping cowl shadowed any expression in her eyes.

Oh! My God! Suddenly I felt a sharp jerk under my feet, as if someone had pulled a mat away. I lost my balance as the bridge swung wildly and grabbed for the hand rope on my right, dropping my sword, which spiraled down and landed with a clang on the rocks far below. Alas! There was nothing there – the rope was gone – only empty space. I could not stop myself from pitching off the bridge through the gap, and hurtling downwards as an evil cackle came from the chapped lips of the Hoodwinker.

Falling, I rolled into the correct position and spied, sixty feet below me, a small but deep pool in a river eddy. I twisted into a steep dive and aimed for it. If I missed, it was certain death on the rocks beside my sword. I held my breath.

I hit the water hard and sliced down into the depths. Then, surfacing, I swam to the side of the pool, avoiding the swift current that swirled around the great boulders and jammed logs in the river. Swimming along the shore, I looked for a place to scramble out, but the rocks hemmed me in. The Hoodwinker stood on the bridge, throwing small stones at me and laughing. I became exhausted, partly from shock, and I reached out in desperation. My hand touched the material of a blue cloak, and I clung to it as someone slowly pulled me over a pebbly beach to the shore.

Hawkley wrung out his wet cloak. "The Hoodwinker tricked you. Her name is Pride, and she planned to make you fall. Please remember, you are not at your goal yet. Now, look at your sword of willpower. It's badly bent, but it's not broken. We can get that fixed somewhere."

He flew down and perched on my shoulder, folding his cloak around my shivering body. "I had to stand by. I couldn't help you, for it was a learning curve for you. Pride comes before a fall, you know. Lucky for you, it was a skilful fall and not to be despised. Now, we will go to a sword smith I know and leave the sword there overnight. He'll fix it for you. While we wait, tomorrow we can complete the sacrifice."

Hawkley took me to his library, where he showed me a simple cot to sleep on. I commented on his numerous books about esoteric subjects, and he told me he was compiling a great book on Secret Teachings. I hoped that he would manage to finish his research, for I wanted to read his book. He explained to me that I was ready to experience my return to my original position in Malkuth, but that I would experience mundane existence on a different level. By accomplishing the seven steps, I would be empowered within the Lesser Stone, but this demanded that I give up something.

The hawk led me outside, where the gazelle was grazing. She had grown old, and was tottering on her frail legs. I wondered how much longer she would last. I wanted to take her essence into my own body again before she died, but I was not sure how. As we stood there, a rattle of chains sounded, and three figures appeared. The two maenads held Belvedere between them.

"I asked the maenads to bring your Ego here. He has served time in Purgatory Jail for assault upon the person of Lucifer, and has repented. He wishes to serve you, yes, serve you obediently and ardently in future." The hawk nodded sagely, his blue bonnet tipping over one bright eye. "You must make a hard decision. The gazelle is an old Soul, you know. She would be better off riding in your solar plexus from now on. You must decide whether to keep her with you, or your Ego, Belvedere. One of them must die."

What a difficult choice to make! Belvedere heard and immediately set up a loud wailing. "Master, choose me! I will serve you better. Please, I beg

of you, spare my life for I do not want to die." He began to cry. "For pitys'
sake, I have been by your side your whole life. You cannot let me go now."
He fell to his knees with a deep sob, clasping me to him, his eyes rolling
up in their sockets, and fainted away.

My brain was still on fire from the effects of the Vitriol I had swallowed.
Nevertheless, I tossed up the figurative coin cautiously. The gazelle was
old but I felt it was important to continue the quest with her alongside of
me. Belvedere had recently been a nuisance, and the more aware of him
and his puppet trickery, the more I realized he was not really a part of me,
especially if I was to board the Chariot shortly and be with my Higher
Self. Therefore, I decided to get rid of Belvedere.

I was about to speak when Hawkley interrupted me. "Think of the
sacrifice, the sacrificial fire. One must thoroughly cook the victuals. I don't
think that Belvedere would fit on the spit, as it is only six feet long. It would
be hard to turn. I usually do it myself, but it's tough on a hawk, and last
time I caught my blue cloak alight. Something smaller would be preferable,
and more manageable. Do you see what I mean?" He gave me a piercing
glance and an unmistakable wink. I admired the hawk for his erudite
teachings and loyalty on my quest. His manner indicated the gazelle.

I understood what he was hinting at. The gazelle was old, and would
make a fine dinner for twenty. However, I needed my Soul, and I was
reluctant to keep Belvedere, who was extremely annoying. The maenads
were slowly fanning him back to consciousness.

"I will choose the gazelle." I announced quietly. "I trust that I have
made the right decision."

Hawkley nodded without saying anything. Preparing a bower of fresh
flowers and plants, he led the gazelle to it and she lay down. He produced
a tiny syringe and pierced the gazelles hide, whereupon she closed her eyes
calmly and passed away. At that moment, I felt a stirring in my solar plexus,
as if a babe was fluttering in there, and I knew her spirit was with me for
eternity. Nevertheless, I was crying desolately as we skinned her. We cut off
her head as a trophy to mount on an oak shield, in the manner of those who
hunted and fished. Hawkley started a roaring fire and we spitted her with
reverence, gazing quietly into the flames as Belvedere volunteered to turn
the spit. When the meat was ready, we sat down at a picnic table, inviting
the two maenads to join us. We loaded generous portions of venison onto
the plates with chunks of good bread, and began to eat. I noticed that
Belvedere was staring at his plate, trying to jab a fork into the bread, but
missing his mark.

"What's up, Belvedere? Not hungry? Dig in, or it will get cold." I encouraged him.

"You didn't give me any meat! I have the bread, but no meat." He was upset. "My plate is empty, can't you see!"

Hawkley clacked his beak. "Belvedere. You are the Navigators Ego and you can't eat the Soul of the Navigator! I'm afraid it's just bread for you, and be thankful it's fresh." The hawk turned to me. "Now I can tell you that it is only when you eat something that it truly becomes a part of you. That's why your choice of the gazelle was unavoidable if you were to continue with your Soul intact. The gazelle has bonded with you and is now a part of your bodily energy. That is how it must be." He put down his knife as I nodded dumbly and we rose from the table. The time had come to make my entrance to the Path of the Chariot. Hawkley bid us goodbye and Belvedere and I set off across the luscious green grass towards a low bank of clouds on the horizon.

First Path of the CHARIOT

Tiphareth is the junction of eight paths. I had already experienced the five lower paths that joined it during my alchemical trials. There remained three paths still in front of me, and I chose the center one that headed due South – the Path of the Chariot. Belvedere remained by my side, very chastened after several weeks in Purgatory Jail. I felt that my choice to sacrifice the gazelle, my Soul, rather than him, had given him faith in me and the new decisions I would make that came from my Higher Self. I hoped he had finally overcome his egotistical pride.

We set out across a sward of smoothly mowed grass where a tall maypole stood, around which young girls and boys danced, their colored ribbons floating and swirling in a light breeze. I had seen them through the clouds on my previous flight over the Island, and my desire was to remain here with them in Tiphareth, and to go no further on my quest. I eagerly ran towards them, wanting to join the dance, and seized a ribbon, beginning to prance around to the sweet hidden music that made my head whirl and my brain go numb. The beauty of the Island and the mystery behind it was drawing me ever closer. Now and again as I whirled around with the other joyous dancers, I saw Belvedere, his shoulders hunched, watching me in disapproval. Hawkley must have given him my sword, for he was holding it silently.

The pace of the dance quickened and strange perfumes filled the air. The dancers began to let go of their ribbons and stagger off to one side, where they fell into heaps, inert and trancelike. A haze came in front of my eyes and I struggled to maintain consciousness. The bright sunlight seemed to burn me up, and I began to sweat profusely. I felt dizzy and my head was hurting. I could dance no more, dropping to my knees and rolling away from the maypole, and blackness overcame me.

I woke to Belvedere shaking me and calling out my name. Sitting up, I saw that we were at the very edge of a cliff that fell away below us for thousands of feet. This abyss had no bottom, just swirling grey clouds that came and went. In front of us, on the very edge of the cliff, was a sign that rattled in the wind. It said the Chariot would come by every hour on the hour, and that passengers should be ready to jump in with their umbrellas folded. I did not have an umbrella, which was a pity, as a light drizzle was falling and the sun had faded away. As I wondered how long the wait would be, Belvedere knelt before me, holding out my newly furbished sword.

He bowed his head humbly. "Oh, Navigator mine, I humbly offer your sword of willpower and with it, my unassuming obedience and constancy for evermore. Will you accept this sincere and modest submission before you leave to join your Higher Self in the Chariot?" Tears were running down his face as he knelt there, his purple velvet suit ragged and worn, and his feet clad only in shoes that had lost their soles.

"Belvedere! I welcome your continued presence in my life as an esteemed servant." I gently took the hilt of the sword he offered me and touched the tip to his shoulder. "Rise, Sir Belvedere, and may your courage be rewarded." I was crying with joy as he stood up and we embraced, feeling unified at last, as I told him. "I must leave you here, but we will be together again."

A bell rang out and a disembodied voice announced. "Five minutes to the next Chariot arrival! Adjust your canopies and prepare for your jump!"

I looked around, but did not see anything that resembled a canopy or an umbrella. Then we saw two horses, one white and one black, emerging through the mist at a steady trot. The announcer bellowed. "Crouch and focus on the interior of the Chariot as it passes, for it will not stop. You must pretend it is a London bus, and make the jump."

Lowering myself into a tight ball, the Chariot came level with me and I launched myself towards the narrow opening, grabbing the rail and attempting to swing my legs inside, but the vehicle was jiggling to the movement of the two horses, and I lost my grip and slid under it, into the space below.

A voice announced coolly. "Failed. Canopy missing. Try next time."

An agonized scream from Sir Belvedere was the last sound I heard as I plunged down into the enveloping mist.

Path of the HIEROPHANT

My fall slowed and I drifted lazily through the mist. Glimpses of black and white below, like the floor of a cathedral, caught my interest. As I floated nearer, I could see two figures standing each side of this floor, like sentries in cardboard boxes. When they saw me approaching, they hurried forward and spread out an intricately woven cloth of yellow fibers to catch me. I bounced into the flexible cloth legs first, and shot into the air again. It was like a trampoline, and absorbed the shock of my landing.

Sitting in the middle of the cloth, I stared at my two rescuers. They were large brown bears, clad in red shorts that covered them in front, but with no back to them. They stood on their hind legs behind two red poles, and one bear carried a wooden ceremonial crook, painted gold and symbolizing mercy, and the other, to my right, the traditional flail of the Pharoah, representing severity. They smiled gruffly at me, showing their yellow teeth in grins that left me feeling extremely nervous, as they were considerably taller than I was. The black and white tiled floor occupied the center of the room, while a wide track of brown bark ran from one wall to the other beyond it. A number of robed and crowned people sat on thrones placed alongside this track.

"Welcome to the Path of the Hierophant." The silvery voice came from a tall woman, who stood under an arch at the back of the room. A vibrant animal skin tunic clung to her form and dark green robes flowed from her shoulders. "I am the goddess Cybele, keeper of Mount Meru, the center of the earth. I rule over caverns and the peaks of mountains, and all wild beasts are in my retinue. I wield the flail, instrument of strength, and my consort Attis, the shepherd, carries the crook that dispenses mercy. Thus, we balance the world of the Hierophant. Come, we will go to the bull pens to catch the wild bull that will be sacrificed today."

Cybele took my hand and led me along the broad track at the back of the room. I didn't want to tell her that I was frightened of bulls, especially as we approached a herd of massive aurochs that grazed in the nearby field. At our approach, the feral animals raised their heads and snorted a warning, pawing the ground. They tossed their great horns, which were at least six feet wide and displayed sharp pointed tips.

"How are we supposed to catch the wild bull?" I asked plaintively. "The herd are standing their ground and forming an impenetrable barrier."

"These wild bulls represent the lower natures of those who reach the high level of the Hierophant, and your lower nature is the bull on the right." Cybele pointed to an especially large bull, magnificent in his powerful energy, his hide glistening and giving off a greenish-yellow glow. He lowered his head, shaking it as the dust rose from his stamping hooves. "You have passed through the seven trials of your lower nature, and you have attained the intuitive knowledge of the Lesser Stone. To prove that you are completely fearless, you must catch this bull and then join the youths and maidens who are waiting to vault their own bulls. Look over there." She pointed to a low pavilion with open walls where a number of nude young people were standing. In a pen at the opposite end of the bull track, several wild bulls were milling around. "They have chosen their bulls and the bull vaulting performance will begin soon. We must hurry."

Cybele gave me a stick with a hook on the end to snag the ring in the bulls' nose. Whispering instructions to twist the ring to keep the animal under control, she pushed me through the gate and I found myself staring into the eyes of my selected bull. His glance was so vivid that it drew me into him, and I saw flashing before my eyes all the times that I had allowed my Malkuthian nature to overcome me. These instances of yielding to my lower nature flickered before my eyes like a kaleidoscope, constantly turning. I saw my weakness in the past and the pull of lust, greed and cunning trickery that held me in thrall until I started my crossing of the Mystic SEA. I couldn't move for what seemed like hours, until the feral bull tossed his head and the point of his horn grazed my thigh.

I leapt back, quickly remembering the stick. Taking a step forward, I hooked the ring and held on while the bull jerked back, twisting the stick slightly. Immediately the animal calmed down and I was able to lead it over to the pen, where grooms brushed down the bulls ready for their entrance into the bull run. I then went to the pavilion, where an orderly told me sternly to take off all my clothes.

"Why must I strip for the vaulting?" I asked, giving him my lemming skin cloak and pulling the hemp tunic over my head. "It's cold in here."

"Your clothing might catch in the bulls' horns when you make the leap. You might fail to complete the jump, and fall. Your bull would trample you to death in an instant. Many young people die in this way – it is the law of the Hierophant. Your mind must be clear and your soul faithful to the Way of Return, for he brooks no dogmatic practices or the lure of false religions, then you will succeed in vaulting the bull."

He folded my garments neatly as the sound of a trumpet vibrated through the air. The first bull came out of the pen at a fast run and a young, handsome man ran towards it, his feet pounding in the dust of the track. As the galloping bull lowered its head to strike, the young man grasped its horns. With a mighty leap, he somersaulted over the wild bulls' head and landed behind it. Still lightly on his feet, he raised his arms in a gesture of triumph as an official escorted him off the field to the cheers and clapping of the onlookers, who bent their heads and murmured amongst themselves.

The next bull and the next came out of the pen in quick succession and the young people, who must have been training for months, completed their leaps neatly. Then disaster occurred. A beautiful blonde girl ran at her bull, but tripped at the last moment and went under its trampling hooves. Not even time for a scream emerged before two orderlies picked up her ragged body and carried it off the track amidst the disapproving grunts of the audience. I hoped to do better, although I had not been in training at all. It would be touch and go! My nudity embarrassed me and I tried not to shiver in the cool air, slapping my thighs to keep warm and limber.

The greenish-yellow glow of my bulls' hide was visible at the end of the track as he was led forward, then poked with the ox-goad. He bellowed loudly and lunged towards me, as I stood poised at the other end of the track. I glanced swiftly down the track, judging the moment to begin my run so that it would coincide with the lowered head of the bull. I felt my feet pounding along the track, but my total focus was on the head of the wild bull as the distance between us rapidly narrowed. Its horns were down, right in front of me. I spread my arms wide and grasped them, pitching forward in a low somersault as the bulls head came up sharply.

There was a roar of laughter from the crowd as I landed on the bony spine of the bull, holding onto his raised tail, and then slid off into a large patch of fresh dung, which splattered all over me. The bull ran on as I got up, wiping the shit out of my eyes, and faced the crowd, who were holding their sides with mirth. I didn't care. I had vaulted the bull, and I was still alive! I acknowledged their mirth and walked slowly and purposefully down the track, where an official greeted me with a bowl of water and a towel.

Bathed and dressed again, Cybele led me to the edge of the black and white tiled floor of the main room that ended in a steep drop. This side of the room had no walls, but disappeared into empty space – the direction I had initially come from. The two bears stood each side of the drop in their boxes, holding the stranded yellow net between them. Underneath the net, far below, the shape of a pentagram glimmered, and from its' center, a figure of light slowly ascended, its arms outstretched. The face of the man was hidden by an iron Mask with bloodstone teeth, obsidian eyes, and a gleaming quicksilver nose that I instantly recognized. He was the Prince I had found in the Sepulcher, during my visit to the Path of Fortune! He was wearing nothing but a small lambskin g-string with the head of a lamb in the center, and a curious red cap on his head. In his right hand was a ball of yellow thread, the end of which hemmed the edge of a pale yellow veil and ended in a knot of threads between his knees. In his other hand rested a curved dagger or harpe, and a blue trumpet stuck out of his left ear; while his legs were bound together by a thick yellow cord.

He was an amazing sight as he came to a halt, hanging in mid air in front of me, the tip of his strange cap waggling in the air. Cybele brought over a curved new moon and he stepped onto it carefully, taking up a stance that resembled a crucified body. The strange Mask completely covered his face, just as I had replaced it when I found him buried inside the gyroscopic clock, but I knew the staggering beauty that lay beneath it. Cybele genuflected, then gently took the ball of yellow thread from his right hand and gave it to me.

"What is this for?" I asked, puzzled. "It's attached to this veil and ends in a really twisted knot. I don't think anyone could untie that knot."

"That is the Gordian knot of your hidden shame and guilt. This thread is the skein of your gut instincts, for the Prince, who is also the Hierophant, represents the art of Intuition, as you saw in Yesod. You must take this ball of thread with you and enter the labyrinth, which lies below us. If you find your way through the dim maze down there, you will reach the center of your possibilities. There you will confront your darkest repressions, which you must master before you can return through the maze. You must also get rid of that."

She pointed to the bedraggled Shadow that still encircled my right arm. "If you fail to resolve the remainder of this repressed material and resolutely put it behind you for good, you may become lost and never return. That's why you fell from the Chariot." She paused. "The Hierophant has given you the thread out of gratitude, for you found the pieces of the Mask he must wear before all who do not truly know him, and he hopes for your safe return." She indicated the woven cloth, and I stepped onto it. The bears lowered the cloth gently until I was several floors below them, then, seeing the entrance of the labyrinth in front of me, I stepped off the cloth and entered its impenetrable depths.

Groping my way in the dark, I first attached the Gordian knot to the doorpost of the labyrinth. Not wanting to waste time, I decided to sort it out when I returned. Holding the ball in my hand, I allowed the thread to run out as I moved forward, using my intuition to guide me in the right direction. I had previously negotiated a maze during my trials in the Knight of Wands, so I had some idea of the baffling arrangement, and remained calm. The walls of the labyrinth were of baked clay, and towered above me, so there was no way of climbing them to make a short cut if I found myself trapped. I wished for light, but the blind darkness enclosed me completely. A stuffy heat made me gasp for air and I began to sweat while I delved into the repressed thoughts I had shelved over the years of my life. Hours seemed to pass as I twisted and turned around the clay walls, feeling their rough surface with my groping fingers. I had to let go of these memories. I was here now, nowhere else, and all that had passed was merely a learning experience. I hoped the ball of thread would not run out, but, in fact, it seemed to remain the same size, although yards of it must lie behind me.

After some time wandering around corners and backing away from dead ends, retracing my steps and trying other directions, the walls appeared to recede and I felt incredibly relieved and buoyant. All apprehension of the future fell away and a spasm of joy gushed through me. This open space must be the center! I returned to the last wall and felt my way slowly around the dark space, keeping the wall to my left and gradually spiraling in towards the middle. I could see nothing, hear nothing, and feel nothing in the air. No sound of breathing came to me and I could not sense the heat of an unknown body. I finally came to a halt in what I believed to be the heart of the labyrinth. Shuffling my feet around in the dust, my big toe touched an object. I bent down and picked up a small box that slid open like a matchbox. Feeling inside, I took out three wedge shaped nails, which I arranged on the floor in the shape of the letter T.

As the points of the three nails came together, a blinding flash of light enveloped the small chamber and I could see the T-shape on the floor clearly. Crumpling into a heap and holding my solar plexus in agonizing pain, I felt my guts torn apart as I watched the light form a rough circle and attach itself to the top of the T. I picked up the still warm ankh as the light slowly faded. A buzzing sensation filled my brain and a ball of white light smote away every thought I had. The sensation of floating free in a chaotic universe washed through me, and my Shadow dropped from my arm and sank to the floor with a laqst groan. Immediately the walls of the labyrinth fell away and I found myself outside, next to the doorpost where I had left the Gordian knot. A second neat ball of yellow thread sat there, attached to the ball in my hand, and I tried to wind up the excess thread between them, but somehow the thread obstinately remained loose. With the two balls of thread, and the loop dragging behind me, I waited to see what would happen next, wondering who had come by and spent so much time undoing the difficult knot.

Without making an effort, I found myself rising gently up to the throne room, where Cybele awaited me. "Congratulations! You have passed the barrier of your horizon by completing the lower part of the cross with the three nails of the crucifixion. Above that horizon - the limit of the Mark of Cain - you are now holding the circle of the blessed ankh. Guard it well and never lose sight of your progress." The goddess moved swiftly across the black and white floor towards the Hierophant, who hung just above the ground in a meditative silence, the Mask still covering his face.

Many questions were crowding into my mind. Cybele, who was reading my thoughts, answered them. "The two balls of thread symbolize your center and the center of the Hierophant. There is still a length of thread separating them. Over your remaining time here – whether it is brief or lingering – the intervening thread will gradually become shorter, and your inner ball will wind up more and more thread, until it has absorbed the enduring Intuition of the Hierophant." She pointed to the cap that the Hierophant wore. "That is called a Phrygian cap. It symbolizes the transference of procreative energy from the genitals to the mind – forming the ultimate Philosophic Stone. You will also note the dagger in his left hand - a harpe, a special dagger curved for sacrificial purposes that kills with one swift blow upwards into the heart of the beast. The Hierophant will permit you to use it for the sacrifice of your wild bull, for when you jumped that bull, even though your vault was not perfect, you sealed its fate."

"I'm sorry about that. What about the lambskin around his hips?' I queried. "Why do they choose that particular animal?"

"The lamb is the symbol of innocence. By taking human form, innocence is shattered, for none are born into Malkuth deemed perfectly free of guilt, carried by their karma from one incarnation to another. The Hierophant and all those who strive for perfection, such as the Masonic guild, wear a lambskin apron to signify their desire to rise through the grades and achieve the 33rd degree. He has succeeded and, as you will note, is no longer bound to the earth by gravity. You may remember the story of Cain and Abel, and how Abel gave God a lamb. That was his complete Self."

"How is this transference of energy carried out?" I asked. "Is it Kundalini who carries the energy upwards?" A flash of intuition struck me. "Oh! I know there are 33 vertebrae in the spine. The Kundalini force must mount upwards one at a time, passing through the seven chakras along the way."

"Yes, the seven chakras, or States of Being, are similar to the seven alchemical tests. From time immemorial this process has been symbolized by seven fixed stars. You will see these stars represented in ancient amulets and sculptures, and few know their real meaning. It is sad." Cybele sighed. "That is what we are here for, to gather all of existence together on the peak of Mount Meru, the mountain at the center of the earth, once they have achieved enlightenment. Until that day, I will remain the guardian of the mountain."

"That's amazing, and it answers many of my questions. The adepts that I met along the way have hinted at this. Now, the black and white floor tiles represent duality, don't they - the duality of the lower worlds? I've seen these tiles on the floor of many cathedrals. Did our current religions steal that symbolism?" I paused, gazing intently at her.

"Yes, regrettably, that is so. You will also see that where the squares disappear behind the yellow veil of the Hierophant, they become dimmer and begin to merge together, to a point where the idea of duality vanishes within the body of the Hierophant."

She withdrew the harpe from his hand and took my arm, leading me towards the bull pen. My heart sank. I did not want to kill the magnificent wild bull.

"I know what you are thinking now. You do not want to see the bull die. But, remember, he represents your lower nature, and when you sacrifice his body, you will understand something more profound. Have courage, now!"

The few remaining bulls scattered around the pen nervously. The young people who had vaulted their bulls successfully were over at the slaughtering ground. Many bulls were roasting over huge fires, the fat dripping tastily into pans below the spit. I hooked the stick into the nose ring of my bull, leading him meekly towards the fires. Flower girls came forward and placed wreaths of beautiful flowers around his neck and horns, then a priest, clad in animal skins, shook some liquid from a pine cone he carried onto his brow. We positioned the animal between four poles, tying ropes under his body so that he would not fall to the ground. Creeping towards his left flank, I pledged myself to make a determined stroke, plunging the harpe behind his left elbow and driving it upwards forcefully. The bull snorted once, and died instantly, his body slumping over, but held by the ropes.

Cybele came forward, scattering leaves and fine earth over the massive body as she vibrated an incantation. As she did, I saw a bright greenish-yellow glow over the bulls body form itself into the shape of a small bull. This vision rose up and then floated over us, landing firmly on the ground some distance away. It bellowed once and galloped away, and I remembered the ever-renewing aurochs that I had slaughtered during my stay with my Guide, and how it would never die. A feeling of tremendous release coursed through me, and I understood that I had given the bull its freedom. It would remain in spirit form until the call came to reincarnate and serve humanity again.

After the banquet, the youths and maidens who remained took ship again for the north, free at last. The Hierophant requested an audition with me, and I joined him in his private quarters, hovering over the abyss, while the two bears controlled the flow of air around him with thin strands of yellow thread.

"I have some very good news," announced the Hierophant. "I have received a message from my runners that the Bride of Malkuth approaches on her white camel, accompanied by her attendants. She is ready to marry me, and I am very joyous. I would like you to give her away. Would you do that for me?"

"I would be delighted at the honor." I cried. "Will you than be able to take off your Mask?"

"I will. For she can now see me in my true light. In the meantime, while we await her train, I will dress myself for the wedding." He descended slowly below the black and white floor. I could now see where the opposing black and white melted into one in the center. A single trumpet blew, followed by a chorus of trumpets, and the Bride and her retinue came into the space, where they were received by Cybele. She took the Bride, who had an extremely long train, through the arch and up the mountain behind, where she prepared her for the wedding. The room suddenly became full of people, all dressed most sumptuously in their best clothes, and they formed around a center aisle, talking eagerly amongst themselves. At the rear of the room, the dirt track was replaced by long tables, loaded with every imaginable delicacy, and servers were standing by another table where a punch bowl of the black drink was waiting.

Cybele brought the Bride back through the arch, and I took her hand. I was overwhelmed with the honor, and felt very nervous, but she squeezed my hand and murmured encouragement. Her beauty was such that one could not reasonably take it in, for it was beyond any description available to man. We moved slowly to the head of the aisle and the wedding march began.

At the same time, the Hierophant, who was also the Prince, rose from the depths and there was a gasp of astonishment! He had removed his Mask and his inner glory showed clearly before the whole company. He stepped towards a small dais, where the person who was to marry them was standing.

This was something I had forgotten – the priest! I leaned forward, trying to see who it was, but the figure appeared fragile and indefinable.

An inward moving core of bright vibrations hovered over the space, and I could see all the company was also trying to make out who was there. Now the Prince, who was also the Hierophant, took the Cup of blood that Ediug had brought from the Moon and, sprinkling a little on the floor, drank down the Cup. He followed this with a small sliver of fresh baked bread.

Wiping his mouth surreptitiously, he looked up the aisle at us as we slowly moved forward, the long train of the Bride sprawling behind her, filled with all manner of beasts, extinct and living. The admiring glances of the company were focused on her, and she smiled and nodded to everyone. When we reached the Prince, I stepped back a little. I was expecting the usual ceremony, where the officiating priest asks who gave the Bride to be married, and I would then have replied. But no such request came from the dancing ball of light that now sparkled between the two. Instead, they kissed, and a huge display of fireworks exploded around them. These were so bright that no-one noticed the couple had disappeared to their own quarters.

Some days later, the Hierophant, looking extremely content, spoke with me. He bent his left ear, with the blue trumpet lodged in it, towards me. "I am perfectly happy with my Bride and her long train of creatures. Thank you for representing her." He paused. "You have confronted all the Shades on their home territory, and although you realized how vulnerable you were, you reconciled with them and let go of the baggage they represented. You have also fought the Hoodwinker and left your Shadow behind here. You will be going to Geburah next. That is a dangerous Island, but Chesed is, in fact, more subtle. You will have to watch out and guard your vulnerable Self in both these Islands."

"How can I best deal with those two Spheres?" I asked him. "It seems that there will be a direct confrontation in Geburah, but that Chesed is far more cunning."

"You will need your sword of willpower for both, but you will activate it differently. During your time in Geburah, you will be using the sharp, cutting power of the Sword, and in Chesed you will need flexibility, for the obstacles are softer, more subtle, and often hard to recognize."

He indicated the blue trumpet in his ear. "Hear, and believe the word of Spirits' power. That is all I can tell you. The bears will now take you to the threshold, where you will cross from one state of being to another. Remember, do not doubt what you have learned for a moment, or you will lose faith."

The two bears stepped forward and led me towards the great arch at the back of the room, through which one could see the towering bulk of Mount Meru. We paused at the threshold under the arch. I heard many shrieks and cries wafting up from below. The bears pointed to their backless shorts and told me to beware of a bare behind – in other words to keep my rear covered. I was about to step forward when the bears pulled me back. Just in time, I saw that there was no ground in front of me, only a dark, swirling abyss between me, and the gaunt mountain. Brownish grey forms struggled and fought below me, screaming out their hatred of each other and their desire for vengeance.

One bear pointed downwards and shook his head, clearly indicating that was not the way to go. Instead, they stretched their cloth of yellow fibers out and sat me in the middle of the cloth. It began to undulate up and down, faster and faster, until I shot up in the air and over the threshold, landing with my feet in shallow, steaming water on a beach where roils of white hot lava hissed into the sea. Beyond the beach, fires sprang up everywhere and the sky was tinged deep scarlet. I felt sure I had arrived in Geburah.

Island of GEBURAH

The Martian influence of Geburah was visible everywhere. Shattering noise surrounded me as I scrambled up the beach, the hot pebbles burning my feet. Over the top of hummocks, their sharp sand particles battering my face in the gusty wind, I came to a yard where all kinds of wrecked vehicles were piled. There were bicycles, prams, chariots, biplanes, roller skates, cannons and even sleek sports cars that had met their fate rather suddenly around a telephone pole, replaced by newer forms of transportation, such as a hearse. Behind them, the Bessemer furnaces of a steel factory, with a line of waiting trucks, loaded clean sheets of steel that were recycled. Over on the left, a huge crane wielded a wrecking ball that was crashing against the walls of a derelict building, the bricks and mortar crumbling and crashing to the ground in a surge of dust.

The sound of marching feet came along the metallic road and a group of soldiers tramped by, meticulously in step, with their iron clad leather skirts swinging to the sound of a beating drum. One of the soldiers spotted me, and rather than stop, he gave a high pitched whistle, at which their sergeant halted them and turning, saw me. He strode over and saluted, carrying a short scourge with him.

"Have you come to enlist? If that's the case, follow us down to the barracks, and I'll deal with you there." He swung on his heel, gave the command, and the soldiers marched on. Out of curiosity, I followed them, not exactly keeping in step. We soon arrived at their barracks and he dismissed them to return to their meager quarters. The sergeant beckoned to me and I followed him into a small, stuffy office built of corrugated iron. A gust of strong wind flurried the courtyard and a dust bunny whirled away, seeking prey, as I sat down in a wobbly wooden chair.

"Fill in these forms - here, here, and there." The sergeant pushed some paperwork towards me. "Hurry, for we don't have much time. The army of the Shriek of Yaboo needs recruits urgently."

"Just a minute!" I pushed back my chair and began to rise. "I am not here to fight a war. In fact, I only recently visited the Island of Tiphareth, the most peaceable spot along the Way of Return. I have no intention of fighting, and I won't sign your paperwork."

The sergeant was annoyed. "Don't you understand? We have a deserving cause. The Viceroy of Muckabad has invaded our territory and blown up all our business centers – those donated to us by our friendly neighbors, the Hodians. Now they are laying waste to our commercial interests. The Shriek instructed me to prepare a large force to drive them from our land. The Viceroy had no right to attack us without warning." He sat back in his chair. "You look like an intelligent person. Maybe I won't send you to the front – we usually keep that for cannon fodder – but you might be useful as a spy, infiltrating the enemy lines to gain information. How about that?'

"As long as I don't have to carry a gun and shoot people, I could do that. I've met the Shriek of Yaboo. I am, in fact, an old friend of his, as he took me to his desert vault while I was in the Nine of Cups, thinking I was a famous archaeologist. I'm not sure that his conclusions about the Viceroy of Muckabad are correct. I would like to hear the other side of the story."

His brow darkened. "There is no other side. The Viceroys' motives are totally unacceptable, and I don't even want to hear them. The Lord is with us, for I've had a sign. A donkey peed on my right foot! That means good luck and indicates we are in the right. How can you question a sign like that?"

I was well aware that donkeys had no discrimination when it came to relieving themselves. Maybe his foot was in the wrong place at the right time. Or, the right place? However, I decided to sign up with the Shrieks' army, as they had offered me the experience as soon as I arrived in Geburah.

"I will sign the forms, and I will enlist as a spy and infiltrate the army of the Viceroy of Muckabad. He was a generous host sometime back when we met in the Three of Cups, and he will not imagine that I am working against him. On the other hand, I did steal his cushion....." A flash of frightful guilt overcame me, and I blushed scarlet. To hide this, I bent forward and signed the forms.

The sergeant gave a sigh of relief. "You will not regret this. The Shriek rewards those who are loyal to him generously. Please go now, and get your disguise from the costumery. It's over there."

He pointed to a vast warehouse near the barracks. I walked over and opened the door. What a surprise! From floor to ceiling, the warehouse was filled with every army uniform and weapon you could imagine, dating from the times of the Pharoahs and before. Cavemans' clubs hung beside the most recent designs in uzis; battering rams were propped against the walls; the latest in unmanned drones were suspended from the ceiling, while tanks and chariots with cruel cutting blades on their wheels stood side by side.

A midget approached. In a squeaky voice, he asked what I needed.

"I have signed on as a spy in the Shrieks army, and I need a suitcase of disguises and some spy equipment. I don't want to carry anything too heavy, though."

"I have the very thing for you. We are very motivated and always come up with something new. It's our latest collection of disguises in lightweight materials. Would you like the models to come out and display them? I can call them out on the runway."

"That would be very nice. Then I can see what the latest design in spy ware is, and make a choice." I waited a few minutes and then he pushed back a curtain at the end of a wooden runway, and the models began to flounce towards me. They were both male and female, but looked very similar in their behavior. The pants, kilts, jackets and scarves were very fetching, and I was astonished to see several completely transparent outfits.

"Excuse me. Aren't those disguises rather revealing?" I pointed to a man wearing tight plastic shorts. He was extremely well endowed, and I feared that his disguise would draw attention to a vulnerable spot.

The midget laughed. "No, exactly the opposite. The enemy will be so fascinated by looking at his genitals, that it will be easy for him to operate a remote camera and even steal secret cheeses right over their heads. Distraction is the key, you know. Oh, yes!"

I chose five unusual outfits, but left the transparent ones alone. The midget then gave me a small briefcase. "Everything you will need is in here – microphones, cameras and radar interference signal receptors, along with several pairs of dark sunglasses, blonde wigs and moustaches. I wish you the best of luck. The front line of the Viceroys' army is five miles away, the other side of the city. We have transport for you."

He brought forward a small donkey, who brayed sonorously. The donkey nuzzled me and seemed very friendly. I looked more closely as I patted him, and recognized my old friend Mandrake, who had carried me for many miles, and whom I had last seen in the russet quarter of Malkuth. I was delighted, and eagerly leapt onto his bony back ready to start my new adventure.

Mandrake trotted happily through the deserted city streets, since most of the population had fled, except for some hard liners who, hidden behind windows with their sharp shooting rifles at the ready, waited for the enemy. I could hear distinct laughter up there, for I was wearing a fetching pink satin frock in the style of Louis XIV, with a 1920's boater on my head, and purple fishnet stockings above ski boots. Mandrake added to the disguise with some red striped socks I put on him and his tail stuck out of a large Depends diaper. We therefore made rapid progress and nobody challenged us. Reaching the enemy lines, I set myself up as a comedy act, with donkey, to amuse the troops. They were only too happy to have us perform, as the long days since their first attack passed slowly while they waited for the opposing army to muster its troops. They felt it would not be fair unless both armies had exactly the same number of soldiers.

I remarked, in a witticism, that it might have been better if they had attacked sooner, but I was told that it was impossible to actually win a war in Geburah, because that would spoil everything. For one thing, any victorious leader would set himself up as a despot and refuse to allow any further wars, demolition of antique or outmoded buildings, or general destruction. It appeared that they greatly valued devastation as a prelude to creation, but had, regrettably, never managed to rebuild, since they were always busy planning strategic war maneuvers.

My performance to a large audience of troops was a grand success, and they feted Mandrake and I at a special party they gave for us, where they had set up large vats of black liquid drinks. I quickly recalled the effects of the liquid, but it was too late, I already had a drink in each hand, and couldn't let go of them. My satin skirt was dragging on the floor and the crazed dancers were trampling on it. Finally it tore away, leaving me in my purple fishnet stockings, garter belt, and a frothy pair of green knickerbockers. The donkey, who had imbibed a large bowl of black liquid, was doing the Charleston, while I joined in a merry romp of catch the thimble. Since I was holding a glass in each hand, this game was not very successful.

Mandrake and I slept the next day off under a bush. When I rose, I dressed in a more suitable outfit – Charlie Chaplin short pants and boots with a blue and green soccer shirt and a large Ascot hat. I added a moustache for flavor. Leaving Mandrake munching the bush, I infiltrated the back of the theater, and behind the scenes, I made my plans. It was important to let the sergeant know that the Viceroys' troops were waiting for him to finish recruiting. It should be clear to him, then, that it was unwise to complete the Shrieks' army under those circumstances. But that might mean that, if he was not busy recruiting, he might get bored, so he must be given something useful to do to take his mind off it.

I hit on the best idea. The prisons on Geburah were full of convicts, since there was an overwhelming police force with little to do but arrest people, mostly for minor drug offenses. They enjoyed the decisive snap of handcuffs and the hollow slamming of prison doors. I arranged a comic performance for the guards of the largest prison and slipped them some of the black liquid. It was easy after that to open the cell doors, and the convicts poured out, shaking my hand and promising me many gifts for Christmas. It was a wonderful feeling – grateful murderers, rapists and petty marijuana growers became my fans overnight. I decided to form them into a third militia and take over the city, since neither the Shriek nor the Viceroy seemed to be ready for battle. We called the new band the Vicious Shriekers, and we raided the ammunition dumps of both armies and took over the city hall, quickly establishing ourselves throughout the urban boundaries. Our aim, of course, was complete and utter anarchy, so we encouraged suicide bombers, because that reduced the population, which was too large anyway.

Geburah succumbed to a three-way stalemate, since nobody knew who the enemy was, and quiet settled over the city for some time. The Sergeant went on a long, paid vacation and both armies began to make scrapbooks of their exploits. One day I was strolling down the shopping mall, gazing at the fine weapons and armor displayed in the windows, when a large Raven flew down and perched on my shoulder.

"Do you remember last November?" The bird croaked. "My name is A. Lyster Crow, cracking clams blow by blow. Now I am fully fledged - as a Raven, but on edge, and I have come to make some trouble to liven things up in this rubble."

"Of course, I know why you're the worst. We met when I was duty bound, abruptly near the Darkest Ground. The Ten of Pentacles, I believe, and also, when you took my sleeve, in the Moons' mad mystic card, where you became a Raven bard."

A. Lyster Crow was pleased at my reply, and nodded his head vigorously, whereupon several feathers detached themselves and left a large bald spot. "I hear you lost your deer, but what will happen here?" He became more serious. "Have you read my Confessions yet? It's very notorious and suitable for light bedtime reading in the hot nights of Geburah."

"Indeed, I've read it now. It's extremely interesting, and I'm sorry that it's just a pack of lies." I challenged him.

"Óh, no!" He fluttered his eyelashes mockingly. "I never intended that. But, as you know, most lies are well worth telling, for life would be so dull without them. I know you've been searching for the Truth along the Way, but how do you know when those that claim the Truth are not lying? Explain that to me." The Raven preened a blue-black feather derisively.

"All I can do is to express the truth as I know it best. My understanding is growing, and I realize that what seems to be true on earth is not necessarily true in the divine world. The meaning of good and bad is confusing." I stroked the Raven thoughtfully. "You have always believed one can only be true to ones own nature. Now, I am in a leadership role in Geburah, the sphere of katabolic destruction, yet I am a believer in constructive and organized thought. I wonder if my thought patterns could influence the Geburians to turn their warlike tendencies to something productive?"

"Certainly, the same energy runs through this Island – there is motivation, the power to build, to take care of ones' family, and the success behind the human struggle for survival. Geburahs' energies are beyond ego survival – for ego is built after the nascent child is born. These energies have been subordinated to the desire for conflict, wasted, as it were, when so much of benefit could come from them." A. Lyster Crow scratched his head with a claw. "Let us set up a new regime here. We can invite all those who wish to convert their energy productively to join us. We can rebuild Geburah and wrest it from the influence of the Hoodwinker, who represents cruelty and destruction." The bird paused. "Of course, we must first get rid of the Hoodwinker herself, for she will defy us at every turn. That will be your job, and I will accompany you."

"Hey! You just landed me a big problem. I might not succeed. She has a huge influence over the Island. Count me out." A shiver of anticipation ran through me. "The rhythmic movement towards her abolition may not have arrived."

"I'm sorry, but you have to do this. You've already encountered and overcome all seven of the Shades. Why not the Hoodwinker too? It would make a big difference in Malkuth if we could convert this powerful energy in a positive way. Do you see what I mean?" The Raven hopped down onto my desk and strolled back and forth, thinking of a plan. I watched him for some moments, and then I picked up a pen and began to write.

The result of our discussion was to begin attracting people who had seen our advertisements for the new plan. We organized them into work groups and they began dismantling the war machine. At the same time, I had to ascertain where the Hoodwinker was hiding, for I knew in my heart that I would have to confront her. Would it be high or low? Hiding in the forest or climbing a mountain? Flying over a vast plain or lurking deep in the earth? I tried to visualize the best environment for her. I saw a big building with pale green and white walls. A figure in a white coat moved swiftly along the corridor and pushed open the door to an operating room.

The hospital! I would go there first. Could the Hoodwinker be masquerading as a surgeon? It seemed hardly possible, and I dreaded the effect on her patients. I sprang from my chair and the Raven flew to my shoulder. "Where is the hospital?" I demanded, as we hurried from the room.

The very building I had visualized was in the center of the city. We entered the emergency room, looking about us for a surgeon that did not seem to fit. Soldiers from the Viceroys army, who had succumbed to the black liquid, filled the emergency room. Many were on life support, still lying on the gurneys that had brought them in, while others, strapped into straitjackets, raved and ranted in the corridors. The first operating room was set aside for brain surgery. I put on a white coat and mask, hid the bird under my arm, and entered in the middle of a difficult surgical process. The surgeon in charge bent over the unconscious man, surrounded by her helpers. They were peering closely at something. On a cart nearby lay an enamel container. One of the nurses, responding to a brief order from the surgeon, went over and lifted the lid. I was close enough to see her take out a tiny dragon with the forceps and hand it to the surgeon.

I crept closer to the surgeon and saw her insert the dragon into a cavity she had made in the patients' brain. I was shocked! That must be how the evil spirit of Geburah perpetuated itself. Now I watched the surgeon closely as she sewed up the cavity, finishing with a neat reef knot in the twine. It was impossible to see her face under the mask, but as she moved away from the table, a whiff of foul air escaped from her garments, and several lice and bed bugs fell from her coat onto the scrubbed floor, where she quickly stamped on them.

Now I knew who the surgeon was. I hurried out of the operating room, removing my coat, and found an empty gurney. I crawled onto it and lay down, covering myself with a thin blanket, while A. Lyster Crow perched underneath. Soon they wheeled me into the operating room and placed a mask over my face. Fortunately, the Raven was able to divert the stream of anesthetic away from my mask and towards the surgeon, who was sharpening a scalpel at the instrument table. The effect of the chloroform on her was devastating. She began to scream and dropped the file and scalpel. She seemed to be shrinking, the white coat becoming looser and looser, until the coat lay on the floor, empty. The Hoodwinker had vanished.

The group of nurses and interns in the room had stepped back in horror, one of them knocking against the table and spilling the contents of the container. Tiny dragons were clambering out, taking off from the table and buzzing low over our heads. I put up my hand and caught one in mid flight. It hissed at me and shot a little tongue of fire into my palm, which left a blister.

"They are real, then." I said as I got up and addressed the group. "Do not open the door! We must catch these dragons and replace them in their container before they escape. You did not realize it, but your surgeon was the Hoodwinker, who spreads violence and destruction everywhere by the insertion of dragons. When these little beasts get inside peoples' brains, they wreck havoc with their thoughts and turn them into resentful, vindictive automatons with hatred in their hearts. The Hoodwinker is vanquished, for now, but she will arise again in due time, for she is never-ending, and when the pendulum swings back in her direction, she will be ready. We have much to do before then. Will you help us? The Raven and I have made plans to convert the evil energy of Geburah into something positive. We must accomplish this before it is too late."

Many of them stepped forward and joined us. It took a while to catch the dragons, for they burnt through a butterfly net and scorched the nurses' hands as they grabbed for them. Eventually we replaced every one in the container, and welded the lid down.

During the next few weeks, great activity spread across the Island of Geburah, as we stopped all demolition until we had inspected any condemned buildings. Piecemeal destruction was wasteful. Maybe the buildings could be converted and saved. Our growing group also worked on recycling materials; converting energy; sponsoring peace talks with their neighbors; and firing their politicians, who were constantly arguing, instead of debating bills to pass them in a minimum of time.

Our new regime, headed by the Raven, A. Lyster Crow, ran smoothly at first, but as more and more Geburians joined, eager to use the motive power in their Island to useful purposes, dissent grew amongst the ranks, and eventually a serious argument erupted between the Raven and the head of waste disposal. The man came to me complaining that the bird was siphoning off some of the liquid and hiding it in a special tank. I asked the Raven what was going on, but he was very evasive, so I decided to inspect the tank and put the contents through a series of microbial tests.

The scientist assigned to this job found considerable amounts of gold dust in the tank. We had to find out where that had come from. I called A. Lyster Crow before me to question him. He refused to answer and took the fifth amendment, so I sent out detectives to discover the source of the gold. They found an undersea pipeline connecting the golden hexagram of Tiphareth to a mulching machine that broke down the gold as it was slowly sucked from the hexagram. This was a most serious transgression, and I was deeply disappointed in the Raven, who had turned out to be a two-faced liar.

I sentenced the Raven to five months probation and shut down the gold operation. Unfortunately, he had many supporters, who were looking forward to getting their share of gold dust, and they gathered in the streets of the city to protest. The situation deteriorated rapidly and our original group began to argue, and formed two opposing camps, threatening to attack each other. The Raven, who was still free on probation with a tracking device on his leg, gathered his own group together, and I sent for my entity Bazoom, to make him general of our group. We began to stockpile weapons again, and searched through the piles of wrecked cars to find steel for bombers and tanks. Bazoom remained closeted in the map room with his closest allies, planning strategic maneuvers, while some of the lieutenants drilled and trained our burgeoning army. Once the juggernaut of war had been set in motion, there was no hope of reconciliation. Communication ceased and a feeling of distrust set in amongst those who had previously been friends, working side by side. All attempts to defuse the menacing state of affairs were met with failure.

They declared war soon afterwards, and Bazooms' army quickly took over the city, pushing the Raven to the suburbs, where he dug in, taking over a number of comfortable motels. The stalemate went on for weeks, but food was running out in the city as the siege continued, and Bazoom was unable to break out. The situation became desperate, so we formed a plan to attack the flank of the Ravens' army and slip by them to safety on the surrounding plain. In the dark of night, Bazoom, leading a battalion of our best soldiers, attacked on the right flank, but failed to breach the enemies' ranks, as someone, obviously a spy, had informed them of our intended strike.

The fighting was fierce, and I wielded my sword of willpower at Bazooms' side. He was an expert at close combat, able to throw himself at the enemy with incredible speed, although he was no swordsman, as he had no arms. Then disaster struck. Bazoom hurled himself at the Raven, who had flaunted his superiority in the midst of the battle, and landed on the point of the Ravens' lance. A. Lyster Crow cawed with pleasure as he plucked my little warrior off the sharp point and flung him back in my face. I caught my entity Bazoom in my arms and rushed him to the hospital, where he underwent emergency surgery to staunch a critical wound in his stomach, but the doctor warned me that there was little chance of his survival.

I remained at his bedside, weeping silently, while the sounds of battle raged outside the hospital as the Ravens' advancing army set fire to the buildings we had restored, until the whole city was ablaze. The hospital was in grave danger, so I took the semi-conscious Bazoom in my arms and made a run for it out of a side door, where I found some shelter behind a Lamborghini sports car in the wreckers' yard. It was there that Bazoom was able to speak his final words in a weak voice.

"I have stood by you throughout your journey, and when you were angry, I leapt forward to assist you." He paused, gasping for breath. "You have conquered your angry feelings now. You…. do not need me…..any longer." He was sinking fast, but raised himself on my lap, his sharp eyes searching my face. "The pendulum will ever swing between Geburah and Chesed. Allow what is inevitable to exist and rise above it." Bazoom fell back, his chest heaving, and a trickle of blood escaped from his lips as his mouth opened to show the rows of sharp teeth that had so often defended me. "You……will conquer the Sea of Sorrow and …….reach your goal." His breathing grew slower and I bent close to hear his last words. "We will meet again, for this is just a dream……." His body fell back and went limp. Bazoom was dead.

Path of STRENGTH

I t had been impossible to guide the powerful right arm of Geburah in a positive direction and expect it to remain there. I understood the predestined swing of the great pendulum between the Geburians and the Island of Chesed on the far side of the Mystic SEA. I must cross the fiery sea towards the Path of Strength, my next port of call. I wept as I wrapped the body of Bazoom, whose prickles were now flaccid, in a piece of aluminum foil and laid it in a nearby trashcan, murmuring the ritual from the Tibetan Book of the Dead. Then I made my way to the shore of the Island and sent out a telepathic message to Joana, my cricket, who swung in her cage over the chart table of my vessel.

To my surprise, the boat that hove into view, skippered by my faithful Pompeybou, was no longer the cruising ketch, but a lean, 75 foot racing schooner with the latest equipment. Pompeybou explained that my Guide had come by and replaced the ketch with this new boat. I was very excited. Jumping on board, I examined the heavy racing winches from Lewmar and the roller furling jib and staysail. The mainsail was a new design out of high modulus carbon fiber that furled into the mast, and the Navigators' position had every new electronic device ranged above it, from a GPS system to the fish finder, depth sounder and bow thruster switch.

During my travels in the Mystic SEA, I hadn't spent much time sailing, and I missed the freedom it gave me. I suggested to Pompeybou that we take the schooner out for a cruise before landing me in the Path of Strength, so that I might recover from the sadness of Bazooms' death. It might not be the ideal cruising ground, with the oppressive heat and gusty winds, but we felt we could deal with it. Leaving the shores of Geburah behind, where the sounds of strife were erupting again, we set a course of 135 degrees and, under reefed main and staysail, fought our way clear of the Island.

The weather grew cooler as we tacked along, and the winds lighter, but the thermometer showed a steady drop in temperature each day. We expected this to be a normal low, but Joana was very restless in her cage. One day she was clinging to the bars of the cage, shivering. The atmosphere outside was frigid and ice was beginning to form on the rigging, which kept Pompeybou busy with the ice axe.

Joana sent me a telepathic message."You must turn back! You are outside the boundaries of the Mystic SEA. You have taken a wrong turn." I could hear her chirping inside my head. "The edge of the Universe is only one days' sail ahead. The drop off is instantaneous and violent. You won't even have time to regret your decision."

Feeling Joanas' tumultuous thoughts, I knew she was unable to give out her usual weather report. I trusted her counsel and besides, the weight of ice was beginning to make the schooner roll heavily from side to side. If she capsized, we would not last long in the frigid water. I looked at the chart on the ECDIS and dialed in a reciprocal course of 315 degrees. We swung the schooner head to wind, put her through it, and ran off on a broad reach, making excellent time. The weather gradually grew warmer, and our speed would put us close to the Path of Strength within a couple of days.

It was during the final night of our approach that we spotted the lights of another ship to starboard. I had not seen any vessels at sea while I was spending time on our boats, but Pompeybou, who was sailing continuously, said he had passed several. The other boat was stationary in the water and carried the red-white-red masthead signal that she was "restricted in ability to maneuver." We came up a few points to the wind and went to investigate. As we drew closer, I could see a plank stretched out from the side of the boat, and a bound figure, hands behind her back, standing on the deck close by. A priest was reading the last rites in a somber voice, but the woman prisoner flung her head back in defiance, shouting at the priest to shut up, for she did not believe in his incantations.

We passed close by, but they did not seem to be aware of our presence, and I wondered whether we were in another dimension, for our schooner was a large boat and not easily missed. The priest flung down his book in a fit of rage and two members of the crew guided the woman to the plank, where she stood for a brief second, vibrating her words in a strange tongue, before she calmly walked to the edge of the plank and jumped into the sea.

Being unable to swim with her arms shackled behind her, she managed to tread water until the strange boat moved away. We quickly launched the dinghy and rowed over to pick her up, dragging her by her armpits over the side. She took a minute to spit out some water, and then graciously thanked us for her rescue. It was a shock to me as I recognized my entity Pullows, who had lost weight since I last saw her on the Island of Netzach, where she had given an outstanding emotional performance.

"Pullows! It is you, isn't it? I can hardly recognize you – you look so trim and fit!" I untied her bonds and gave her a wet hug. I was full of questions. "Whatever happened? I'm so glad we were close by! You might have drowned, alone on the edges of the Mystic SEA. Who were those people? Why did they make you walk the plank?"

Pullows shook her head. "They were the old school of thought – believing that a woman was inferior to a man. Most of them are priests of the religion that is now in a steep decline. The people associated with that school of thought are persecuting many women for taking back their lives and acknowledging their personal power, which comes from Geburah. I was on my way to the Path of Strength myself, as the owners of the grand arena there had signed a contract with me to appear as a gladiatress. They have trained wolves and lions that match my energy and the populace of Strength are looking forward to this contest."

"That sounds very interesting. We have to go to the Path of Strength, as you know. We should be there in about 24 hours sail. We will deliver you, safe and sound, to the arena, and then book seats to watch your performance." I remembered she was collecting tarot cards, and I had assembled quite a few Major Arcana cards during my travels, so I handed over all I had. "Here are several important cards. Your deck is nearly completed now. I believe there are only eight more cards to conclude the deck, so you should have seventy now."

I watched as she counted the deck. "Yes, that's right. This is absolutely thrilling! I've always wanted a full deck so that I could do tarot counseling. I really feel it benefits people in a positive way."

"Then I'll collect the remaining eight, and hand them to you at the end of my journey – for there will be an end, won't there?"

"Well, not exactly." Pullows nodded sagely. "I was recently at tea with the Archpriestess, where we had cucumber sandwiches and tea cakes. She told me that many people believed there would be an end to their journey. She said they were wrong, for their souls lived eternally. If that's true, I'll be able to use this tarot deck for ever!" She laughed ecstatically. "That would be an incredible rush."

The following day we reached the shores of Strength, where Pullows and I left the schooner and set foot on dry land once more. One could feel the influence of Geburah below, but there was also a stable, steadying effect from the Island above us, Binah, the dark mother from which sprang the veiled Archpriestess. Evidently, Pullows knew her intimately, but most people could not pierce her veiled countenance.

An envoy from the arena manager drove up in a London taxi and we jumped in. Our trip to the arena took a couple of hours, which gave us time to visit and catch up with each other. Fields of blue flax billowed in the wind on each side of the road, while farm workers were cutting grain and tying the sheaves into corn stooks that dotted the fields in neat rows. We passed orchards where fruit hung heavy from the trees and toiling hands plucked the harvest and placed it in tiers of boxes. The Path of Strength appeared to be very bountiful, and I was pleased to experience something more positive after the difficulties of Geburah.

Drawing up at the massive gates of the arena, we stepped out of the taxi. The stairs led to the lower levels, where the animals were caged and where the dressing rooms for the gladiatress' were located. Pullows now had to don her costume, a helmet with the twin horns of the goddess Hathor surmounted by a sun emblem, and a Celtic torc around her neck. She put on a thin g-string with attached stomach lamen, and took up a small flail and her venomous snake, an orange banded krait that glared at me unkindly. Pullows handled the krait with ease as it wound around her right arm. Bugles were blowing to announce the contestants, so I wished her good fortune and she suggested we meet after the show.

At her remark, I voiced some doubts. "Suppose, well, suppose you don't make it? Survive, I mean? You have to fight a wolf and a lion. Do you feel prepared?" I was concerned. "If anything goes wrong, would you like me to plant blue flax on your grave?'

Pullows grinned. "Don't you worry. I know what I'm doing. I have a plan – how to conduct the fight. I am well versed in strategy, just watch me closely."

She walked to a small opening in the arena through which we could see the bleachers on the other side. The seats were almost full, and they had reserved the front row for seven strange looking people who had hollow torsos, for I could see right through them. To their left, a tight group of seven robed figures gathered on a large, black cube that stuck out from the side of the bleachers.

Pullows pointed them out. "The seven people in the front row are the Seven Sons. They carve seven holes in space for the seven original planets, and they are anxious to become complete by the installation of the Seven Seals, which also represent the seven chakras. Six of the Seals are already in the black box, where the Nefilim, or Watchers, who are the Keepers of the Seven Seals, are guarding them." She indicated the strange group. "You see that group over there. One remaining Seal has to be broken, and the solar lion is in charge of that. We hope all will go well, for it is my job to bring the lion to heel and tame him."

A low humming now came from the waiting crowd, and a rush of excitement overcame me as I gave Pullows a final hug. She strode through the gate into the wide arena, her bare feet kicking up the reddish sand, flourishing the krait, which had became stiff and malevolent. I quickly ran up some stone steps and found a seat near the front, on the opposite side, so that I could watch the Nefilim, or Watchers, themselves while the display took place..

The bugler gave a final flourish and a loudspeaker blasted out. "The black lunar wolf will enter the arena first to challenge Strength. This wolf represents the dark and repressed thoughts and nightmares of the gladiatress Pullows, which she has to combat. This wolf is an expert at the art of stalking, and it is very difficult to discover it in the mind and make friends with it, for it is extremely secretive."

A low black door opened in one end of the arena, marked by a crescent moon. Out of it ran a great dark wolf, its jaws slavering and bones showing through its matted coat, the stiff hairs on its back bristling with menace. The half starved animal was obviously crazed, and a shiver of fear ran through me as Pullows took up her position of Strength in the center of the arena. The lights began to dim and I could just see the wolf by the malicious gleam in its eyes. Crouching low, circling, creeping ever closer to her - the drawn inrush of its breath was palpable. She turned to face the animal as it circled, keeping the orange krait ready as a protective staff and vibrating the words that signified her past life, for the wolf was a symbol of that which is over and done. The animal seemed to hesitate, raising its head and staring in her direction, then lowering its muzzle to the ground and beginning to approach again.

Pullows flung the words out repeatedly in a vibrant chant, allowing the animal to draw closer, until it was only a few feet away. She drew a protective circle around herself with the krait, which, at this point, was looking more and more like a glowing wand. The wolf appeared even bigger when it was close to Pullows, but she did not move a muscle, and it seemed confused, as if it expected her to turn and flee. A low growl came from it, and it bared a row of yellowed teeth, saliva dripping from its mouth.

She feinted, daring it to come closer, raising the krait above her head, where flames began to lick around it. I saw the wolf in this orange glow hunker down and gather itself, ready to pounce. Her face was tight and her eyes had a strange glitter that revealed her concentration. Then, with a fierce growl, the animal threw itself at her, clawing at her Achilles tendon to disable her, but she struck it a blow with the krait, driving it off. There were teeth marks on her leg where the wolf had bitten and it circled, crouched and pounced again, this time flinging its body at her and knocking her to the ground, where it stood over her, its gaze held by hers and transfixed. They remained thus for a few moments, while it seemed that an electric current passed between them, and then she reached up and held out her hand for the wolf to sniff. Cautiously it rested its nose in her palm, and then sat down for her to stroke its matted fur. Pullows petted it and then rose to her feet, resting her right hand on its back.

The crowd came to its feet and yelled applause. But I knew all was not yet over. With the wolf still in the arena, a red gate, surmounted by a blazing sun, opened at the other end of the arena. A massive lion stalked towards her, its mouth open showing a long, curling tongue that searched its lips hungrily.

A bugle trilled and the loudspeaker gave out strident new information as the lights went up again. "The lion symbolizes Pullows' solar self, the daytime consciousness that she has to monitor every second, to make sure that she harms nobody by angry words or misplaced sentiment. This means being focused on one's ego consciousness, questioning decisions, and making sure they are made in compassion and full understanding of other peoples' situations." The audience nodded assent as the loudspeaker clicked off.

The huge lion padded silently towards her, as she watched it with a shrewd expression, while the wolf sat on the sidelines licking its chops. Suddenly one of the Keepers threw a rolled parchment down onto the sand, and the lion moved over to investigate it, picked it up gently in its mouth and took it to the center of the arena. Pullows gave a sharp command and the animal sat down, allowing her to open its jaws and remove the parchment. It was torn open at the seventh Seal, which fell onto the ground, broken, and the lion roared, swiping her with a clawed foot.

She backed away, blood running from her leg and pooling on the sand. Raising the flaming wand over her head, she called out in a terrible voice. "Kundalini, lord of my spine, come to my aid! I have passed the Seven Seals, the chakras, and learned the meaning of each one. You are raised up to my throat, and now you must come out to defend me."

From the center of the torc around her neck, an opening appeared, a mere slit, and the head of a large green anaconda emerged. The snake slithered down her body, winding itself around her in a caress. The lion drew back, its tail between its legs. as the snake hissed and moved towards the beast with intent to swallow, but quickly changed its mind.

"I'm thirsty. I need some lubrication before I can ingest a lion. Give me a drink!" The anaconda ordered, and quickly a server ran onto the field carrying a tray with a bottle of wine and a glass balanced on it. He wiped the bottle carefully with a starched napkin, showed the snake the label obsequiously, and drew the cork. The snake smiled as it tested the wine with its forked tongue. "Ah! Vouvray 2001 BC – a fine vintage, and brewed by the Pharoahs in Egypt. Pour it down my throat." The server reached up, his legs trembling in fear, and the anaconda drank the wine rapidly and then swallowed the bottle and the tray. The server managed to dodge and escaped, carrying the empty glass.

Pullows was very amused. "I didn't know Kundalini was a wine connoisseur. I guess it must be in my blood."

I thought of my own Kundalini, the faithful rattlesnake, and wondered how he was doing. I hadn't been paying attention to his movements, but I hoped he had managed, at least, to rise to the sixth thoracic vertebrae.

Pullows gave the lion a hug. "The lion has now opened the Seventh Seal, and I will give it to the Keepers of the Seals. We will now be able to fill the holes in the Seven Sons."

Immediately the crowd rose to their feet in great excitement and rushed down the bleachers, pushing at each other to get down to the arena, where they milled around. The two beasts were surprisingly tame and the lion allowed Pullows to ride on its back in a victory lap around the circle, while the drunken anaconda tactfully withdrew into her larynx. Fourteen people, in twos, escorted the Seven Sons to the center of the arena, laying them down on their backs in a neat row. The crowd stepped back and made a passage for Pullows to walk to the black cube, where she curtsied and waited for the Keepers to speak. The tallest Watcher came down the steps gingerly, trailing his long gown, and shook hands with Pullows.

"From now on, you are no longer Pullows, nor are you Swollup, but you are the very epitome of Strength, and that is now your name for evermore." He moved over to the bulkhead and began taking down the six Seals, handing them to her in a neat pile. He then summoned the remaining six Keepers and each of them took a Seal from her and walked with it to a Son, where they attempted to insert the Seals.

Unfortunately, the Seals were muddled, and did not fit. This caused a great deal of confusion. One of the Keepers was struggling to force the Seal into a Sons' torso, and the poor man was screaming in pain, while others gazed anxiously from the Seals back to the Sons and shook their heads. Strength – it was her name now – collected the Seals from their Keepers and laid them out neatly.

"We have to find out which is the right one for each torso." She said. "There must be minute differences between them. Of course, each Seal is different and each Son is different. No two are alike. There is only one correct fit for each. Let me think….. " She put her head in her hands. "Now, the seven chakras all have names and colors. If we can match the names with the colors, the Seals will fit. Stand up, you guys, and answer to your name as I call it out."

They scrambled to their feet and stood in an untidy line. Strength read from the register in the parchment. "Chakra # 1 – Muladhara. Which of you is this chakra?"

A small, rather ragged looking Son wearing a brown tribal bonnet and carrying a tree root stepped forward humbly. "It is I, my lady Strength."

"Good. What color is your chakra?"

"It is red, madam. I will be glad to get it back, for on winter nights the wind howls through my lower intestine and keeps me awake."

Strength stepped over to the row of Seals and touched each one with her krait wand. They lit up in different colors, and she picked up the red one and inserted it in Muladharas' center, stepping back to admire her work. "It feels very comfortable. " He said.

"Next! Chakra # 2 – Svadhisthana. Where are you?"

"Over here." A thin, bent Son stepped forward, clad in purple robes and carrying a bottle of semen. 'I have the Seed of Life, which I have carefully bottled. Would you like some?"

"Not right now. I would have to lie on my back for several hours and I'm too busy for that. What color are you?"

"I am orange, madam. I will be glad to get my Seal back, for I have serious erectile dysfunction which is annoying my girl friend."

Strength handed over the orange Seal and helped him to settle it in place. Immediately he smiled in glee as a monstrous erection rose from his loins, and he turned and rushed to the arena gates, where a woman was already stripping herself naked.

Strength ignored this discourteous charade. "Chakra #3 – Manipura. Who is Manipura?"

"Here, Ma'm. My chakra is yellow – that one. I will be glad to get back the yellow Seal, for my emotions and my reasoning are in constant disagreement, and I am exhausted, trying to choose between them."

He received the appropriate Seal, which fitted nicely, and broke into excited flurries of speech, at the same time mopping tears from his eyes. Struggling not to break down from joy, he sat down on the ground.

Strength touched a Seal with her wand, and it flashed green. "Whose is this? Speak up! They are getting impatient, for they want to start the parade."

'It is I, Anahata, madam. I will be glad to get my Seal in place, for I feel no compassion towards anyone, and it is as if a cold wind blows over me when I see someone in trouble, and I turn away. Now I will feel like giving my spare change to the Homeless who stand at each crossroads, holding placards. Thank you, thank you." . Anahata began turning out his pockets and distributing what coins he had.

"Right. Now we have Chakra # 5 – Vishudda. The throat chakra. It must be you. There he is!" She waved at a small Son, dressed in alternate blue and red stripes, his throat wrapped in a heavy scarf. "Is your larynx cold?"

"It certainly is! Why, every time I try to speak I end up gurgling and I always belch loudly after food. Since I'm supposed to be very quiet, it has become a problem."

"That's not good. I hope you will feel better now. Next is Chakra # 6 – Ajna. That is the right and left hemisphere of the brain. Come forward. I have your purple Seal here."

This Son was obviously manic-depressive and carried a crook and a flail. He had a long white beard, but was dressed in fancy womens' clothes, and fluttered his eyelashes at me. "I'm totally bewildered. I can't decide which is the most important, the left hemisphere or the right. Getting my Seal back will help me distinguish between the two. In the meantime, I have been practicing drawing with the right side, and writing with the left, which I feel should, actually, be kept for mathematical problems." He patted his Seal proudly. "Now people won't be saying I'm crazy anymore."

"Excellent!" Strength stepped towards the remaining Son, who stood absolutely still without replying. "You must be the owner of Chakra # 7 – Sahasrara." Softly she pressed the indigo Seal into his space. He kept his eyes closed without comment, but managed a little sigh of relief, and from the top of his head a cork popped out, revealing an unknown fizzy substance.

"We have replaced the Seven Seals in the holes of the Seven Sons! Let us now make merry and reap the rewards of harvest time!" Strength called out.

The crowd swelled and parted, and through the gates came a fantastic parade of twenty-one floats, displaying all kinds of harvest produce. The god Cernunnos, crowned by a magnificent pair of ten-point horns, sat in the last float surrounded by white chickens. The Celtic god greeted the crowd, his stag head nodding affably as they swarmed around the float, begging for blessings. His attendants threw eggs into the multitude, and those that caught them were more fortunate than those that did not. There was general merriment as yolk-covered revelers smeared each other, eggshells sticking to their hair and clothes. The procession wound its way to the center of the arena and formed a circle around Strength, by now seated on a high throne built of faggots of wood. The women formed up on one side, and the men on the other, as skirling bagpipes howled out a rousing square dance. The dancers wound in and out, passing each other, sometimes facing, sometimes back to back, their arms akimbo and their skirts and blouses fluttering.

Cernunnos began to climb the pile of faggots, which seemed a little unsteady. He had obviously had too much barley wine and fancied a significant encounter with Strength, who sat firmly on top. Just as he reached her and stretched out his hand, she set fire to the wood with her flaming wand, and the dancers gave a cry of horror and stepped back hastily, gazing upwards. The pile of faggots caught alight and the fire began to blaze merrily. Flickering flames reached Cernunnos. He let go with a shriek! He fell heavily to the ground, banged his head, and broke off one of his horns. The attendants rushed in to help him, while a shudder ran through the crowd as the flames licked up around Strength. She rose to her feet, waving the flaming wand, and it began to snow, whirling flakes coming down thick and fast, until the blizzard obliterated the wood pile and put the flames out, as she laughed out loud and remarked. "Let no man, even if he is a god, lay hands on Strength without her permission."

Meanwhile, they were treating Cernunnos for concussion at a field hospital, while the dancers were shoveling snow away from the floats, which were loaded with fruit and flowers. Fortunately, the blizzard stopped as quickly as it had started, and the merry crowd was able to continue with their dance, while others unloaded the baskets of fruit, the ears of corn and Cauldrons of Plenty and placed them on long tables covered with white cloths. They brought in spits and set them up, as butchers sacrificed pigs, lambs and goats and set the joints to cook, their juices flowing in great sizzling drops into the fires. Barley wine, beer, and a vat of the strange black drink stood at the side, and a long line of revelers waited for their share of the booze

A server brought Strength a large glass of the black liquid, which she drained at one gulp. Then, placing her hand upon her stomach, she began to groan loudly.

"Help me! I am with child and about to give birth!" Two midwives who were in the crowd rushed forward, and made a space for her to lie down.

People began muttering amongst themselves. "Surely he didn't have time?"

"I thought I saw him raising his tunic, though."

"He must be a very fast worker – of course, she is very attractive."

"How did they do it? We were all watching!"

"Shut up, all of you! The baby is coming......."

The midwives bent low, and Strength pushed hard and silently. A cry went up. The midwives raised the newborn on high for all to see. It was a beautiful child, and the remainder of the anacondas' tail was just disappearing between its buttocks. Strength got up immediately and took the child, placing its tiny hand in hers.

"Remember, trust in yourself and all will be well." She said.

Path of the EMPRESS

W hen I came round after drinking too much of the black liquid, I found myself lying half in, half out of a cool spring deep in the woods. It was night with a luminous moon that shone brightly on sparkling water. Standing beside me, knee deep in the stream, was a red stag missing one antler. The moon seemed to signal to me through its silhouetted antler, which formed a heart shape. I didn't know where I was, for I had not remembered leaving the Path of Strength at all. This landscape was completely different, and I wondered how I got here. Drops of water began splashing on me, and I looked up to see dew falling all around me, and the red stag was there, and spoke.

"I am the spirit of Cernunnos, and I brought you here riding on my back. I felt it important to rescue you from Strengths' arena, for they were about to start a chariot race, and you might have been trampled to death. You were somewhat drunk. We are now in the Path of the Empress, and I am the stag that urges on the hunter, Parsifal, who seeks the Grail as his quarry. He is becoming close to me, and I must try to stay ahead of him."

"Who is Parsifal?" I questioned. "I have heard the name from medieval sources. Doesn't he chase around after a lady called Cundrie?"

"He is known as the Accursed Hunter, for he is constantly looking for the answer to the meaning of life. He doesn't realize that the Grail is inside him, and that he need not look for it any other way."

"Why would he chase you, then? You are not the answer to his questions, and killing you would not give meaning to his life." I remarked. "Besides, you are beautiful and full of grace."

"Yes, thank you - but I embody the material world, which he must overcome. During his quest, he must embrace the ugly Cundrie and give her a kiss, which is like the story of the princess and the frog, and he must also kill the most beautiful thing in the material world – the swan, for this magnificent bird is but a pale reflection of the bliss of divine unity." The stag raised his head, his ears alertly pointed. "Hark, I hear the hunters now. I must flee......"

The animal leapt gracefully out of sight amongst the trees, leaving me alone, as the sound of blowing horns and the din of galloping hooves passed close by and faded into the distance.

Now I heard the echo of laughter and music filtering through the trees nearby. Someone was playing the panpipes, and a lyre player and drummer set time to the melody. I got up and walked unsteadily through the bushes in the direction of the sound, coming to an open grassy space beside a large lake that reflected the orb of the moon. Three dancers were twirling around in a circle, while amongst the trees the strangest musicians were playing for them. The fellow clad in goatskin legs was obviously Pan with his pipes, for I had met him during my visit to the Path of the Devil. The second musician was wearing green and his face consisted of woven green leaves that trailed in and out of his nose and mouth, while he strummed an Orphic lyre. The drummer had on a Punchinello mask with a huge nose. He beat in rhythm to the music and sang a ditty in a raucous voice.

The musicians called a break and put down their instruments while the dancers came towards me. They were three very different women, one of Asian descent, one African, and one Caucasian. I introduced myself and the African woman greeted me breezily. "I am called Golette, and I symbolize the Past. To achieve freedom, one must let go of the Past."

She moved back and the Caucasian stepped forward, shaking my hand. "I am Donowa, of European ancestry, and I represent the Present. It is important to focus on the Now, for that is all we have. People do not understand that."

The Asian girl bowed slightly and spoke. "My name is Hopeleen, and I represent the Future. The Future is never set in stone, for when you visited the Path of Fortune, you learned of the parallel universes that encompass us in the material world. In making your choices today, we must, however, hope for the Future, for the ideas we embody in the Present can take form when we have intent."

They told me that, together, they symbolized the passage of Time in the creative and destructive world of the Empress, and that their dance celebrated life itself. I was impressed, and asked them to continue their dance.

"Only if you join us!" Said one, taking my hand and leading me into their midst. The musicians took up their instruments again and began to play a merry jig. Standing in the center of the three encircling dancers, I watched them weaving and out, now taking my hand and turning me this way and that, handing me to the next, and then placing me in the center again. I began to feel dizzy, trying to focus on one object - I closed my eyes, but felt as if I were falling. The dancers spun ever faster and faster, and my mind went with them, until past, present and future mingled into one continuous movement, and I was floating above Time as I understood it. I knew then that time did not really exist, but that everything flowed into each other in a single, everlasting moment. Feeling myself sinking to the floor, I let go and forgot the dancers, the music, and the moon that shone upon the vast lake.

Later, regaining consciousness, I felt a deathly hush creep over the surrounding countryside. The silence was broken by the silvery note of a sistrum, tinkling from the far hills. I opened my eyes and got up. The dancers and musicians were gone, yet the moon still shone upon the lake, and over the surface a great white swan glided towards me with a woman on its back, landing on the lake shore. This attractive woman, dressed all in green with her diaphanous cloak swathed in every kind of orchid flower one could imagine, moved towards me with a lilting step. She carried the sistrum, which she rattled from time to time to chase away any lurking demons. A red cone hat with a green mamba trim was poised on her head, pointing at the green planet Venus. I could see that the woman was at least eight months pregnant, and displayed her extended stomach with pride. The swan moved beside her, opening its widespread wings and preening gently.

For the first time, I noticed two trees at the edge of the forest that were very different from the others. One tree was bare and dead, its leaves having fallen to the ground, and an axe was buried deep in its trunk. The other, near it, was perched on the edge of a dip in the ground, its roots hanging over the sandy edge. This tree was in full leaf, and within the trunk, I thought I discerned a human form.

"Those two trees - they are unusual. I hadn't noticed them before." I pointed to the trees. "What is it about them that attracted me?"

The Empress, for it was she, told me that the trees always traveled with her, and that was why I had not observed them before. "They guard the underground cave that I call my womb with a view. " She smiled with a beneficial expression. "Would you like to see it? It is there we keep vigil for the advent of the unborn."

"Yes, that sounds fascinating." I was eager to visit the cave, but first I asked about the strange trees. "What do the two trees mean?" I asked her.

She was about to answer as she stepped down towards the cave when the sound of hunting horns vibrated through the wood again.

"Drat it!" The Empress exploded, her expression changing rapidly to one of sudden rage. "That Parsifal fellow never leaves us alone! Forever chasing up and down, in and out, and forward and backward through the forest, searching without finding and letting his arrows strike where they may."

A stray arrow flew through the air and the swan gave a loud squawk of pain and sank to the ground, its wings outspread. The Empress hurried over to the bird, frowning deeply, as a thin stream of blood came from its body. She pulled an arrow from its feathers.

"Thank heaven – not a fatal wound. That aggravating hunter is always trying to kill my swan, but he has not succeeded yet. There, my beloved, rest and I will staunch your wound." She hurried to the lake and scooped up a handful of water, which she applied to the wound. The bird wound its neck around her in a very familiar gesture.

"Let me see, where were we?" Her face quickly resumed its calm appearance and her eyes twinkled. "Oh, yes, I was going to show you my underground cave. Normally there is a babe in the bed, who is conceiving, but – regrettably - my last little one, Reficul, escaped and went down to earth, where he is imprisoned now. I hear from passers by that he has been consecrated King and rules over the Island of Tiphareth. I am sorry that he felt he had to descend into the land of the ignorant. Maybe you met him while you were there?"

"I did indeed. He has reverted his name from Reficul to Lucifer, which he claimed was the original. He is a bright light down there and is doing good work, I assure you, even among the ignorant." I changed the subject, remembering the trees. "You were going to tell me about the trees, weren't you?"

"Oh, yes. The dead tree with the axe still embedded in it is a birch. People use the flexible rods from this tree to flog each other and themselves. Neither self-mutilation nor punishment by blaming others is acceptable here, so I asked my woodman to cut down the birch tree. Unfortunately, a passing dragon burnt him up before he managed to finish the job. Now I must find another worker." The Empress paused, her green mamba eyeing me tentatively from its perch, flicking its tongue in and out to test my odor. She continued. "The other tree, a willow, contains its' own nymph, who makes her way up the tree through her own willow power. This gives life to the tree and growth through the rhythm of the moon and its tides, which are so important here."

The swan settled down and tucked its head under its wing, so we felt able to leave it and move towards a rather muddy tide pool at the entrance to the cave, where a large hippopotamus was wallowing.

The Empress told me. "This is my little Mother, and I sprang from her, for she sucks impure water and cleanses it through her great mouth." .

The hippo slowly made her way over, leaving a wake of turbid water behind her. "Yes, I am sacred to the god Set, for I come out of the waters of the unconscious. Did you know that my babies are born underwater? It is much the best way to give birth, and I thoroughly recommend it to humans, who seem to have such a hard time birthing their young. Their hospitals have no idea how to handle a mother in labor."

"Yes, Mother." The Empress looked irritated for a moment. "You always tell us about that. You're a bit of a lecturer, you know. It's tiresome." It was amazing how quickly her moods could change.

The hippo blew a spout of water into the air and sank beneath the surface calmly. It was clear that she was used to the Empress' rapid mood changes. Wading through the shallow water at low tide, we reached the interior of the seven-sided cave, which was quite large. An enormous bed stood at the far end with a candle burning on each side, as if for a vigil.

Someone had thrown back the covers and damp footsteps on the floor led towards a set of steps to our right that disappeared upwards into a long tunnel. The walls of the cave were of pulsating red velvet, and throbbed continuously, now and again squeezing inwards as if to practice labor pains.

The Empress moved towards the bed, lifting the disheveled covers, and gave a little shriek. "Oh! How disgusting! Bed bugs. No wonder Reficul had to leave. I must get my handmaidens to eliminate them." She paused, clutching her stomach and grimacing. "Ouch! I feel my labor pains are coming on early. It's those damned walls – I should never have ventured down here. Handmaidens! Come here instantly, and bring the hippo midwife. My babe is coming early......" She sank down on the bed, then jumped up again. "Oh, my god! Maybe I sat on a bug!" She brushed down her robe frantically. "Ah! Here come the handmaidens and the midwife."

Two strange women came into the room, followed by the hippopotamus, carrying a bathtub. They were very different in appearance, one being small and rather meek, with a blue cloak covering her hair. A light hovered above her head, while the other – well! She was dressed in black gothic style, a short skirt with goose shit green embroidery; a blood colored blouse; black fishnet stockings; high-heeled tarnished silver sandals and a long chain of skulls that hung around her neck.

The gothic woman introduced herself in a dictatorial fashion. "I am Kali, and this is Mari. I don't want the hippo to do this delivery, although she is the official midwife. I need to birth this babe."

She briskly filled the tub with warm water and undressed the Empress, bidding her step into the tub, where she assumed the birthing position. The quiet Mari stood by, complaining tearfully that it was her turn to assist at the birth.

"Then, which of you is the midwife this time?" The Empress questioned irritably. "Make up your minds and get on with it. I can't lie here all day, there are too many ideas waiting for creation in my boudoir." She let out a small scream, and her face took on a snarling, ugly expression.

The two women stood each side of the tub, glaring at each other. Mari dashed the tears from her face and spoke to Kali. "It's my turn. You didn't let me have my turn last time, and look what happened. My little Reficul, on whom I placed so much hope for the future, escaped. He is now down in the material world when I wanted to keep him up here. You are rude and mean, Kali, and you always push in front of me."

At this point, she elbowed Kali aside, setting her skulls jingling, and crouched down by the edge of the tub, where the Empress had already begun to push. But Kali seized Mari by her long hair and dragged her away from the tub, throwing her down on the ground and taking up the midwives' position. A long cry rose from the birthing mother. Mari scrambled to her feet and, leaning over, drove her sharp fingernails into Kalis' eyes, at which they fell to the floor together in a fierce wrestling match, kicking, clawing and screaming. Kali managed to get Mari's arm and twisted it behind her back, murmuring nasty remarks in an undertone. Meanwhile, I was bending over the tub and saw the babes' head crowning, so I bent down, my arms in the water, and delivered the child by myself. Seeing this, Kali was furious and Mari was sobbing hysterically. They both yelled out at me, for I had thwarted their intentions.

"You just can't behave like that during childbirth!" I exclaimed in annoyance. "The baby is here now. What shall I do with it?"

"Put it in the bed, you fool!" The Empress was beside herself. "Then it can be nurtured until it is fit to leave the cave."

"What about the bed bugs? Nobody has had time to spray them and change the linens. The baby will get bitten." I was trying to be practical.

"It's all your fault." Shrieked the Empress. "If you hadn't showed up, everything would have been correctly organized. Now look what has happened. Oh! I'm so frustrated. " She raised herself painfully out of the tub. "I suppose I'll have to deal with the bugs myself. Hang on to the child for a moment."

She walked painfully over to the bed, stripping off the linens, where Mari picked them up and fled. Leaning over the bed, she gave a brief command, and the green mamba over her forehead sprayed a thin stream of venom onto the mattress, at which the bugs who had managed to escape certain death by hiding in the cracks formed themselves into a brigade, jumped to the floor, and marched off up the mysterious flight of steps.

"Give me the child." The Empress beckoned to me, a sweet smile on her face once more as she bent solicitously over the tiny babe. "There, there, my little one. Rest yourself in this bed and grow into your full potential. We will keep vigil beside you and make sure your candles are always lit." Mari came back nervously with fresh linens, and together they tucked the little creature into the covers.

I signaled to little Mari, and whispered to her. "I have met your son, Reficul. Nepthys, sister of Isis, introduced him to me as a baby. They were looking after him when I was in the Path of the Star. He is amazingly intelligent, and even as a small child he was able to question an interloper, Prince Amgodovich, when he disseminated false doctrines during a convention in Miami. I observed that while I was visiting the Queen of Swords."

I paused and observed a tender smile brighten Maris' face, then continued. "He is now working to balance the interaction between Geburah and Chesed in the Island Of Tiphareth. There is much work to do there, and his work may take Aeons, so be patient."

By now, the Empress had recovered from her delivery, yet to my eye, she still seemed to be pregnant, and it wasn't just my imagination, for I could clearly see the next babe kicking vigorously under her diaphanous robes. This seemed very strange, but I didn't want to mention it, so I changed the subject and walked over to the flight of steps. "Where do these steps lead? I saw the bed bugs disappearing up here and I think Reficul went this way, too."

She walked over to the steps, dismissing the two handmaidens and the hippopotamus with a brief wave and telling them to be ready for the next birth in six hours, after the tide turned. "These are the secret steps that lead to my husbands' abode." She blushed modestly. "Normally I don't show anyone this hidden passage between us, but you are an initiate, and therefore this is the way you will leave my domain and enter that of the Emperor. Before that happens, I want to go back and see how the swan is doing, and whether its wound has healed. We can just make it before the next high tide." She led the way out of the cave and we waded through the shallow pool, where the hippo was peacefully floundering, and sat down near the swan.

During our absence, the bird had built a large nest by the pool, and when it rose from the nest, there were two magnificent eggs resting there. I was extremely hungry. "Look, the swan has laid two eggs. Let's have them for breakfast!" I picked up the still warm eggs.

"Not so fast!" The Empress warned, a cautious look on her face. "Hold them up to the light before you boil them. They may have been fertilized."

I held up the first egg to the light of the moon, which was brighter than ever. It was true, the egg was a reddish double-yolker, and two tiny fetuses were wriggling around inside. Carefully laying it down, I picked up the second egg. This also had two yolks, although they were floating quietly in their whites and it was hard to see what was inside.

"You're right!" I exclaimed. "Both these eggs are double-yolkers. What could be inside?"

The Empress gave a tender sigh. "I have waited many aeons for the swan to lay double-yolkers. I think I know what they contain, but we must wait for it to complete the incubation. It would be fatal to crack them open now. Put them back."

I gently laid the two eggs back in the nest and the bird fluffed its feathers and settled down gratefully.

Looking serious, the Empress explained. "While we are waiting for the twin chicks to be born, let me clarify who I am. You may wonder why I am often very moody. Sometimes I am happy and soothing, and then I change and become fierce and demanding. That is because I am Eve, and my consort, the Emperor, is Adam. Eve gives birth to everything that exists. EVE-rything! She also destroys everything, for without destruction, creation could not manifest. There would not be enough space to contain all the new forms. Imagine living alongside dinosaurs, cavemen and computer nerds, all at the same time." She laughed. "It would be impossible. I have to destroy old forms in order that the universe may progress, for we are evolving rapidly."

"Oh! I understand. So, you and the Emperor are the paired impulses that create the world as we know it." I was amazed as she continued.

"We both also represent the gods Shiva and Shakti, and, for my part, I symbolize the receptive, formulating principle while the Emperor is the propulsive, thrusting principle in the universe. We work together to form ideas from the two Islands above us. I emanate from the Island of Binah, representing understanding and foundation of earthly objects, and my path goes to Tiphareth. The Emperor, who also goes to Tiphareth, embodies the wisdom of Chockmah in an abstract force, and it is important for him to penetrate my staircase, for without me his impulsive images would never be manifested."

"I have visited Tiphareth." I said soberly. "They seem very happy there. People yearn to emigrate to Tiphareth, for is it not the ultimate Island, the greatest joy they can attain to?"

"That is what they imagine, for they can visualize nothing further. When my son Lucifer arrived in Tiphareth, he came with a message. That message was contained in the lantern he carried and his emerald. But most people thought the lantern was not important – just a light that shone on its surroundings, when really, the lantern revealed the path upwards, which they could not see, for they looked at the light as if they were blind." She sighed, looking forlorn. "It will take many Aeons for the secret meaning of the lantern to be understood, except by a few who truly question their mundane existence. So be it, time will reveal everything about Atlantis."

Not being aware of time passing, for we were beyond earthly time and space, I observed the rise and fall of tides outside the cave, which appeared to flood at high tide. I wondered, then, whether the rising water would drown the babe in the bed and swamp the vigil candles. I decided to go back to the cave myself, since I was a strong swimmer, and the Empress had retired to her bower to rest. Lowering myself into the swirling waters, I bumped into the hippo, which raised her head.

"Don't go into the cave." She advised me. "The tide is up to the ceiling, and you wouldn't be able to breathe."

"I can swim underwater." I protested. "There must be an air pocket in there. Besides, I want to see if the baby is all right."

The hippo gave me a secretive look. "I am merely advising you. There is no air in the cave when the tide is full. What is more, if the Empress finds out that you have ventured in there, she will be furious. She may assume her worst manifestation, that of Kali, and kill you."

"I thought Kali was a separate person!" I said. "How can the Empress be Kali? I saw them as two separate beings, and Mari was there, too."

"Mari and Kali are the Empress, for she represents the vital energy in every female. The three are unified. You saw them as separate beings because you still think in terms of multiplicity. I, myself, am also a Shakti-aspect, although I do take after my father, Set, in some ways." She snorted coyly and a plume of water shot from her nostril and drenched me as I trod water next to her.

Ignoring her warning and taking a gigantic breath, I stubbornly swam underwater into the cave, feeling my way along to the bed, where the candles glimmered faintly in the turbid water. Waves washed in and out of the confined space, making it difficult to progress, for every time I reached the bed and was about to pull back the covers, a wave would suck me away. I was beginning to run out of air after five attempts to see the child. I turned and swam towards where I thought the entrance to the cave would be. It was not there. I began to get alarmed and tried not to panic, conservimg my breath.

Groping around the seven sides of the cave, I came to the steps, and with a great effort, I felt my way up, step by step, until I reached the surface of the water. Giving a gasp of relief, I sucked in the clean air, sitting down in the tunnel above the tide to wait for it to fall. Hours seemed to go by, and the water was still just as high. What had happened to the tidal flow? It must be out of rhythm. Farther up the steps I could hear the sound of a drum and marching feet. Another army? There were shouted orders that sounded like a drill for soldiers.

A shaft of pre-dawn light now came from the top of the stairs. I got up and scrambled towards it, reaching the open door to see a battalion of soldiers, dressed in red and black, approaching the entrance. They were carrying an enormous red battering ram, whose size was bigger than the tunnel itself, and I was between it and the door! I quickly dodged to one side, tripped, and fell into a disgusting cesspool by the path. The soldiers carried the ramrod to the tunnel, put it down, and pressed a switch at its base. Immediately the object began vibrating up and down and moving forward and backward, gradually disappearing into the tunnel until the darkness swallowed it up.

Thankful that I had the presence of mind to avoid the dreaded rod, I found myself in a delicate situation as I scrambled out of the cesspool. I knew I was already in the Path of the Emperor, but I had not finished my time with the Empress, for the two swans' eggs were about to hatch, and I needed to be there with her to help with the process. I wondered how I could get back, since the rod was busy occupying the tunnel, and I was not sure how long it would be there. I was afraid I would be cut off when the sun rose.

There was a flutter of wings above my head, and a large Atlas moth that I had seen with the Empress came floating down, landing on my foot. A faint, dusty voice spoke to me as I craned my head down to hear it. "I can lead you back to the Empress, but you must wash first. You're smothered in primeval soup, a nasty smelling liquid that contains the elements of the universe. You must cleanse yourself, so follow me. We will have to get this done before dawn, when the Emperor wakes up."

The moth flew towards a giant computer screen, set above the tunnel in a series of ascending locks. It indicated a basin of pure water above the screen, so I prepared to dive in. The moth fluttered in front of me, shaking its antenna. "No, not that way. Go through the screen to enter the water. Put your finger on the screen, and it will open up."

I touched the screen, and a vista of Mediterranean blue appeared before me – a gently sloping sandy beach leading down to lapping waves. On the beach was a lounge chair, with parasol, striped towel and a set of new clothes. I ran down to the waters' edge and gleefully dived into the foaming waves, fully clothed. Swimming up and down, I rinsed the filth off my clothing, then toweled off. I kept my original hempen tunic, though, for I did not like the outfit they had left hanging on the chair. It was a pair of black pants with a red tunic and a bearskin helmet, the uniform of a palace guard.

The Atlas moth led me back by a roundabout path through the dense woods. I could hear Parsifals' hunting horn far away, as I reached the Empress in her bower safely. She was just waking up, rubbing her eyes and saying in a vague voice that she had dreamed her consort visited her during the night, and it was wonderful. I politely refrained from asking whether the battering ram had anything to do with it.

The swan stood up, revealing one of the eggs between its feet. There was a definite crack in the egg. Beckoning to the Empress, I showed her that the twin chicks were on their way out. We watched in fascination as the shell fell apart in small slivers. Out of the first egg, two tiny red-faced chicks staggered to their feet, swaying uncertainly. I had to look closely, for although they looked like regular chicks, they had human faces, and I recognized them immediately. They were the twins from the Passage of the Sun, Kerry and Kerri! Barely a moment later, the other egg burst apart and revealed two silvery chicks, the twins from the Passage of the Moon.

The Empress welcomed the four sweetly. "Here you are, my lovelies! Right on time. We are starting a new universe today, so take your positions in the sky. Once you are settled, we can begin to arrange mountains, forests and seas." She looked down at her bulging stomach tenderly. "I am great with child, and impatient to populate our new planet." She turned to me with a glare. "Now, as for you – I am aware that you violated my cave while I was resting in my hammock. Rather than put you to the sword, I have decided to exile you. You are condemned to visit the sphere that is not a sphere, Da'ath. I sincerely hope you will find your way through that enigma. Be gone from my presence this minute."

The Empress pointed to the West, where the Path of the Emperor lay, beyond the mysterious Island of Da'ath. She evidently had no further interest in my company.

Path of the EMPEROR

I had to leave the Path of the Empress, knowing I had disgraced myself by violating her cave, and could not return to the Emperor through her tunnel. It was, however, in a good cause. Reficul had escaped, and the incoming tide may have swamped the new babe, although the vigil candles were still burning and I had to assume the babe was alive underwater. I sat for a while in the wood, not knowing how to leave, until a quiver of wings on my shoulder told me the Atlas moth was there.

"Follow me." It announced. "I will lead you to Da'ath, the sphere that is not a sphere. If you can guess the riddle, you may enter the Path of the Emperor safely."

The moth set out through the moonlit wood. In the distance, faint music played and dancers laughed. A mist rose from the ground, almost obliterating everything in front of me, even the faint, bobbing shape of the moth. We left the wood and came to the edge of a high cliff, shrouded in fog. The moth glided over the edge and told me to follow. I hesitated, teetering on the brink of the Abyss, then jumped into empty space, fixing my intent on a safe landing.

There was no sense of falling through gravity, and time and space disappeared, as I floated idly, suspended in a vast unknowingness. I tried to clear my thoughts. I had heard someone speak about Da'ath. Who was the person that had come down from Da'ath? Thick mist dripped down my back as I hung helplessly in the miasmic void. I remembered the enigmatic Reficul, who became Lucifer. Born from the Empress, he had mysteriously disappeared from her cave. He manifested in the Path of the Star, grew up, and then showed up in Tiphareth. Of course! That must be it. He was the one who told me that he came down from Da'ath, bringing the Emerald Tablet and the lantern with him. Evidently, he brought great knowledge with him, but nobody understood his message. Da'ath – Lucifers' knowledge had come from there. Therefore, Da'ath was no longer a sphere. I wondered if it had been robbed of its power and no longer contained the knowledge of all things? The Fall of Lucifer might have taken that knowledge to Tiphareth, where it remained, unappreciated by all.

Immediately my flight resumed. I had answered the riddle of Da'ath, which I hoped to reach later, and I was able to complete my journey to the Path of the Emperor.

It was dawn when I arrived. The strident crowing of a rooster rang out as the sun tipped over a range of jagged mountains. The vast lake of primal soup lay before me, its varied colors flashing and rippling, and reflecting an enormous triangular sign that rose from its depths. Hearing the sound of a hammer on wood, I wandered over to a small boat yard where a Druid was replacing a plank in a little rowboat.

"There – that's fixed now." The white robed figure straightened up, rubbing his back. "Now I can go out on the lake again to fish." He suddenly noticed me. "Want to come fishing today?"

"Sure, that would be very relaxing." I agreed.

"It's the only way to kick back here." He complained. "Everything is in everlasting motion, and the Emperor is always anxious to press forward. It's very exhausting. Contemplating the primal soup helps, and you never know what might be in your net when you haul it in." The Druid pushed the boat on greased rollers back into the lake and we climbed in, taking an oar each. The fishing net spread out behind us as we made slow progress through the dense liquid in the silence of dawn.

We remained on the lake, trolling up and down until something big snagged in the net. Hoping for a big fish, we began to haul it in, dragging it over the stern. The object was very heavy – definitely not a small fish. Maybe we had caught a marlin? Closer the net came, and the head of a ram broke the surface, its horns entangled in the net.

The Druid paused. "Darn it! No fish. I don't think I want that ram in my boat. It might struggle and capsize it."

"Well, we can't leave it here. It will drown." I was concerned for the animal. "How about bringing it close to the boat and towing it to shore?"

"That might work." We pulled in the net tightly so that the animal could keep its head above water, and began to row back to the boat yard. The ram dragged heavily on the little boat as we struggled with the oars. Our progress was slow, but we were close to shore when a bugle blared loudly, panicking the ram who thrashed around, spraying us and tipping the rowboat over. It capsized and threw us into the primal soup.

"Help me!" The Druid cried as he clung to the upturned boat. "I can't swim. I can't hold on – the boat is too slippery. I'm sinking underwater."

"Hold on there, I'm coming." I swam over and slid my arms around him, striking out backwards and dragging his heavy weight towards safety. The ram, trailing the net and the upturned boat, followed us. I laid the old man on the beach and did some CPR, and he quickly recovered. He seemed very familiar on second thoughts

"My goodness!" I stared into his face. "I know who you are! You're my Guide!" He gave a weak smile and winked as he got to his feet.

I was overjoyed, but meanwhile, with its hooves safely on shore, the ram made a run for it, pulling the net and the sinking boat with it. I leapt for its horns and held it down while the old fellow untangled the net, letting the ram go free. It plunged rapidly over a low hedge into a ploughed field alongside. The animal was now floundering in deep mud up to its neck, and slowly sinking, when a young boy, hiding in the folds of earth, came to rescue it

"Phew!" My Guide mopped his brow. "I'm glad David was able to secure the ram. He's been hiding in the furrows waiting for Goliath to come along. He has his catapult ready, but there's been no sign of the giant. I suggested he took a shot at Napoleon instead. We're really tired of his troops marching up and down. It's making the whole ground shake and that jiggles the jigsaw puzzle and tosses the pieces out of alignment."

"Where is the jigsaw?" I glanced around. "I can't see it from here."

"You won't be able to. It is in the center of that city over there." The old fellow pointed to skyscrapers on the far side of the lake. "It's in a huge park where the people go to work out. Instead of running around in circles, tossing a ball, or climbing a manufactured wall, they have to place the pieces in their correct positions. That's not as easy as you would think. The pieces themselves are huge and weigh many tons, but they can still be dislodged by violent ground movement, such as an earthquake."

"What is the theme of the jigsaw?" I asked. "When will it be finished?"

"Theme? Representation? There is none. Finished? Of course it will never be finished – if it was, the Universe would cease to exist." My Guide nodded sagely. "We don't want that, do we?"

"Well, why even bother with it, then? It doesn't make sense to try and complete something that will never be finished." I remonstrated. "They could have a nice space with lots of trees and benches to sit on when they run out of breath."

"If you examine the idea, you will understand that, although people think they often finish a project, such as a temple, a painting or even cooking a meal, those things are impermanent, and will eventually be destroyed by entropy. The temple will end in ruins; the painting will be stolen, or fade, or will be destroyed in a territorial war; and the meal will be eaten – that is the most transient of all. The influence of that witch Melusina, goddess of unfinished projects who lives with the Devil, is all powerful in the material world."

"Then, how can we build something permanent that will last?"

"We build only in the world of visions. All your efforts, even the tarot cards you are collecting for Pullows, will end in certain failure. You can only create something out of your Self, and that is why I am here to instruct you." He went on. "I became a Druid many years ago, and since then I have been a priest investigating many different cults. It is here, in the Path of the Emperor, that we finally see there is no difference between all beliefs. They have only one root. If people understood that, all wars would cease and peace would reign because no-one would disagree with anyone else."

He moved towards a series of descending locks that led out of the lake. "Here are screens which you can look at, placed here by the Memorizer from the Aeon, where you can see what you have screened out from your memory over the years. You must go back and recognize what you have omitted."

I walked out over the second lock gate, looking up towards the screen above me. A dozen distorting mirrors reflected my image back at me from every angle. I looked from one to the other, trying to focus on my real image, but it was very confusing.

"I can't see myself at all. This screen doesn't show me anything. It is split up into dozens of different images. How can I tell which one is mine, for I can't get back those memories."

"The mirrors represent the images that other people have of you. They only know their own distorted account of you, not the true version. You need to get past those reflections and find yourself. Close your eyes. Visualize the screen in front of you. The locks in your memory are clouding your real self. As the locks clarify the descending water, purifying it, so your mind will clear itself, and you will find the key to your real nature."

I closed my eyes. Multiple images - contorted, distorted, tortured - swam into my vision. Calming myself, I searched for who I really was. A vision hung, purified, in my minds eye, and I knew the answer.

I opened my eyes and signaled to my Guide, but his back was turned and he pointed into the ploughed field. "Look what's happening now."

All over the field, soldiers were sprouting from the furrows, digging up their horses, and developing a mounted battalion of troops, clad in black trousers and red jackets. They formed straight lines and galloped by, saluting a small figure who sat on top of a cube by the lake. Beside him, a fountain in the shape of a dragon spouted red liquid from its mouth.

"Is that a hamburger stand over there?" I asked plaintively. "I see the tomato ketchup, but not the mayonnaise. I'm hungry!"

"No, that is not tomato ketchup – that is blood that has been shed for the Rights of Man – millions of gallons that pour into the fertile soil, ready for the seed. We will sow the seed in due course. The cockerel will see to that." The Druid indicated a large rooster that was strutting nearby. The bird jumped up and perched on a log, giving out its traditional call "Cock-a-doodle-do!"

"Oh, don't do that to me!" Cried my Guide. "I'm too old for that. I've moved past my need for fertile pleasures, so just clear off." He gave the bird a swipe and it jumped up indignantly, spilling a basket of seeds beside it.

"Now look what you've done! I suppose we'll have to pick every seed up, for we can't afford to lose any." He took up the basket and we began to gather the seeds and throw them into the basket.

"Should we plant these before they get spilt again?" I questioned. "Some of them may be lost otherwise."

"That is true. Unfortunately, some of them do seem to disappear into thin air. They are ideas that never reach maturity in Malkuth. They present themselves again and again, and sometimes they are taken up by a genius. But, there aren't that many geniuses to capture them. If there were, humans would progress much faster. It's their greed, apathy, and ignorance that holds them back."

We walked along the furrows as we talked, placing the seeds carefully apart, so that they would have space to grow, and covering them with earth. I remembered the multicolored seeds of my future life that I had sown in the Path of the Aeon. I hoped they were sturdy and growing strong.

The sound of a light seaplane circling overhead interrupted our task. The little red plane flew past, waggling its wings, and then came in to land smoothly on the surface of the lake, taxiing into a small dock.

"There he is!" The old man exclaimed. "It's the Emperor at last! He pilots his own plane, for he likes to be in the cockpit as often as possible. Let's go over and greet him. He represents the Lord Shiva and Adam to his Eve." He set off at an unsteady run, his frail limbs trailing in a decided limp. A tall figure clad in an old-fashioned pilots' helmet and goggles, and wearing a purple leather pilots' jacket, jumped from the plane, followed by a magnificent cheetah, and shook his hand. They walked over towards me.

"This is the Navigator, my Lord. I am in charge of this person throughout the present life. You will be proud of the efforts that the Navigator has made to get here." I stepped forward and bowed deeply. I noted to my surprise the Emperor was not wearing any trousers, but had on a pair of multi-colored underpants. He was obviously well endowed, for the bulge in his pants was significant. The cheetah strained against its leash, for it had sighted the rooster, who thumbed its beak in defiance from a safe distance.

"How about having a cock-fight? I love the competition." The Emperor suggested with glee. "I saved that rooster from many other fighting cocks, as he was the biggest. I was going to present him to the Empress, as her special cockerel, but now I see he thinks too much of himself and deserves only to die." He released the cheetah that bounded after the bird and caught it in his mouth, bringing it back to the Emperor gently. He took the bird, holding it by its wings. "Thought you could get uppity with my beast, did you? Well, you looked ridiculous flapping your wings and running. You forgot you can't fly, and the cat can get you every time."

The bird cocked a bright eye at him, trying to sound sincere. "No, Sir! I really didn't intend any impertinence. I was merely cocking a snook at Napoleon. He was strutting around, trying to pretend he was a rooster himself. He is so foolish, like all dictators. They forget that the cock rules everything, and will certainly cause their downfall." The rooster went limp and began to snivel. "I'm feeling claustrophobic. Please let me go."

"Well, I will, if you restrain yourself. Otherwise you'll be in the next cock fight, and you have no spurs." The Emperor released the bird. "Go play with your key, and stay away from the seed basket this time." The rooster pulled a large and rusty key from under one wing, and stalked off with it.

"What is that key for?" I asked. "It looks very ancient."

"That is the key to the lock on the Hermits' loincloth. He hasn't unlocked the cloth for ages, and I fear it is now welded in place, as he doesn't bathe very often. He isn't interested in going down in that area any more – just allows his double to wander around looking for the Abbess. He's more interested in taming the eagle these days." The Emperor pulled a polished boomerang out of his pocket. "Want to see my boomerang fly?"

Without further ado, he launched the boomerang in a wide curve, and it spun through the air, coming back to his hand perfectly. "This boomerang is a great symbol for propulsion. What you give out, both in word or deed, comes back to you. It's called the boomerang effect. If your intention is positive, you will receive favorable responses. That is the law I project, written by the Archpriestess and passed to me to operate, since she can't throw a boomerang to save her life. It always gets tangled in her veil." He threw the boomerang a few times and then, impatient, suggested the three of us inspect the cock-fighting ring.

This evidently involved a flight in the seaplane, a flimsy looking biplane dating from the early days of flight. I was a little nervous as we walked along the dock and stepped on the float to climb into the tiny cabin, where we crouched down. My Guide took the passenger seat and I sat amongst the baggage, which consisted of some fishing rods, soup ladles, parcels of different salts and various bottles of mercury. The Emperor sat nonchalantly in the pilots' seat, started the engine and taxied out on the lake, picking up speed to take off.

With our extra weight, the plane rose sluggishly from the surface of the lake, and failed to gain height. The Emperor, used to flying by instrument, did not appear to notice we were approaching the large triangular sign in the middle of the lake. I gritted my teeth nervously. Would we manage to clear it?

We did not. At the last minute, the plane caught the tip of the triangle and the sign collapsed and disintegrated into the lake, emitting a strong smell of sulfur and a cloud of foul smoke as it hit the water. The plane staggered a moment, the engine sputtered, and the Emperor wrestled with the controls. The engine stalled and we went into a low glide over the primal soup, which seemed to have changed character and become rather glutinous, like a bowl of brown jelly.

"Damn it!" Our pilot shouted. "We'll have to ditch! I don't want to do that here. This is going to be a problem Prepare for the worst!" He took the plane in a shallow dive, barely touching the surface. It came to rest delicately "Don't move, either of you! When the sign for sulfur hit the water, it mixed with it and formed nitro-glycerin. If we make even the slightest movement, the whole lake may explode!"

Without moving a muscle, I asked, with a quiver in my voice. 'What do you suggest, then?"

"The nitroglycerin must be made to sink below the surface. To do that, we must add salt to the water that suspends the compound. Look amongst my baggage. Do you see a package marked sodium chloride?" The Emperor looked cautiously over his shoulder. "Don't move them around too much."

"Let me see. Sodium phosphate, sodium bisulphate, sodium carbonate – ah! Here is sodium chloride....." With trembling fingers, I slowly extracted the package from the pile of baggage, and slid it over to the Emperor. He opened it and carefully placed the compound in a large atomizer at the front of the plane, and pressed a button.

"Mistake! Serious error!" Came a voice from the void, where I floated alongside my Guide. "That was mercury fulminate! It's the detonator for nitroglycerin. You gave me the wrong package. We are in limbo now, but fortunately at this level we do not need the physical presence of a plane to keep us aloft – merely the belief that we are still alive!" The Emperor sounded faint but clearly identifiable, and my Guide whispered to me.

"Do not worry. We have suffered a large explosion. However, as you will observe, we still exist. In fact, I am sure you did not notice any difference as we were blasted out of existence." The old fellow paused. "Existence, that is, in the mundane sense."

"Well, I'm not sure that I like it." I complained. "I still prefer some contact with the ground. Can we descend again? I haven't completed my quest."

'The Way of Return, yes. Your quest can be continued equally well up here, since you are now at a high level of thought. In fact, it was your own deliberate intention to be up here, since you selected mercury fulminate instead of sodium chloride."

"Don't blame me!" I objected. "My eyesight isn't that good and I'm not trained in chemistry. Never was interested in that field. I am who I am, and that is how I wish to finalize my journey. Don't try to make me into something I'm not."

"OK, ok! No need to get huffy!" My Guide placated me. "If you like, we can go down now, even though I really enjoy it up here. Still, just to please you, we will find ourselves back in my rowboat, floating placidly on the primal soup."

"There won't be any soup left." I was despondent. "It blew up! We'll find an empty basin, I'm sure, and the boat will be at the bottom of it."

"The primal soup contains everything, all matter and antimatter. It cannot disappear from a mere explosion." My Guide remarked calmly. "That only affected a small part of it – there is plenty left. In fact, the elements that caused the explosion have now reverted to their original forms in its constitution, and will not bother us in the least."

"All right, then. I'm ready to go down." I braced myself for the fall, but nothing happened. The boat rocked gently on the primal soup, and in my hand was an oar.

We rowed back to shore. There was no sign of the Emperor or the little plane. Sounds of cheering were coming from the center of the city, so we decided to go over and see what was happening. It meant taking the boat, but it was a pleasant day to row, and all was placid on the lake with no indication of an explosion at all, except that the sign for sulfur had sunk below the lake, if, in fact, it had survived the explosion. We docked the boat at the city wharf, where people were busy unloading large pieces of jigsaw puzzle with a crane and driving them on ox carts through the cobbled street. Following the column of carts, we came to a vast open square where many people clustered. Some were unloading the carts and dragging the jigsaw pieces into the center, where a crowd of people was trying to fit them together. Three quarters of the jigsaw was finished, but they were having difficulties at one end. It was a picture of a huge figure, dressed in a plain three-piece grey suit, the pinstripes matching the muted color of the grey tie, which set off a grey shirt perfectly.

It was evident that the head was not coming together as it should. Shifting the gigantic pieces around was no easy task. A group of people pulled on a rope while others used wedges to settle them in place. There was a lot of cursing if the piece did not fit, for then it would have to be levered out with crowbars and moved to another area. All the pieces were now waiting in the carts, ready to fit. I looked around for the Emperor, hoping that the explosion had not killed him, although I personally thought he was a bit of a fool to meddle with chemical elements.

A couple of hours later – although time was not a factor up here – the last piece of the puzzle fitted into its temporary place. They had attached ropes to its head and run them up through a set of blocks and tackle to a crane, which pulled the huge figure upright gradually, and its feet were set in two brackets to hold it firm. The giant looked very smart and he reminded me of a Wall Street stockbroker in his neat outfit.

"Goliath! Goliath!" Shouted the crowd in a frenzy. "Open the Exchange! The Exchange! We want to invest our money." There was great excitement. I waited to see what would happen next. Many of them began throwing money at the giant, and others followed in a frenzy, until the heap of investments was up to its knees in bills and coins. "We want stocks and bonds! Get us a good return, won't you?"

The great figure remained unmoving, staring out through sightless eyes at an unmentionable horizon, their investments lying untouched at its feet. The people became restless, and some ran forward and began grabbing handfuls of money, little caring whether it was theirs, or not. At this, some cried out that they were being robbed, and hundreds wrestled and fought over the spilt fortune, trampling paper bills in the mud, where they became worthless. A mob scene developed, as screams, shouts and wails rose ever higher, and then, suddenly, the crowd fell silent as the throb of drums reverberated in the hazy air, coming rapidly closer.

The Emperor rode into the square, surrounded by his minions, each carrying a specific banner. A slight figure perched in front of him on the saddle. It was David with his sling, and rumbling across the cobbles behind them, pulled by twelve men, came a giant onager – a single armed catapult powered by a large skein of twisted sinew ropes. Everyone cheered as they assumed a position in front of the jigsaw and set a large rock in the arm of the catapult. The people stood as if transfixed, and then gave a great shout.

"One, two, three!" Yelled the crowd. "Let her fly! To the third eye!"

David gave the signal and the arm of the onager rocketed upwards, the great stone shooting out and hitting Goliath square just above the eyes. A thin wisp of blue smoke ascended and a distinct round hole was visible in the center of his forehead. Slowly the jigsaw giant raised his right arm, then moved a leg, nodded his head and stepped firmly out of the brackets, moving slowly over the trampled money, across the square, nodding, greeting the multitude and shaking hands with people in the crowd. The giant was grinning happily as he began to hand out fistfuls of money, scooping it up from the ground and adding more from his own pockets, which hung down, heavily loaded, to his knees. Everyone lined up and received what they needed, and there was still enough. David threw back his head and laughed.

"See what happens when you get stoned!"

Path of the HERMIT

I t had been decidedly rowdy in the Path of the Emperor, and I was glad
to be leaving. My Guide and I performed a ceremony for the solstice
before I said goodbye to him and committed myself to a tedious walk
along a stony beach towards the region of floating islands, which I could
see in the distance, as they languorously drifted past each other. One of
them must contain the Hermits' cave. It might be hard to find, as the islets
were very numerous, but I was determined to root him out.

Far off along the beach billows of smoke arose from a large fire.
Dancing figures circling around caused the intermittent flickering of
flames. Beyond them, a stepped pyramid rose to a great height, its terraces
overflowing with every kind of green foliage in wild profusion. At the top a
magnificent temple, built in Palladian style, glittered as if covered in gold.
I was soon close enough to see the nine dancers as they spun around, their
white skirts spreading out in strange cone shapes as they gracefully turned,
their arms stretched wide and their heads with the tall brown hat cocked to

the right. Recognizing them as whirling dervishes, I respectfully sat down cross-legged on the sand and tuned in to their trancelike motion.

When they ended the dance, the central figure came forward, and I recognized the Shriek of Yaboo, whom I had met previously in the Nine of Cups. He sat down beside me as the dervishes relaxed, their faces calm and filled with a strange joy. I also served briefly in his army during the wars on the Island of Geburah. He was a very helpful friend, and it was with his permission I had been able to search the desert vault and discover the tomb of the masked golden Prince.

"It is good to see you here, Navigator." The Shriek nodded. "You have come far, and you have experienced much and passed many tests. Through your poetry and witticisms, you have gained entry into our number, the Sufis, for you have reached the state of detachment from the world ordained in the Path of the Hermit. Your Ego, Belvedere, you recently raised to knighthood for his total submission to your Higher Self, and that is no easy task." He paused. "You seek the island cave where the Hermit keeps himself, both in meditation and in perambulation, for he must be, at the same time, in the world and out of it. At the present moment, he is visiting the Abbess and sampling her bread. While we are waiting, may I show you around our ziggurat?"

He rose to his feet, and I followed, walking towards the massive stepped pyramid. We mounted a wide staircase, stopping to walk a spiral ramp at each level to admire the beauty of the flowers and foliage. At the second level we entered a tall doorway between pillars, moving into the third level of knowledge. As the Shriek explained, the pyramid represented the three Sufi crossings that took an initiate from the fourth level of existence through the second and third level, to the final level of enlightenment. At each level, the aspirant shed certain character traits that, otherwise, would hold him back from his ecstatic encounter with divinity.

We paused to examine an exotic hibiscus plant, its gorgeous flowers extended towards us as if in supplication. "This beauty will shortly fade. Is there no way to retain it?" I asked. "We dream of heaven as a garden, don't we?"

"When you become old, you would lose hope if you did not imagine what lay ahead. Maybe there is a beautiful garden with everlasting flowers. But we do not know that! It is only in our imagination, in our heads, in our mind. What is mind?" The Shriek gazed at me intently. "It is all there is. Therefore, we carry our imagined thoughts with us wherever we go, alive or dead. We think in dreams and we think even after death. There is no end. That is why we must love eternity and purify ourselves in readiness, for otherwise we would make eternity a hell with our wrong thoughts. Fortunately, we have been given the opportunity to reincarnate many times, for our experiences on the earth plane prepare us for divinity, and we must reach certain standards before that occurs."

We continued our stroll upwards, arriving at the doors of the Palladian temple, perfect in its symmetrical proportions. "Palladio has always appealed to me." I remarked. "There is a calm simplicity in his buildings that beckons to my inner being, and I find joy in contemplating such an edifice."

"Indeed. Sacred geometrical forms are the visible gifts of pure mathematics. You must know of the golden division?"

"Yes, I acknowledge that in my practice." I nodded as we entered the temple.

The main feature inside the temple were two exceptionally beautiful statues of the lovers Tristan and Iseult that stood apart from each other, their yearning arms outstretched, reaching for ultimate unity. The Shriek explained that their earthly love, although consummated, could not last and was a pale echo of the divine, everlasting love they sought in each others' arms. The temple was dedicated to the search for that love.

He told me that the Hermit had been one of their number, a leading light amongst the dervishes, but that he had slipped from favor because of his attachment to the Abbess, whom he had met at a garden fete. Her honey had won many awards for its smooth texture, and the Hermit went for it, thinking that a spoonful or two could do no harm. Soon, apparently, he was spreading it on bread, and from there, he introduced butter – a fatal flaw. We knelt and prayed for the soul of the Hermit, that he could regain favor in the eyes of the gods.

The Shriek then helped me to prepare for my flight to the floating islands. He told me that my whirling action would transport me upwards, provided I got it right. I practiced for many weeks, finally feeling myself lifting off the ground on several occasions. The Shriek then announced that I was ready to take flight, and gave me his blessing.

On a sunny day, I began my whirling on the beach, gradually lifting higher and higher. Soon I was easily airborne and steering high between the floating islands, looking for any sign of a cave. A tall island, covered by snowy mountains with numerous glaciers cascading down its slopes, hovered nearby. I made out several ice caves in the glacier, so I angled my body in that direction, landing on a grassy meadow by a lake of freezing glacial water where a herd of ibex were grazing. A large eagle flew by, some nesting material in its beak. It must be spring, I decided, as the ibex abruptly scattered, their noses snuffing the cold air in alarm.

A snow leopard had suddenly appeared on a rocky ledge directly above us and was peering down, crouched in readiness to pounce. I swiftly moved away from the overhang to a safe distance. It was easy to move around up here, as the pull of gravity was much less noticeable. The leopard sprang off the ledge and onto the back of an ibex, but failed to hold the terrified animal, which shook it off and leaped away, following the startled herd. The leopard, disgusted, howled miserably, moving off in the direction of the ice caves, and I followed it cautiously, hoping to find the Hermit in one of the caves.

On the other side of the lake, the face of the glacier rose up before me. The caves were high up in the broken ice, and did not seem to have ledges in front of them. I whirled around a few times and rose up to the level of a large cave. It was true, the cave was inhospitable, and any fire lit inside would have melted the ceiling, causing a possible collapse of dangerous proportions. I had to look elsewhere.

Standing just inside the cave, I shadowed my eyes against the bright sun and examined the other islands as they floated by. My eyesight being exceptionally good at these heights, I could make out a small island which was not covered by snow and had a large cave on it that must be a good place for a Hermit, and, in fact, the faint glimmer of a fire came from its dark interior. I was about to take off for this island, when a larger island nudged its way between us and took up the intervening space.

There was activity on this island. Someone had built a large Gothic abbey in the center, surrounded by plots of land on which vegetables and corn grew. In the midst of this garden, a woman, dressed in a revealing blue robe with a translucent veil, stood arguing with a tall bearded man. This must be the Hermit! He had on a thin goatskin robe with nothing but a loin cloth underneath, and held a long, stout staff in one hand. The woman, who wore a medieval head dress, was offering him a loaf of bread, but he was shaking his head and backing away, raising his hand in a gesture of refusal, whereupon she pressed forward, confronting him more vehemently.

It looked as if the Hermit was having second thoughts about his relationship with the Abbess, even through the smell of fresh bread that drifted to my nostrils was extremely tempting. The Hermit turned and began taking great strides away from her, covering several yards with each step. The two islands, still moving, nudged up against each other again and then drew apart. At that moment, the Hermit gave a huge leap, landing on the edge of his island amongst some snowdrops that were scattered in front of the cave. The Abbess gave a loud cry of dismay, standing forlornly on the very edge of her island. It was evident that she could not make the jump to follow him, as the two islands rapidly parted again.

Now that I had the location of the Hermits' cave, I made ready to fly there. Unfortunately, I had not calculated the space inside the ice cave, and there was no room to whirl. Without this ability, which had to be repeatedly wound up, like a grandfather clock, I might not be able to float. I gingerly examined the sheer drop below me. Should I jump in the hope that sufficient whirling power upheld me? There was no other choice. I launched myself into thin air, feeling the upward draft as I fell rapidly towards the lake below. My whirling power had run out! Preparing myself for certain death in the frigid waters, I felt unnaturally calm, and as the rigid surface of the lake rushed up towards me, I closed my eyes, accepting my fate.

At the last moment, I felt a clawed grip catch me up as the rush of powerful wings swooped above me. Hanging from the eagles' talons as it headed over towards the Hermits' cave, I felt grateful for the faith that saved me. The bird soared over the small island, then dropped down in a wide turn and deposited me in front of the cave on a bed of snowdrops, where I lay, recovering my breath. Over me stood the Hermit, his staff in his hand, stroking his dark Assyrian beard thoughtfully.

We contemplated each other for a few minutes in silence, and then a grin spread across my face. "I know who you are!" I exclaimed. "You're Aurelio! The beard threw me off for a moment. How are you?"

"I am well." Aurelio responded in a deep voice. "You can see that I did build my own pillar, as I hoped to do when you met me in the Six of Swords. After quitting my academic background, I spent my time investigating different religious theories suggested by the glyphs on the pillar - bell, book and candle, you recall."

"And then we met again at the White Pyramid!" I interrupted in excitement. "You were visiting Braimind, the Ace of Swords, and we went together to your city, Alexandria, and I studied astrology, and then I became Court Astrologer." I finished breathlessly.

Aurelio smiled under his tonsured beard. "My! You are an excitable individual. Never mind, you will soon calm down here. The cold air will lower your body temperature and slow your heartbeat. In this way, you will be able to undertake further studies with me." Aurelio showed me into his cave, where a small altar fire flickered. At the back of the cave, motionless, a figure sat in the lotus position.

"Who is that?" I asked, narrowing my gaze to make out the features of the sitter. "He looks very familiar."

"It is myself." The Hermit Aurelio said serenely. "I am in deep meditation. It has been several years since I moved my position."

"But – you are here, talking to me! How can that be you?" I was mystified.

"I will explain. I became a master astrologer in Alexandria. I studied under Chaldean priests, who invented the art. But when I completed my analysis, I felt the need to discover more. Astrology was potent, but it was not the whole answer. I retired here, to the floating islands, and began to meditate. Now I am able to leave my seated body and take my energy wherever I am needed, to help people in difficulties that visualize my particular vibrations." Aurelio paused, frowning. "Unfortunately, a certain woman, the Abbess of a bogus Gothic edifice, appealed to me on a very high level. She wanted spiritual help, and I responded. I leaped to her floating island, and there she attempted to seduce me by offering me honey, spread on bread. At first I refused, but her smile was so sweet, I forgot myself and took a bite, ruining my years of fasting. Tasting the forbidden meal, I wanted more. The honey melted in my mouth, but it sank into the bread. I needed a barrier – butter!" The Hermit began to weep. "I went on my knees, begging her for some grease. When she gave it to me, it melted into my beard, and made a terrible mess." He wiped away a tear. "I was undone – filled with shame. I backed away and, getting to my feet, I managed to escape. I knew she could not leap, because of her skirts, so I waited until the gap between the islands widened before I jumped back to the safety of my cave." Aurelio mopped his eyes with a corner of his robe.

"That's terrible!" I commiserated. "So, even at this high level, you can still be tempted. After all the years you have dedicated to study and refining your personality, a mere woman can still trap you with her honey."

"That is true. Now I can only redeem my transgressions by committing myself to educating you. By arriving at the right time, you may help to save my reputation. I sent my eagle to rescue you when you jumped from the ice cave. We allowed you to fall until you were a millisecond from hitting the water, and the timing was perfect."

"So you and the eagle are in league. Is the bird your ally?" I asked.

"Indeed. When I first came here, I would watch the eagles as they soared past my island. They were so free, so independent. I wanted to tame an eagle, but I knew they had sharp talons. I debated making myself a glove from ibex hide, but, after consideration, I knew that was a cowardly way to proceed. I had to allow the eagle to land on my bare hand! There must be no barrier between its body and mine." He paused. "I began breeding chipmunks, for there are many that share my cave. They had formed themselves into a society – MUCK, or Merciful Use for ChipmunKs. They were willing to make the sacrifice. Anything was preferable to facing pointless annihilation from passing vehicles at their base on Chuckanut Drive."

"They are fine creatures." I agreed. "But it is their own fault if they end as road kill.. They don't stop to think. The only way to avoid them is to watch the tail, which they often carry in the air like a flagpole. Then you can brake in time."

"Yes. So I wanted to offer them another, more meaningful way out. Their society MUCK agreed to arrange regular sacrifices that would be preceded by suitable rituals. Each martyr munk would then offer its body, dangling from my bare hand, to attract a passing eagle. It worked very well. As the eagle – and there was a particular one that passed frequently, realizing the offer of free food – grew used to my outstretched arm, it finally landed on my wrist, its talons digging painfully into my flesh."

"Ouch! I don't know how you withstood that!" I was filled with admiration.

"Not to worry. I was overjoyed! I had finally found my ally, and the bird has been with me ever since. I am immune to its pricks now, and we work together to help other people soar. When I travel astrally, the eagle comes with me as my disciple. We have healed many who feared they could not rise above themselves. It is rewarding work." Aurelio fell silent.

I attempted to continue the conversation, but it seemed he had gone far away in thought. His body still moved around the cave preparing a simple meal for us, but our conversation ceased.

After several days of quiet waiting, during which I attempted to meditate alongside his seated body, I grew restless. His island was small and, apart from the chipmunks' regular weekly meetings, there was little to occupy my mind. I decided to do a whirl and see if I could fly to the island where the Abbess lived. I wanted to talk to someone, as the continual silence was getting on my nerves. Whirling cautiously outside the Hermits' cave, I timed my flight as her island came floating by randomly. I landed, painfully, on top of the Gothic building, filled with sharp spikes and horrible grinning gargoyles. Bruised, I nursed myself up in the bell tower, where I met some interesting bats. They were intrigued to learn of the free chipmunk dinners, but, on consideration, decided it would be as well to stick with mosquitoes, which were considerably smaller.

I spent the night up in the bell tower, and took the opportunity of the wonderful morning view to absorb the scene around me. Floating islands were everywhere, as far as my eye could see, each one having a small figure living on it. In a way, their separation reminded me of the Hodians, who lived within their own bubbles of protection. Why was it necessary to perpetuate separation? Even up here, in the higher latitudes, it seemed to be the norm. I would find out more about that philosophy when I could.

The next day I descended the spiral staircase in the tower and found myself in a small, enclosed loggia open to the sky. The Abbess sat on a garden bench, absorbed in her crochet work. I hesitated to disturb her, but she looked up at my approach.

"Ah! You've come over to see me. I've been focusing on you, for I saw you up there with my beloved Aurelio, and I was jealous. He has never allowed me to visit him, for he fears my influence." She cocked her head to the right, looking at me slyly. "Tell me what you're doing up there. Are you having fun?"

"I'm afraid not. He hasn't spoken a word for several days. I got bored, so I whirled over here. I made a bad landing on one of your gargoyles, and I have bruises to prove it."

"Never mind. Bruises are part of life. You must take risks sometimes. For myself, I am content to remain here and tend the beehives of my mistress, the Archpriestess. She cannot extract the honey, as she is too busy organizing reincarnations. You can imagine the number of people who pass through the Society of Enochian Anchorites on a daily basis, interviewing for their next Destiny. It gets more hectic every day, especially when there is a war or a natural disaster." The Abbess set down her crochet work on the bench. "Come, I will show you around my island."

She took my arm in a firm grip and we set out on a winding path amid the vegetable beds. I was astonished at the power of her hand on my arm, and I felt the need to break free, but I didn't want to offend her. The sunlit paths, bordered by rows of radishes, pumpkins and peppers, enthralled me. I felt as through I could wander forever in her garden, sampling a raspberry here, a carrot there, and the path wound on and on. After a while, considering the size of the island, I began to wonder where it would end. I felt we had been walking for miles, as her light conversation kept me occupied while we strolled onwards.

The vegetable beds ended and gave way to regular rows of shrubs – spiraea, glossy abelia, and a host of others that gave off a cloying perfume, making my head spin. The sunlight now filtered through low trees, and the path grew darker as we entered a dense wood. Still her melodious voice rippled on and my head was filled with thoughts of fresh salads, bowls of fruit, and the unique taste of ratatouille, my favorite dish.

"Here we are." She announced firmly, as we came to a small clearing with an old well in the center. "This is where I must ask you a question, sadly. If you cannot answer, you will have to join the others."

She shifted her grip on my arm and quickly twisted it behind my back, holding me firm as I bent forward over the lip of the well. The pain in my arm could not distract me from the sight at the bottom of the well, where, through the glimmer of translucent water, I discerned a pile of bodies of all different races and creeds. A pang of terror shot through me.

"What are you doing?" I managed to gasp, although my thinking was blurred. "I don't know anything. Let me go!"

"The question is – where is the key to the lock on the Hermits' loincloth? That is what I need to know." She turned me around to face her, still retaining her grip. The hood of her dress had fallen off her face, and, with a gasp, I knew I was a captive of my own Shadow, the Hoodwinker! "Where can I find the key? If I can unlock his loincloth, he will be mine, mine! I can't wait to rip it off!"

Knowing where the key was, I decided to remain silent at first, but as she forced me further over the lip of the well, I was soon hanging head downwards, and at that point I felt it necessary to tell her that the cockerel held the key, and that it was in the Path of the Emperor.

"Blast it!" She cried. "Are you sure? The Emperor will blow me away if I try to enter his domain. I must find another way to entice the rooster to come here. Unfortunately, it can't fly, so I will have to go down and get it." She released her hold on me and seemed to have quickly lost interest in my fate. "Why don't you just leave?" She said rudely. "I must prepare to descend to the beach and ask direction from the dervishes. What a come down!"

Without further ado, I began to whirl and was soon able to soar back to the Hermits' cave, where he awaited me.

"Your education is coming along fine." He said admiringly. "That was a close call! At least you told the truth when I would have expected you to lie. It is no good protecting the Emperor, for he breaks through every barrier set up against him. He is force itself, and cannot be halted." Aurelio patted me on the back. "Now we will continue your education. I have lost my lantern and I've searched everywhere, but I haven't been able to find it recently. Can you tell me where it is?"

I began looking around the small island, and then searched the inside of the cave thoroughly. "It's not here. It should be at the top of your staff, so that you can show people the Way of Return."

"You are correct. Now, look up at the top of my staff." He pointed upwards.

I found myself momentarily looking straight at the sun, and hastily lowered my eyes. "I can't see the top of your staff. The sun is blinding me." I rubbed my dazzled eyes.

"I can't keep a secret. The sun is my lantern, for it never goes out. People imagined in distant times that the sun went to bed in the evening, like everyone else, but it was hiding on the other side of the planet. Finally they discovered it, which was a relief; since they were afraid it would not come back. There will come a day, however, when it will burn up, and long before that, humans will cease to exist in their present form, as the moon, of course, is also moving away from the earth and its influence is dwindling imperceptibly. These are transient phenomena!" Aurelio laughed happily. "Only one thing is permanent, and you know what that is, don't you?"

I nodded sagely. "I'm sorry I became trapped by the Hoodwinker again. She seemed so friendly. I keep reminding myself of the danger she represents as my Shadow, yet she lures me again and again into foolish deeds."

"That is what you are here to learn. At least you are fully aware of her. As for the key to my lock, it is not the key that the cockerel holds in its beak, after all. Instead, ask your friend the rattlesnake, who lives inside you now as Kundalini, about the real Key. It will tell you when you are ready – at the thirty second level." As Aurelio moved his staff out of the suns' glare, I saw that the end of it was shaped like a crook.

Island of CHESED

I left Aurelio filled with new hope from his teachings, and made my way northwards towards the Island of Chesed, the next stop on my travels. Because I had fallen from the Chariot on my first attempt, I felt I was backtracking on my path, but there was no other solution. I knew that the Way of Return involved a continuous spiral climb, with frequent lapses that set me back. However, the influences of Chesed seemed to reach out to me and draw me within, almost as if I were born for the first time into the temporal world.

Images began to form in my mind before I reached Chesed, sometimes known as Gedulah, the Island that balanced the Martian influence of Geburah. The katabolic red blooded atmosphere of Geburah had been extremely disturbing, although I could see, if those forces were used wisely, that they could be very beneficial and motivating. As I traveled north, the sky overhead became filled with the shifting and nebulous colors of the Aurora Borealis, a sight so beautiful that I longed to ride on those filaments of light. No soon had I visualized this, than I found myself amongst the waves of light, riding along in the flow of subtle colors that passed me from one strand to another effortlessly, so that I wound like a thread from pink, to blue, to turquoise. I was indeed reluctant to observe the Island of Chesed beneath me, its serried ranks of pyramids lined up along the flood plain, yet it glimmered in the same way. The filaments seemed to emanate from the center of the Island, where an indefinable cloud shaped itself into a vast throne, on which sat none other than Aurelio, clad in a kings' garments, and bearing a scepter and an orb in his hands. The skeins of light set me down delicately at his feet, and I bowed down obediently.

"Welcome to the island of archetypes." The Hermit intoned in a low vibration. "You are here to work in the realm of images – thoughts that are formed in the higher mind before they are made manifest on earth. This is the magic of Chesed, the anabolic blue-blooded sephirah, which builds up multiple visions that can only be manifested through the motivation and focus of Geburah. Many of these hazy thoughts never come to fruition in the violent atmosphere of Geburah, which breaks them down. Yet ever more abstract images are constantly made in Chesed and stream forth on their way to formation, if not now, in the future of mankind." Aurelio gazed past me into the surrounding clouds. "Man does not, or cannot, always take advantage of these images. Take, for example, the image of a flying machine. An excellent idea, yet at the time it first came to a man of genius, the technical problems associated with it had not yet been solved. The time was not right, and the image was put back on the shelves in the warehouse of Chesed for several hundred earth years."

"I remember. Leonardo da Vinci even designed the machine, yet he could not get it off the ground, because the need for speed and the science of pressure on the wing of an aircraft had not been discovered, even though the idea was ready to depart from Chesed." I frowned. "Why does it take so long for such an idea to make its way down the Tree to Malkuth, where it can be made manifest?"

"The problem is not in Chesed, for the images are free flowing here and can be grasped at any time. Alas! They are held hostage by the very apathy and inertia of Malkuth, where the majority of people never rise above the comfortable level of mundane existence. They do not ask questions, nor dream of great things, but fortunately there are a few, a very few, who have received the gift of genius, and they are the beacons that lead mankind forward, despite all odds pitted against them by Geburah. In fact, it is those who persevere through all that Geburah throws at them who will finally succeed."

"Perseverance, yes, that's the key. For myself, I'm anxious to complete my journey on the Way of Return. Do I have far to go still before I can become free of all desires?" I asked plaintively.

"The very tone of your voice shows that you are not entirely free of Sir Belvedere. I suspect that your Ego is lurking nearby, and you cannot be free of karma until you let go of all egotistical desires – even that of the desire to be free of desire." Aurelio began to chuckle to himself. "Do not worry, though. We are pleased with your progress, and you have come here to release yourself from the Wheel of Life and Death, and we will help you, provided you show true humility and creative supremacy in your dealings with us. Inevitably...." Here the Hermit looked at me with a piercing stare. ".... You must first deal with the Shade of Chesed, whose bigotry and hypocrisy are causing great strife amongst us. This is a greedy Shade, whose great appetite must be curbed by discipline. Unfortunately, the Chesedians tend to be too merciful, and they are dreadful enablers, always trying to see the point of view of those they defend, without realizing the mayhem that creates."

"By Jove! I see what you mean. Enabling people to continue on a path that is disastrous for them is not a good idea. It is a mistake to think you can change a persons' Destiny by interfering, although you can alter their life choices." I agreed. "In fact, it's an ego trip, mainly because a person does not want to cause waves, or to have confrontations, that they weakly allow those they love best to stray from a rewarding path. I am ready to tackle the Shade. Tell me where to find it."

Aurelio pointed upwards to a magnificent cloud formation that towered overhead. "You will find the Shade in that storm, for it eats the very energy that jumps from cloud to cloud as lightning. Go now, and the waves of color will sweep you up into the storm. May you be successful in your search, and take with you this gargoyle, gathered from the bogus Gothic edifice on my last visit."

The gargoyle stuck out its tongue at me in an extremely vulgar way, waggling its ears. In spite of this, it allowed me to climb on its back, and we shot straight up like an arrow into the massive thundercloud, which took on the shape of a huge fat man as we approached. Hovering in front of him, but keeping a safe distance away, I watched as he sat, his anvil head dress streaming in the wind above him, and devoured flash after flash of lightning, which ran across and from top to bottom of the surrounding clouds. His eyes, dark slits in the cloud, were glazed, as he reached for yet another streak of light and stuffed it into his mouth.

The gargoyle shuddered in disgust. "See the way he behaves! I've never seen such a greedy fellow. He never stops eating, and when he does manage to spit out a few words, he is always raving about unnatural practices and falsehoods, which he loves. He's the biggest hypocrite I ever met. I consider myself above such things, as I live without nourishment at a very high level on my edifice, and I am never tempted by all the vegetables that surround me."

"Well, I have to defeat him. He's very large, and he could easily swallow me in one gulp. What do you suggest we do?" I said. "How can we deflate him and make him rain, for then he would dissipate entirely."

"Aha! I hadn't thought of that idea. He's always been swirling around, especially when it gets hot and humid. Sometimes he even farts tornadoes – the rush of wind from his rectum is so violent that it can knock over pyramids and kill people. It is not a fart to be reckoned with, I can tell you." The gargoyle sniffed loudly.

"I have an idea. Of course, Chesed is the very best place for ideas. We can use a method called cloud seeding to produce rain where it is needed. If we were able to get enough seeds, he would have to go on raining until he petered out." I suddenly knew where to get the seeds. "Fly me down to your vegetable garden by the bogus Gothic edifice. I'm sure the Abbess must have stored away plenty of seeds in packets. We can use those."

The gargoyle objected. "I know I belong in the Path of the Hermit. I am only here on the Island of Chesed on a four day visa. The customs officials would not allow me back in if I crossed over to get the seeds."

"H'm. I didn't know they have customs here. Is this a border?"

"Of course it is! The Hermit is on the barrier between the real and the numinous that exists in the Island of Chockmah above him. They call it the Limbic Threshold. Nothing passes here without close scrutiny, and you may even have to strip off and let them paw you all over – horrible!"

"We do need seeds from somewhere, though. The rooster has a basket of seeds in the Path of the Emperor. We could go there."

"Not likely! My cousin, a handsome gargoyle with a very long tongue and pointed ears, was knocked completely off his perch by the Emperors boomerang. He was broken in two and lost his head. He never recovered, as there were no available donors willing to offer him a new head."

"No good being a coward." I remarked. "I'll watch out for you. The Emperor is probably off on a jaunt in his cockpit. You can take me due east and, with any luck, the people will be busy with a new jigsaw, and we can remove some seeds. I hope the cockerel won't catch us, but we'll have to take that chance."

We touched down near the basket of seeds. There was no sign of the Emperor, but a new biplane was doing dangerous loops and aerobatics over the lake. The rooster was sitting on the basket of seeds, asleep. We had to get him off somehow.

I approached the snoring bird slowly. "Good morning, Good morning. Time to get up! Get it up! Early morning is the best time to fertilize your furrows." The bird opened one cold blooded eye, and I jumped up and down in a frenzy. "Up! Up! Up and down, up and down."

The rooster rose haughtily from the basket. "All right, all right! I'm getting up. Shut your noise, you interfering wretch. I'm going to crow now." He stalked off, whereupon we loaded as many seeds as we could into my tunic pockets, and stuffed some more into a pouch that the gargoyle was carrying.

We took off at a run as we saw the bird who, when overexcited, reverted to his barnyard language, hurrying back. "Youooo hypooocrites! Yoooou've stooolen my seeds." He crowed. "What am I to do, to do? Cock-a-doodle-do."

He was too late. It took us little time to soar above the anvil shaped cloud and begin to scatter the seeds. We could hear people down below complaining that they had never experienced such heavy rain, and they were wondering when it would stop. The fields became flooded and many people took to the boats, but the fat cloud shrank and the lightning ceased in the flooding downpour, and even the tornadoes fizzled out. The sky soon cleared, and a great cheer came up to us from the freshly watered ground.

"The Shade is gone! The Shade is no more." It was true, for the Shade never showed its face in the Island of Chesed again.

I bid goodbye to the helpful gargoyle, who returned to its edifice. Since the King of Chesed, Aurelio, being able to levitate, was still in two places at once, I went back and asked him what I should do next.

"Down on the plain are many large pyramids." He replied. "One of them is a Weaving Institute, as we card and spin wool here from our many sheep. We like to keep sheep as they are very complaisant and never disobey us, so we never have to punish them. The Chesedians do not like to punish people. They will do anything to avoid confrontation, and often let bad behavior continue rather than admonish the perpetrator, for they are truly merciful here. This is not always a good thing, as we have problems with gangs of disobedient teenagers, who roam the streets, mugging and knocking off stray transients and old crones withdrawing their last savings from the bank." Aurelio continued. "Anyway, the head of the Weaving Institute is waiting to greet you, and you will be joining many other weavers who are working on the colored skeins of the Aurora Borealis, to make a fine tapestry. When this piece of creative art is complete, it will change the world, for it will replace the old wall-hanging that has worn out."

"What is this tapestry?" I asked. "It sounds vague to me. What is wrong with the old tapestry?

"The tapestry itself is woven into a way of behaving by changing the skeins. Down in Malkuth, people cling to old ideas because they are familiar, and they are afraid of change. These old ideas, which were woven into the old tapestry, are outmoded and prevent mankind from moving forward. Our aim here is to keep pouring inspirational ideas into our weaving, and to promote these images to the few of genius in Malkuth, that they may carry the people forward. The new tapestry is a changing pattern filled with new images – for example, the great recession that is now plaguing the world. You will find it most interesting to work on." Aurelio pointed towards a colorful pyramid. "They are ready to start now, and they will welcome you."

I walked over to the Weaving Institute, where I met the head weaver, a fellow with an unnaturally large thumb. The four weavers were lined up in front of a single loom, so I joined them. "Are you ready?" Came the command. "Steady, Go!" The shuttle began flying to and fro at breakneck speed, and the weavers were shifting threads of wool at an incredible rate. I found it impossible to keep up with them, and my thread became wound around one of the flying shuttles. There was a terrible crash, and the loom broke down, the shuttle taking off and heading in the direction of the moon that shone overhead.

"This is a disaster!" The head weaver moaned. "How did this happen? You people are no better than chipmunks. I suppose it's your parents' fault. They never spanked you, and so you have no discipline and can't work as a team like the Gedulians."

A weaver spoke up. "It wasn't one of us! It was the new weaver who just came in. I know it's the Navigator who made a mistake and lost the thread of the whole picture. The Navigator should be thrown out!"

A murmur came from the group. "Yes! Get rid of that person! Our tapestry will be ruined. The Navigator should stick to the compass, and not bother us. We can go on strike, you know. The owner is very loving, and will not blame us if we do."

I thought it was rather feeble of the owner to allow a strike under such circumstances, but I decided to leave the Institute and find something else to do. The moon now had a large black spot on it where the shuttle had landed. I felt somewhat guilty as I wandered among the dozens of pyramids, each dedicated to a particular task, and came to a black pyramid with a blank door. I wondered what was inside, and tried the knob, which opened easily under my hand. There was no light visible, but the sound of faint breathing, coming from a hundred tiny throats, filled the air. I struck a magic match that flared up, revealing rows of incubating chambers with a baby in each one, hooked up to breathing tubes.

"Can I help you?" In the matches' dying glow, a tubby black and white bird, dressed in a nurses uniform, strutted towards me, its head crowned by a burst of small yellow feathers behind a reddish eye and a tough looking beak. The bird touched a switch, and a faint green light illuminated the awesome scene.

"I am Eeleye Fastlever, the penguin you met during your river journey. Do you remember? I gave you the magic matches you now hold.. Very soon you will face the terrors of the vast ocean we call the Sea of Sorrow, which lies between Chesed and the Island of Binah, the foundation of all. You must cross that Sea to complete your journey."

"I'm very intrigued by the babies incubating in this pyramid. Are you their nurse?" I gazed towards the babies.

Eeleye turned and beckoned me to follow him. "Here is where all the newborns that come from the Passage of the Archpriestess are kept, until they have adjusted to their material bodies. You must realize that birth into the world of matter is a terrifying ordeal, and almost all babies are filled with Fear, when they emerge from the birth canal. If this fear is not dealt with early on, they retain it in their unconscious, but they forget they are frightened as they learn the world about them. Unfortunately, their fear, manifested in Chesed, has not gone away, but as they move on to Geburah, they become angry – angry that they have been separated from their divine father and mother, and unwilling to face life on earth. These babies grow up, and each of them carries this deep anger within them throughout their lives. It is then usually triggered by a brief remembrance of their initial Fear."

"The poor things! I completely understand." I walked along, looking at each tiny mite in its little cot. "We have all come down here for a purpose, but we arrive confused. The Cup of Lethe we drank before birth made us forget our Destiny. It was ordained by the Society of Enochian Anchorites, for to comprehend one's Destiny would be too great a burden in life, and many would prefer death rather than face that knowledge."

"That is why we recommend the protective talismans that Isa Real Gardy gives to each person. The penguin gave me a piercing glance. "Still, you obviously think you can manage without one."

"That's not true. I have activated my talisman and I keep it in my inside pocket." I had mixed feelings. For one thing, I resented any sort of authority, and if told what to do, I almost always did the opposite. It came to me that, on this occasion, I would appear more appealing to the magician Eeleye by actually agreeing with him, for once. Therefore, I bowed my head, and in a muffled voice, consented to learn more about the talisman. Chesed seemed to be the one Island where I was forced into leaving, constantly coming and going, as I had already visited the Emperor with the gargoyle, who was now far away, sitting on the Gothic edifice. For the first time, a shiver of fear went through me, and I felt a hand on my shoulder. I turned around, and there was little Paragut, proudly displaying the Order of Nonexistent Empire that he had been awarded,. many aeons ago.

"Remember, you have put aside fear. I was your fearful entity, and you liberated me a long time ago. Why are you now fearful?"

"It's good to see you, Paragut. I'm afraid because this bird has told me I can't proceed towards the Sea of Sorrow without the protection of a talisman. I never believed in them before, but now I doubt my abilities, for the test ahead of me is most severe."

"You distrust your higher self – your own Guide. The talisman would not do any harm, and it might help. Would you like me to get it?"

"Please! That would be so calming. My Guide left me in the Path of the Emperor, and I have not seen him since. I will wait here and watch Eeleye Fastlever tending to the tiny ones."

Paragut left, heading for the coast, and took with him my blessings. Meanwhile, the penguin was ministering to the babies in the incubators. He stood behind a lectern, reading from a strange book, and each child listened through a soft speaker in its cot. The words were unfamiliar to me, but sounded like ancient Egyptian, and they cast a spell over the children. Their faint cries of uncertainty became still, as the little ones heard the truth of their roots in past lives, and they understood in a simple fashion that their spirits were part of a continuum, an eternal transformation, and that whatever lay ahead, they could trust in the Destiny they had chosen before birth. The soft words of Thoth, god of thought, reminded them of their karmic debts, and how they could remedy their previous mistakes by thinking the right thoughts. Eeleye finished, and as I walked along the rows of cots, I saw that every child was peacefully asleep.

My little Paragut promptly returned carrying the parchment talisman. He gave it to the penguin, who muttered some words over it and placed it on a small cubic altar at the east side of the pyramid. We knelt down, and heard the words of the magical sigil chanted over us. I felt Paragut edging closer and closer to me, and I was receptive to his approach. At last he was right up against my solar plexus, looking up at me with his pleading yellow eyes, and I embraced him. At that moment, every doubt fled from my mind, and a sense of pervading peace overcame me. I looked down, and saw that Paragut had vanished. I had absorbed him and he was now inside me, unifying me with my own fear as it dissipated, just as the thunder clouds had done.

I heard my magical word on the talisman again, and Eeleye warned me never to repeat it to anyone, for silence was important along the Way of Return. I had reached the point where great danger lay ahead, but I must not speak of my trials, for the ears that noted slips of the tongue were uncomprehending, and would take my words and twist them into malevolence. This method was used against all those who sought enlightenment, to drag them back to earthly dogma.

The penguin now prepared me for my second attempt to board the Chariot. He told me that I would not necessarily need an umbrella, but that I must have some sort of head covering, for the bats in the narrow defile that we must pass were constantly dropping guano. He devised a pink helmet for me with a small flexible plastic shield perched on top, which I thought looked rather ridiculous. I remained silent as he tied the strings under my chin.

"Now you are ready. The canopy will deflect any droppings from above. But be warned by an experienced magician. Even if you manage to jump into the Chariot, you will immediately find the path narrowing down rapidly into a gorge with rocky walls. Do not look up, or the horror that would meet your eyes may tear your courage from you. I will not tell you what is in the walls, you do not need to know. Keep your gaze forward and urge on the horses, for ahead of them you will see the edge of Binahs' cloak, which spreads itself over the Sea of Sorrow to aid you on your path. You will find the edge of the cliff four leagues from here. Go now, and may Jupiter be with you."

I thanked Eeleye Fastlever for his invaluable help, and set out to cover the distance to the Chariot stop in the mist.

Second Path of the CHARIOT

I reached the Chariot stop quickly and stood waiting by the post with the sign that clanged in the gusty wind, the schedule underneath being unreadable due to water damage and mould. I had now acquired the correct head gear, which I adjusted, and then I heard a call from behind me.

"Hey, there! It's me, Sir Belvedere. Welcome back to the Path of the Chariot. I've been waiting here for you. Are you going to try again?"

I felt a rush of annoyance at the sound of his familiar voice. So, he calls himself Sir now, does he? I then recalled that it was I who had knighted him, on my last visit to the Chariot. I didn't feel like responding, though, as I caught sight of the Chariot coming through the mist, the two trotting horses slowing down a little as they pulled past the stop. Crouching down, with one hand holding my helmet, I leaped for the narrow opening, and managed to pull myself into the small space inside the Chariot, at which the two horses pulled up to a stop. The white horse, I could see, was impatient to continue, and he reared up, prancing and snorting, but the black horse stood steady and turned her head towards Belvedere, who knelt on the cliff edge.

A quartet of large bats flew by, carrying a microphone on a stand that they placed near the horses' head. They took the long cord attached to it and inserted it into Sir Belvederes' trachea, then they dangled upside down in a row on the microphone stand. The black horse then cleared her throat and neighed into the microphone for some minutes. I could not understand what she said, but then Belvedere began to translate her message.

"I am Yin, the black horse, and my partner the white horse is Yang. I am here to warn you, before it is too late, to get out of our Chariot, for you risk your life if you continue on this journey. Many have tried before you, and almost all have failed, their bodies now petrified. It takes great courage to ride the Chariot, for we have no reins. We are guided only by your will power. If that should fail, we would run amok, and the chariot would overturn and crush you. Your passage through the narrow defile is fraught with danger, and even beyond that, the Sea of Sorrow, which consists of the tears of every human being since time began, can drag you down into its depths. Misery will be your lot, and the only hope is to cling to the outspread cloak of Binah, the goddess of Understanding, With luck, she will see you through, for I already see that by your stance, you are determined to continue with us and face the terrors ahead."

The black horse Yin raised her head and shook it, pointing her ears forward as if she heard something stirring in front of her. The bats removed the microphone and Belvedere pulled the cord out of his throat angrily. "They duped me! Those bats led me to believe I was going to get a shot of pure oxygen, not the ramblings of an old mare." He looked at me, and I saw tears of frustration in his eyes. "Don't go, Navigator. It's too dangerous, and I can't be with you to ensure your survival. I'm afraid this is the end of my possibilities. I beg you, come back, and we'll manage together. We can still have a good life!"

"No. I can't turn back." I remonstrated. "I must bid you goodbye, for this is my Destiny, and whatever I face ahead, I will try to vanquish my failings." I gave him a last wave, clucked to the horses, and they set off at a gallop for the rocky gorge. The Chariot swayed dangerously from side to side and I crouched down to balance myself, holding onto the two railings. Then a face appeared in front of me on the inside of the vehicle, a woman with her hands raised above her head.

She spoke to me. "If you recall, when the two Lovers were finally united, a smoky child was born from their union, inside the garland of yellow flowers. I am your Genius, Ediug, of that meeting - with you now - and I will keep you safe, but you must do as I say. We are approaching the defile rapidly. On no account look up at the walls as we pass through, for certain death awaits you if you do. The magician Eeleye Fastlever warned you about that already, and so did the Hermit. Make sure your helmet is in position, for most of the bats in the gorge have bad diarrhea. Quickly now! We are nearly there." She put her finger to her lips in the vow of silence.

Our path through the mist narrowed rapidly and a slender gap showed ahead in a wall of twisted black rocks that rose up into the brume. The horses dashed for the gap and I held my breath, for it looked too narrow for the Chariot. However, we passed through with less than an inch to spare on either side, and gloom fell upon us. Yin and Yang slowed to a walk, for the path was rutted and scattered with black scull-like stones that had fallen from the high walls on either side. I remained kneeling on the floor of the Chariot and keeping my head down. I wondered how long it would take to get past the unknown danger.

What was that? It sounded like Sir Belvederes' voice! Up high, somewhere on the right. What was he doing here? This was forbidden ground for him.

The call came again. It was unmistakable. "Navigator! Come and save me! I'm stuck up here, high on the wall of the gorge. I need your help. I'm afraid I'll fall, and my foot is caught between two rocks in a crevice. I may die here! Please help me."

The insistent voice went on and on, and finally I could stand it no longer. Besides, I felt extremely guilty about leaving him behind. He wasn't such a bad guy. I mistakenly looked up, to see where the voice came from, and immediately a horde of bats swooped down and took me in their clutches, lifting me out of the chariot and dragging me over the jagged rock walls upwards, until the defile became so narrow above that they let me go. Instead of falling back, I found myself stuck to the rock wall in a sprawling position, and unable to move a muscle.

It was then that I saw the composition of the walls surrounding me. They were made up of bodies, sagging stiffly one on top of the other, and all of them turned to stone from the continual seeping of the lime in the surrounding rocks. I was horrified! Belvederes' voice had faded away in a syrupy chuckle, and I knew I had been duped. The call for help was a scam. I was about to become part of the petrified wall of bodies. The steady dripping of the lime would calcify me over time along with those that had failed by looking up and fallen into the same trick as I had when they heard the voice of their Ego.

By twisting my head slightly, I could see my Chariot far below. The horses were standing still. Inside the vehicle, I spotted a movement, as Ediug stirred from her position in the chariot and emerged, treading lightly over the rutted path.

"Remember the transformation you went through in the Path of Art." She called up to me in great excitement. "It was there that you experienced calcination. I had forgotten that for the moment. You cannot be calcified a second time. That would be double jeopardy. You will not turn to stone, even if you were to remain up there for ever." She beckoned to me. "You

can free yourself by exerting your willpower, and I'll be here to catch you."
She shook out a net of yellow cords and spread it between the two horses,
who moved apart to accommodate her. She tied the ends of the net to their
harness, and told me to jump. I had difficulty convincing myself that I
was not stuck, and could move my limbs, as the wall was so vertical I was
afraid to move at all. Slowly I dislodged my right foot from between two
rocks, lifted my right arm, and felt my body sway forward away from the
wall, and then I was falling and bouncing into the net. The horses took the
shock and nickered hopefully, for they wished to continue their journey
without delay.

I remounted the Chariot and Ediug took her place in front of me as
the horses moved on and quickened their pace to a steady canter. A flat
stretch of grey mud lay before us, and the edge of a vast sea that roiled
and fumed from one end of the horizon to the other. Far off, across this
expanse of menacing water, a city gleamed on the horizon, with domes and
minarets, steeples and towers, and in the center a wide doorway opened
under a magnificent arch. On a black throne in the center of the doorway
sat the Queen of Queens, Binah, and cascading from her shoulders on each
side spread a wide purple cloak that floated like a sheen of thin oil on the
turbulent waters, calming them.

"For the first time you are looking at the City of Jerusalem, with
its twelve gates." Ediug explained. "See how fair it is! In that place are
combined all the religions of the world, joined in perfect union, so that
there is never a moment of discord between them. There is the seat of
judgment, where the Enochian Anchorites carry out their investigations
into the lives of those that have passed over the Limbic Threshold."

"Does that mean I can't reach the city until I'm dead?" I asked. "Then,
even if I were able to cross the Sea of Sorrow on Binahs' cloak, I would be
refused admission at the gate?"

"What makes you think that you are alive now?" Ediug smiled gently.
"You may be dead already! You must understand that your spirit knows
no difference between life as you know it, or death and the world beyond.
For the spirit, an unbroken continuum exists, and it pays no heed to the
state of the present body it inhabits."

I ruminated over this statement, as the horses pulled up at the tide line
and I descended from the Chariot to take a closer look at what lay ahead.
Binah was too far away to make out her expression, and the cloak I was
supposed to tread on seemed delicate in the extreme. I could not visualize

this thin film of undulating fabric supporting me, if I hastened across towards the fantastic city that I longed to enter.

"Are you ready to make the journey now?" Ediug asked me. "You cannot turn back on the Path of the Chariot, you know. You must go onward and persevere in your quest. I regret that I cannot come with you, for I am unable to swim."

"What! You were born on the surface of the water, between the Solar Man and the Lunar Woman, and you can't swim? That is preposterous!"

"Not necessarily. I was born in a little mist that rose above the water, and I should, by all accounts, remain floating in the air, so that I can reach your mind through your airy thoughts. You must face the Sea of Sorrow alone, for the tumultuous influences that lurk in the Sea would threaten my destruction, as so many that were blessed with Genius failed, and sank into madness."

"I've read about those people and the thin veil that divides their brilliance from lunacy. Madness often overcomes them. It seems as if the universe stands guard against such people, placing great difficulties before their delicate minds." I responded thoughtfully. "Why is that? I would have thought that divinity would welcome Genius, for it is Genius that leads humanity forward to higher things."

"That depends on the type of Genius. A Genius for burglary or serial murder would not be as welcome as a great symphony or an accomplished work of art. But now you must go forward. I will stay on this shore and watch you as you tread carefully on Binahs' cloak. And my blessings go with you."

I stepped reluctantly to the edge of the water and tested my weight on the oily cloak. It supported me, so I gradually made my way out to sea, balancing like an acrobat as each wave passed under me with arms outspread. I was halfway across the expanse of water when I spotted, coming towards me on the surface of the water, thousands of Portuguese men of war jellyfish, their tiny sparkling sails breaking the surface like so many bright stars. But I knew them to carry deadly poison, and they were in my path. I stepped cautiously between them, trying to avoid their stings, but they became so thick around me that I finally succumbed to them. When the sharp pain of their stings coursed through me, I began to panic, thrashing about, and breaking the sheen of the cloak. I sank, screaming, into the depths of the Sea of Sorrow.

Island of DA'ATH

S ubmerged in the Sea of Sorrow, many distressing sounds overwhelmed
me. Wails, moans and the wrenching of grief stricken sobs were all
around me. It was a terrible, unending nightmare. In a vain attempt
to escape these heart-rending cries, I descended to the sea floor, a dreary
stretch of mud inhabited by catfish, dogfish and parrot fish that dashed out
of sight as I felt my way along, clinging to the crumbling rocks to keep my
balance in the strong underwater surge. Groaning human forms swam by
in the shadowy water, chasing each other, wrestling and scratching at each
others' eyes. The way ahead was murky, as strings of filth slithered past my
face and dark, darting creatures sped away from me.

Gradually the sea floor began to rise until I reached the surface and
scrambled out onto a rocky shore cast in gloom. Desperate cries, screams
and howls still pulsed in resonating vibrations beneath the waves, and
occasionally an inconsolable body broke the surface and splashed helplessly
before sinking down again. All was swathed in perpetual dimness as
I made my way steadily uphill on a narrow, cobbled street with a few
dilapidated hovels on either side. At the top of the hill, a flickering sign on
a battered movie hall announced several films to be screened. I read them
off - there was a documentary by "Our Librarian Einerline;" a musical
opera by Huckslee "The Doors of Preoccupation;" a BOTOM production
"The Cube of Space;" and a comedy "Escaping Illusion" by the chipmunks.
I decided to see the Cube of Space movie, and addressed the large anaconda
curled up in the ticket office.

"I'd like to buy a ticket for the Cube of Space movie. How much is it?"
I enquired. "What time does it start?"

The snake swiveled its head around uneasily. "The movie is on all the time. We don't have ON or OFF up here. Be reminded that there is only one screen, though. Now, do you have the price of a pomegranate?"

"I don't have a pomegranate, but I could get an apple from somewhere." I frowned. "You have billing for four movie events. How can you run one movie on the only screen all the time? What about showing the other three?"

"You are an ignorant fool. Once you have decided on a movie, and paid for it with a nice pomegranate, all you have to do is sit down and look at the screen. The movie you have decided on will be playing, even though there are others in the audience watching different movies on the same screen. It's all in the mind, you know." The anaconda frowned at me. "I remember you from the Passage of Strength. You didn't do much to help Strength in the arena, did you? Well, there aren't any apples growing here in Da'ath, so go look for a pomegranate, because you won't get in without one." Here the snake split a juicy pomegranate and began devouring the countless seeds greedily, spilling some on the office floor.

I soon found a pomegranate tree with ripe fruit hanging temptingly from its branches. Sitting underneath it, deep in study, was an odd, bent figure, pen in hand, an absent minded expression on his grimy face. It was my entity Einerline, with the suitcase full of books from the Vatican library at his feet. I could see his incredible neurons whizzing around, faster then they had ever worked on earth, the tiny intermittent flashes lighting up his transparent skull. I cleared my throat loudly but he did not raise his head. There was a little bell hanging from a branch. A sweet, reverberating tone came from it as I rang, and he looked up, blinking.

"Why, it's you, Navigator! Come for your pomegranate? That's all there is to eat up here. Fortunately, I live on Air, which is the element of rigorous and logical study, and I don't miss the fast food I always scoffed as quickly as possible down in Malkuth, especially as the grease often dribbled onto my books." Einerline went on. "Going in to see the Cube of Space, eh? It's a long program. I don't expect you to come out for quite a while. Pawel Phustercus, the owl, you know, cooked up a difficult theme with that. Did you know he is here now? He lives up at the top of Trestleboard Summit in a Masonic Hall that was built by the Chaldeans."

"Oh! I haven't seen Pawel since he helped me in the Island of Hod. I would love to spend some time with him. I consider him almost as wise as you, Einerline."

I loved to flatter him for he was completely oblivious to adulation. I reached up and picked a luscious pomegranate. Einerline was once more engrossed in his studies, as always, so I returned to the movie house and gave the anaconda my pomegranate, which he seized rudely, and went into the darkened theater.

I groped for a seat, but could not find one unoccupied. I touched several people who gave small yelps of surprise, then accidentally parked myself in the lap of a very large person of uncertain genus, who shrieked and gave me a sound cuff across my ear. I finally sat down on the soiled carpet of the ramp, where I was kicked about by people going in and out, who stumbled over me continuously in the blackened theater. The program on the Cube of Space was long but engrossing, and contained references to the tarot cards and zodiacal gates. My interest was so keen I scarcely noticed the suppressed laughter, hawking and wheezing exhibited by the other patrons. When it was over, I got up, stretched, and was immediately thrown to the ground and trampled by a horde of people rushing towards the exit, for evidently all the programs had simultaneously ended. When the last person had trodden on my outstretched arm, I rose to my feet in a dignified manner, brushed myself off, and went off to look for Einerline, nursing my bruises.

There was nobody under the pomegranate tree, but I was able to follow shuffling footsteps through the dust to an ancient building, where a pair of worn out shoes lay discarded on the doormat. There was a little bell by the pitted oak door, so I rang it. The door opened a crack and a bleary eyeball gazed at me. Ascertaining that it was me, Einerline opened the creaking door and led me inside. He shambled forward, his unwashed socks filled with holes and dragging loosely on his feet, into a vast room that seemed to stretch on for miles and miles. Shelves ran along each side of the room and reached up as high as I could see. Without speaking, Einerline showed me a particular shelf part way along on the left side of the room, where he took down a book and gave it to me.

"Open it." He said with a crooked smile. "You will find everything you need to know inside. At first you may see nothing – for the pages appear to be blank – but with concentration, you will find that the story of your entire life is written in that book, up to the present moment. It is very intriguing."

"I didn't know everything was written down. Do you mean that all my experiences, both good and bad, are published here? It's as revealing as the Internet!" I leafed through the pages, at first seeing blank paper, but as I progressed, faint signs of type, grey at first, began to show, and soon the type was plain in black on the white paper. I read through the book quickly, recalling with shame and embarrassment the mistakes I had made, and then set it aside.

Einerline had waited patiently for me to finish. "Interesting, isn't it? There are many more books discussing your previous lives along your personal shelf in the Infinite Library. The Library is where the record of every ones' life on earth is filed. We call it the Akashic Records – the imprint of human and animal behavior over the centuries of reincarnations that all have experienced – every detail written down by the Society of Enochian Anchorites as their lives progress, so that the Board can make an accurate assessment of each ones' karmic debt." He looked grave. "They elevated me to Keeper of the Infinite Library after they researched my previous lives and saw the assiduous manner I kept at my studies. I was overwhelmed by the honor, and take my assignment very seriously. But now I grow old, and long for final peace in the lap of Wisdom. It remains for another to take my place here, and they are aware of that as they interview prospective souls as the next Keeper."

"I can't imagine you getting old." I said sadly. "I expected you to go on forever, because you are my intellectual entity. Doesn't that outlive death?"

"Well, in a way it does. The intellectual self is always asking questions. It seeks to have answers - to be satisfied. Only when it comes to knowledge of itself in Da'ath can it stop asking questions, for all the answers are here." He scratched his chin thoughtfully. "I have gnosis now. I don't need to seek any further, to have any desire in particular. I am filled with the Knowledge of Da'ath, the sphere that is not a sphere. You know, of course, what happened here long ago?"

"Was it – was it when Lucifer fell down with the Emerald? I met him, and he told me that he had planned to bring the knowledge of the emerald stone of eternal youth to mankind. "

"Yes, he deliberately left Da'ath, where all knowledge lies, in an attempt to bring it down to Malkuth. Unfortunately, he got stuck in Tiphareth, and could get no further, for the general inertia and ignorance associated with Malkuth proved to be too great a barrier for his fragile essence to overcome."

"I thought that might be it. Does that mean he will never reach Malkuth?"

"It is unlikely, but they are working on it. The ignorance and obstinacy in Malkuth is gradually yielding to wiser influences. Let us hope that, in time, he will be able to get through."

"He will be able to, I'm convinced of that." I sighed and began thinking of the Library again. "I visited a library like this once before. It was in a vision. I am writing a book about it. Although my task is almost complete, we do not know whether it will ever see the light of day in its entirety, for, as you know, ideas are slow to catch on in the mundane world."

"Nevertheless, I am duly impressed. It is not important to let the world know what you have created. The creation exists in itself, complete. You have done what the Enochians asked for and can rest assured that in the circles we belong to, your work will be appreciated." He led the way back to the main door and bid me goodbye. "I will meet you again, once more, in the Island of Chockmah, where I hope to reside permanently. Until then, may you complete your journey safely. By the way, you may find some of your earlier cast-off entities down by the shore. They are seeking resolution themselves."

I left my entity Einerline sadly and wandered down to the shore, where I sat down on a rock, staring out into the Sea of Sorrow. Whispers and hisses, the sound of lapping water and soft feet on the sand roused me from my reverie. In the dim light, wraiths were emerging from the water and gathering round me with pleading eyes. One or two of them reached out tentatively to touch my face, gazing at me with head lolling on one side, their mouths beseeching soft entreaties of me. Amongst them, as I began to see their faces more clearly, were many that I knew. My greedy entity, Aquirot; my lazy, fat Spredaloth; my moralizing entity, Pulpidoro. All these were left behind in limbo during my journey: cast off as and when I thought fit, without so much as a goodbye. Now they sought to be free. They wished to leave the Sea of Sorrow, for they felt they had done their jobs of educating me. It was very true – I had never respected them and their valuable teaching.

I glanced at each in turn, their soundless pleas understood. It was important to interview each one, and then absolve it, so that it could re-enter the Sea and return to the material world, where it would attach itself to another neophyte and begin the teaching again. We gathered together on the shore of Da'ath and, after much discussion, each one was liberated, and in their turn they dived back into deep water and struck out for the far shore happily. The last one was Numbyling, which was to be expected, as she was the most apathetic of all.

"How are you two getting along?" I questioned, as I knew that she had fallen in love with my organizing entity, Endevvy. "Does he ever slow down?"

She replied in a faint whisper. "He has taught me to step up to the plate. He told me I should not spend my life as a listless couch potato. I have learned how to make decisions for myself, and not to simply let life flow along meaninglessly. My presence in his life has helped him to be less rigid and controlling, and to act more spontaneously, as he responds to his feelings." She gave a little smirk. "I think it is a good match!"

I hugged Numbyling, who felt like smoke in my arms, and then let her go.

The wraiths of my entities that were attached to me during my river trip could now be free to follow after new people who exhibited their particular traits. Again and again they would attach themselves, remaining with them until they were recognized, dealt with, and let go. However, there was another group of people that had been on my mind for some time, and that was the Clan. I last saw them in the Queen of Wands, where they were given shelter after their ice cave collapsed. Their Shaman was determined they should learn Intuition. In order to do that, they had to perfect their speech, as intuitive ideas had to be expressed in language rather than by vulgar arm movements. The Island of Da'ath seemed to be a good place to find Shaman Reeve and his group, for here was the very root of all language as it had developed from earliest man.

They would probably be in a cave, I decided, unless they had grown soft during their visit to the Castle of Fire where the Queen lived. Their sojourn in Death had been brief. I set out across the island, seeking a good spot for caves, and came across an amazing sight. The land was broken up into pillars of sundried mud that rose up like so many steeples across the rough terrain. It was clear that man had been at work here, for little doorways had been cut in the sides of the stacks, and the concave areas blocked with dried bricks. They stretched for some leagues along the floor of a shallow valley. Not knowing which to choose, I looked among the stacks for one that might be somewhat larger, or display some decorative object across the doorway. I found one in the center of the group with the head of a young cave bear, its mouth open revealing rows of white, pointed teeth, mounted above a varnished door, where I knocked.

The door was opened by a man with low, overhanging brows and an apelike jaw, who presented a terrifying appearance. He was wearing a long cape made entirely of ermine fur, the black tipped tails hanging in neat rows underneath a neck ornament of fanned eagle feathers. Under this robe he had on a pair of shorts and a T-shirt with the slogan "Cats Suck" and a picture of a dog enjoying a cat in a compromising position. His bare, horny feet shuffled the dust as he gave a shout of joy. It was Shaman Reeve.

"It's you! Come and greet the Navigator, wife, and bring all our seventeen children as well." The Shaman beckoned to a nervous woman peeping out behind a curtain. "Wow! Am I glad to see you! We thought you might have gotten lost on your journey. It's been such a long time."

"No, I'm well and hoping to reach the end of the Way of Return shortly." I replied. "What's been happening with you?"

"After our visit to the Castle of Fire, the Queen plied us with many goods and stores, and gave us pack armadillos to carry the heavy items. For several years, we wandered, but I had never forgotten Gofer and the Wands of intelligent inspiration that he always brought us at great peril to himself. I knew it was important for us to learn to speak better." Shaman Reeve continued enthusiastically. "Although, as their head man, I had a good command of language, most of the Clan still conversed in grunts and sign language. I felt that if we could reach the Island of Da'ath, which is the Word, the clan would be able to form a significant language between them. Unfortunately, we mistook the Path of Death for Da'ath, and we were stuck there for a while. When we reached this Island, we decided not to live in caves any longer, since our totem, the cave bear, was extinct." Here he wiped away a tear. "We still revere him, of course. These spires and mounds seemed just the place to settle down, and it is much warmer here. You remember we were living in an ice cave that collapsed on top of us, and we were lucky to escape. Well, the original Clan that consisted of thirty people are now three hundred and thirty three! Each family has built their own house and we conduct a busy trade on this route – for those that pass are looking for dictionaries and encyclopedias to further their knowledge. We built a printing press and we trade these valuable books for objects we need, like spices and silks from the Orient."

"I'm delighted to hear you're progressing so well. Now that the Clan has perfected the command of speech, have they remained aware of their Intuition?" I questioned.

"Indeed, we still nurture the Eternal Flame of Intuition, and each family has a small altar in their house where it burns." As he spoke, a Black

Dog bounded up to him and licked his hand. "You will remember our dog. He is still here with us, although many years have passed. He never grows old, for he is a constant reminder of the evil that we must combat at every moment. It is good to have a Black Dog, and each person in the Clan now owns two Black Dogs, and there are six hundred and sixty six of them. Would you like one? They breed fast, and we have several to spare."

"Alas! Unfortunately, I have to travel alone to make a rapid ascent, and at the moment I'm in the middle of the Sea of Sorrow. I hope to return and catch my Chariot again as I wish to conclude my journey to the City of Jerusalem that I have seen from afar."

"At least take a meal with us before you go." The Shaman took my arm. "My wife is a very good cook, and we have chipmunk stew hot on the griddle."

I was happy to eat with them. The meat was lean and tender with no fat, very tasty. I wondered where they had found the little creatures, and hoped they hadn't been scraped off the road. I left the non-existent Island of Da'ath the following morning after a cozy chat and sleep at their spire house, and made my way back to the shore of the Sea of Sorrow, where I plunged into the water and struck out for the northern pass.

Path of the MAGIAN

I t was a long swim in the cold and murky water of the Sea of Sorrow before I pulled myself out on shore near the northern pass, where I had previously become stuck on the wall in the narrow defile, and saved from certain petrifying by double jeopardy. I looked around, but my Chariot was not there. Instead, a cunning grey fox with a bushy white tipped tail ran up to me, its eyes sparkling.

"Anal, the hunchbacked White Dwarf, told me you had lost your way, and he sent me to get you." The fox barked sharply. "We've been watching your progress from here - the Path of the Magian, for we are capable of seeing the whole picture. You didn't make it through to the City of Jerusalem this time, and you failed dismally last time as well. You only have one more chance – three strikes and you're out – so we felt it was important for you to come to us and learn some vital truths before you make your final attempt to ride your Chariot into the City itself."

"You're right, I did mess up. The first time, I fell out of my Chariot before it had even started, and the second time I foolishly listened to my Ego, Belvedere, who was trying to call me back. My Genius Ediug was quite upset." I spoke intently. "Can you help me complete my journey? I have traveled far and experienced many things, and I am anxious to reach my goal."

"You will find the Path of the Magian has two parts - the two hemispheres of the brain. I am from the right hemisphere, as I am the emblem of native cunning and intuition, and I have a fine brush with which to create my paintings." The fox picked up his tail with one paw and stroked it. "See, it is very full and long. Now the Magian and the White Dwarf preside over both hemispheres, but the ibis, like me, only symbolizes one - the left hemisphere, for she is the logical scribe who attends to reading and writing. Come with me and we will go first to the right hemisphere, where two friends of yours are waiting." The fox grinned, showing a perfect row of sharp, white teeth. "I will not tell you their names. It will be a pleasant surprise! Just follow me."

"Wait a minute! Why is he called the Magian and not the Magician?" I was puzzled.

"The Magian is the Magus, from the ancient Magi, the three wise men who visited the Christ principle at his birth into the mundane world. A Magician – well, that is a person who merely does magical tricks in front of an audience." The fox wrinkled his nose. "You can tell the difference. The Magi are far superior."

"Oh! I see. That makes sense. A higher order, as it were." I ruminated, as the grey fox darted off with surprising speed, zigzagging between the rocks on shore. Although I ran as fast as I could, I was hard pressed to keep up, and we were soon out of sight of the Sea as the countryside became greener. The sleek animal headed a little to the east, in the direction of two high transmission towers shooting forth crackling sparks of lightning. A dark forest of evergreen trees surrounded a small lake, and in the center was an island from which came the throbbing beat of a drum. The fox stopped at the waters' edge and gave three sharp barks. The water parted, and a huge manta ray leapt out, soaring towards us.

"Here is your ride." The fox announced. "I will swim, because I enjoy that. It throws hounds off my trail. See you over on the island." He jumped into the lake, his bushy tail floating behind him on the surface, and paddled steadily towards the island.

The ray glided right up to me, thrashing the water, and slid its wide head onto the beach. It looked very slippery and I wasn't sure how to balance on its back, but I crawled up and hung onto the edge of its wings as it gently drifted into deeper water and made its way to the center of the lake. In the middle of the island was a bizarre capsule, resembling a huge round Cup on three legs that looked like swords with their points stuck in the ground, and inside the Cup an odd figure was spiraling in circles, as if in perpetual motion. To one side Anal, the White Dwarf, beat on a small conga drum vigorously with his fists, which seemed a little unusual. He was obviously an expert, though, and the acrobatic figure in the cup followed the Dwarfs' rhythm perfectly.

I slid off the ray and walked over to the Dwarf. "Hello, Anal! I wondered what had happened to you. Last time I saw you, I was afraid you had drowned off the Path of Death, but then I had a vision. I thought you were riding in a little chariot, drawn by two fishes! Could that be true?"

The White Dwarf seemed to sink even further into his curved back as he eyed me suspiciously. "I didn't know you saw that. I had to get back here secretly. The Magian was starting an important ritual, and I had to make sure his magical weapons were clean."

Anal looked at me, narrowing his eyes slightly. It was obvious he had made up a quick excuse. I would have to find out what was behind that. Why wasn't he telling the truth?

The fox interrupted my thoughts. "Come with me. I will take you to meet your two friends now." We descended a spiral staircase with grimacing faces carved in exotic woods decorating each side, and reached a level under the island. A large brain lay pulsating in the underground space, the opening of a long grayish tube in front of us. I followed the fox into it. On either side of us through the thin walls, neurons flashed and glinted as messages passed between them at astonishing speed. The grayish pink tube coiled on, twisting and turning in a neat, layered fashion, until we reached the center, where the hippocampus protected a small cage with a pea sized pineal gland inside. It was the first time I had seen this incredible gland up close. It was hard to imagine that such an insignificant, rather dull blob of matter was capable of incredible feats of psi vision and out of body experiences.

The fox barked three times and two women that I immediately recognized walked towards me from a hidden corner. They were the two Aces from the White Pyramid; Sensawaria, the Ace of Pentacles, and Liquilim, Ace of Cups, representing the passive elements of Earth and

Water. I greeted them cheerfully, although I recalled clearly the mistakes I had made during my trials at the Pyramid, which I hoped they had forgotten.

Not to be! They had not forgotten - but to my surprise - Sensawaria, a short female dressed entirely in white skintight clothing, her generous figure covered with white gold and diamonds in strange earthy patterns, and wearing a gold belt across her breast, shook my hand with a smile and said smartly. "I'm very glad to see you. I wanted to let you know that the robot mole you invented came back to us. It had second thoughts. I was happy to see it and I apologized profoundly. In fact, we are using it at present in the gardens at the Temple of the North, where it has proved to be very efficient at plowing neat rows in preparation for planting."

"Don't thank me. My entity Einerline was the one who thought it up." I said. "I'm really pleased it has turned out to be so useful. How is Cosmo, the Guardian of the First Crossing?"

"He is doing well. He and Adonia have added a daughter, Melania, to be a sister to their son Dysis." She turned to Liquilim, whose liquescient form seemed to melt and coalesce with astonishing rapidity, since she was the element of Water. She was a beautiful blonde, slim and graceful, and moved towards me with sinuous poise, taking my hand between her soft, moist palms.

"I always enjoyed your astral journey as the mother-in-law! You were really quite a wicked old lady, weren't you?" She laughed, the sound tinkling like the dripping of liquid from a fountain. "I'm glad you got rid of your envious entity, Covvymor, too. Now we meet in the right hemisphere of the Magian."

"Are we actually in the Magians' brain?" I asked. "What are you both here for, anyway?"

"Yes, we are in the center of his brain. We were summoned here during an invocation ritual by the Magian, aided by his faithful hunchback, Anal. The Magian needs us to morph into the two passive magical weapons, the Pentacle and the Cup, for he needs all four of the weapons to make a great ceremonial rite he is planning. He will obtain the other two active weapons from his left hemisphere, the Sword and the Wand. You will be meeting those two Aces shortly." Liquilim paused and turned to Sensawaria. "It must be nearly time to morph now."

The fox agreed and led them to their dressing rooms behind the hypothalamus, and then we went upstairs to await their appearance on the small ceremonial circle under the great cup. A fire had been laid in the center of the circle, which was drawn carefully around it, and a fire stick lay by a soft wooden log to make the spark. The two Aces came up from their dressing rooms and Sensawaria began rubbing mud from the edge of the water on her face and arms. Liquilim went into the lake fully dressed and splashed water over her head. They then sat down, Sensawaria to the north of the fire and Liquilim to the west. The throb of the drum grew more rapid and the pounding beat made my head spin as I stood outside the circle watching. We could see the Magian over our heads in his transparent cup, twisting and whirling ever faster, when with a fearful shriek, he leapt from the cup and stood before us, his dark red cloak with the Uranus symbol on it swirling around his gangly frame.

I couldn't believe my eyes! The person standing in front of us was none other than my trickster entity, Kracklewergen. I recognized him instantly from his long, beaky nose and the toothy grin that puckered up his cheeks so that they looked like two round apples. A few locks of spiky hair decorated his balding skull.

"Kracklewergen! It's you, isn't it? I didn't know you were the Magian!"

"No! Er-hem, I never saw you before. You are er-mistaking me for someone else, hem. Maybe another er-true hedonist, who loves a party, eh?" He looked shamefaced.

"You're a liar! But that's perfectly natural. Even if I didn't recognize your face, I would know the unique way you have of speaking, with all those pauses – it's like a bad politician! I shook my finger at him. "Come clean, now."

He gave me an engaging grin. "All right, hmmm. You win. You didn't know how er-powerful I was, did you, eh? That's because I was, er- always joking and playing around, hmm. That is my façade." He held up the mask of a pink baby face and disappeared behind it, making little cooing noises. "See! I always approach er- attractive women that I meet like this, and that arouses their nurturing instincts, hmmmm. It is only when I am lying er-hem, in their arms that I demand a titty to nurse. Well, of course, it's all over after that….. so easy, hmm" He looked dreamily out across the lake with a gleam in his eye, then suddenly whirled around and crouched down by the fire, picking up the fire stick and thrusting it into the log, twirling the stick between his crafty hands until a little wisp of smoke arose. Carefully he transferred the flame to the tiny twigs under the fire, and a merry blaze sprang up.

The Magian took some palm leaves from a cycad plant that was growing on the island, spreading them around the fire, and plucked one of the reddish cones. The two Aces sat cross-legged, staring into the fire. Kracklewergen asked them if they were prepared, and they answered in agreement. Taking his red cloak, he spread it around Sensawaria, dipped the cone into some liquid from a tiny vial, and sprinkled it over the cloak, muttering secret words. I wondered if it was a spell.

Then he took the wand that he held in his right hand, touched the cloak, and spoke. "Root of the Powers of Earth, reveal your weapon, the Pentacle!' He pulled the cloak away and a small platter lay on the earth. It was wrought of silver with a design, etched most beautifully, of the entwined Hindu yoni and lingam. The edge of this pentacle was studded with softly glowing moonstones. It was the platter that Swollup had given me when I left her parlor in the Nine of Swords, promising me that it would be valuable later on. Now I understood her words so long ago and thought gratefully of my friend Pullows, her inverted form.

But where had Sensawaria gone? I had no time to think, for the Magian was already swathing Liquilim with his cloak and sprinkling the libation. He touched the cloak with his wand and spoke. "Root of the Powers of Water, reveal your weapon, the Cup!" He swept away the cloak to disclose a goblet of pure copper, encrusted with a design of gazelles and doves entwined in jade around its rim. I saw the goblet in which Little Laboria had offered me a drink of clear water during my travels in the Seven of Swords, and I was delighted that these two valuable pieces, which my Guide had kept for me, were now revealed in the possession of the Magian.

"Where are the two Aces?" I hastened to ask Krackenwergle. "Are they OK?"

"Sensawaria and Liquilim, whom you think of as real people, are numinous patterns of the elements they represent. The platter, or Pentacle, and the goblet, or Cup, are also elemental patterns. Therefore, the two Aces are still here, only changed into their alternate selves, the Magical Weapons, which I will use for my ceremonial rite later on, at the ball I intend to give." He cocked his head on one side and took my arm, and the Dwarf came forward, picking up the two weapons and hurrying down the spiral staircase with them. I walked with Kracklewergle to one side of the island, where he pointed towards the two transmission towers that stood on the far side of the lake.

"Do you see the golden chain that links the towers together?" I noted that he had lost his annoying way of speaking. "Observe the chain, which includes my own capsule in the large Cup. That chain represents the hidden oaths that link all magicians together throughout the world, and they are known as the Illuminati. Many folks are afraid of them, and think that they have too much power, for they control the political, economical and legislative branches of every government, and make the capitalistic world turn. The rest of you just keep going, oblivious of their machinations. I am one of them, a white magician who seeks to do only that which is good in the cosmos – a guru, if you like. I put on the trickster with the funny accent because it is easier to mix with people that way. But I am really serious underneath."

He squeezed my arm. I looked at him and saw a small tear run from the corner of his eye and course down his cheek. "I have given my word to remain on earth through many incarnations, in order to help assuage the suffering and grief of humankind. So do not think badly of me."

"You are my beloved Kracklewergle, for evil and ever." I assured him stoutly. "Lead me, and I'll follow you wherever you go."

"Now that I can talk normally with you, I would like to show you around my private bazaar. After all, we first met in a bazaar, didn't we?"

"Yes, I remember it well. You threw me a gold velvet cushion with red tassels." I said, as he picked up a large nautilus shell lying on the ground. "What are you going to do with that?"

"This is the bazaar. Please step inside, and you will see." Krackenwergen waved his wand, and the shell became large enough for us to venture inside. We followed the spiral and soon came to rows of colorful stalls on each side of the passage, their goods laid out for inspection. I was surprised to see these were quite different from the usual wares. We first inspected a stall featuring Memory lists and Attention spans; next to it was a stall selling checkerboards and miniature models of race cars and planes; then a display of books entitled "How to Activate the Creative Process" and a demonstration of different colors and shapes flashing on a large HD television screen. Further along, a sign swinging on a curtained booth announced "Consult Madam Tarot to resolve Emotional Issues."

"This is very unusual." I remarked as we came out of the nautilus shell. "Why don't they sell Turkish delight and leather handbags?"

"We are in the right side of the brain, remember. We only sell useful things that are relevant to our position. There are other things for sale on the left side. I will show you when we get there, but first I am inviting you to witness one of our fun events here. It's the Nightona 500 meter gecko race, which is held each month here to keep the skills inherent in our reptile brain from becoming stale. The race course is in here." The Magian opened the door to a square room hidden under the roots of the cycad plant.

Immediately the sound of revving engines burst out, drowning our conversation. A lizard waving a flag ran across the floor, followed by about 35 little cars driven by geckos. The flag went down and the lizard jumped niftily out of the way, as the racers shot across the floor, up the wall and over the ceiling, where the leaders hit the front of the pack and led the field down the other wall. The noise was deafening and the smell of dope from the cars' tiny engines unbearable. I blocked my ears, and Krackenwergen laughed as he placed bets on the miniscule contestants. To my horror, halfway across the ceiling one of the cars went into a skid and hit two others, unseating them, at which they dropped to the floor in front of the leader, who was at top speed on his dash across the floor. His car flew into the air and landed in front of another, who attempted to steer out of the way, but skidded across the floor to the side of the room. Immediately four iguanas ran forward and quickly changed the tires, repaired a broken fender, and sent the racer off again, his tiny face and bright, intent eyes fastened on the wall ahead of him and his sticky feet glued to the steering wheel. His car quickly climbed the wall and drew ahead of two geckos who had got out of their cars in the middle of the ceiling and were arguing a point. The Magian obviously enjoyed this immensely.

"Suppose some of them get killed?" I shouted above the racket. "They are so small and fragile. Are you sure this is a good idea?"

"The main purpose of these races is to keep my learned skills, contained in my reptile brain, or cerebellum, razor-sharp. Geckos are two-a-penny. It's especially important for a Magian to be skilled in many different activities. Besides, it's a novelty and right brain loves new and unfamiliar experiences. They coalesce into the intuitive function, which, as you know, is invaluable for mankind. Sadly, people do not use their Intuition much any more. They rely too frequently on what they are told or what they read, without questioning facts, and therefore they are frequently duped by those who take advantage of them."

We left the gecko racing after Krackenwergle had won several bets, and as evening was descending, he showed me to the dressing room where I could get ready for the fashion show later that night. Many different costumes were hanging on the walls of this room, and so I spent some time amusing myself, trying on different outfits and parading in front of his distorting mirrors outside in the corridor. I settled on a very tight satin salamander suit that fitted like a glove and zipped up the front, which might come in useful later on. The suit was, basically, black but had symbolic red flames embroidered on each side and green spots scattered over a pale belly. With it was the head dress – a flamboyant black hat with fake peacock feathers that swept over one eye, making it hard to see, and a pair of red high heeled thigh boots. It looked even better in the distorting mirrors, and I couldn't stop laughing, in fact, I laughed so much at my image that I was bent over and couldn't straighten up. I became nervous and tried to stop, for I was afraid I would choke. Just in case, I positioned myself leaning over the back of a chair in the solo Heinrich maneuver.

A shriek of mirth echoed behind me from Krackenwergen, as he came to get me for the fashion show. He held out an arm and I took it mincingly, pretending to be a poufter dame, and we waltzed into the show together. It was a huge space, cut out of the base of a large tree, and the tree roots formed a picturesque design on the walls and ceiling. The floor of the room was of oiled teak, and had a number of circles carved into the wood, with different sigils around them. A long raised walkway for the models stretched from the end of the room. A band called the Seven Caterwauls were setting up, tuning their instruments and mewing amongst themselves. The odd sight of seven cats, one playing a violin, another on the glockenspiel, along with a ginger tom on the drums and two maio-maio vocalists was very unusual. It was clear there would be dancing before the fashion show began.

The Caterwauls soon struck up a merry waltz and Krackenwergle insisted on having the first dance with me. He whisked me around so fast I was afraid my salamander suit would split, and my hat tipped even further over my face, blinding me, but I didn't care, for I was ecstatic. The music changed to a foxtrot and I cut in on the grey fox and trotted him away, the Magian chuckling to himself as he swept a fairy into the complicated dance. The showroom was filling up with all kinds of folk. I saw a gnome and a troll dancing together, treading on each others' feet, and the elves weren't following the music at all, but rocking around the corner clock by themselves. The people on the floor were all wearing costumes for the show, so it was impossible to tell who was there, but I thought I saw a black feathered head and a pale owl face rolling amongst the revelers.

Someone blew a trumpet, and the dancers came to a sudden halt as iguanas with trays made of hub caps handed round glasses containing a black drink. Everyone took a glass and raised it for a toast to the Magian, then tossed back the liquid. I was only too aware of what I was drinking, but I could not stop myself, and joined in with the others, hoping the drink would not treat me as badly as it had before.

"Have you tasted it?" Came a voice from a figure in chain mail. "By Gad! It's damn good – I'd like some more. Wonder what's in it?'

"You're right! I've had three glasses already." Agreed a small woman dressed as Minerva with an oversize helmet wobbling on her head.

I downed my third glass and went over to the bar for more. Certainly, it was delicious! A mixture of coconut, Devonshire cream, Grand Marnier and.......My mind swayed and everything became blurry. I staggered to the side of the ballroom and lay down next to the sarcophagus of a witch who had been a close friend of the Magian. My head soon cleared again and everything seemed incredibly sharp, sending forth colored vibrations that enveloped the scene around me. The witch jumped out of her tomb and scurried onto the dance floor, meeting up with a fellow in the costume of a secretary bird, complete with quills sticking out of his head. They conferred for a few moments and then left the room, while others began to leap to an Irish jig that the cats were fiddling with.

Now there was a commotion in a corner near the band. I edged my way through the crowd to see what was going on. Three people were arguing over a troll, who lay on the floor with his eyes shut. It looked as if he had been crushed in the rush to get to the bar, but why weren't the three trying to help him? I crouched down and felt his pulse, which was very slow. Not knowing the regular heart rhythm of a troll, it was not much help. I stood up quickly to signal for a doctor, and my zipper broke, revealing the entire front of my body. People started to laugh, but I was reasonably drunk, and did not care. Let them gawk if they wished!

I got an arm around the troll, who smelt very badly of fish, and was about to get him off the dance floor when one of the three people stepped towards me, whisking off his giraffe mask. I nearly let go of the troll, who was groaning loudly, when I saw wild-looking Festerbash standing in front of me.

He was grinning and hiccupping loudly, his blond hair spiking in every direction. "I'm Fes'erbas', I am. Yer party man, I am. Re'ember yer hedonish'ishtic self, thatsh me!" He burst into a fit of giggles while the other two stood looking on with distaste. I turned my attention, sharpened by the black drink, on to them, dropping the troll, who crawled away and hid under the bandstand Of these figures, one had a very poor disguise, his French beret barely covered his handsome raven face, while the dungarees he wore were torn to ribbons and shiny black feathers burst through. The other was dressed in a pale monks' robe with a pair of outsize spectacles adorning his owl face.

"Excuse me, but aren't you A. Lyster Crow and Pawel Phustercus? I'm sure I recognize you both." I exclaimed, trying to pretend I didn't know Festerbash. Why did he have to show up at every party, I thought to myself.

"You are correct. Three of us are here now in the right hemisphere, as you seem to think we fit in better here. Personally, I consider myself a left brainer. But of course all magicians should be able to use both sides of their brain equally, which would make us all mid-brainers." The raven, who was A. Lyster Crow, reminded me that he had become a raven during the Path of the Moon, when he had succeeded in leaving his inferior crow status behind. The owl, who was Pawel Phustercus, was quiet, but his strange eyes mesmerized me as he turned his head from side to side in a wide circle.

"Where is the third magician? I thought I saw a tall bird with quills on his head conversing with a dead witch, and then they left hurriedly. What's up? It looked very suspicious."

"We can go and find them, if you like." A Lyster said, smirking. "But I suggest you get your zipper fixed first – it is rather revealing."

I had completely forgotten, in the excitement of meeting them, that I was practically bare to the groin. I wondered where I could find some safety pins. Fortunately an old dame carrying an embroidery frame came by, and I stole some pins from her pincushion, which she had placed on the top of her head. Somehow my suit was forced together and pinned so that it was halfway decent, and we went in search of Isa Real Gardy and the witch.

Up the spiral staircase to the island again, we found a causeway had appeared above the rapidly retreating lake. This convenient pathway led into the forest by the two towers, and hurrying across it were the secretary bird and the witch, carrying something in a small bag. The three of us followed them deep into the forest, winding their way swiftly between the serried rows of tree trunks. They came to an octagonal shed that appeared to have no doors, for we glimpsed them disappearing straight into the wall. We hunkered down nearby, considering whether we should surprise them, if we could get into the shed ourselves. With two other magicians, that should not be too difficult.

Voices came from the shed in murmurs and soft chuckles. Then the night was split by a piercing scream, and begging sobs came from inside. "No! No! Please don't experiment on me. I don't want to know what it's like."

I heard the voice of the Magian. "We chose you for the experiment out of many who would be glad to try it. Don't have second thoughts now and back out! The laser beam will not hurt you."

"I have seen the others - the ones who have had the experiment. It is not funny! They are completely out of their minds. I have a wife and children to consider – I don't want to be enlightened yet. Maybe after the kids have graduated."

I could distinguish at least four people in there, and the Magian was one of them. What was Krackenwergle doing? And who was the endangered fourth person? We decided, rather than burst in on them, we would spy from outside without disturbing them, although I was concerned about the victims' situation. A. Lyster had a spy glass, and Pawel a drill, for he was a Mason, so we quickly drilled a small hole in the side of the shed and carefully pushed the spyglass through.

On one side Isa Real Gardy and the witch were firmly holding a woodcutter from the forest between them. His head had been shaved and a terrified look crossed his face as the Magian took a small laser gun out of the bag and pressed it to his forehead with soothing words.

The gun popped and the woodcutter gave an ecstatic shout. "Oh! The marvel of it! I had no idea. Thank you, thank you…..." His voice trailed off and he gazed around him with new interest in his surroundings. They let him go, and he walked through the wall and out of the hut, singing a little song.

"So! They are trying the Experiment here." Burst out A. Lyster Crow. "I suspected it!. I'm glad we followed them. Now we know what's going on."

He turned to Pawel, who nodded sagely. "False enlightenment! They zapped the guys' pineal gland with a laser. Causes coagulation of the gland, and it goes through a substantial change." The owl coughed politely. "Unfortunately, a great deal of damage is caused, for the gland should be gently heated over a period of years by meditation in order to experience the true results. In this case, the sudden change will send the woodcutter off his rocker. In fact, look at him now." Pawel paused and pointed to the nearest tree. The woodcutter was high up in the branches and climbing fast. Reaching the top of the tree, he positioned himself on a branch, looking down.

"He thinks he can fly now. There's nothing to be done for him. Just let him jump, he'll never come back to normal again, anyway. It's sad, but inevitable." We turned and watched the woodcutter launch himself off the branch, spreading his arms as if to fly. He crashed to the ground and showed no further signs of life. It is possible his children never graduated.

A dark mist rolled across the forest, casting everything into gloom, and I found myself alone as the four magicians and the witch slipped silently away into the shadows. I returned to the fashion show, but found that most of the audience were so drunk that they had cancelled it. One of the cats had fallen over and ripped the drum with its claws, and another had a squashed tail, blaming Festerbash for the injury, as usual. How I despised him......

I was glad to move on to the left hemisphere, thinking that events there would be more controlled. The way across was not easy, as the path was very faint. I was forced to stop many times, to trace signs of a trail such as broken twigs, animal scat, or prints. A firm and recent set of three-toed footprints in a muddy section of the path reassured me. I knew some way ahead of me walked an ibis, certainly the black and white ibis who was the Magians' scribe. I hurried along, but it was not until the sixth day that I saw the bird.

The ibis turned and regarded me serenely. "Welcome to the left hemisphere of the Magian. I am he who writes and he who classifies thoughts. Please follow me. The Magian awaits your arrival."

The bird strode off, his pace increasing, and I broke into a trot. Although I ran as fast as I could, I was hard pressed to keep up. It was not far, fortunately, before we reached the familiar island in the center of the lake.

"Here is your ride" The ibis announced. "I will fly, because I enjoy that. It throws the man with the bird net off my trail. See you over on the island." He took off over the lake, swooping down in a low curve onto the shore by the Magians' capsule. The manta ray was waiting to carry me over to the island, and I was happy to see that a meal of curried chipmunk with mice was prepared for us. I was ready to eat anything.

After the meal, the Magian took me down the spiral staircase to the next level, passing quickly through the right hemisphere to the center of the brain, where the hippocampus protected the small cage with the pea sized pineal gland inside. The Magian opened the cage and squeezed the gland vigorously, whereupon it let out a piteous squeak. A glass partition walling off the left hemisphere rolled back, giving access to a long, grayish tube that we entered, winding on until we emerged on the other side of the left hemisphere.

The two active Aces, Braimind, the Ace of Swords, and Percepto, the Ace of Wands, were feasting at a dainty table covered with a white cloth that was placed in the center of a cottage garden blooming with myriad flowers. We pulled out the two remaining chairs and helped ourselves from a three tiered cake stand in the middle, loaded with tiny triangular sandwiches of cucumber, salmon and egg mayonnaise. I was already full, but managed to force down a few dozen sandwiches and three rock cakes.

Braimind regarded my greed with disgust. He was a serious and dedicated man dressed in a skintight white suit with a peaked helmet and a long, narrow necklace. A hefty sword rested in its sheath by his side.

"Do you have an entity that you would like to train as a spy?" He asked thoughtfully. "It would be to infiltrate a familiar territory that has set up boundaries against us, for we need to analyze their sequential categories. We fear they are muddled up and are not in the right order."

"I suggest the ibis, who is a representative of Thoth, would be the very one. He can fly over the boundary and gather information from the air by trapping vagrant thoughts. Shall I fetch him?"

"No, that will not be necessary. He is already here." Braimind slid his hand into the neckline of his suit and brought out the ibis, who smiled widely at me. "I was just testing you to see if you would pick the right spy. By the way, your conduct while you were staying with Aurelio at the observatory was rather shocking. I hope you aren't going to indulge yourself again at this level?"

Shaking my head vigorously, I assured Braimind that I would behave myself, as I swallowed a large piece of Bakewell tart. Relieved that he hadn't chastised me further, I turned my attention to Percepto, who was sitting on my left.

He had pushed his firey red hair under a curious tight skull cap and his fierce body tattoos spoke with the roar of an uncontrolled wild fire. "I will always be grateful you restored the Phoenix, bird of rebirth, to us. I saw you summon Nuit to build your bridge over to the Bar, too, and I was most impressed. What is your mission here?"

"I've come here to be trained in the use of the four Magical Weapons. Two of the Aces have now dedicated themselves as Weapons to the mission, and it only remains for Braimind and yourself to join us in your altered state." I wiped my mouth surreptitiously on the edge of the tablecloth.

"You might at least use a napkin!" Braimind snorted. "I suppose during the years of your long journey you have forgotten your manners. Pity!"

"I'm truly ashamed. The learned tasks of my youth have been obliterated by time. I am not as detail-oriented as I once was." I secretly resented his judgmental attitude, and hoped that Krackenwergle would soon start the ceremony, for then Braimind, having the quality of Air, would metamorphose into a mere Dagger.

"I heard what you thought." The ibis broke in. "Remember, I am Thoth, god of all thought, and it's easy for me to pick up telepathy. Do not for a moment consider the Magical Dagger to be less than the Ace. It has far more power. You must be careful to censor your thoughts during your time here, and, I suggest, also until you reach Kether, your ultimate goal."

Feeling somewhat trapped, since I was apparently banned from thinking negatively, I subsided and waited patiently for the Magian to leave the tea table. To pass the intervening time, I selected a large banana split and set to work on it.

A sharp order from the Magian made me drop my spoon on the gravel. A waiter came, whisking the dessert away before I had finished. "It's time for the ceremony! Let us go upstairs to the fire pit." Kracklewergen rose and walked stiffly back into the left hemisphere and we followed him along the grayish tubes of the brain.

We gathered at the fire, where he quickly had a little flame going and fed it with twigs. Braimind, the element of Air, fanned himself vigorously before sitting down on the east side of the circle, while Percepto actually stood in the fire for a few minutes, then, with a satisfied grin, he took the southern seat. The two Aces then sat cross-legged, staring into the flames. When asked, they agreed they were ready to morph. Spreading his red cloak over Braimind, the Magian sprinkled liquid from the vial using the cycad cone, and then touched the cloak with his wand.

"Root of the Powers of Air, reveal your Weapon, the Dagger!" He pulled the cloak away and a magnificent Dagger lay on the ground, encased in an elephant skin sheath patterned with Celtic roses. Picking it up, he

404 *Julia A. Turk*

withdrew the sharp blade, which ran in a zigzag pattern, the engraved handle set with rubies.

Gazing at the beautiful design, I murmured. "It's the Dagger you gave me originally in the Five of Wands, up at the mountain pass. My Guide took it and said he would keep it safe until later. This must be the time."

Without answering, the Magian threw his cloak over Percepto and repeated the ceremony. "Root of the Powers of Fire, reveal your Weapon, the Wand." The cloak revealed a Wand that took on a crystalline form, a substance that shot back all the colors of the rainbow like a perfect prism. I reached for the Wand, but the Magian was quicker, and picked it up. Two servants appeared, carrying a portable altar, and set it down. They were followed by Anal, the White Dwarf, who arrived with the Pentacle and the Cup. Krackenwergle carefully placed the four Magical Weapons on the altar, murmuring to himself. I wondered what the four Aces were thinking as they lay there, inert. I presumed it was their Destiny, and since they were not made of material substance anyway, the change had probably not disturbed them unduly.

"We must invite all the people who were dancing at the show!" The Magian announced. "This is to be a fine evocation, now that I have my Magical Weapons back. Where are the other magicians? There were three I saw dancing – I don't know where they went to – and the other four should be joining us soon. The seven magicians, with myself, make eight. Eight is a good number for the ceremony." He looked about him, then turned to me. "Someone, go and round up the magicians. While we're waiting, I will show you the bazaar here."

The White Dwarf scurried off to look for the magicians while we strolled over to the tip of a spiral fern, that was about to unfold itself. Waving his wand, Krackenwergle enlarged the fiddlehead and we walked inside, passing along the frilly green tube that unfolded before us. We came to a store selling white picket fences, and next to it, a stall with myriad crossword puzzles and brain teasers of different kinds. Set back from the walkway was the School of Analytical Judgment, with several earnest looking professors conducting classes inside. Beyond that, a book store, the titles carefully classified into categories, caught my attention. I stopped to examine one of the books, but it proved to be rather dull – just a set of logistical sequence verbs. A crowd had gathered around a storyteller, whose narrative powers were recognized by everyone, while some children at the side were playing with lettered bricks. Personally, I found the bazaar at the right hemisphere more interesting, but I knew I was a mid-brainer, so I made an effort to focus on what I was viewing. We watched a group of seniors doing Tai Chi, their movements carefully copied from the instructor.

"It's time to go back for the evocation." Krackenwergle announced, steering me back towards the point of the fern spiral.

.

We stepped down as servers arrived and set up several long tables and a bar with a large bowl of the black liquid. Twilight had fallen, and soft nightly sounds from the surrounding forest stirred the heavy air. A sense of foreboding crept across the grounds, and even Krackenwergen was sniffing the sir suspiciously with his long coyote nose. If there was another drinking party, I hoped Festerbash would not show up again, for he always made trouble. The four Magical Weapons lay neatly on the altar, and a small fire burned in front of it. On the other side of the room, a row of cheap plastic glasses stood on the bar, filled with the black liquid. People began to arrive, still clad in their fancy costumes from the fashion show. Time seemed to stand still as they picked up their drinks and formed small conversational groups. Krackenwergle circled around, looking here and there for the missing magicians.

A straggling group of figures arrived, led by the White Dwarf. They were four of the magicians - Hawkley P. Mann, a noble peregrine falcon; the short stumpy figure of Eeleye Fastlever, the penguin; a squawking parrot, Arty Weight; and the bug eyed owl, Pawel Phustercus. The other three were still missing. I decided to hunt for them myself, and I ran over the causeway into the forest.

It was very dark in there as I wandered from tree to tree. Then I was startled by a loud squawking, and a flurry of activity came from my left. There was an argument going on. Some feathers floated through the air. They looked like chicken feathers and I thought maybe McSmother Feathers was being attacked by a marauder, so I hurried in that direction, bumping into trees and bruising myself in the process. The squawking became hysterical and a heavy bundle of feathers brushed past me in the dark, followed by the silhouette of a raven. After them, the secretary bird Isa Real Gardy ran past me on his long legs.

They were heading for the causeway. That was the right direction, at least. Maybe they didn't know the evocation ceremony was about to begin. I followed them at a distance. Then a fourth figure came up behind me, dressed in a strange robe covered with moons and stars and wearing an enormous black hat on its head. As it hurried past, I put out my foot and tripped it up. It crashed to the ground with a loud cry. I bent over and tweaked off the big hat, to see the familiar tufts of spiky blond hair.

"Festerbash! What are you doing, dressed up like a magician?"

I could see the gleam of excitement in my entities' eyes as the twilight glow faded. He tried to wriggle free, but I had him by the scruff of his neck.

"Let go of me! They're having a party. See the bar, see the drinks, there'll be music too, I bet. I just want to have fun. Don't be a spoil sport." His conniving eyes wandered from side to side and I remembered he had never been able to look me square in the eye, but always prevaricated. I gave him a little shake.

"What was going on in the forest? You saw the three of them. Is McSmother hurt? I saw feathers flying. Tell me what happened." I insisted.

"All right, I'll tell you, if you let me go. A Lyster Crow, the raven, got into it with McSmother Feathers. He really had a go at him - called him a blithering idiot and a complete charlatan. While he was berating him, he held onto McSmothers' kilt, trying to tear it off, but the chicken would not let go, for fear he had no knickers on underneath. McSmother called the raven an egotistical renegade who was spreading secrets about the Gudden Doorn to the public. Then, at the height of this name-calling, the secretary bird Isa Real Gardy appeared from the direction of a shed in the forest, and sneered at A. Lyster Crow, telling him that he intended to publish even more revealing facts. Well, the chicken was so upset he attacked both of them, coming off much the worse for wear and losing clumps of feathers, which they tore out with abandon. He has almost been plucked and seems to have gone crazy." Festerbash sniffed. "Now leave me alone. If you want to pester anyone, go and see what your idols have done to each other."

I let him go, giving back his stupid hat, and he laughed illogically and hastened towards the party, which was in full swing. Annoyed, I walked to the bar and took a black drink in each hand, taking a large gulp of the liquid. The first four magicians had formed a band and were playing reggae music, and as I got closer, I saw Krackenwergle sauntering up with the remaining three magicians, who were trying to arrange their ruffled feathers and look cool. They picked up their instruments and joined the band, strumming for a moment to pick up the key. The eight magicians struck up together, perfectly in tune, and played magnificently. The crowd went wild, and I could see Festerbash, his hat trampled underfoot, dancing madly just under the stage.

Many of the celebrants were still drunk from the thwarted fashion show, and had not bothered to change their clothes. I looked down and saw I was still wearing the salamander suit, held together at the front with a row of safety pins. I decided to go and change into my tunic before I was overcome by the black liquid again. As I passed the bar, putting down my two empty glasses, I saw Festerbash, his hair awry, balancing five glasses in his hands. Curse the fellow! There was sure to be trouble. I hoped he hadn't noticed the portable altar standing in a corner. Hurriedly I ran to the changing rooms and put on my tunic, flinging the lemming fur cape over my shoulders.

The party got wilder and wilder, and I wondered whether Krackenwergle had been wise to serve drinks before the evocation ceremony. Personally, I felt my solar plexus fluttering nervously at the thought of a drunken venture into the occult. But in spite of that, I myself cast caution to the winds and took another glass of my favorite drink, tossing it back recklessly. Across the tumult, I heard the Magians' voice, summoning the revelers towards the altar and asking them to sit down, so that the evocation could begin.

His voice seemed to have an amazing effect, for most of the people trooped up and arranged themselves in rows, some sitting on benches at the side, and others on the floor. Krackenwergen raised his wand, and spoke in a sonorous vibration, forming a circle on the floor around the altar and the sacred fire in front, and then proceeding with the normal ritual. His voice assumed a strange quality that seemed to mesmerize the audience, and they watched with bated breath as he approached the altar, bending over it and focusing on the four Magical Weapons. The room fell into a hush, and a feeling of awe and devotion swept over the crowd, who sat silently watching.

CRASH! As the Magian jumped back in astonishment, the portable altar tipped over and fell into the sacred fire, tossing the spinning Magical Weapons onto the ground near the audience, who shrank away in dismay. A figure rose up from behind the fallen altar, waving its arms and cackling loudly in a drunken frenzy.

"I did it! Ha! Ha! Ha! Didn' wan' ter interrup' th' party. Stupid ceremony, if yer arsks me. Lesh get back ter the dance – com'on, now, ever'body." It was Festerbash.

I instinctively cowered back into the shadows, for Festerbash was one of my entities. This was a major disaster. I had let him get out of hand. Now what would happen? I saw out of the corner of my eye that Krackenwergle was in a towering rage. The audience was rapidly retreating, except for four figures that lay very still on the floor by the altar.

"Dead! They're all dead! Killed by the Magical Weapons!" The Magian shrieked insanely, his bristly hair crackling with sparks. "Look what you've done – my evocation is ruined."

At this point he seized Festerbash, who was too drunk to escape, grabbing him by the throat. Festerbash staggered back with a hollow gurgle, trying to defend himself. I leapt forward, forcing my way between them to save my entity, and thrusting Kracklewergen back, so that he staggered and fell to the ground on top of the four corpses. Grabbing Festerbashs' hand, I dragged him off to a side door and we made our escape over the causeway and hid in the forest for the rest of the night.

In the morning, I found that Festerbash had made use of the darkness. I couldn't feel any sorrow when I spotted his limp form hanging from a nearby tree, and seated around the tree were the seven magical birds. I crept up behind them, readying my jeweled bird net, for this was the first chance I might have to capture them all together. Silently I flung the net that swirled wide over the seated birds. It fell down onto their heads and trapped them. But, as I ran forward to gloat over my catch, I found only a kilt; a pair of spectacles; a quill and a parrots' brightly colored tail feather under the net.

A ghostly voice echoed in the early mist. "Nothing, not even the magical net, can contain us." With a final snicker, the seven magicians had escaped once again.

A stealthy figure behind me had me trapped, its hand over my mouth to stifle my screams. Dragging me struggling to the water, it hurled me from the causeway with a bitter curse. "Go, infidel, and take your partying friend with you." The Magian had his revenge.

Island of BINAH

The magicians faded from my mind as I surfaced, gasping and spitting out water, my limbs tingling from the stings of Portuguese men of war. It seemed I had failed to cross the Sea of Sorrow once again. The dark mist that engulfed me made me forget where I had been. It gradually grew paler, and an Island made entirely of obsidian, the black, volcanic glass often used for flint tools, appeared in front of me through swirls of clouds. I swam on until I reached the beach, climbing from the water dripping wet. A series of undulating hills formed of the black glass alternated with flatter areas that swooped down into deep clefts in the terrain. Nothing grew on the Island, for the harsh obsidian had not broken down into dirt. Nature had not set foot here, and the black mounds swelled up and down, rank after rank, with no end in sight.

A movement caught my eye and I crept forward to the bottom of the nearest knoll. A throne was there, carved out of the black rock, and on it sat a silent figure, a mature woman dressed in a voluminous robe that concealed her body from head to foot. She was weeping copious tears that ran down her face into a bowl that she held on her lap, and from there, in a little rivulet that snaked its way towards the sea. I knelt at her feet, overwhelmed by her sorrow, but when I tried to assuage her grief, she put a finger to her lips cautioning me not to break the moment, for not even the twitter of a bird echoed through the hushed landscape.

I moved on, uncertain of what to do, coming to a narrow path that wandered through a cleft in the rolling hills. Following this path until I emerged on a wide plateau, with a small encampment near a pool at the far end, I came to a waterfall splashing into the pool over a gap in the rocks above. There was a cave behind the falls, and a moment later a thin, undernourished woman brushed past the spray and walked towards me. She bowed, murmuring "Amen!" but nothing more, and beckoned me to follow her, leading me behind the falls to a small tent in the cave, where she pushed open the tent flap and ushered me inside. I found myself face to face with a wizened old crone sitting behind a desk, her worn face a mesh of a thousand wrinkles and her expression severe.

"I am Ama, the dark, sterile Mother. I have never given birth, but with my life experience I counsel those who come here, to help them pass the tests that Saturn sets for them. Please be seated."

Reluctantly I sat down on a wobbly canvas stool. She regarded me relentlessly, at the same time pulling a large file from a cabinet at her feet, which she placed on the desk and opened. "Let me see now. There are numerous complaints in your file from all sorts of people who have run up against you during your lifetime. What a pity!" She thumbed through the paperwork with a grubby hand. "However, Saturn has left a message for me to test you on one particular fault that you have, so we will concentrate on that." She pulled out a sheaf of papers.

"What is the fault?" I asked tremulously.

"This is a report from a certain woman, we will call her the Baggot. You know who that is, don't you?"

I nodded miserably.

"Well, the Baggot claims that you are a moocher, and that you have mooched off her, her husband, and numerous other people during your lifetime. Do you deny this?"

"I don't know what the Baggot means. I have accepted hospitality many times, and I have always tried to give back by helping out with some necessary task, like painting a house, or weeding a garden. I thought a moocher was someone who came to visit, ate food without paying for it, lay down on the couch, and then would not leave. That is not what I do." I started to feel challenged.

"Well, the Baggot says here that you mooched their car, and that you tried to mooch a free breakfast off them. Also, you always looked hopeful when they mentioned having a barbecue, and she knew you wanted to be asked, and felt that she had to, but it was against her nature. These are serious charges. How can you defend yourself?"

"I remember the breakfast incident. The Baggot and her husband had invited me to their house at a certain time. I got up early and had my breakfast, and then set off for their house. Alas! I made the mistake of arriving early, which is a habit of mine, and they were still eating. The food was disgusting, biscuits and gravy – really unhealthy stuff, and I didn't want any of it. But they must have thought I had come specifically in time to mooch their breakfast. That was not my intention at all." I was angry at this unfair accusation.

"Well, I believe you, for you sound sincere. My advice to you is, next time she asks you to her house, make sure you are late, so that she can be kept waiting. She would also have time to finish her tardy breakfast, and as a result, she would be unable to accuse you of mooching if she had eaten all the biscuits and gravy."

"That is an excellent idea. I will always make sure to be late for the Baggot, even though I may be early for other people."

"Well, you want to make sure, if you are early, that you don't arrive in the middle of a meal, otherwise you may get more people accusing you of mooching."

"Yes, that is a good point." I looked serious. "I will not help the Baggot any more. I hope you understand why I feel this way?"

"I do understand. Even though I am dark and sterile, that does not mean I am not fair. We do know that the Baggot claims to have the gift of compassion. We are watching her when she weeps over fat people on the television. We hope that she will step forward when it is necessary." The dark mother Ama pulled out another file and wrote a short note in it. I wondered if that was the Baggots' file.

The interview was over and the scrawny woman, who had waited quietly while we were talking, rose and ushered me out and across the cave to another tent that was draped in dried flowers and colored ribbons. She pulled back the tent flap and I walked in, to find a youngish, cheerful looking woman sitting comfortably in a large recliner, dressed in bright woven garments with a coronet of silk flowers in her hair.

"Welcome to my abode! I am Aima, the bright, fertile Mother, representing the other side of Binah, the Sphere of Foundation. My job is to help you set up the groundwork on which to build for the rest of your journey here, and certainly for the remainder of your current life. Do have a seat." She indicated a comfortable armchair with a foot rest in the corner of the tent opposite her.

"You have just come from Amas' tent, and I know how she can be - strict and demanding. However, she is unbiased, and so am I, for we operate in Binah far above normal human emotions and feel total detachment from their cares and tribulations. I know Ama brought out the paper work that she felt was important. You felt anger and great disappointment when you heard the Baggot speak bad words behind your back. You feel she is a hypocrite, a traitor, and betrayed you." Aima gave a slight smile. "Now, with my help, you can turn those feelings into compassion for her."

"Would that make me feel better?" I frowned. "Would my anger go away?"

"Indeed, if you follow my reasoning, you will release yourself from any regrets over the Baggot, for she is ignorant of what she has done."

"She always seemed so excessively thoughtful – but underneath I felt her disapproval."

"Well, she is trying to get along as best she can. I know that you have spent much time and trouble over the years to help her and her family when they needed you. That stands to your credit, no matter what they think of you. It is written here, in your book of poetry….."

Here she produced a slim volume bound in leather, with gold trim…..."Never regret what you do for others. They may not think to respond. But they are your sisters and brothers. And there is a common bond."

Aima shut the book and settled back in her chair, closing her eyes for a moment. Then she sat up. "Every good deed sends vibrations out into the universe, and every thoughtless condemnation returns to the place from which it came. Do not now condemn the Baggot, or you lower yourself to her position."

"I see what you mean. Is it better then, to remain silent, rather than to indignantly remind her of what I have done for her? I feel like cutting her out of my life – not just her, but all of them. Is that so wrong?'

"That is the normal Ego response. But you are now in Binah! You would not have arrived here if you had not dispensed with your Ego, Belvedere, and nullified his control over you, so that he is now your servant. But even servants can be disloyal. Belvedere will try to creep back and get your attention from time to time. You must let him go, and that means any resentment he carries with him." Aima leaned forward in her chair. "I would like you now to meditate for a few minutes. Just relax and feel forgiveness towards the Baggot – she can't help herself, being caught in her own net."

I sat quietly with my eyes closed, my feet on the flat obsidian floor of the cave. Gradually I let go of any feelings of anger towards my betrayer, and understood that my desire to remind her of everything I had done for her was the thought that my ego, Belvedere, whispered in my ear. I pushed him from me and a feeling of relief flooded through me. My vindictive feelings sped away, leaving a tender void. I opened my eyes slowly.

Aima was gazing at me with quiet sympathy. "You understand now. That is the foundation on which you must build. It is written, when someone wounds you, turn the other cheek. Never was a truer word spoken. It is the path towards enlightenment that you seek, and that you will succeed in reaching, if you continue to react favorably. As you know, your Akashic Records are in the Infinite Library on the Island of Da'ath, where all knowledge is stored. When you begin the Path of the Archpriestess, you will go before the Society of Enochian Anchorites for analysis. At that time, they will tell you what your Destiny will be for your next life, which depends on your achievements in this one. You may go now, and experience the strange and wonderful sights on our Island of Binah. I sanctify you." Aima stood up and gave me a hug. I had not realized until then that she was a midget.

The thin woman led me in silence to a bunk room and indicated a simple pallet that had been made up with clean sheets. I slept well that night, the Baggot failing to invade my dreams. Next morning I left the plateau and set out across the rolling hills. There were frequent dips in the hills, and at the bottom of each one there were holes in all shapes and sizes. I went along until I came to a large rectangular hole and sat down beside it, for I could see movement down at the bottom of the hole. Straining my eyes, I made out a lawn tennis court, and four figures were playing a game of doubles on the court. It was like looking at Wimbledon from the rooftops.

I soon made out the contestants. To my astonishment, they were the four Queens. I saw the Queen of Pentacles serving. She was rather clumsy and her ball went into the net, whereupon a ball girl ran across, picking it up. Her partner was the Queen of Swords, who cussed at her when she missed a shot and was very good at backhands, but not so good at forehands. Playing against them as a team, were the Queen of Cups, who insisted on hitting really high lobs, where the ball would almost disappear into the stratosphere and, in fact, whizzed past my nose on several occasions. The Queen of Wands studied her shots carefully, and excelled at low, fast forehands that just topped the net, the ball spinning so that it was almost impossible to hit it back.

I felt the game was well matched, for the two passive Queens were partnered with the two active Queens, so that it was hard to guess who would win. They played for a long time, and I was beginning to get bored, although I enjoyed tennis, when the Queen of Swords caught a high lob from the Queen of Cups in mid air and smashed it down by the net. Unfortunately the Queen of Pentacles was in the way, and was hit on the head by her racquet and laid out cold. They all rushed forward, pushing and shoving each other out of the way to get close to the unconscious Queen, while an umpire imperiously blew a whistle, hoping to calm them down. One of them got her robes caught in the net and tore a big hole in it, then dragged it across the court and tripped up the Queen of Cups, who landed on her face, bumping the machine that was producing tennis balls.

With the contestants arguing amongst themselves, no-one noticed at first that the ball-making machine had gone wild, spitting out ball after ball until the tennis court was full of bouncing balls that formed into piles everywhere. The floor of the court began to sag under their weight, and the Queens began to slide towards the center amongst the flood of tennis balls. They struggled to save themselves, clutching each other, and managed to wrap the broken net around them, where they hung as the floor split in two and released a deluge of tennis balls into the Island of Chesed below. The balls bounced into the room where the babies' incubators were, causing great distress and forcing the penguin to summon help to gather up the balls.

I couldn't watch any more. I left that hole and moved on to the next curvaceous valley, where I found something far more interesting. While examining a round hole, to my surprise real dirt began spurting out of it and forming a pile in front of the hole. Something underground was digging, which proved there was earth on this island underneath the obsidian after all. I watched by the hole, and soon a tiny feathered head with two bright eyes peeped out. A little burrowing owl scrambled up the pile of earth and stood at the top, its head cocked to one side. Then a second owl appeared, but this one was different. It came out slowly, straining its head from side to side, because it was blind. I wondered how that had happened. The blind owl was not sleek and well groomed like the other one, but had fluffed itself up into a big ball and carried its wings far out from its body. The first owl saw me, crouching down a little, but did not flee.

I decided to ask them a question. "Excuse me, I know that owls are normally silent, but if you could explain my concern, I would be more than happy. I'm very sorrowful, for you appear to be blind. I'm wondering, though, why you are also fluffed up?"

The blind owl spoke in a whisper. "Ah, yeth, the fluffing. Well, ith's twue I can't thee, and my fwiend over there keepth a lookout for me. Hith head ith permanently cocketh ower to the lefth. Fell out of his netht, I fear. Ath for me, I wath bown blind. I fluff mythelf up becauthe it maketh me look bigger. That way, all thothe who path are afwaid of me and thtay faw away. They don't thee that I'm blind and wulnerable, you thee. It workth for me."

"That's a very good explanation. I can see you've accepted your sad state and you're able to deal with it successfully. I would like to take you both for a trolley ride. Would you enjoy that?"

The two owls jumped up and down with glee. "Oh, yes!" The other peeped. "That would be fun. This burrow can get rather boring, you know, because, being a hole, we have to keep digging it, and we can never actually build a significant mound or a pile of earth, for this is Binah, and everything on this island is receptively female and flat. Anyone who tried to make an obelisk or set up a pole faces immediate arrest." The owl looked around. "Where is the trolley? I have never seen one here."

The blind owl spoke up. "I couldn't thee a twolley if there wath one. Let'th jutht imagine it! I am wewy good at that. We will take the forthe in the atmothphere that ith coming fwom the Ithland of Chockmah all the time, and conthruct a twolley from it. We can give it fowm, and build it wight here, and then we can imagine wailth for it to wun on anywhere we want to go!"

I clapped my hands. "Great! You go ahead and imagine a trolley on rails, then. I'll imagine a city with big hills that go up and down, and we will have an exciting ride."

The blind owl, even more fluffed out, settled down quietly, putting its head under one wing while the bright-eyed owl stood by solicitously. Around us, lines of force appeared from the direction of Chockmah, running over the hills from the west and gathering around the blind owls' head. Slowly the bulky shape of a bright red trolley car formed next to us, with a conductor who imperiously blew a whistle, expecting us to board the gleaming car.

I held out my arm and bright eyes hopped onto it, while I gently picked up the blind owl in the palm of my other hand, its soft feathers brushing my skin tenderly. We boarded the trolley, which set off at a smart pace, running up and down over the obsidian hills like a roller coaster.

The owls loved it, their feathers blowing in the breeze, and the blind owl was twittering to itself and flapping its wings freely, as if flying. We spent several hours exploring the island in this way, and when we returned at nightfall I escorted the owls to their burrow.

"Will you come back tomowow?" The blind owl asked. "I would like to thee you again."

"You will see me now." I passed my hands over the birds' little face, and blessed it. When I took them away, two bright eyes blinked at me in amazement. The blind owl could see! The owls gazed at each other, their eyes locked together in harmony. I crept away quietly, allowing them to celebrate their meeting.

Leaving the owls' burrow, I felt drawn by some inner force towards an area of Binah as yet unexplored. The rolling hills led downwards gently until I felt we must be well below sea level, and I followed the faint path that led round and round in a spiral towards an enormous hollow beneath me. Many people were digging in a vast clay pit, and amongst them the four Queens, dressed in long aprons, were up to their elbows in moist black clay. They were muttering amongst themselves. Above this industrious scene sat a horrifying woman on an ornate black pillar named Boaz that carried a throne. Her eyes glittered with the sheen of obsidian; her teeth were blackened and sharp, and her hands reached out on the arms of the throne in long black claws as she clenched them angrily.

"Soyla! Amferna!" She commanded threateningly. "You are not forming your clay fast enough. You have to catch the lines of force quickly as they come in from Chockmah, and convert them to form before they evade you." She banged her fist on the arm of the chair. "And there's another thing. I have a suspicion you may be plotting against me, and, if so, you know you can never succeed. My minions will throw you into my dungeons below."

The four startled Queens hastily bent their heads to the task of spinning the clay on their carousels and molding it into different forms. The other workers glanced furtively at the woman, ceased their muted chatter, and focused on digging up the clay and patting it into shape. Her ghastly head came up and she noticed me teetering on the edge of the pit. I tried to make myself as small as I could, but of course with no trees or bushes to hide behind, it was impossible.

Her downward gaze fixed on me and she almost spat out the words. "What are you doing here? Snooping around? This is a work area – put on your apron and get busy immediately. What are you going to form?"

I hastily told her that I would form a monkey out of the black clay, and I bent down, sinking my fingers into the cool clay and bringing up a large lump of it, which I put on an empty carousel near Fluvia, whose face was streaked black as she wearily pulled back a stray hair.

I pretended to look earnestly at my clay lump, and patted it smooth while questioning Queen Phere under my breath. She was making a stork. "Why are you and the others working here?"

Phere heard me and snapped back, being rather severe at the best of times. "Of course we are here! All four of us belong to Binah, our foundation. This is where the Queens get their power."

Stung by her curt attitude, I moved over to question the Queen of Cups, Fluvia. "Who is that supervisor woman sitting up on the pillar?"

She gave a surreptitious glance up at the supervisor. "That is the Terrible Mother. She rules here in Binah, and she makes sure that we supply a continuous sequence of forms for their individual birth and eventual death."

Dissatisfied with her answer, I struggled through the sticky clay, dragging my legs one by one with a faint sucking sound, to the Queen of Pentacles, Soyla, asking her. "Why are you down here on Binah with the other three Queens?"

Soyla responded, lazily punching her clay ball into shape. "We are consorts of our Kings in the four elemental castles by the Lagoon, as you saw when you visited us during your travels in Gulftide. But we have to return here at regular intervals, to remind us of the limitations and discipline required by Binah. It is like a boot camp to keep us regulated."

"Thank you." I murmured as I passed her and leaned forward to speak to the Queen of Wands, Amferna, with another question. "Why are you forced to model black clay into forms?"

She tossed her head, her green eyes taking me in. "As for the forms, well, Binah catches the wayward forces that come from the Island of Chockmah, to the west of us, and brings them to a halt, for otherwise they would melt back into the atmosphere and nothing would ever come of them. Here, we make the forms out of clay and send them down the Path of the Empress, where they are animated and enter the round of birth and death ruled over by our planet, Saturn."

"Ah! I have seen the Empress' cave, where she watches vigilantly over the unborn." I whispered. "Are you allowed to choose any form you like? I am molding a monkey." A faint recollection of the red monkey I had feasted on went through my mind as my fingers swiftly formed the monkeys' shape. I cast a glance at the Terrible Mother. Two of the Queens were throwing clay at each other, and she rose from her seat with a formidable glare, slid down the pillar and stalked over to them.

"Active Queens! Your behavior is not appropriate. Now look what has happened - Malkuth has sent up a messenger, the Navigator." Here she turned to me and said. "Yes, I know who you are, believe me. It is most disturbing to see you here, rare, indeed, to realize that someone from Malkuth actually made it as far as this. It speaks well of your work." She turned back to the Queens. "The Navigator is witnessing your appalling conduct. How can Saturn expect us to make the forms in chronological time and send them down, if you refuse to work sensibly?"

The Queen of Wands, Amferna, spoke up. "We're tired of doing this mucky work. After all, we are Queens." She called over to the two passive Queens, Soyla and Fluvia, who were trying to finish their clay models. "We're going on strike! Are you going to join us or not?"

The Queen of Swords, Phere, actively backed her up. The other two looked doubtful. "We don't want to cause any trouble." Said Fluvia. "We may not be allowed to return to our castles."

"So you're willing to go on with this filthy work, are you?" Phere used her most sarcastic tone. "Well, take that!"

Phere threw a large lump of clay at Fluvia that hit her square on the head. She toppled and fell, clutching at the robes of the Terrible Mother, who was watching their outburst in utter astonishment. There was a ripping sound and the Mothers' outer robe of concealment tore in half. With a loud scream, she attempted to cover up, for underneath the robe she was nothing but a jumble of clean picked bones. The bones collapsed slowly, clanking together in a cumbersome heap that gradually sank under the clay. The Terrible Mother was gone. Or was she?

Now I was ready to go to the Path of the Archpriestess, but I was not sure how to leave Binah and find my way, so I climbed the hill to get a better view of my surroundings. Since I had swum in the Sea of Sorrow, everything appeared imprecise. At the brow of the hill, I saw nothing but undulating hills on three sides of me, but to the southwest a luminous stretch of sand, fading from black obsidian through grey to gold beckoned me. I strained my eyes and felt sure I could see a little group of palm trees some way off. Was it an oasis or a mirage? It was hard to tell in the glistening rays of light. I had to go down the hill and find out. I made sure my water bottle was full at a little stream on the way, and set off towards the vast desert that stretched in front of me.

Path of the ARCHPRIESTESS

Coarse sand scrunched underfoot as I made steady progress towards the palm trees. They became more real every moment. I could see black tents pitched under them and a herd of camels by the water hole, tended by a man in a purple robe. In a couple of hours, I reached the oasis and found shade under the palms, where I sat down and drank from my water bottle. A camel brayed somewhere, and the man looked my way and then started towards me. As he came closer, I recognized him and the camel that was following. It was my friend Tabansi, and my camel Lemig was close behind, snuffling my scent on the breeze.

Overjoyed, we embraced and Lemig came up to me, pushing his nose into my hand and begging to be petted, his long eyelashes fluttering winsomely. Tabansi looked well, and had obviously never returned to drinking. I enquired after his mother, Ediug the crone. He told me she was well and had recently won a medal for downhill skiing. I was astonished, since she was.....how old? Tabansi laughed and said she was an expert shape shifter, and had simply taken on the appearance of an Olympic ski racer because she fancied the idea.

"Where have you come from?" I asked Tabansi. "It seems synchronous that you would be here with Lemig, when I need a mount to cross the great desert to the Path of the Archpriestess."

"It is not chance, but good planning." Tabansi insisted. "I have been with you many times during your journey, and I have committed myself to your welfare, since you saved me from a worse fate – the bottle. I estimated the time it would take you to arrive here, from the last time we met, when you had to leave Lemig with the good nuns to recuperate from his fall in the snow. I decided we could be here on time, and Lemig shall be your mount to cross the desert, for no other camel is as faithful as he. The Archpriestess would like to meet him, for she has nothing to sit on, and has heard a great deal of his abilities as a couch. I will not be able to accompany you, as I have my own fleet of camels now, and I have built up a large trade in solar panels, which are much in demand around these desert regions. Here, you will need this." He handed me a passport and Lemigs' rein, reminding me to make sure he drank enough water, for the trip across the great desert to the Archpriestess might take several days.

I said goodbye to Tabansi sadly, for I knew in my heart I would not see him again, since Lemigs' future lay with the Archpriestess. After a good night's sleep, I loaded Lemig with a comfortable saddle and some provisions for the journey, which included hearing aids, sunglasses and a foghorn. I had heard rumors that the desert journey played havoc with a persons' five physical senses, and that I would lose my senses one by one, beginning with the sense of speech. My sixth sense – Intuition - and my camel were the only guides I would eventually have. We both drank at the water hole and I filled a leather bag with water. It was still early in the morning when we set off, and although the sun quickly became hot, I enjoyed the vast desert scene where low, tufty bushes and straggly trees grew randomly amongst the boulders. From time to time distant groups of palm trees emerged and the glint of water shimmered on the horizon, but the mirage would vanish as we moved along. My eyesight began to get blurry, so I rubbed my eyes, thinking that sand had gotten into them, but my sight remained dim, so I put on the sunglasses. I was thankful that I could rely on Lemigs' clear eyes and steady padding across the sands.

We passed shepherds with flocks of sheep and, far off, I distinctly saw a caravan of some thirty camels heading towards the oasis we had left. The first night we slept close to a group of trees, where a small pool of water quenched our thirst. The next day we reached some giant sandstone mountains, cut into strange shapes by the incessant wind that blew in our faces. I found it strange that the wind made no sound as we sought shelter in a narrow cleft between the towering rocks. Was my hearing fading as well as my sight? We followed a winding sandy path in through the reddish rocks, coming to some ancient petroglyphs scraped into the rock face. I studied them, screwing up my blurry eyes with difficulty and attempting to decipher their symbolic meaning, but my sight was so bad it was hopeless.

Turning the next corner, we found ourselves in front of a beautiful building carved out of the rock face, and I knew we had reached the "rose red city, half as old as time" that was held in the memory of earlier ages. Feeling I was going back in time, that night I slept inside a tomb cut into one of the many mounds outside the city, Lemig keeping guard outside. Mysterious dreams troubled me, and I fancied I saw a man with the head of a hawk beckoning. I was boarding a boat moored by a dock, and before us was a wide bay with headlands that left a narrow entrance out to the open sea beyond.

I woke strangely disturbed, but I thought it was probably the desert atmosphere. Lemig had left a steaming turd outside the tomb, but I could not smell anything. I groped for the saddle as he knelt in front of me and mounted him with difficulty. We moved slowly on. It was becoming hard for me to breathe, my breath coming in short gasps and long exhalations. My tongue felt like a dead clam in my mouth. It was hard, even, to hold onto the camels' shaggy mane, my fingers felt numb and clouds of sparks flickered in my inner sight. Powerless to prevent it, I felt my whole body slumping to one side as Lemigs' pace increased to a fast lope. I remembered no more......

White, red and black flashes passed in front of my eyes. I opened them to a row of bead sellers sitting in front of a wide river, with a hempen tightrope strung across it. One of the bead sellers displayed a row of short, red sticks laid on a white cloth.

"Buy my obolus, buy my obolus," He chanted, and I felt curiously drawn to him. Of course, I didn't have any money, so I offered to barter something useful to him. He told me that I needed the obolus to hand to the puppet of the Archpriestess, for only in that way could I gain entrance to her chamber. I couldn't offer Lemig, for he was already promised to her. The bead seller said he would take my body energy instead, for it was essential for me to have an obolus. That was not so hard, as I already felt separated from that energy, which had dragged on me increasingly towards the end of my journey, so I pulled on the silver cord attached to my solar plexus and handed over the small package to him, selecting a fine obolus in exchange. With the stick in my hand, I led Lemig forward. The tightrope did not look very safe, but I spotted a small boat pulled out on the rivers' bank with a surly boatman sitting by it. I offered him the obolus, but he shook his head, scowling at me.

"I can't accept your obolus, I'm afraid. I will take the camel, but you must cross on the tightrope. The Archpriestess ordered that when you arrived I wasn't to make it easy for you. I'll deliver the camel safely to her, though." He sniffed lugubriously. "Let's load him into the boat."

It was a tight fit, and poor Lemig had to crouch down to keep the boat on an even keel. The boatman grumbled a lot and I felt desperate at the thought of losing my camel. Why, the little boat might capsize in the rushing waters and Lemig would drown! The boatman cut short my concerns by pointing silently to the tightrope and pushing off with one oar. I watched as the river caught the boat and whisked it downstream, with Lemigs' head peering over the bow and the boatman manipulating the oars with surprising skill.

I turned to the tightrope, clutching the obolus in one hand, and gingerly set forth, one foot at a time, my toes instinctively curling around the thick hemp rope. It was now that I noticed my senses had returned to me, but in a vastly heightened state. It was truly amazing! I could see further; turn my head far around; hear every tiny sound; and feel every inch of the hemp cable I walked on with the soles of my numerous sucker feet. I moved forward stealthily, my antenna waving to-and-fro, discerning every slight irregularity in the rope, my long back humping up and down. I clung to the rope with my sucker feet as the wide river rushed by underneath me, water boiling as the rapids ran between boulders below, while surging waves constantly jostled each other aside. Out of the corner of my sharpened eye, the boat with Lemig swung far out across the surging water, heading in the same direction as me, but swept downstream by the powerful current.

I couldn't see the farther bank, but I sensed with my heightened awareness that I must be half way across, when two golden swallows, carrying a voluminous yellow veil in their beaks, dived towards me in a sudden attack that nearly knocked me off the tightrope. I shrank back, attempting to hide under the rope, for I was a tasty morsel, the veil brushing my face as they flew by. The little birds were determined, however, and although they missed me at their first pass, they turned and approached me again at great speed. This time, the veil caught me, and in a second the flimsy material was wrapped around me, pinning me tightly in a fetal position, my head near my feet. I staggered, lost my balance, and fell, the veil catching around the tightrope, leaving me swinging upside down sixty feet above the roiling river like a mummy, afraid that the veil would tear and drop me into the water, where I would surely drown. Where was my Guide, I prayed, as the two little birds flew away, abandoning me in my desperate position over the rushing water.

The drone of a small medivac helicopter approached and the little machine made a quick pass overhead. Seeing my plight, they lowered a man on a rope. As he came level with me, I was surprised to see that he was quite old, as they normally used younger people for rescue work. But as soon as he spoke, I knew it was my Guide! He got a bridle around my cocoon and we were hoisted into the helicopter, which revved its engines and made fast time towards the far bank of the river. My Guide alighted from the helicopter, and within minutes my cocoon was lowered onto a stretcher. I hoped that someone would help me get rid of the suffocating fabric, for although I could move my head a little, my body was pinned by the tightly fitting veil. Barely able to see through the veil, I pleaded in a muffled voice.

"Help me out of here! It's really uncomfortable I'm hungry – do you have a nice angora sweater I could eat?"

The old fellow smiled. "In a minute. You are cocooned for a reason. Those swallows are a nuisance, I know. They guard the Archpriestess, for she always hides behind a veil. But sometimes they are over zealous, and when they see anyone approaching, they want to stop them from coming near her, and many people have been lost in the raging river because of those pesky birds. However, I was watching for you because you are in grave danger up here, high on the Tree of Life, and only great courage and careful discrimination can see you through." He laughed. "Instead of complaining, you ought to be grateful the birds didn't knock you off into the river, which is so cold it would freeze your bones in a second. Instead, they wrapped you in a cocoon, which saved you. You may not be aware that you are a caterpillar, and that's why you have to wait a while before we try to unwrap you, otherwise you may emerge without wings."

Struggling to speak, I mumbled. "So, am I going to become a butterfly? That would be fun! How long will it take? I could use a meal – say, a woolen glove or two."

"I'm sorry. You are going to emerge as a clothes moth. That is why you are hungry for wool. You are in a cocoon, not in a chrysalis, which is an object of gold, and transformation within it is only allowed for the chosen few. The moth state is good enough for you, since you will be coming through here again many times. You have not yet experienced all the twelve disciplines. Your present incarnation is not your last, by any means. Never mind, I will be with you again and again." His words reassured me. "Go to sleep, now, and the conversion process will go by quickly."

Some days must have passed, although, of course, one did not measure Time on this level, a fact I found hard to adjust to. My cocoon gradually grew looser and one day I emerged, wobbling slackly on my six legs and spreading my tiny wings out to dry. My Guide brought me a meal of mink coat, which I greedily began to eat.

He plucked the coat from under me and I flew up into the air, fluttering my frail wings. "Hold on, there! This is for your caterpillars. As a moth, you don't eat any more. Hurry up and lay your eggs on this coat for the next generation."

No more food! How long was I supposed to last before I starved to death? My outraged thoughts were soon answered.

"You will probably only survive for a couple of days as a moth, for you will find a flame. In that moment, you will return to what you believe is your former shape. When that happens, we can proceed."

Within a few days, I had found a mate and laid my eggs on the mink coat. I passed away quickly without being burnt, and regained my previous form, and my Guide told me to watch out for the puppet.

"The puppet? What puppet?" I looked alarmed. "I know all about puppets. After all, I've gotten rid of a large number of them. Who controls this puppet? Who's pulling the strings?"

"All right, take it easy. There is only one puppet, but it is a mean manikin – a sour and frustrated puppet, and it belongs to the Archpriestess. She likes to play with it and make up stories, and then together they enact the stories on the scroll that unrolls below her – the scroll of constant conflict. You will see it when you reach her anteroom, and remember, it is rare to catch a glimpse of her, for even if those swallows have taken one of the veils, she has many more of them in all different colors, like a peacocks' tail. The puppet was once a Magian, and through necromancy he forfeited the rights to his elevated position. He was forced to become the plaything of the Archpriestess, and he is not happy with his demotion."

My Guide walked with me towards a large building, which hovered in the swirling mists that surrounded this side of the river. "This is the customs house. You must show your passport. It is here you will be interviewed before you are allowed to cross the border into the Path proper. There will then be further interviews with the Society of Enochian Anchorites, who decide your future course." The old man pursed his lips, "Yes, so it will be."

He led the way through a series of barriers manned by altered creatures, some of which had the heads of lions and the tails of serpents; while others were birds that hopped on frogs' legs; and a third was a fish with human legs. I displayed my passport to all of them and each one stamped it and sealed it with a wax seal depicting the head of a commanding woman.

"These are creatures who couldn't decide what they wanted to be." The old man said. "They vacillated for too long and, sadly, ended up neither fish nor fowl. Since one has to follow strict rules to be born in Malkuth, they were unable to manifest on that level, for they would have been laughed at and shunned. They are, therefore, put to work here until they make up their minds."

We passed through the customs house. The creatures patted me down, searching for any sign of contraband, their pawing hands fondling my figure. I showed my obolus to them, which made it easier, as they seemed to respect the red stick, and I had no luggage for them to search through. Outside, my Guide bid me goodbye. "I will stand by, watching, but I cannot be with you all the time. You must face the puppet alone. I will see you later on."

"Wait! I have one important question before you go." I waved to attract his attention, and he turned back. "Everyone here is presumed dead, at least, they are wraiths with no bodies. I can't help wondering – what is the meaning of death? Why are we all here?"

"I can assure you nothing in the universe is wasted, likewise, although death seems to be the waste of a life, even if the person was creative, intelligent or sensitive to the needs of others, they all die with a greater purpose than when they lived."

"What do you mean? How could they have a greater purpose than their life purpose?"

"Their death purpose was written on the blueprint of their Destiny. Some of them, for example, may die in a plane crash. The result of their sacrifice is that the wreckage is carefully analyzed by the officials, so that they learn what happened. They can then make adjustments to ensure that it will not happen again, thereby saving the lives of many others. It is the same rule that applies to a person who is battling cancer. Through the treatments they agree to endure, much is learned about the disease, and if they die in spite of it, they have, nevertheless, advanced their karma. Many cancer sufferers will benefit from their sacrifice, and eventually a cure will be found." The old fellow nodded to himself. "So you can say that each death is as noble as any life might be."

"That's a great philosophy." It was clear to me. "Thank you for explaining death's mystery. I'll remember that." I bid him goodbye cheerfully.

The old fellow stayed behind as I set off, still holding my obolus, towards the august chambers of the Archpriestess.

Everything in the Passage of the Archpriestess was fluid, hovering in the air – not anchored on firm ground. Above me, hundreds of peacock eyes wavered in the sky, their iridescent colors sparkling in the darkness. Stark against the sky, a brilliant green carpet edged with gold trim floated by, pedaled by a small Pekinese dog. The carpet moved slowly away, vanishing behind a veil, and then reappeared, this time carrying a puppet that swung from it by a set of strings.

I took one look at the puppet and my knees gave way under me. It was Krackenwergle, my trickster friend and the Magian I had just visited! What could have happened to bring him to this state? Surely he hadn't fallen foul of the Archpriestess in such a short time? Then I recalled that time here was meaningless, and how I had passed by the Fortress of Time, where my Guide had explained the true meaning of time. Time was not measured here in the same way as it was on earth.

The carpet slid to a stop and the trickster puppet stiffly unhooked itself and got down. He didn't really land on the ground, for we were both suspended in mid air, and I found I could easily maneuver around him, which I did to keep some distance between us. But he was too quick for me and rapidly intruded into my space, his face close up to mine and his hot breath scorching my nostrils.

"So! You are finally here. Well done, indeed – I don't think! It's because of you that I'm in this fix now. It's your fault!" He snarled at me. "If you and that maniac Festerbash hadn't ruined my ceremony – the ritual for charging the four Magical Weapons with energy – I would be a free Magian at this moment instead of a stuck puppet." His voice rose to a frenzy as he ground his sharp teeth at me. "A curse on you! I'll rid myself of you and your meddling ways....."

He broke off abruptly and leapt at me, his teeth bared and his long fingers with their sharpened nails ripping at the remainder of my clothing, reaching for my neck. I fell backwards, clutching at thin air, feeling his knotted fingers closing on my throat. Putting up my hands, I tore at his wrists to try to free myself. I could feel his grip tightening and cutting off my air supply. Gasping for breath, my windpipe bent and cracked under the strain and my eyes bulged almost out of their sockets. Desperately I freed a hand and reached into my pocket for the magic matches that Eeleye Fastlever, the penguin, had given me. Striking a match, I put the tiny flame to his loose pants, and they flared up in a great burst of fire.

The puppet Krackenwergen gave a hollow scream and relaxed his grip on my bruised throat, trying to beat out the flames that were quickly gaining hold, as he was made of wood and flammable glue. It was too late. He exploded in a blazing pyre and was quickly consumed, his ashes falling down like feathers through the air, to settle on the mysterious scroll below.

A thin wail rose from the scroll, and a three-dimensional picture formed itself on the surface of the rough sea. Floating on this sea were many different craft, from coracles to Spanish men-of-war, destroyers, aircraft carriers and nuclear submarines. Overhead flew several different planes – bombers, dirigibles and rocket firing drones, and they were all engaged in a fierce combat, with smoke pouring from their cannon and puffs of flak filling the air around the bombers.

I was mesmerized by the sight of this fierce battle, when a voice spoke in my ear. "You see, now, how the Scroll of the Law operates – a tooth for a tooth, as it were – and how conflict never ceases on the plane of manifestation." My Guide stood close by, his hand on my shoulder. "Yet it is this conflict that moves the world towards excellence, for every battle that is fought and resolved becomes the springboard for new ideas, new behavior and new actions. In this way, the Universe completes its goal – the goal of perfection in everything. Would that we could reach it today, but that is not to be." He sighed, handing me my obolus, which I had dropped during the struggle. "But it will come, it will come."

Feeling weak after my combat with the puppet, my Guide took pity on me and summoned his little hut, where I was able to rest. He put cold compresses on my throat to ease the bruising, and in a few days, as I measured time, I was able to swallow again.

"Now that you are recovered, it is time for you to meet the Archpriestess. You will hand her your obolus, which, if you recall, was the object you exchanged for your life energy. In return, she will stamp your passport with her seal, and you will be allowed to come before the Society of Enochian Anchorites in their boardroom." He floated in front of me, leading me through an intricate corridor between the shimmering peacock eyes, to a staircase bounded on each side by two great pillars, the left one black with a scrolled Doric capital, and the other white, surmounted by an Ionic design. We mounted the stairway to a golden door, emblazoned with designs of cosmic dimensions, and I tapped on it with my obolus.

"Enter!" Came a commanding female voice. I pushed open the door, to find myself surrounded by a myriad of hovering veils of every different color that emerged from the peacock eyes as an eternal woven web of lights. Beyond that, I could see nothing as I felt my way forward in the direction of the voice.

"Wrong way. Over here." The voice of the Archpriestess became gentler. I turned towards the sound, feeling sure I would soon come face to face with her, but again the voice, chiding a little, now explained. "Not that way! I am more to your left. Turn a little, now."

Her voice grew softer. "You may give me your obolus now."

"Where are you? I can't see you." I was peering around me nervously. "I want to make sure you accept my obolus. It's very important."

"Don't worry about that. Just let go of it, let go, and it will find its own way to me. Then I will stamp your passport." She sighed. "It is so hard for people to let go up here. They don't understand that it is for their own good, and that they must interview with the Enochians before they reincarnate." She gave a little gasp of relief. "Ah! I have it in my hand now. My! It is a powerful stick! It is vibrating even as I hold it to my bosom." She gave a little laugh. "By the way, I just wanted to tell you that your camel Lemig makes a very comfortable couch. He sends his best regards."

"Could I see him one more time?" I begged her, almost in tears. "He has meant so much to me on my life path."

"No, I'm sorry, but that is no longer possible. You are now a wraith, a ghost of your former self. Your old life is over, finished with. You have to let go of the camel, along with everything else. Do not worry, I will appreciate Lemig and he will stay with me always. Now, leave me and go to the boardroom, where the Enochians await you."

I turned and, tears pouring down my face, groped my way towards the door and passed through it, drifting towards a sign that said "To the Boardroom of the Society of Enochian Anchorites of the Mystic SEA."

Moving in the direction of the sign, I heard the sound of many voices echoing in the stratosphere, and I soon passed through a set of iron gates emblazoned with the sign of the Zodiac into a long corridor, whose end was not visible. On each side were immense cubicles, each with a Zodiacal sign over them – Aries, Taurus, Gemini, and so on. Many wraiths were milling around in each cubicle, moaning and chattering in confusion, reaching out their arms to me with indignant howls, yet bound by an invisible wall that held them. Guards who resembled the half-breeds I had encountered at the customs were patrolling up and down the endless corridor, now and again taking a wraith from one of the cubicles and ushering the poor creature up the corridor towards an opening in the ceiling, from which the bottom of a steep ladder protruded. There they were poked and prodded until they reluctantly climbed the ladder and disappeared into the space above.

A guard approached me and asked to see my passport. I handed it over and he seemed satisfied, so I ventured to ask him a question. "Why are these wraiths categorized into cubicles? They don't seem very satisfied with the arrangement."

"Each cubicle holds those who have just completed their lives in that particular sign of the Zodiac. They have never been content with their lot on earth, and now it is over - whether they expected it, or not. Of course, since they did not become perfect, they must continue to learn new lessons by being born into a different astrological sign, whichever the Society thinks will benefit them the most. Each wraith must pass before the Enochians, who will decide and map out the Destiny for their next reincarnation, and then give them a blueprint to follow when they are reborn. But people are rarely happy with these arrangements, and have a habit of forgetting them as they travel down the birth canal, thus arriving in the earthly world with no idea of what happens next. It is only those who are far advanced that can recall their Destiny, and follow it while they grow up in Malkuth."

"That's very interesting. I appear to be a wraith myself, although I feel perfectly normal – whatever normal means on this level." Pausing, I heard a loud crying from the Virgo cubicle, and walked over to find two small chipmunk wraiths arguing, while a third wept copiously, spattering tears over the nearby wraiths that glared and brushed them off brusquely.

"What's the matter?" I asked the chipmunks, as the guard looked on. "Tell me about it. I met you before, you know."

"We had a house on Chuckernut Drive and it was foreclosed on." Sobbed the wraiths. "The Old Oak Bank refused to loan us any more nuts. The trees were bare, as winter had set in, and we had not bothered to save any nuts for the lean times. We blamed each other, but in the end we decided to commit suicide together. We waited days for the right car, practicing by darting across the road at precisely the right moment. Finally a Rolls Royce, driven by a very old lady, came around the corner. We chose the moment, and ran, three abreast, under the front wheels. You would have thought that was the end, but when we arrived here, we found the old lady, also born in Virgo, in the cubicle with us. She had died of a heart attack when she saw what happened to us. Furthermore, all the wheel nuts came off the Rolls Royce and it crashed over the bank into the sea. This superior car was also born under the sign of Virgo, and it is here with us, waiting to be interviewed. We are feeling very uncomfortable in this position. We are responsible for the old lady's heart attack and the wreck of the car." The little chipmunk wraith gulped and wiped away a tear. "We can't escape our feelings of guilt."

"That's why suicide isn't a good option." I said. "It always affects someone else. Since we're all bound together as molecules, people, chipmunks and cars, our vibrations are entwined, and cannot be separated."

The guard nodded and took my arm, leading me to the Libra cubicle. There I found a giraffe, a skyscraper and a Cistercian monk, all born under the sign of Libra, and we set up a brisk conversation.

A few days – such as no time was – passed and I had mingled with numerous other Librans, including a whale shark, a pork pie, and a bicycle with the same sign as myself. They wondered whether they had a chance of becoming human. I told them I didn't recommend it. Too complicated, I said.

The pork pie sighed. "It has to be better than being eaten. Why, I was scarcely out of the oven when a drunken sot in the Pub spotted me and ordered me - with piccalilli, if you please! I hadn't even time to cool before I was struck by a set of teeth the size of a horse and immolated! What sort of a life is that, I ask you?"

"Sometimes a short life is good. You had no time to go moldy or stale. You probably got rid of a lot of bad karma. Being eaten is one of the best ways to advance cosmically."

The pork pie cheered up. "That's good. Maybe I'll try being a sausage roll next, then. Stay in the same Pub, you know, because I'm familiar with the boozers there. It's a little place up on the Isle of Iona. Ever been there?"

"My goodness! Yes, I have. What a wonderful reception I got from the locals. Free beer, and all that. They were warning me not to go over to Hughs' temple, for fear of the monsters. Of course, I listened, but it was my Destiny, and together with my shadow, the Hoodwinker, I vanquished them."

The pork pie nearly burst with excitement. "That's amazing! My aunt, a Cornish pasty, was eaten by Hugh. She was shipped over to his temple with a load of stores, and could not escape. He never came to the Pub – a strange guy, he was."

"Yes, he had his problems. Personally, I would shoot for a quiet life for you, back in that Pub, where the surroundings are familiar and you don't have to deal with rude people from the big cities. Why don't you try reincarnating as a Scotch egg? That would make your life even shorter." We all laughed as the guard came to the cubicle and beckoned to me.

"Your turn next, sea wanderer, or whatever you call yourself. Up the ladder, now."

The vast room at the top of the ladder in which I found myself was flanked on one side by a curved table of the finest marble. Sitting on the far side of the table, each isolated in a small dark cubicle, were nine strange figures writing busily on parchment scrolls in front of them, each one having ear trumpets and a microphone attached to their simple tunics of sacking. The strangest thing about them was their heads. Instead of a normal human head, they were elongated into the shape of a telescope, pointing upwards into the starry night above them, for there was no roof to the boardroom. How they managed to write and speak without eyes or a mouth, I could not fathom, so I seated myself in the only chair, facing them in the center of the table.

"The Navigator, I believe?" The voice was no more than an echo that surrounded me, so that it was impossible to tell who had spoken. "We have the details of your most recent life and we have perused this information with care. How do you speak for yourself?"

Well, I didn't know who to address or what to say. I had expected them to give a judgment of my conduct themselves, but they had now put me on the spot. I stammered out a response, immediately going on the defensive.

"Well l l l…. I have made some mistakes. I have, on occasion allowed my better judgment to be clouded by personal interests and survival instincts. There was the time…."

"Stop! We are not interested in excuses." The nebulous voice shattered my line of thought. "We are only concerned with a positive assessment of your life experiences. Kindly speak well of your Self and don't run down your dying personality in the sign of Libra. The balance always causes problems for Librans, since they can always see both sides of a situation. We want your truth – if you had to be ruthless, unreliable or vacillating, remember that is the fault of Belvedere, your Ego, not of your Self, who we are judging here."

Opening my mouth to reply, a sudden scuffle attracted my attention at the head of the ladder. Someone was trying to force their way up into the boardroom. I felt resentful. It was not their turn! My emotions, which I was convinced were under control after my long journey, suddenly flared up again. I fought to keep the surging fear that had always undermined me from surfacing. After all, the interloper, who was now struggling with the guards and shrieking loudly, was nothing to do with me, but I had come this far and waited for my turn to be interviewed patiently. Now the Enochians were distracted and looked up, breaking off their focus on me. As the intruder was forced down the ladder again by two guards, I gritted my teeth and tried to stay calm, putting on a bland expression for the benefit of the Enochians, who now turned back towards me, their telescopes wobbling unsteadily above their shoulders.

"We observe through your vibrations, to which we are sensitive, that you are in a state of volatile pathos, and you are attempting to cover it up." A pause ensued, followed by a polite cough. "Under the circumstances, we feel it would be better to curtail this interview and send you back to the Libran cubicle until you have reasserted your higher Self. We regret to say that your ego, Sir Belvedere, as you call him, is standing right behind you, visible to all of us."

"No!" I yelled in desperation. "Please don't send me away! Please continue the interview – I'll banish Belvedere with all my might – give me another chance, I beg you!" I was on my knees, weeping and crying out to them, as a feeling of incredible dread suffused me. What was I to do? I felt completely powerless and insignificant. I slumped forward onto the floor under the marble table and broke into hysterical screams, which took over my body as if an evil wind had blown through the room.

After a while I lay exhausted, hearing the scraping of chairs. Were the Enochians leaving? A long silence descended on the boardroom. I crawled out from under the table and looked up. The nine strange figures were all sitting quietly in their cubicles, and they spoke with one voice.

"Resume your seat, please. This was a test. We had to find out whether you were truly committed to the Way of Return, or not. By introducing a diversion with the intruder, we now know that you are connected most deeply with your inner suffering, although on occasion you try to mask it by bravado. We have the blueprint for your Destiny in your next life right here. It has been ready for you for Aeons, for your deeds and misdeeds are registered in the Infinite Library of the Akashic records immediately they occur, which we study on a regular daily basis. Come forward and take your blueprint. And congratulations......." Their chairs shifted slightly as the bodiless voice ceased and I stepped forward. A somber owl flew down and gave me the blueprint, which I tucked into my tunic. I bowed deeply, thanking them, and was ushered through a door on the opposite wall and down a ladder, the last rung of which hung over deep space. I jumped off......

Island of CHOCKMAH

I landed with a tremendous splash in the Sea of Sorrow. Swimming against the current, I observed that I was not alone. An all too familiar figure had joined me, her bedraggled cape floating behind her, and her hood pressed tight against her face. The Hoodwinker swam amazingly well, with swift, short strokes, keeping pace with me, and from time to time, casting a mystifying glance towards me. We passed many limp and lifeless bodies that floated obscenely by, all heading in the direction of the Archpriestess. Certain wraiths must have left their bodies behind, overcome by the intense feelings of anguish and despair they had encountered. They were people who had, in fact, successfully passed through the narrow defile on their Chariots without being petrified on its walls, but, on entering the Sea, had been unable to withstand the truth that all those they loved would eventually perish and, in fact, that the life of planet Earth itself would inevitably end. The feelings of those who fought for the environment on earth and ecological change were invalidated, as they finally understood their fight to save the planet was merely in their own human interests.

Yet as I swam against the current in the opposite direction, heading for the Island of Chockmah, I knew that those transient events were directed by the eternal Cosmos, and its deep caring and compassion for the creatures it had birthed. This gave me hope, and through these beliefs I was able to have faith in an unknowable future.

Exhausted from fighting the current, I trod water from time to time, but that swept me back, and so I lost ground. I had to keep going, or drown and give up my wraith, which I had just rescued from the Enochians after much trouble. I gritted my teeth and swam on until the tips of grey peaks ahead of me signaled my approach to the Island of Chockmah. Keeping up a steady breast stroke, the Hoodwinker dropped behind and I lost sight of her. The peculiar mountains that made up the island grew closer. Each peak was separate from its neighbors and rose up steeply to great heights, possibly ten thousand feet, without any connection or visible support from those beside it. From one peak to another, fluctuating lines of force like neurons in a giant brain shot out and made a confusing zigzag pattern that obscured any clear view of the Island.

Landing on an unknown shore, I had to swim over several creeks and a lake, for the path was along tidal flats and became boggy as I reached the Island of Chockmah. As I pulled myself wearily from the dark waters, not expecting assault from any quarter, I was stunned by a thud against my chest as a random line of force deviated from its track and struck me. I fell back into the shallows, flailing my arms and struggling for breath. Getting to my feet, I attempted to step forward again, but a stinging strike on my right arm left me gasping. I had to find safety on this Island, so I confronted the rapidly striking lines of force with determination and, after a considerable battering, during which I felt an army of archers was shooting at me with longbows, I managed to conceal myself in a small dry cave above the high water mark. Finding a heap of dried seaweed, I fell to my knees thankfully, massaging my bruised limbs. Then, curling up on the makeshift bed, I gave in to the sleep I craved.

The morning broke with a pale, luminous light filtering behind the grey peaks. It was not the sun, but something more subtle, and the soft blues and pearl grays soothed my heart. After drinking at a small stream and eating some moss, I set out on a winding path through the mountains, which rose abruptly to stunning heights on each side. Soon I came to a large square, divided into smaller squares with strange words written in each square, bounded on each side by numerous rows of tubes, while from a massive rock in the center of this square ghostly filaments of light flared out continuously and disappeared down the tubes. I approached the rock cautiously, and found that these lines or flares passed right through me without hurting, reminding me that I was a wraith. They were much softer than the lines of force I had battled with on my arrival at the Island.

I came closer to the rock and saw that it was roughly shaped into four sides. A statue stood in a deep niche on each side, and I realized with astonishment that they were the four Kings, Compos, Atmos, Jetspur and Cinarburn. Each King stepped down from his plinth and shook my hand as I noticed they all had transportation. King Compos carried a skateboard; Atmos a paraglider; Jetspur had a surfboard and Cinarburn a lavasled. In the background, strains of sweet music arose from the band Abba, one of my favorite groups.

"We are devoted to your cause." Atmos, King of Swords, said quietly. He was the King who stood apart, the studious professor and the least accessible. I felt privileged to be received by them, for they were the four Fires, of Earth, of Air, of Water and of Fire itself. They looked far more splendid than at their castles, for each King wore his finest regalia, sparkling with every jewel in the crown of heaven, and the sight almost blinded me.

Cinarburn, King of Wands, next stepped forward, with a sly glance at me and a wink. "I'm very pleased to see you again," he purred, pinching my arm. "I hope we can experience another explosion together."

I couldn't help grinning to myself at his remark as Compos, King of Pentacles, lumbered over, slapping me on the back. "Seen any good boars lately? The hunting up here is exceedingly meager. They haven't invented animals yet – that happens over in Binah. So we have to hunt each other – play tag, you know – it's a good exercise but not much fun. One can't get the thrill of downing a decent boar, and I feel really bereft."

I commiserated with him and turned to Jetspur, King of Cups, the last to greet me, who looked a little embarrassed, for he remembered that I had caught him with Anahita at the bottom of her pool. He smiled cautiously. "I felt your sorrow as you traversed the Great Sea recently. Pour your sadness into my Cup, and I will turn it into light." He stooped and gave me a hug.

We all walked over to the edge of the square. Everything here was visible only through straight lines, and these lines moved constantly in front of my eyes, as if searching for a point on which to rest, for nothing was, as yet, fixed. Some lines seemed to form themselves around abstract shapes, yet the shapes themselves did not yet exist. The Kings explained that the triangle – the primary shape created by joined lines - had not yet been invented. It was up to the workers in Binah to form that idea. We stood at the edge of a precipice, gazing down on rolling clouds, and as we looked, the clouds shaped themselves into a great city, surrounded by ruined temples of every kind, their roofs collapsing and the statues lining the narrow tracks between them in a state of destruction.

"What happened here?" I asked in surprise. "It looks as if there's been an earthquake!"

"You'll have to ask the Supernal Father about that." Atmos explained. "He is our liege Lord and rules over us. Although we are permitted to dwell here, we are merely mundane kings compared to his glory. He has his reasons, you know – he's always busy evolving and revolving ideas in embryo. Personally, I think it's a waste of time, but he wants to get it perfect. For myself, I have studied enough philosophy to know that the world is perfectly imperfect, and that's all there is to it." He sniffed lugubriously.

Atmos had a tendency to be cynical, so I ignored him. I wanted to go down into the ruins and examine them, so I asked if one of the Kings would accompany me. Atmos said he was too busy, as he had to return to his books and complete some important research for a thesis he was writing. King Compos lay down and went to sleep, snoring loudly, while Cinarburn glanced at me so meaningfully I decided I had better not find myself alone with him. I chose Jetspur, the King of Cups, who was the most sympathetic of the four.

Since the lines of force had not yet formed themselves into steps, Jetspur invited me to step onto his surfboard and slide down to the level of the cloud city. The surfboard slid easily, as if it was riding an imaginary wave, and I was able to keep my balance behind the King. We scooted the board along a street flanked by broken statues of lions, each one snapped off above the hindquarters as if by a deliberate hand.

"What were these lions for?" I asked Jetspur. "Where are their heads? The heads must be lying somewhere here, even if they have been broken off."

Jetspur laughed. "The statues were not lions. They were phalluses. In the time before time, the phallus was worshipped as the giver of life, but a sinister and authoritative religion arose that saw the phallus as sinful, and to be despised." Here he paused, and a dark shadow crossed his face. "Iconoclasts came here bent on the destruction of the old, pure religion, which had its roots in Earth nature and its branches in Wisdom. They left the area scorched, and Famine ruled the land. The inhabitants of these times died of starvation, fled, or were made prisoner during the struggle to save their way of life and were carried off by the invaders. They were forced into slavery and their sacred temples were left ruined and deserted."

Sadly we surfed on, leaving the broken statues, which faded into an evanescent mist. Rolling forward on a wave of radiant cloud, we came to another area where the smell of burning wood and flesh polluted the air. On either side, smoldering buildings, their roofs collapsing and their walls crumbling, gave off flickers of fire in the devastation. It was clear that the people who lived here had run away, for there were still upturned pots and charred food on the tables.

"As you can see, there was a terrible war here." Jetspur explained despondently. "A long standing feud between early tribes erupted again, and the enemy tribe laid siege to this city. The siege was long and hard, and they grew impatient to break it, so they used catapults to hurl flaming balls soaked in tar over the walls, and the fire consumed the city, killing most of the people."

I nodded, feeling the horror of those times deep inside me as we maneuvered the surfboard with skill, shortly arriving at a third group of buildings. These were ramshackle huts built of the cheapest materials and leaning perilously on each other, but they were still standing. On each door was a black cross, a warning that disease, its virus carried through the air by foraging rats, had paid an appalling visit to the homestead, and I dared not push open one of the doors for fear of what lay inside, for it must have been the Black Death. I shuddered as we passed dusty mounds of earth marking the mass graves around the edge of the village.

"We are seeing the results of visits by the Four Horsemen of the Apocalypse, aren't we?" I observed. It was hard to believe that on the Island of Chockmah the plagues of Famine, War and Disease had reached so far up on the Tree of Life. I knew, as we moved on, that the next and final scene would be that of Death, and I was right. We came to a place of watery dissolution, where soundless mourning over never-ending gravestones marched to the horizon. "Why, why should these horrible aspects of life intrude into Chockmah?" I asked in despair.

Jetspur put his arm around my shoulders. "My friend, I am the King of Cups, and I represent the Watery element. All emotions run through me. Chockmah is the Island of Wisdom and its title is the Illuminating Intelligence. How could one learn Wisdom without first experiencing emotional and physical suffering?"

I thought back to the many encounters I had been through during my journey on the Way of Return. Jetspur was right. It was only through the question "Why" that one received the answer, and it was necessary to ask "Why?" many times before the true dimensions of karmic justice became clear. The path of the cross was essential, to see the luminosity that lay beyond time and space which we all sought.

"Now the cycles change!" Jetspur commanded, taking his Cup and throwing the contents into the air around us with a sweeping motion. Instantly, the scenes of apocalyptic despair vanished, to be replaced by joyous laughter and brilliant music, as a group of dancing Bacchantes swirled around a great stone circle built in the middle of a cloud plain. Their dresses were woven of the finest thread, and flowed about them in every different shade of pearl, the palest blues, pinks and opalescent colors making up a river of delicate light as they celebrated the power of the massive standing stone in their center. The dynamism of Chockmah was immediately apparent in the instability of opposing energies with this rapid change, and even as I considered joining the dancers, they came to a sudden stop, all looking upwards and pointing at a tiny bright dot in the sky that was fast approaching. I watched as the dot resolved itself into a daring green man surfing with great skill on the tail of a comet that burned in front of him. The Bacchantes formed a large circle and he landed in the center, whereupon they all ran towards him, each trying to be the first, holding out their arms to receive the powerful lines of force that emanated from him. He was dressed in motley, a multi colored T-shirt and swim trunks in a black, white and red pattern.

An invisible musician struck a golden chord that vibrated through the air as the girls swarmed all around him, crying out. "It's the Fool! The Fool!" He laughingly shot sparks amongst them, which they leapt to catch in mid air. "My girls - how I love you!" He cried. "I can't stay long. I'm always on the way to nowhere. Take your chances with me and I'll be back again."

"No! Don't go yet. Stay with us a little longer! Join us in the dance, won't you?" They tried to tighten the circle around him, so that he could not take off again. One of them put her foot on top of the comet, but leapt away with a shriek as the fire burnt through her shoe.

"Ah! Don't get too close, now. You'll get burned. Here." The Fool took an armful of snowflakes from his pocket. "This will cool you down!" As the flakes fell to the ground, they became tiny sparks that darted from one Bacchante to another, tickling them. They all wriggled and laughed and then he was gone, whizzing up into the sky again. We watched until he had vanished.

"Does the Fool come here often?" I asked them.

"All the time. He brings new emanations with him. We are all in love with him." Here the girl who spoke looked sad. "He's married, you know. Has a consort. They don't spend much time together, but they are inseparable cosmically. So there's no hope for us."

"Who is his wife, then? I can't imagine anyone marrying a Fool."

"Well, he is called the Fool, but of course he is the wisest of us all. He is Harlequin, and she is Columbine to his foolery - she takes the serious side. You may have met her already. She is the Archpriestess."

"Oh, yes. I have just come from her Path. I thought she was a spinster. Many priestesses do not marry, but remain virgins. And she acts so serious, I can't see what attracts him to her."

"They are opposites. He is always coming, and she is always going. He creates new forms, and she takes the old forms and disposes of them. Like you, each wraith has to hand her an obolus. It is a gift of their life force. After she has received their obolus, they pass into the boardroom, where they are interviewed by the Enochians. But of course you know all about that."

"Yes, I have passed the interview. I don't know how. There are nine Enochians. They each have separate cubicles and they don't seem to communicate with each other, and therefore, when I heard a voice, I couldn't tell who it was coming from."

"It is like that up here. We are no longer grounded, and live in a state of constant fluctuation. It is very pleasant. But now, it's time for us to escort you to the Supernal Father, who is our great King here." Two of them took my hands and we ran up a grassy knoll, where we came to a tall white pillar with a throne at the top.

"This is the pillar of Joachin that sits at the head of your left side – the Pillar of Mercy. The Pillar of Severity, black Boaz, you saw on the Island of Binah." The girl on my left made clear. "These two pillars are also in the chamber of the Archpriestess, and they are often called the twin pillars of Hercules. For many centuries, people have been looking for the island of Atlantis, which is supposed to lie beyond the Pillars of Hercules. No-one has ever found it, although there are different theories as to its geographic position."

The other girl laughed merrily as she took up the tale. "Of course, we know there never was an island! It is a metaphor. Beyond these two pillars, Boaz and Joachin, lies the real Atlantis, for its very name gives away the secret. Atlantis means "towards the shining lantern." It is a symbol for enlightenment. Each person must travel between the pillars of Severity and Mercy on their Way of Return, striking a balance on the middle pillar, to reach Atlantis. It is the sacred heart that is the center of the City of Jerusalem, where they will remain in the pure light eternally."

"And Hercules is the original Hero!" I added. "The path of humanity is hard, indeed. All those who pass through are truly courageous."

Gazing up the length of the white pillar, I saw an old man with a long silvery white beard elevated on his throne, holding the Rod of Power. He gazed down at me, but I could only see the left side of his face.

"Hi, there you are!" He chortled, getting up and sliding down the pillar with amazing speed. He stood before me, and I shaded my eyes from his splendor, for he wore the Inner Robe of Glory, which no one could gaze upon without being blinded by its rays.

The scintillating King of Chockmah, the Supernal Father, continued. "I'm exhausted with these emanations. The Fool keeps sending them down, and I know he is packed full of them, for he is obliged to receive them from the One Spot, Kether, and when he is overloaded, he has to pass them to me. But I can never decide what to make with them, so I have to send them on to Binah. I heard recently that a couple of burrowing owls formed a shiny red trolley from these forces." He sighed. "How I wish I could ride in a trolley like that! But it is not to be – I am committed to my role of mystical prophet, for Chockmah is the source of all inspiration."

I noticed as he spoke that a large crown hovered over his head. From time to time, he reached for the crown, but it evaded him, and he gave a shrug of frustration. "That's another thing. This darn crown is always floating just above my head! I can't seem to bring it down and wear it like a normal king. My head gets cold, for it's breezy up here with all these clouds."

Just then, a tiny creature peeped out from the Kings' robes. It had a round face with a large, drooping curved nose, more like a dew drop than anything else.

"What is that, Sire?" I indicated the little creature, which retreated inside his robe bashfully.

"Oh! That's my Yod. It's devoted to me and I couldn't do without it. It's very shy, so don't stare at it for too long. Eye contact can make it evaporate, and we don't want that, do we?" He gazed down fondly as the little Yod poked out its head again, and tickled it, at which it shook itself and spattered tiny drops of light down the front of his robe.

"Allow me to take you to the Association of Whizzes near here. All our whizzards are gathered there, gliding around on their vehicles. I expect you saw the skateboards and surfboards the kings use. Well, everyone here has to move at great speed, and they all have different methods of doing that. This is the birthplace of the ideas for downhill skiing, bungey jumping and even for the circus clown who is shot out of a cannon! Yes, the only problem is, they all have to travel in straight lines, since the curve has not been invented yet. Some idiots say there is no such thing as a straight line. That may be true on Earth, which is a curved ball in the sky, but I can assure you we have straight lines here."

"What about slalom skiers, Sire? They must race through the gates down a curved course." I pointed out.

"Ah! I'm afraid that is outside our comprehension." The King replied, as we drifted along. "Those decisions are made on the Island of Binah, for when they begin to take the forces of Chockmah and create forms, then they have to invent curves, otherwise it would be very difficult to have living things. I suppose they could stick with skyscrapers, though."

We arrived smoothly at a misty space, where dozens of whizzards were scooting from one area to another on their vehicles. A large toboggan pulled up in front of us with a reclining figure on it, swathed in a blanket. A peaked nose peeped out from under it. It was a shock to me – I knew that nose! No, it was not the nose of my trickster, Kracklewergen, for I believed him burnt up, since I had set his puppet on fire recently to save myself, but my intellectual entity.

"Einerline! How can you be here? I last saw you down in Da'ath, you were sitting under the pomegranate tree, and then you showed me the Infinite Library." My heart sank as I moved closer, sensing the pall of death upon him as he attempted to sit up. "You don't look well."

"That's true. I am dying of old age." A faint chuckle came from Einerline as the blanket fell away and revealed his emaciated body. "I am worn out, and it's time to discard my body and take what I have learned forward into my next life. I wanted to pay a last visit to the other whizzards, for I have colluded with them for a long time. I made my own way here, but after we gathered together, I became very sick, and I knew that my time was near. Fortunately, all the Wisdom I have gained has now been passed to the others, and so nothing will be lost, for Chockmah is the repository of Wisdom at all times." He paused, wiping his drooling mouth with the edge of the blanket. "But, how are you, now?"

"I am well. It has been a long journey on the Way of Return, and your help and counsel have sustained me, especially when we managed to raid the Fathers' library!"

Einerline chortled weakly. "My! I remember that! What fun we had. I was able to obtain books that became a source of unparalleled information. All the whizzards have been informed of that now, and can pass it on. Nothing should be hidden, for the age of transparency is close upon us." He sank back on his pillows, coughing. "This darn cough! It must be from

all the dusty books I've worked with over the years. I feel I'm sinking fast."
His eyes closed momentarily - then flicked open. "I'm so glad you arrived
in time. Come closer – I want to see you clearly."

With dread in my heart, for I knew I was going to lose him, I crouched
by the toboggan and took his paper-thin hand in mine. "I am here. All you
have taught me is distilled in my thoughts. Do not fear. I will carry your
Wisdom far and wide, for it came from the hidden vaults of the ancients,
and you revealed it to me."

His eyes were closed, and his breath came in faint gasps. "Lean closer.
I am going….." His hand relaxed in mine, and his eyes opened, gazing at
the splendor of the King, who stood in front of him. He whispered. "I am
blessed…….." With a final gasp, his wraith rose from within the blankets
and made its way towards the Path of the Archpriestess peacefully.

I could not refrain from weeping, although I knew he was in life
eternal and that we would work together again in our future Destiny.
My tears were brief, for I remembered that beyond sorrow there lay a true
understanding of joy, and the King was smiling as I drew a blanket over
the head of my beloved entity Einerline.

The Kings took me to a sumptuous banquet with the associated
whizzards, where we toasted Einerline and spoke of his intelligence and
dedication to the research of ancient manuscripts. We told stories of the
dangerous missions into distant lands which he undertook, and how hard
it was to distract him from his life purpose. When the celebration of his
life was over, we laid his body high on a hill, where the forces would take
it and mould it once more into an earthly body that he could inhabit. I
almost envied him, but felt it was not yet my time

The following day – of course, there was no real day or night up in
Chockmah, but somehow I had to keep track of time – the four Kings took
me to the round coliseum that contained the circle of the Zodiac.

The first comment I made was about the round building that contained
the wheel of the Zodiac. In an environment that contained only straight
lines of force, which had not even formed the simplest triangle or curve,
how could a circle exist? The King of Pentacles, Compos, explained that,
once the Fool had discovered DNA, he had to find a place to put it, and
he searched for years and years through the Universe to find a straight
place for it, but all the planets that inhabited the Universe were round,
and even the asteroids had curves. Finally, fed up with looking, he picked

a round blue planet that took the DNA gladly and appeared eager to use it. Then the problem arose, that all the creatures that caught on to this wonderful idea wanted to be born at once, and in the beginning that was very confusing, because there would be a plethora of births, and then, after those life forms had died off, a vacancy of forms would occur. So he decided to make a round circle that would look like the Earth planet, and divide it into 12 segments, to which he would give different names and symbolic meanings. The only one to object to this arrangement was the Moon, who wanted 13 segments, but she was over-ruled and has been sulking ever since.

King Atmos continued, explaining that when the round circle with 12 segments was made, the Fool divided all the creatures that wanted to be born on Earth into 12 categories, so that they could be born in sequence and inhabit the Earth together. Some would be born early, and some later, so that they overlapped, and that made them feel more comfortable. He called the 12 segments "disciplines", because in each one the creatures that were born according to the position of their stars had special attributes, so that each birth enabled the creature to work with those astrological attributes to overcome past karma, which they had built up by eating each other. Eating is a bad thing, since it involves immolating other living beings, such as cows, chickens and lettuces, all of whom resent their sacrifice. But, eating it had to be, because all the creatures on Earth could no longer live without food.

King Jetspur took up the tale next. A fellow came along called the Christ, who collected about him a motley group of peasants, fishermen, and advocates. They trudged around after him, listening to his words, and he called them disciples. You would have thought they might have been called assistants, or maybe followers; possibly fans, or students; maybe hangers-on or groupies, but no, they were called disciples. That is because they represented the 12 disciplines of the Zodiac. Unfortunately, the real meaning of the 12 had been lost, for they were exalted by later scribes and over time it has been assumed they were real people, but there is no proof of that. Furthermore, there is no proof of a real human Christ, but merely the Christ principle itself made simple for the layman by creating an androgynous metaphor, so that people could understand this Truth in a basic way.

When the Kings had explained the Zodiac, I asked King Cinarburn how many times a person might have to reincarnate through the astrological signs. Would it be exactly 12? Or would a person need specific disciplines and therefore go through more then one sign twice? He told me that the astrological signs were very flexible, and that, for example, a person might want to experience his sign, Sagittarius, several times. So, the reincarnations could be infinite, until that person rose beyond the need for reincarnation. That was up to them, and constituted their individual Destiny, for only if they were aware, through Intuition, of their personal bliss and sincerely followed it in a lifetime, would they tend to advance. Otherwise, if they were oblivious of what they should be doing during their life, they would not get anywhere.

This was extremely instructive and I thanked the four Kings for their Wisdom and wished them well. The time had come for me to meet the Fool in his Path, so I once more sought out the Sea of Sorrow and entered it, swimming slowly to absorb the real meaning of grief, until I met a pod of orcas, beautiful sea mammals that were highly intelligent, and one of them befriended me.

Path of the FOOL

An orca swam alongside me, making it clear that I should slide onto her back. I grabbed the huge fin that stuck out bravely and, by allowing the animals' speed through the water to wash me on to her broad back, I found a safe seat, my head out of the water, able to see all around me. The pod of orcas made its way rapidly through the Sea of Sorrow, heading in a south westerly direction. All around us stretched the dark sea, the waves churned up by gusts of wind that came from different directions. It would be impossible to sail here, I reckoned.

But that was not the case. A boat hove into view before us – a beautiful racing schooner with all sail set, running before the fluky winds. I watched anxiously, for the boat was running goose winged and in grave danger of gybing, rolling from side to side, with faint snatches of a sea shanty coming from a figure in the cockpit, one foot casually steering on the wheel, while he gulped down a bottle of beer. We got closer, and soon the orca pod was racing alongside the schooner. I got a good look at the skipper......

Of course! It was my vessel, and that was my sailing entity Pompeybou at the helm! I hadn't seen the boat for some time, since I had traveled by different vehicles on my path – a manta ray; a chariot; a camel and many other forms of transportation.

"Hi! Pompeybou! It's me. Look over your starboard quarter – the orcas – I'm riding on the biggest one! Here – on its back by the fin that's sticking out of the water." I waved frantically, our speed, as we overtook the surfing schooner, probably at least 15 knots.

He saw me and jumped up, throwing the bottle of beer down. Quickly he reached for the man overboard pole and heaved it in our direction, but we were past it before it landed, the little flag fluttering bravely in the gale. Pompeybou looked distraught. He had forgotten to make the line on the pole fast to the stanchions, and it disappeared far astern.

"I'm OK!" I shouted. "I'm riding on an orca! Don't worry about me – we're heading for the Path of the Fool. How are you doing?"

It was evident he was making a solo passage, and his competency in handling the schooner rig alone amazed me. He called back. "I'll see you soon. I'll be waiting at the dock for you when you're done."

I didn't know what he meant by "done", and I wasn't sure where the dock was, but I waved agreement as the orcas sped up and swiftly outdistanced him, pulling ahead with powerful tail strokes as they steered through the rising seas, their flippers outstretched. As their speed increased, they began breaching, hurling themselves up and out of the waves as I hung on for dear life. Fortunately, my ride was coming to an end, as I was getting tired and finding it hard to cling to the slippery fin. Ahead of us, a curious multi colored strand of material stretching from the heavens down to an unseen destination twisted and turned, and riding down this spiral on the tail of his comet came the motley Fool.

The orcas swung in towards the Fool and I jumped off. The animal I was riding slid to a stop and remained, lying quietly. There was no apparent ground, but it felt as if I had landed on an enormous trampoline, a trampoline so large that it stretched to both horizons. There was a black and rubbery sensation in my body. The Fool motioned me to hop onto his surfboard, which I did with difficulty, as my legs felt like elastic bands. I grabbed him around the waist as he shot off, making a wide circle towards an enormous air bladder that hung above him in the sky, surrounded by a scattering of stars. Pausing by the bladder, he pulled out a stopper and put his mouth to its neck, drinking in the air as if it were water.

"May I have a drink?" I asked plaintively, for I was thirsty and encrusted with salt after my swift journey.

He handed me the neck of the bladder. "It's not water - but pure oxygen. I live on it. I don't need food, for I'm an airhead, you know. People call me stupid, and even a lunatic, but they have no idea of my potential. In fact, their world would not be populated at all if I didn't direct the coils of DNA to the right places."

"That's all very well." I grumbled. "I can only exist if I have regular food, since I am from the lower worlds, where everyone eats each other. But for now, I think I'll take a swig of that air. Maybe it will restore me." I took a long suck at the neck of the bladder, and it began to deflate quickly.

"Hey! Take it easy! You're only supposed to sip the oxygen, so that it diffuses in your bloodstream evenly. You are a mere mortal, even though you consider yourself an adept now. Pure oxygen is only suitable if you have some terrible lung disease. I don't know what the Swords would say if they saw you using up so much Air."

I dropped the neck, feeling rather giddy. I hung on grimly as the Fool looped about and caught some stars in his right hand. From his left hand, a swirl of snowflakes drifted down towards the earth.

"I make them out of the stars. Every one is unique. Each flake animates the babes that are born in Chockmah. They are desirous of incarnation, and their desire stems from the stars." He chuckled. "They think it's better down there – that they can live out their Destiny, but many of them forget their purpose and become apathetic, leading meaningless lives, seduced by the material goods they find down on Earth. A pity....."

He threw down more handfuls of snowflakes, and as they wafted downwards, I thought of the future bodies they would inherit in Malkuth, and hoped that at least some of them would seek a higher purpose.

The Fool shifted to face backwards on the surfing comet, poising with grace, while the comet continued on its balanced course. "I would like to introduce you to some other fools, for all fools originate from this Path. Some say the fool is divinely inspired, and you have many examples of this in Malkuth. We have built the Hall of Famous Fools – out of straight lines, of course. In the Hall their perfected images, transformed into wackyworks, are displayed, so that we can remember the benefits their humor created for mankind."

"I would like to visit your Hall." I tottered a little on the surfing comet, stretching out my arms to keep my balance as we sped along. "I've heard of Madame Tussauds Waxworks, but not wackyworks. What does that mean?"

"Fools always do wacky things. That's why their images are cast in wacky. It is a different substance, suitable only for our Path." He resumed his position and steered the comet towards a gigantic obelisk, made up of straight lines. It soared into the sky above us, its tip enveloped by consuming fire, and the front of this building was covered by countless small, square windows. We slowed down and entered by a square door in the foot of the building.

Inside the obelisk an elevator stood in a square cage in the middle of the floor, while all around it were mounted numerous wacky figures of fools through the ages, which reached up the walls, each statue resting on a small, straight shelf in the walls. We took the elevator to the top of the building, about 33 floors. At the top, a large bound atlas lay on a lectern, its pages marked with strange hieroglyphic maps. I looked at the maps, but could find no resemblance to my own world. The Fool pointed to a bent, wizened dwarf, very realistically fashioned, that stood at the lectern.

"That is the statue of Atlas, the fool who decided to hold up the world. Alas! The world became heavy with so much folly, and he shrank and shrank, until he remains as he is, at present, in the hope that he may be able to straighten up eventually."

The angled figure wore a jesters' three pointed red cap, with bells hanging from each point, and bells on the tips of his shoes. His costume was in red and gold, scarlet hose with a gold embroidered tunic, and he carried a bauble, or mock scepter. His sightless eyes seemed to mock us as we began to descend. At each statue, on its shelf, the Fool stopped and told a tale of the character. One was named Buffoon, and stood on one leg; another the Juggler, who threw a dozen balls in the air at once; a Wit-cracker came next, interviewing on a TV screen; now there was a Prankster, planning another trick up his sleeve, and finally a Moron, who seemed vaguely familiar to me.

"You can see how important we fools are." My escort explained. "We express wisdom in our folly, and we are the only ones who are allowed to criticize our betters, for we do it in a jocular fashion, and that takes the edge off it. But we walk a fine line, for if we are too bold, we may be whipped or even banished, and if we are too truthful, we may be executed, for no-one likes to hear the real truth about themselves, or to be seriously criticized. We hold up the mirror of projection, so that people can see how they blame others for their own faults. We are not bound to any creed or faith and we have no wish to promote ourselves or gain fame. But we are notorious, and we will be remembered. What is more, they need us in their lives, for without humor and laughter, it would be hard to get through some of the tough aspects of life We are considered pets or mascots, and we are often deformed, ugly, or old. In that way people can look down on us as being inferior. That makes them feel better about themselves. "

"That is a sad truth." I mused. "It is true that people always laugh at a person who is humiliated for some reason. Why is that?"

"People are relieved when someone else is brought down. It wasn't their turn! But when it happens to them, they don't like it. The secret is, to be able to laugh at yourself. Then you are not humiliated, but humbled, and there is a great deal of difference in those two states."

The elevator bumped to a halt and we climbed out, leaving the obelisk behind as we mounted the Fools' comet again. We shot off to the shore where I had originally landed.

"The orca that carried you in also carried another passenger. You didn't see that because he was invisible to you. I hear the groans of the creature, for she must give birth to her burden very soon. You are about to witness a sight that few ever have the opportunity to observe. Be very quiet while the orca gives birth, and don't disturb her."

We pulled up by the side of the orca as she slid her groaning body into the water, her head resting on a flat rock. Along her sleek form strange movements could be seen, as if a living thing was moving inside her. She gradually opened her vast mouth, revealing rows of sharp, backward facing teeth. I leaned forward, looking down her gullet as she grunted once more, her mouth wide and her tongue hanging to one side. From my position I saw a round object, colored indigo blue, thrusting itself up against her natural swallowing reflexes. She groaned again as the thing slid in pulses out of her throat, and two nubile arms came free and caught on to her teeth, pulling the body forward. With a final lunge, a young boy slithered out of her mouth and lay upon the rock, carrying an egg in his left hand.

The Fool stepped forward and raised him up, then sank to his knees, and I did likewise, bowing my head, for I understood that this was Horus, the blue babe, who personified the quintessential spirit. He had emerged from the darkness of the whales' belly.

As I raised my head, the boy looked directly into my eyes. "Do you not recognize me?"

I racked my brains, but I felt sure I had never seen him before, although I knew of him through my study of ancient literature. "Forgive me, Lord, I do not know you." I looked down at the ground, ashamed.

"You have had many conversations with me during your travels on the Way of Return." The boy reminded me. "I am your Guide, your Holy Guardian Angel, and I appeared before you both as an old man and as a crone, Ediug, which, of course, is Guide inverted. You have reached the end of your journey, and it only remains for you to return once more to my Chariot, for you failed twice in your attempts to cross the Sea of Sorrow safely. Now it is time for your third effort to reach the City of Jerusalem, with its twelve gates, which are the twelve disciplines of the Zodiac." He stopped talking suddenly and walked away, raising his finger to his lips in a gesture of silence.

The Fool explained. "He is exhausted after fighting Set, your repressed nature, within the depths of the whale. He must purify himself with Fire and then feed the hawk Horus, his emblem, for this bird flies high in the empyrean of the heavens." He sighed. "He doesn't talk much – only when someone arrives who can have a sensible conversation. But, as your Guide, it is imperative that he works on your behalf. Otherwise, he prefers to remain silent."

"I feel honored that he would consider me a candidate for his knowledge. I am ready to make the final attempt in my Chariot." I banished any doubts from my mind. "I will succeed in crossing the Sea this time, but before I go, I have always wanted to visit Kether." I announced. "You are so close by here. Could we go and see that sphere?"

"By all means. I can take you there right now." The Fool said, speeding up, as over the far southeast horizon a massive ball of white light began to emerge. I shielded my eyes, although the desire to look at Kether was almost overwhelming.

As we drew closer, the air became hotter and hotter, until I felt I was thrust into a burning furnace. The Fool urged us on, sniggering to himself. I began to beg him to slow down. Maybe we should reconsider my request? I tried to protect myself from the intense glow, as the round ball of Kether rose above our horizon, its shattering brilliance more then I could stand.

I clutched at the Fools buttocks, squeezing them hard to attract his attention. "Turn away, turn back." I begged. "I've changed my mind. Kether is too bright! I feel as if I'm shriveling up. Please, please take me away; this is too close for comfort."

The Fool chuckled and slowed down, looping around and surfing away from the blazing globe. I could hear his increasing laughter.

"What's so funny?" I burst out angrily. "You played a trick on me."

"I did exactly what you asked. You said you wanted to see Kether, to get closer. I took you there, as requested." The Fool was smiling. "If you can't take the heat, get out of the kitchen, that's what they say, isn't it? So, don't think of doing something you know nothing about. Get more information about a risky move before you try it."

We were surfing into cooler air now. He continued. "I would like you to meet my little fox terrier. He goes with me everywhere. See, he is over there, balancing on that rocking horse." The Fool pointed to a small, fierce looking black and white dog that moved in rhythm to the steady rocking of a wooden horse. The horse was painted in a natural shade of green and had a saddle cloth with the sign of Pluto embroidered on it in black. Beyond the ever-moving horse, the spiral of DNA led down, down, towards a blue world that spun slowly on its axis far below. We stopped beside the green rocking horse, and the little fox terrier jumped down and trotted over to the Fool to be petted.

"It's time for you to move on now." The Fool announced, stroking the terrier. "Mount the rocking horse. He is the pendulum of the Universe. To-and-fro, to-and-fro, he goes, like the waves of the sea, up and down, up and down, from riches to poverty, from sickness to health, from one experience to another, ever changing."

As he spoke, I obediently slid onto the horses' back. The wooden animal rocked slightly, but I held still, listening to the lyrical words of the Fool. "I don't want to go – on. Can't I stay here with you? We could surf the Universe for ever."

"Not yet." He admonished me. "You must return around the buoy of Malkuth. Your race is not yet over. Begin to rock, now. The horse will take you where you need to go."

I shifted my position, leaning back and forward, and the wooden horse began to rock. Faster and faster we went, and I felt as if I could never stop. The rocking became a blur. I felt my brain struggling to break free, and I drifted into a trance.....

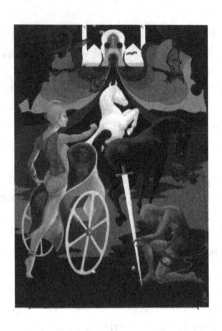

Third Path of the CHARIOT

L ying in the arms of my Guide, I came to my senses once more. The rocking horse had vanished. I allowed my Guide to carry me back to the Chariot, which was waiting at the bus stop. He placed me on the ground, where I stood uncertainly for a moment before pulling myself together and putting on my protective helmet. Then he – or was it she – climbed into the Chariot and took up the correct position on the front panel of the interior, arms upraised, gazing at me intently as I jumped into the vehicle with consummate ease. I felt sure that we would make it through this time. I knew of the dangers in the narrow defile, and now Sir Belvedere could no longer distract me from my purpose – to reach the City of Jerusalem. I understood that there was only one reason I had sunk into the Sea of Sorrow. I had lacked faith that the cloak of Binah would hold me up and protect me from the Portuguese men-of-war. I had allowed them to sting me, and the pain distracted me from my purpose.

The two black and white horses leapt ahead at my command. I controlled them with my voice, as there were no reins. We quickly reached the constricted defile, and I heard once again the dreadful cries of those who had become petrified on its walls. I prayed that they might be released from fear and complete their own interrupted journey. We came out of the canyon at a gallop, the horses straining and frothing at the mouth, their sides wet with sweat, as they drew near the shores of the Sea of Sorrow.

I commanded them to halt by the edge of the Sea, where small waves lapped the beach. It was a windless day, and the black cloak of Binah rested lightly on the waters, undulating softly. My Guide Ediug whispered to me from inside the Chariot.

"Remember – Knowledge and Understanding will help you to cross the Sea safely, and Wisdom awaits you on the far shore. Go now. I will be with you evermore, so banish fear and doubt. Fare you well - pupil of my eye."

I advanced onto the edge of the black cloak as it washed along the shore and began to tread cautiously on my crossing. Keeping faith in my heart, my confidence increased with every step I took, and I focused on the distant figure of Binah as she sat on her throne, and the path of the cloak that gradually narrowed as it came up to her. Then I felt solid ground under my feet as I stepped to the foot of her throne.

Binah, the Great Mother, in her aspects of terror and sympathy, looked down at me. I dropped my glance, unable to face her questioning eyes.

"You understand the meaning of the Sea of Sorrow." She murmured. "Now climb the steps that lead into the City and make your way to the inner sanctum without delay, for any hesitation on your part will be fatal."

I nodded my head silently and moved past her, mounting the stairs one by one, as if in a dream, and entered the great gates of the City. The streets were swathed with gold cobblestones and gossamer banners hung from every rooftop. The sound of a harp accompanying ghostly singing was in my ears and all around me surged an incredible sensation of peace. The road grew narrower and the doors of the temple that shielded the inner sanctum rose up before me.

But, before I could reach out to open them, an inward vision rose up. Familiar faces were calling out to me, weeping, and begging me to turn back. Now they were calling my name, "Navigator, Navigator, where are you?" Sounding worried and anxious, I knew it was not yet time. There was something I had to do – down in Malkuth. My hand dropped away from the doors, reaching out for something else......

Epilogue to The Navigators Dream

My hand clutches at the slippery chain. Of course! It must be the Golden Chain of the Magians, I think vaguely. I haul myself up, my orange lifejacket bobbing around my soaking head, water dripping from my nose. I feel the solidity of the buoy above me – I'm coughing up water, and then everything goes dim once more. My last thought is to hang on to the shifting buoy as the chilling waves wash over me again.

"Navigator, Navigator, where are you? Over there! I'm sure I saw something – it's by that buoy." A voice, calling out above the sound of a driven propeller, alerts me. "Do you see that? It looks like an orange lifejacket. Steer over that way, now."

"Ah! Yes, I see it. Can it be the Navigator? When they gybed, they didn't discover the boom had knocked someone overboard. Too drunk, I expect. Shocking!. Someone should have been on lookout." A second voice reaches me through my haze. "God! I hope the Navigator is still alive. Hurry...."

I see the boat coming through blurry eyes. A figure is standing up in the bow as they close in, slowing down as they come up to the buoy.

"It's you! Navigator! Are you all right? Covered with blood! Must have a head wound." The fellow in the bow reaches down towards me, grabbing my arms and passing a line around me, which he quickly ties in a bowline. I can't speak, but I nod my head, spitting out volumes of water. The bowline tightens and I feel two pairs of arms hauling me from the water, over the side of the rubber dinghy and onto the wooden slats of the floor, where I lie prone, vomiting.

"Here – get those clothes off as fast as possible. Wrap a blanket around – like this. Another one – yes, and a bandage for the head. First dry the hair. Conscious, yes, but let's do CPR in case. Must have swallowed a lot of water." My wet clothes lie in a heap as I cough and vomit again.

I am rolled onto my stomach, shivering, my head turned to one side. The GPS rattled onto the boards, still slung around my neck. Someone pumps on my back, causing me to throw up more water and my last meal. The blanket feels good and begins to warm me slowly.

I recognize two of my friends. They look extremely anxious. "You've been in the water over an hour. We were looking for you all over the race course. The crew of your boat came in second. Then there was an outcry when they realized their Navigator wasn't on board. Several boats set out to look for you. Thank God we found you in time. The water is freezing at this time of year. At least you were wearing a lifejacket."

They sit me up, propped against the thwart while the outboard revs up again and the dinghy speeds toward the shore. One of them is dialing 911 on his cell phone. It's really hard to breathe. The cold air smites on me, but I'm alive! My head hurts and I put up a hand to feel blood still oozing from a wound. I don't remember being hit or falling overboard.......

We pull in to the dock and the EMT's are there with a gurney. Although I feel a little better, they insist on strapping me down and carting me off to the hospital. My two friends come along as well and my frantic parents, Lance and Gwen, meet us in the hospital lobby. After they see me safely into bed with warm pyjamas, I am hooked up to an oxygen tank and a glucose drip as the doctors scurry around.

The light slowly fades from the window and I close my eyes and sleep, the sleep of the dead.

I remained in hospital for three days, and then they allowed me to go home to my parents' house. I had an apartment in the basement that gave me the privacy I needed. It was good to walk through the door to my own place and check out my 1937 dark blue Daimler with Wilson pre-selector gearbox sitting quietly in the garage. I was more than grateful to be alive.

For some reason, I walked over to the wastebasket and stared idly down into it. A small smear of damp ashes covered the bottom, and I wondered what it was. Could it have been a fire? I didn't remember putting one out. I looked up at the bookcase, where I kept my owl collection. One of them was out of place – it had fallen on the floor. I picked it up and looked at it. The barn owls' bright eyes seemed to gaze back at me as I placed it on the shelf with the others.

Later that day I went to my office. My new assistant, Miss Wollup, was tidying the bookshelves. She greeted me cheerfully and said how relieved she was that I had been saved from drowning. My significant other had called in a panic, Miss Wallop told me. She had informed the person that they were searching for me in the bay.

"And I found this!" She held out a small box – a box of Tarot cards.

"Where did you get that?" I asked in amazement. "I threw a box like that out the other day. Didn't think I wanted to get into that sort of thing. The occult, you know, it's scary. But maybe I'll take another look. Are they all there?"

"Why wouldn't they be?" Came her reply. "Shall I count them for you?"

"Please do." I said as I bent over my appointment book. Beside it were some notes I had made before I went sailing. Ah! Yes. The ideas I got from the book about multiple personalities. Why, it now seemed perfectly clear to me. Of course everyone had more than one aspect of themselves. We all had many separate entities, like puppets. We pulled the strings, but they were as vivid and vital as ourselves. The whole idea was apparent to me as if I had learned it yesterday. I decided to try the method with some of my more stable clients. A workshop, maybe? I would call it "The Actors on your Stage."

Miss Wollup interrupted my thoughts. "I counted the cards. There are eight missing. Let me see. Strength is missing; the Empress and the Emperor; the Hermit; the Chariot; the Magian, the Archpriestess and the Fool. That's a shame. The deck isn't complete without them. They are all important Major Arcana cards. I wonder where they are." She began searching around. "Did you leave some of them at your apartment?"

"No, I don't think so. Wait! What's this?" I put my hand in my jacket pocket and pulled out several cards. Quickly counting them, there were eight. I handed the remaining cards to Miss Wollup, and she threw her arms around me and gave me a big kiss.

My parents were so relieved at my rescue that they bought me a beautiful racing schooner of 75 feet. We all went down to the dock to have a christening party aboard the boat. There I was introduced to the skipper they had just hired. He was a stout fellow, impeccably dressed with his blue and white jacket and yachting cap, which he tipped to me.

"I'm pleased to meet you. You're done, then. I'm Pompeybou." As I shook his hand, he winked slyly at me.